Editors/Advisory Board

Members of the Advisory Board are instrumental in the final selection of articles for each edition of ANNUAL EDITIONS. Their review of articles for content, level, currentness, and appropriateness provides critical direction to the editor and staff. We think that you will find their careful consideration well reflected in this volume.

EDITOR

David McComb
Colorado State University

ADVISORY BOARD

Staff

To the Reader

In publishing ANNUAL EDITIONS we recognize the enormous role played by the magazines, newspapers, and journals of the *public press* in providing current, first-rate educational information in a broad spectrum of interest areas. Many of these articles are appropriate for students, researchers, and professionals seeking accurate, current material to help bridge the gap between principles and theories and the real world. These articles, however, become more useful for study when those of lasting value are carefully *collected, organized, indexed,* and *reproduced* in a *low-cost format,* which provides easy and permanent access when the material is needed. That is the role played by ANNUAL EDITIONS. Under the direction of each volume's *academic editor,* who is an expert in the subject area, and with the guidance of an *Advisory Board,* each year we seek to provide in each ANNUAL EDITION a current, well-balanced, carefully selected collection of the best of the public press for your study and enjoyment. We think that you will find this volume useful, and we hope that you will take a moment to let us know what you think.

In recognition of the importance of international events, world history courses, next to those about the United States, have become the most popular history courses of the secondary schools. World history, moreover, has spread through higher education in the past decade and a half, and the first generation of scholars trained in world history is just emerging. Increasingly, the U.S. government and its citizens are caught up in a daily vortex of concerns such as exported terrorism, peacekeeping missions, nuclear proliferation, outbreaks of viral disease, illegal immigration, and environmental degradation. It is impossible to comprehend the front page of even a local newspaper without a knowledge of the world. Responsible citizens must become informed about international matters in order to act and vote intelligently about these events for the welfare of individuals, the nation, and the world. Thus, educators and others have become sensitive to the need for instruction about global matters in the classroom.

The organizational problems in world history include the traditional difficulties of scope and relevance. What should be included and what may be left out? How can diverse material be arranged to make sense of the past? In all history courses choices must be made, particularly in the surveys. No one learns all about each country of Europe in the survey of Western Civilization, or all about each state in a survey of United States history, with the hope that such details add up to a comprehensible story. Instead, there is an emphasis upon ideas, technology, turning points, significant people, movements, and chronology. Efforts are made by historians and teachers to place events in perspective, to illustrate cause and effect, and to focus upon what is important.

World history is no exception, but the range of choices is greater. There are simply more people, places, and events in the history of the world. There is more material, and thus world history courses demand the broadest level of abstraction from teachers and students. World historians, consequently, focus upon civilizations, cultures, global systems, and international relationships. Often they attempt cross-cultural comparisons, but some historiographical problems remain unsettled.

Probably the most difficult question involves periodization—how to divide history into time spans. In Western Civilization courses the division of ancient, medieval, and modern works nicely. In world history, however, this division does not fit so neatly because civilizations have evolved at different times. The development of medieval Europe makes little sense for Asia, the Middle East, Africa, or the Americas. World historians, nevertheless, have reached some consensus about the following: the two most important technological events in human history are the invention of agriculture and the industrial revolution; the thousand years before Columbus are significant because of the rise of Islam, development of global trading routes, evolution of civilization in Mesoamerica, and the power of China; and 1500 is a reasonable dividing point for history classes because of European explorations and their consequences.

In this volume, I use a periodization of early civilizations to 500 B.C.E., later civilization to 500 C.E., and the world from 500 C.E. to 1500 C.E. This is fairly traditional, but there are additional units on natural history and culture that include the earliest developments of humankind, the great religions, and exploration. Within the broad units can be found information about women, technology, the family, historiography, urbanization, sports, and other subjects. Since the development of Western Civilization is a part of world history, western topics are also included. The topic guide is a useful index for this varied information. The articles were selected for readability, accuracy, relevance, interest, and freshness. They are meant to supplement a course, to provide depth, and to add spice and spark. The articles do not cover everything; that is impossible, of course. Sometimes older selections have been included to provide balance when nothing current is available. You may know of some other articles that would do a better job. If so, please return the prepaid article rating form at the back of the book with your suggestions. Thank you.

David McComb

David McComb
Editor

Contents

UNIT 1

Natural History: The Stage for Human History

Five articles discuss how Earth may have come to be and how the environment impacted on the shaping of early human society.

UNIT 2

The Beginnings of Culture, Agriculture, and Cities

Six selections examine early milestones in the history of humankind: the origin of writing, the beginnings of agriculture, and urbanization.

UNIT 3

The Early Civilizations to 500 B.C.E.

Six articles consider the growing diversity of human life as civilization evolved in the ancient world.

UNIT 4

The Later Civilizations to 500 C.E.

Five articles discuss some of the dynamics of culture in the New World, Egypt, and Greece.

UNIT 5

The Great Religions

Nine articles discuss the beginnings of the world's great religions, including Judaism, Christianity, Islam, Hinduism, and Buddhism.

The concepts in bold italics are developed in the article. For further expansion please refer to the Topic Guide and the Index.

ix

UNIT 6

The World of the Middle Ages, 500–1500

Eight selections examine the development of world cultures during this period: in the Western Hemisphere, flourishing Mesoamerican cities; in the West, feudalism and the growth of the nation-state; in the East, the golden age of peak development.

The concepts in bold italics are developed in the article. For further expansion please refer to the Topic Guide and the Index.

UNIT 7

1500: The Era of Global Explorations

Five articles examine the enormous global impact of the voyages of discovery, essentially by the Europeans.

Selected World Wide Web Site for World History, Volume I

All of these Web sites are hot-linked through the *Annual Editions* home page:
http://www.dushkin.com/annualeditions (just click on your book title).

The Internet is virtually the ultimate network. It has the ability to link all of the computers in the world through telecommunications and to share the information stored at any of these computer sites. The part of the Internet that is of most interest to students and teachers (in fact, to any average citizen with a computer) is the World Wide Web. It is also the easiest to use. Information is organized on the "Web" through a system of linked sites or "home pages." Every home page has an address, and it introduces a purveyor of information, which in turn has a number of connections called "hot links" or "hyper-links." These links are like windows that open to a wealth of knowledge. For instance, if you call up a home page to a university you will find a number of links that lead to related sites, and at those sites you will find more links, and so on. In a sense, it does not matter where you start; the World Wide Web can be explored by any number of paths. You can start exploring on one of the Web addresses listed on these pages and follow the links to a number of other sites.

The Internet is not a substitute for a conventional library—at least not yet—but it is a very valuable supplement that draws from a worldwide source of knowledge, and it gives you the ability to research areas in ways that were impossible only a few years ago.

Some Web sites are temporary in nature and are continually changing their structure and content, so the information listed on these pages may not always be available.

General World History Sites

ARCHNET: WWW VIRTUAL LIBRARY—ARCHAEOLOGY— *http://www.lib.uconn.edu/ArchNet/*—This archaeological Web site with many links to other sites is reached by geographic region or subject area. Site includes a search mechanism and up-to-date news.

GATEWAY TO WORLD HISTORY—*http://library.ccsu. ctstateu.edu/~history/world_history/index.html*—One section of this collection of resources is an organized tree of history-related links to online resources. Another section searches world history archives. The site also includes a search engine.

THE HISTORICAL TEXT ARCHIVE—*http://www.msstate. edu/Archive/History/*—This award-winning site contains links to world history, regional or national, and topical history and resources. For speed, use text version.

HISTORY OF SCIENCE, TECHNOLOGY, AND MEDICINE— *http://www.asap.unimellb.edu.au/html*—A database of information on science, technology, and medicine with

alphabetical listing of resources, search features, and multiple links.

HYPERHISTORY ON LINE—*http://www.hyperhistory.com/*—At this Web site, click on "hyperhistory" and navigate through 3,000 years of world history. Links to important historical persons, events, and maps.

INDEX OF HISTORY—*http://www.academic.marist.edu/ history/*—Scroll to "hiseuro.htm" for an immense collection of links to sites devoted to different aspects and periods of history, for example, European, Chinese, Latin American, or medieval, Renaissance, ancient, some with graphics and sound.

INTERNATIONAL NETWORK INFORMATION CENTER AT UNIVERSITY OF TEXAS—*http://inic.utexas.edu/*—Gateway has pointers to international study sites for Africa, India, China, Japan, and many other countries.

LINK TO WORLD HISTORY SITES—*http://www.avel.com. community/edu/links/hstwo.html*— Links include Aegean Palaces, Mayan Civilizations, Ancient Greece and Rome, Ancient Egypt Archaeology, Greek Mythology, and Native North Americans.

NATIONAL HUMANITIES INSTITUTE HOME PAGE—*http:// www.access.digex.net/~nhi/*—Web site includes philosophical, cultural, and historical worldwide links, including archives, history sites, and an electronic library of full texts and documents that is useful for research in history and the humanities.

WWW VIRTUAL LIBRARY—HUMANITITES—*http://www. hum.gu.se/w3vl/VL.html*—This main subject index leads to many humanities research subjects, many of which relate to historical studies.

YAHOO'S HISTORY SEARCH ENGINE—*http://www.yahoo. com/Arts/Humanity/History/*—Yahoo's history search engine has links to ancient history, archaeology, the seventeenth through the twentieth centuries, and religions, and specific topics such as military and maritime history, economic history, women's history, and much more. There is a direct link to "Eurodocs: Primary Historical Documents from Western Europe."

Prehistory

TALK-ORIGINS—*http://www.talkorigins.org/*—This is the site of a newsgroup devoted to debate on biological and physical origins of the world. Many articles are archived here and there are links to other Web sites. Be sure to click on "The Origin of Humankind," a comprehensive source for students of human evolution, which has the latest news about new discoveries, a link to an exhibition of human prehistory, and links to many other related sights, including Yahoo's creation/evolution material.

Ancient Civilizations

AKKADIAN LANGUAGE—*http://www.sron.ruu.nl/~jheise/akkadian/index.html*—An introduction to the culture and history of Mesopotamia and to the cuneiform writing system on clay tablets, this site also includes discussion of Akkadian and Semitic languages, book references, and external links.

ANCIENT CITY OF ATHENS—*http://www.indiana.edu/~kglowack/Athens/*—Click on "Athens.html" in the index for images of ancient Athens as well as insights into Greek history and links to other Greek historical sights.

ASSYRIA ON-LINE—*http://www.cs.toronto.edu/~jatou/*—All there is to know about ancient Assyria, including the epic of Gilgamesh and Hammurabi's Code, can be found at this Web site.

DIOTIMA: WOMEN AND GENDER IN THE ANCIENT WORLD—*http://www.uky.edu/ArtsSciences/Classics/gender.html*—Historical information about women in the ancient world is available at this site, which also includes search possibilities.

EXPLORING ANCIENT WORLD CULTURES—*http://cedar.evansville.edu/~wcweb/wc101/*—Eight ancient world cultures can be explored from this starting point. They include Ancient China, Egypt, India, Greece, Rome, Near East, Early Islam, and Medieval Europe.

THE INSTITUTE OF EGYPTIAN ART AND ARCHEOLOGY—*http:// www.memphis.edu/egypt/*—This site offers an exhibit of artifacts, a color tour of Egypt, and links to other Web sites about Egypt. Click on "main.html" for access.

ORIENTAL INSTITUTE—*http://www-oi.uchicago.edu/OI/Dept/RA/ABZU/*—Click on "ABZU.htm" in the index of the University of Chicago's Oriental Institute for information about ancient Near East archaeology and a bibliographic reference on women in the areas covered.

REEDER'S EGYPT PAGE—*http://www.sirius.com/~reeder/*—Click on the tomb opening to reveal a wealth of historical and archaeological information about Egypt, including a tour of the tombs of Niankhkhnum and Khnumhotep.

ROMARCH—ROMAN ART AND ARCHAEOLOGY—*http://www-personal.umich.edu/*—Choose "Table of Contents" and then click on "Beyond the University of Michigan," followed by "ROMARCH" in order to reach this resource, which is the original Roman index and link to over 175 sites. It is also an Internet discussion group of more than 450 professionals and laypersons worldwide.

Middle Ages and Renaissance

LABYRINTH HOME PAGE TO MEDIEVAL STUDIES—*http://www.georgetown.edu/labyrinth/*—Complete information about medieval studies on the Web can be found here. Site also has a search capability.

LORDS OF THE EARTH: MAYA/AZTEC/INCA EXCHANGE—*http://www.realtime.net/maya/*—History, geography, and art about the indigenous inhabitants of the Americas before the arrival of Columbus is available here.

THE MAYA ASTRONOMY PAGE—*http://www.atro.uva.nl/michielb/maya/astro.html*—The focus here is on Mayan civilization, especially astronomy, mathematics, and the Mayan calendar. There are also links to other Maya-related sites. Click on "Maya Astronomy Page."

WORLD OF LATE ANTIQUITY—*http://ccat.sas.upenn.edu/jod/*—Click on "World of Late Antiquity" for interesting documents, many concerning military history, about late Roman and early medieval times.

WWW MEDIEVAL RESOURCES—*http://ebbs.english.vt.edu/medieval/*—This site has links to different resources concerning medieval times. Click on "medieval.ebbs" in the Index.

We highly recommend that you check out our Web site for expanded information and our other product lines. We are continually updating and adding links to our Web site in order to offer you the most usable and useful information that will support and expand the value of your *Annual Edition.* You can reach us at our general homepage: *http://www.dushkin.com/*

Topic Guide

This topic guide suggests how the selections in this book relate to topics of traditional concern to world history students and professionals. It is useful for locating articles that relate to each other for reading and research. The guide is arranged alphabetically according to topic. Articles may, of course, treat topics that do not appear in the topic guide. In turn, entries in the topic guide do not necessarily constitute a comprehensive listing of all the contents of each selection.

TOPIC AREA	TREATED IN	TOPIC AREA	TREATED IN
Africa	15. Out of Africa 16. Daily Life in Ancient Egypt 17. All the King's Sons 22. Cleopatra	Environment	1. In Defense of the Big Bang 2. Among Planets 3. Evolution of Life on the Earth 11. How Man Invented Cities 13. Collapse of Earliest Known Empire 41. Columbus and the Labyrinth of History 44. Easter's End
Agriculture	10. Corn in the New World 13. Collapse of Earliest Known Empire		
Americas	5. Human Presence in Americas 8. Tale of Two Cultures 18. Tales from a Peruvian Crypt 23. Mysterious Mexican Culture 32. Tracking a Vanished People 33. Cracking the Maya's Code 41. Columbus and the Labyrinth of History	Europe	7. Mummies, Textiles Offer Evidence of Europeans 9. Writing Right 14. Herodotus 19. In Classical Athens 22. Cleopatra 37. Reinterpreting the Crusades 38. Making of Magna Carta 39. Clocks 40. Images of Earth in the Year 1000 41. Columbus and the Labyrinth of History 42. Sailors of Palos 43. After Dire Straits
Asian Civilization	7. Mummies, Textiles Offer Evidence of Europeans 8. Tale of Two Cultures 25. Messengers of Light 30. Confucius 34. Imperial Tombs of China 35. All the Khan's Horses		
Buddhism	24. Ancient Jewel 25. Messengers of Light 31. Koran, Gita, and Tripitaka	Geography	1. In Defense of the Big Bang 2. Among Planets 3. Evolution of Life on the Earth 5. Human Presence in Americas 8. Tale of Two Cultures 10. Corn in the New World 11. How Man Invented Cities 12. Old Tablet from Turkish Site 40. Images of Earth in the Year 1000 41. Columbus and the Labyrinth of History 43. After Dire Straits 44. Easter's End
Christianity	26. Thrice-Holy City 27. Rethinking the Resurrection 28. Women and the Bible 37. Reinterpreting the Crusades		
Economics	10. Corn in the New World 12. Old Tablet from Turkish Site 23. Mysterious Mexican Culture 41. Columbus and the Labyrinth of History	Greek Civilization	14. Herodotus 19. In Classical Athens 20. Mystery of Persepolis 21. Old Sports
Egyptian Civilization	9. Writing Right 15. Out of Africa 16. Daily Life in Ancient Egypt 17. All the King's Sons 21. Old Sports 22. Cleopatra	Hinduism	24. Ancient Jewel 31. Koran, Gita, and Tripitaka

TOPIC AREA	TREATED IN	TOPIC AREA	TREATED IN
Historiography	14. Herodotus 27. Rethinking the Resurrection 28. Women and the Bible 36. Master-Chronologers of Islam 41. Columbus and the Labyrinth of History	**Prehistoric Culture**	4. Mapping the Past 5. Human Presence in Americas 6. Dawn of Creativity 7. Mummies, Textiles Offer Evidence of Europeans 8. Tale of Two Cultures 10. Corn in the New World 18. Tales from a Peruvian Crypt 32. Tracking a Vanished People 44. Easter's End
Indian Civilization	24. Ancient Jewel 25. Messengers of Light		
Islamic Civilization	26. Thrice-Holy City 29. State and Society under Islam 31. Koran, Gita, and Tripitaka 36. Master-Chronologers of Islam	**Religion**	10. Corn in the New World 23. Mysterious Mexican Culture 24. Ancient Jewel 25. Messengers of Light 26. Thrice-Holy City 27. Rethinking the Resurrection 28. Women and the Bible 29. State and Society under Islam 30. Confucius 31. Koran, Gita, and Tripitaka 37. Reinterpreting the Crusades
Judaism	26. Thrice-Holy City 28. Women and the Bible		
Middle East	11. How Man Invented Cities 12. Old Tablet from Turkish Site 13. Collapse of Earliest Known Empire 20. Mystery of Persepolis 26. Thrice-Holy City 27. Rethinking the Resurrection 28. Women and the Bible 29. State and Society under Islam 36. Master-Chronologers of Islam 40. Images of Earth in the Year 1000	**Roman Civilization**	22. Cleopatra
		Technology	4. Mapping the Past 9. Writing Right 10. Corn in the New World 39. Clocks 42. Sailors of Palos
Politics	22. Cleopatra 29. State and Society under Islam 38. Making of Magna Carta		
Population	4. Mapping the Past 7. Mummies, Textiles Offer Evidence of Europeans 11. How Man Invented Cities 16. Daily Life in Ancient Egypt 21. Old Sports 41. Columbus and the Labyrinth of History 42. Sailors of Palos 44. Easter's End	**Urbanization**	11. How Man Invented Cities 12. Old Tablet from Turkish Site 13. Collapse of Earliest Empire 16. Daily Life in Ancient Egypt 19. In Classical Athens 20. Mystery of Persepolis 23. Mysterious Mexican Culture 26. Thrice-Holy City
		Warfare	20. Mystery of Persepolis 22. Cleopatra 35. All the Khan's Horses 37. Reinterpreting the Crusades
		Women	22. Cleopatra 28. Women and the Bible

Natural History: The Stage for Human History

The setting for human development has been planet Earth and the environment it has provided for life. Humankind has been shaped by this environment and has used the resources of the surroundings for comfort and survival. It was not until recently, however, and then without planning, that human beings began to influence the environment on a global scale. Coincidentally, and perhaps fortunately, space exploration made us recognize the potential danger of jeopardizing the life-sustaining atmosphere that wraps our planet like the thin skin of an apple. Buckminster Fuller's descriptive phrase of "spaceship Earth" expressed the wonder—how did we get upon this blue planet orbiting In black space—and a warning—it's our only home, we had best take care of it.

The late Carl Sagan in his book *The Dragons of Eden* (1979) imagined all time compressed into a single year. New Year's Day would have begun with the "Big Bang," a moment when the universe was created in an enormous explosion of compressed matter. Neil de Grasse Tyson in the first article of this unit explains why this theory has been supported by scientists. Twenty-four days, according to Sagan in his imaginary year, corresponds to a billion years. This means that the universe is 15 billion years old, that Earth formed in mid-September of his year, and that life began near the end of that month. How life began is a mystery, but in 1986 Roberta Score, a geologist, found a frozen meteorite glowing bright green in the blue ice of Antarctica. This stone, ALH 84001, possessed the same composition as matter found on Mars by space explorers in 1976. The presumption was that the meteorite came from Mars, and more astounding, as was announced in 1996, it looked as if it contained fossils of life forms. The evidence is inconclusive, and the announcement raised a storm of scientific controversy. After all, it could mean that life on Earth came from another planet, and that would tend to confirm the idea of life elsewhere in the universe. Dava Sobel reviews this event in the second article of the unit, "Among Planets."

Stephen Jay Gould, a popular science writer, comments upon the haphazard evolution of life on Earth. Human beings are lucky to be here in their present form, and if it were done over again the evolution might not take the same path. In Sagan's scenario, moreover, humans do not appear until 10:30 p.m. on December 31 and the Akkadian Empire, the first one, does not form until the last 9 seconds. When thinking in cosmic time, such as this, human existence seems both recent and precarious.

It is the human story, nonetheless, that is the main concern of world history. The migration of human beings across the face of the planet has long been of interest, and, since there is no evidence of any type other than modern homo sapiens in the Western Hemisphere, there is a question of when and how they came. Previously, humans were thought to have arrived across the Bering land bridge some 15,000 years ago. Recently, as reported by Pulitzer Prize–winner John Noble Wilford in the *New York Times*, discoveries in Chile indicate an arrival date of 25,000 years. DNA tests by genetic historians and anthropologists, in addition, have provided an accurate tool for tracking migrations. Island Polynesians have been traced to Southeast Asia and American Indians to Mongolia, as explained by Adam Goodheart. In human terms, rather than the last minute or so of Carl Sagan's cosmic year, this seems like a long time ago.

Looking Ahead: Challenge Questions

How do you think the universe, Earth, and life began? What is the evidence? Discuss other theories that might be considered.

How does evolution work? Why does Stephen Jay Gould say that modern humans might not evolve again?

How did modern humans reach the Western Hemisphere? What is the evidence?

What scientific tools are used to probe the distant past?

Of what use is DNA testing in population research? What difference does it make to the world about who goes where and when?

In Defense of the
Big Bang

Yes, questions remain. But the big bang is the most successful theory ever put forth for the origin and evolution of the universe.

Neil de Grasse Tyson

What, you might ask, could possibly induce a rational astrophysicist to believe that fifteen billion years ago, the universe—with all of its matter and energy—was packed into a primeval fireball smaller than a marble, and that it has been expanding ever since? The answer is simple: Regardless of what you may have read or heard to the contrary, the big bang is supported by a preponderance of evidence and has become the most successful theory ever put forth to explain the origin and evolution of the universe.

Scientific evidence in support of a theory sometimes takes you places where your senses have never been. Twentieth-century science has largely been built upon data collected with all manner of tools that enable us to see the universe in decidedly uncommon ways. As a consequence, while we have always required that a theory make mathematical sense, we no longer require that a theory make common sense. We simply demand that it be consistent with the results of observations and experiments. This posture facilitated the rise of counterintuitive, yet remarkably successful, branches of physics, such as relativity and quantum mechanics.

Of all the theories that describe the physical world, the big bang, first described in 1948 by physicist George Gamow, seems to intrigue the general public most consistently. Some people vehemently oppose the big bang, even when they are unaware of its fundamental tenets. Others like to claim that the big bang is "just a theory" and should therefore be discounted.

Don't be fooled. The beginning of the twentieth century saw the end of describing successful theories as "laws." This change of vocabulary came when new experimental domains revealed that the predictions of previous physical laws were incomplete. The adoption of the term *theory* came with the humble recognition by physicists that data from newer and better equipment might provide a deeper understanding of the physical world. This is why before 1900 we had Kepler's *laws* of planetary motion, Newton's *laws* of gravity, and the *laws* of thermodynamics, whereas after 1900 we have Einstein's *theory* of relativity, the *theory* of quantum mechanics, big-bang *theory,* and so forth.

A well-constructed theory must explain some of what is not understood, predict previously unknown phenomena, and, to be successful, have its predictions consistently confirmed. Furthermore, skeptics should not hesitate to question every possible assumption, no matter how basic.

Confidence in the big bang is derived from the strengths of many arguments. Let us start with Edwin Hubble's 1929 observation that we are part of an expanding universe in which distant galaxies recede from us faster than the near ones in direct proportion to how far away they are. Further support came from Einstein's theory of gravity, better known as the general theory of relativity. One of its solutions predicted a universe that expands according to precisely the pattern found by Hubble. Since Einstein's theory preceded Hubble's discovery (by thirteen years), it was to provide independent corroboration of the idea.

If you happen to have a gripe with the big-bang theory's claim that objects with high recession velocity are farther away than objects with low velocity of recession, then consider the existence of gravitational lenses. As first predicted by Einstein, the gravity of a high-mass object in an observer's foreground can act as a lens. It distorts space in its vicinity so that light from a background object along the same line of sight is split into three or more images. Such optical antics have been observed for dozens of quasars all around the sky. In each case, the "lensed" object always has a higher recession velocity than the object whose gravity is serving as the lens itself.

Could it be an illusion that very distant galaxies are receding from us at very high velocities? We can test for this because objects moving at very high speeds should measurably exhibit the effects of "time dilation" predicted in Einstein's theory of relativity. Indeed, supernovae recently discovered in distant galaxies do take more time to explode and to decline in luminosity than comparable supernovae in nearby galaxies.

The most significant supporting argument for the big bang derives from the existence of "cosmic microwave background." Shortly after the notion of a hot, explosive origin for the universe was first proposed, physicists Ralph Alpher and Robert Herman, invoking simple principles of thermodynamics, inferred that the density of matter and energy of the universe must have been much higher in the past. They were forced to conclude that the universe should betray some sign of leftover emergy from its earlier, much hotter existence. As the universe expanded, such a signal should have cooled appreciably to become an omnidirectional bath of microwaves with a characteristic temperature of a few degrees on the Kelvin absolute temperature scale. In 1965, part of this background signal serendipitously revealed itself in data from microwave antennae used by two Bell Laboratories physicists, Arno Penzias and Robert Wilson. For this finding, they were jointly awarded the 1978 Nobel Prize for physics.

If you are skeptical of the claim that some accidentally discovered microwaves are the cooled remnant of a youthful, hot universe, then consider that the big bang predicts a specific mixture of energy with a characteristic temperature. (Similarly, the Sun's mixture of energy, which includes specific propor-

tions of infrared, visible, and ultraviolet light, also has a characteristic temperature (6,000 kelvins) at its surface. The Cosmic Background Explorer satellite measured the cosmic background in every direction and indicated a single temperature of 2.726 kelvins.

You might be skeptical about whether this single-temperature assortment of microwaves actually came from the early universe. Perhaps you prefer to think they were created by your neighbor's microwave oven or by a police radar gun or by some microwave-emitting wall of interstellar material nearby in space. One proof of a distant source uses the hot gas embedded in galaxy clusters, which we expect to slightly increase the temperature of cooler energy that passes through. And when we look toward these distant clusters, we do see an increase in the temperature of the microwave energy along our line of sight, implying that the microwave background indeed hails from beyond the clusters and not from a source in the foreground.

If you are unconvinced that the universe was hotter in the past than it is today, consider that because of the time it takes their light to reach through intergalactic space, we see galaxies not as they are but as they once were. If big-bang cosmology is correct, these distant galaxies were once bathed in a hotter cosmic background than they are at present. To test this notion, we can use selected molecules as "thermometers" that allow us to infer a temperature for the background microwaves that once bathed distant galaxies. Sure enough, the measured temperature is in precise accord with the predicted temperature of the universe at the time the light left those galaxies.

Just for fun, let's turn back the big-bang clock and use current laws of physics to extrapolate the behavior of the observable universe at a time when it was much smaller, denser, and hotter—when the background was upward

of a trillion degrees. (Our current theories of physics actually allow us to describe the behavior of the universe from the first 0.00000000000000000000000-0000000000000000001 second of its existence all the way up to fifteen billion years and beyond.) At these early times and high temperatures, all atoms were broken apart into their component nuclear particles, which themselves were broken into their quark subcomponents.

Combining all that we know of quantum mechanics and all we have learned from busting atoms to smithereens in particle accelerators, we conclude that as the cosmic soup expanded and cooled, nuclear particles recombined to make a specific and predictable assortment of atoms: the universe forged most of its elemental mass into hydrogen and about 25 percent into helium. These are bold extrapolations, but surveys of the most helium-deficient galaxies (those that have undergone very little star forma-

While a theory must make mathematical sense, we can no longer demand that it make common sense.

tion) routinely find between 22 and 27 percent helium, in good agreement with big-bang predictions.

A few other light elements are predicted to have formed in trace amounts during the first moments of the universe. Among these are "heavy" hydrogen (which is simply a proton and a neutron), "light" helium (helium that is missing a neutron from its nucleus), and lithium (the third-lightest element on the periodic table of elements). The measured quantities of these light elements in the universe are also consistent with big-bang predictions.

We didn't just make this stuff up. The acceptance of the big bang represents an unprecedented marriage of astrophysics and particle physics, one in which a coherent cosmic picture emerges from a minimum of assumptions and measurements. Yes, the galaxy velocities are real, galaxy distances are real, the expanding universe is real, and the big bang is real. Whenever very different experiments support the same theory, then the confidence you have in the theory is greatly enhanced.

But alas, all is not perfect in paradise. A few holes remain in the big bang.

Most worrisome is that the mass density of today's universe would have to be remarkably close to the critical value—the point at which the universe is delicately balanced between recollapse and infinite expansion. This scenario requires a little too much fine-tuning among several cosmological parameters in the early universe.

When we go beyond the simple extrapolations from the big bang, we also find that the microwave background is far too uniform from one patch of the sky to the next to have emerged from the conditions we think were present in the early universe. And the subsequent rapid expansion of the universe does not leave enough time for the galaxies to form as we think they should.

Moreover, the big bang offers us no insight into what the universe was doing before time began or, for that matter, why the laws of physics are what they are.

Do we throw out the big bang along with the bath water because of these complications? Or do we retain the theory's successful predictions and see if there is room to modify the details? These sorts of questions have arisen before. In the mid-sixteenth century, the Polish astronomer Nicolaus Copernicus proposed a model of the known universe that placed the Sun, rather than Earth, at the center of all motion. This heliocentric model was much, much simpler than the competing geocentric model because it removed the need for complex epicycles to account for the motions of the planets. But there was a problem. The predicted paths of the planets did not always conform to their actual paths in the sky. Should Copernicus have therefore discarded the entire idea of a Sun-centered system, or should he have modified some of the model's details? His heliocentric view was, of course, basically correct. The problems arose because he naïvely assumed that planets orbited the Sun in perfect circles rather than in ellipses. It would be two centuries before Newton conceived of his universal law of gravitation, which supplied a bigger picture that modified and subsumed Copernicus's view of the world.

Progress has been made toward resolving some of the outstanding problems with the big-bang model. The most significant contribution, introduced in the early 1980s by the American physicist Alan Guth, is known as inflation, which posits that the energetics of the very early universe passed through a phase that spontaneously triggered a period of extremely rapid expansion. When the details are worked out, inflation naturally explains the embarrassingly fine-tuned "critical" density and also allows the cosmic microwave background to be as uniform as it is measured to be. A consequence of the principles of quantum mechanics applied to the fabric of space and time in the early universe, inflation has no household analog. It predicts a universe that was born at critical density and remains there. Unfortunately, astrophysicists have not been able to track down the requisite amount of mass, but current observations have come up with anywhere from 20 to 40 percent of it. Of course, inflation enthusiasts are fervently looking for the rest.

One class of inflationary theories describes a megauniverse with multiple areas of expansion, each of which looks like a big-bang universe from within and sustains laws of physics that may differ from the ones we know. If this model can be tested and supported, then inflation will have subsumed the entire big bang into a larger cosmological picture.

If you choose to discard the big bang entirely, then step lightly. You will be forfeiting an impressive set of successful predictions—far more than most theories in progress enjoy. Nearly everyone in the community of astrophysicists has chosen to work with the big bang, while recognizing that it may one day become the core idea of something even bigger.

> The unprecedented marriage of astrophysics and particle physics results in a coherent cosmic picture—the big bang—based on a minimum of assumptions.

Neil de Grasse Tyson, an astrophysicist, is the Frederick P. Rose Director of the Hayden Planetarium at the American Museum of Natural History. He is also a research scientist at Princeton University.

AMONG PLANETS

In the age of the Hubble Telescope and rocks from Mars, planetary exploration is getting new respect.

DAVA SOBEL

THE rock that sprang to Martian "life" late last summer did not shock me by offering up fossils of an extinct foreign biology. I had long believed—with Stephen Jay Gould, Frank Drake, and other scientists who have considered the odds—that the universe teems with life, and that our failure to find it owes more to our lack of exploration than to an absence of life elsewhere.

No, what amazed me about the potato-size rock that fell from Mars was that it had travelled millions of miles across space to land here, blasted from world to world by a planetary collision of the sort that purportedly killed off our dinosaurs, and had then lain for millennia upon an Antarctic ice field, until an observant young woman in an expedition party picked it up, because she figured that it had come from another world. *How could she know such a thing?* She recognized the meteorite's extraterrestrial nature right away, thanks to several acts of foraging far from the surface of this planet by teams of Apollo astronauts and robot explorers, which have enabled some of us to see pieces of the moon and of the planets for what they really are.

The composition of ALH 84001, as the much scrutinized rock is designated, closely matches the makeup of Martian matter that was analyzed on site in 1976 by miniature chemistry laboratories aboard two Viking Mars landers. As a result of this positive identification, no astronomer—not even the severest critics of NASA's biological interpretation of the rock's innards—seriously doubts the meteorite's Martian origin. And now other planetary scientists are busy determining—from everything they know, from every relevant spacecraft mission and telescope observation—just which crater (among tens of thousands scattered over the Red Planet) marks the ancestral home of this chunk of Mars crust. Researchers think they have pinpointed its former resting place to just two possible sites—a

region called Sinus Sabaeus, fourteen degrees south of the Martian equator, or a crater east of the Hesperia Planitia region. The bold precision of this assessment is for me the most stunning surprise dealt by the rock from Mars—even more mind-boggling than the suggestive traces of something that might once have lived and died in its microscopic fissures.

I cannot resist comparing this new intimacy with our solar system to the shoebox diorama of the planets I designed for my grade-school science fair. I used marbles, jacks balls, and Ping-Pong balls, all hanging from strings and painted different colors. That crude assortment of materials allowed a reasonable representation of what was known forty years ago about the nine planets: Mars was red and had two moons; Jupiter dwarfed the other planets (I should have used a basketball, but it wouldn't fit in the box); Saturn had rings.

If my school-age daughter were to attempt such a construction today, she'd need handfuls of jelly beans and gum balls to model all the newly discovered satellites of the giant planets. She'd want rings around Jupiter, Uranus, and Neptune, too, not to mention a moon for Pluto. If she wanted, she could even leapfrog *this* solar system altogether and pick for her project one of the newly discovered planetary systems that populate more distant regions of the galaxy—planets that circle stars with names like 51 Pegasi, 70 Virginis, 47 Ursae Majoris, 55 rho[1] Cancri, Lelande 21185, and PSR 1257+12.

Our solar system, once considered unique, now stands as merely the first known example of a planetary system. Since October of 1995, astronomers at ground-based observatories in Europe and the United States have announced that they've found evidence of at least seven alien planets orbiting other stars. As yet, not one of these large planets— some of which are many times the mass of Jupiter—has actually been seen through

a telescope; all were detected indirectly by the gravitational effects they exert on their parent stars. Yet, even though we have no picture of what they look like, enough information has been deduced about their atmospheric conditions to grant the nickname Goldilocks to a planet attending the star called 70 Virginis, suggesting that the cloud-top temperature is "just right," as the storybook Goldilocks would say, for the presence of liquid water. Since liquid water, which supports life, is not known to exist anywhere in our solar system except on Earth, hopeful scientists need only a short leap of faith to carry them from the presence of water to the existence of extraterrestrial life. (To raise the spectre of the Mars rock once again, the primitive life-forms that pressed their memory inside it recall an era when dry-as-dust Mars was a wet world, where rivers flowed.)

Thanks to the excitement surrounding these recent discoveries, researchers investigating the planets have found their status suddenly raised. For years, they were derided by stellar and galactic astronomers as "hard-rock guys" and "butterfly collectors," as though they were too shortsighted and fact-oriented to appreciate the grand theoretical arena of deep space. That is to say, compared with the Big Bang origin of everything, or with black holes that swallow anything, planets paled for many astronomers, and were dismissed as a pedestrian pursuit.

But now planets are in the ascendant both in scientific circles and in the popular view, for a variety of reasons, some esoteric and some aesthetic. One is the sheer proliferation of planetary systems, whose existence had long been suspected but was never proved. The number of planets in the universe, it turns out, may exceed the number of stars.

Just last January, at a meeting of the American Astronomical Society held in San Antonio, scientists using images from the Hubble Space Telescope reported that the universe contains at least forty billion more galaxies than had previously been believed. The celestial census thus rose in a trice from at least ten billion to at least fifty billion, with each manifold galaxy boasting from tens of billions to hundreds of billions of stars. And approximately one in ten of those suns, it is thought, has planets as yet unseen revolving in formation. Within our own Milky Way Galaxy alone, many astronomers now estimate, millions of stars are encircled by planets. Indeed, a retinue of planets seems to be a natural consequence of star formation. Given these literally astronomical statistics, the chances loom large that some percentage of the solar systems in question might harbor planets hospitable to life—even intelligent life. Earlier this year, Daniel S. Goldin, the NASA administrator, declared the search for extra-solar planets a priority for the space agency. (NASA abandoned its support of the Search for Extraterrestrial Intelligence in 1993, however, after one too many attacks by United States senators, who read U.F.O. reports from supermarket tabloids into the *Congressional Record*.)

I visited Goldin in Washington, last spring, to talk to him about planets near and far. The NASA chief, who is fifty-six years old and bears an uncanny resemblance to Dustin Hoffman, appeared to have the energy and enthusiasm of someone half his age. Although the day at headquarters had been designated a dress-down Friday, and many NASA employees were wearing jeans and sneakers, Goldin had on shiny black cowboy boots, a blue shirt, and a dark-olive suit. On a coffee table in his office sophisticated adult toys—models of rocket ships to come—represented the latest in aerodynamic elegance.

"My vision, my hope, my dream," Goldin told me, "is to take a picture of an Earth-like planet, within a hundred light-years of Earth, that will let you see oceans and continents and clouds, and maybe even mountain ranges. Just think what that picture would do."

At that moment, I thought I knew exactly the sort of excitement he was imagining. But now, in the aftermath of the Mars-rock discovery, I realize how grossly I underestimated the impact of such a discovery.

"Let's say we find an Earth-size planet by direct detection in ten years," Goldin continued. "It's not impossible. We'd better be prepared to explain what processes might have given rise to the observations we make then. We'll have to have done some ground-truthing"—NASA-speak for laying intellectual groundwork—"on Earth, and some ground-truthing on some other planets in our own solar system, so when we look out there and see things we'll understand them."

THIS solar system that Goldin now views as ground truth consists mainly of a star, nine planets, and more than sixty moons.

Although Mercury, Venus, Mars, Jupiter, and Saturn have been known since antiquity, at least as wandering lights in the night sky, the detection of the more distant planets, Uranus and Neptune, had to await the development of large telescopes in Europe during the eighteenth and nineteenth centuries. The smallest planet, Pluto, came to light only through heroic search measures applied in 1930 by Clyde Tombaugh at the Lowell Observatory, in Arizona. (Not long ago, I asked Tombaugh, who is now ninety years old, what he said on the sweet eve of his success. "That's it!" he remembered exclaiming.) To sight the planets of other stars will require a new breed of telescopes, which will in all likelihood be assembled and stationed in space.

The star that is our sun, along with its planets, condensed from a cloud in interstellar gas and dust that collapsed some four and a half billion years ago. As the cloud spun down, it spread out into a broad disk. The sun formed at the disk's dense heart. The planets accreted around the sun in a flat plane—the same flat plane in which they orbit to this day. In January of 1994, the Hubble Space Telescope captured its first compelling images of the process repeating itself elsewhere—in a region of the constellation Orion, where new stars are forming.

The individual worlds of our solar system differ drastically from one another, despite their common origin, and each planet is defined in part by its distance from the center: On the heat-soaked surface of Mercury, tides of solid rock have

been raised by the nearby sun. Around Venus, an atmosphere run amok has smothered a nearly Earth-size world under a blanket of carbon dioxide and sulfuric acid at least fifty miles thick. Earth might better have been named Water, because its liquid presence—covering most of the surface—is what distinguishes the third planet from all the others. The nearness of Mars, along with its Earth-like features (two polar ice caps, for example, easily seen through a small telescope), has inspired fantasies of life-forms there. In 1877, when Giovanni Schiaparelli viewed Mars from Milan, he saw a maze of straight lines crazing the planet's surface. He described the markings as *canali*, meaning "grooves," or "channels," mapped them, and gave them names—Elysium, Eden, Paradise, Utopia, and the like—but he did not pretend to know what they were. Later, after sloppy translation into English turned the features into "canals," the American astronomer Percival Lowell surrendered Mars to an intelligent race of imaginary beings who fended off fatal drought with a planetwide irrigation network.

Across the asteroid belt from Mars, Jupiter is the quintessential gas giant: it has no solid surface to speak of. Saturn, squashed by a rapid rotation rate to the most oblate of all the planets—flattened at the poles and spread at the equator—has its squatness exaggerated by broad encircling rings. Green and icy Uranus lies sidewise, with its poles where its equator should be. Neptune has white cirrus clouds, fashioned from crystals of frozen methane, moving in changing weather patterns over an ice-slush "ocean" of methane, ammonia, and frigid water. Pluto, the coldest, smallest, and least known planet, raises many questions at the ninth circle of the solar system, having never been visited by any American or Russian mission of robot exploration. (Of the four spacecraft that are heading completely out of the solar system—Pioneers 10 and 11, Voyagers 1 and 2—not one has ventured close enough to Pluto to learn anything about it.) The instrument most actively pushing planetary exploration forward now, toward Pluto and elsewhere—at a time when funding for big planetary missions has dropped far below its former levels—is the Hubble Space Telescope.

ALTHOUGH the primary mission of the Hubble Space Telescope is to probe beyond our galaxy in order to determine the size, age, and fate of the universe—whether it will expand forever or eventually contract—roughly ten per cent of telescope time is spent on solar-system studies. This division of Hubble's labor reflects the demographics of American space science: of the more than sixty-three hundred members of the American Astronomical Society, at the most twelve hundred pursue lunar and planetary studies full time. The rest devote their research efforts to subjects like stellar astronomy, theoretical astrophysics, galactic dynamics, and cosmology. Even the name of the telescope stresses its obedience to majority rule, by honoring the memory of Edwin P. Hubble (1889–1953), the American astronomer who first grasped the immensity and the expansion of the universe. Edwin Hubble made his discoveries through a telescope perched on a California mountaintop. His namesake enjoys a much better vantage point—three hundred and seventy miles straight up, where it orbits the Earth every ninety minutes and its view of the cosmos is unobstructed by the distortion and jiggle of Earth's atmosphere. As a result, H.S.T., as it is often called, can literally see forever.

The Hubble's international retinue of about four hundred astronomers, computer scientists, and technicians runs around-the-clock operations from the Space Telescope Science Institute, a modern five-story building on the Baltimore campus of Johns Hopkins University. In the lobby of the institute, near the receptionist's desk, a small, wall-mounted television screen continually fills with serial images of planets, galaxies, supernova remnants, and comets—trophies of the telescope's reconnaissance.

Overhead in the atrium hangs a full-size replica of the telescope, wrapped in heat-reflecting aluminum foil, just like the real thing. It is a long, large tube, with a hinged cover at one end which can be flipped up and down, like one of those plastic visors people snap on their eyeglasses to make temporary sunglasses: for a few minutes during some orbits, the Hubble Space Telescope must "blink" to block the nearby Earth from its view.

Many yellow metal handles, stuck all over the outside of the telescope, give astronauts a handhold virtually anywhere along or around it. Seeing the handles reminded me that although this instrument was deployed from the cargo bay of a space shuttle to make its observations without the interference of human beings or the air they breathe, it is first and last a man-made tool, dependent on regular maintenance calls. When Keith Noll, a resident planetary scientist at the institute, came to fetch me from the lobby, I remarked on the abundance and the significance of the yellow handles. He pursed his lips and murmured, "Thank God for that."

Everyone at the institute remembers the months following Hubble's launch, in April of 1990, when the telescope was an orbiting embarrassment, depicted in newspaper cartoons as a mechanical Mr. Magoo in space. Then the perfectly executed repair mission, three and a half years later, redeemed the observatory as the most credible witness ever to astronomical events.

Noll, at thirty-eight, represents the second generation of planetary scientists—those whose childhoods were dominated by the Apollo moon landing, and who as young adults watched Carl Sagan's "Cosmos" on public television. Sagan, the best known and loved of the first-generation planetary explorers, availed himself of a series of direct exploration opportunities via spacecraft that had been dispatched to every planet from Mercury to Neptune. Noll, who had begun his science studies in physics, switched to planetary science after thirteen episodes of "Cosmos," because, he recalls, "the idea of studying places where you could actually go someday turned me on."

"Go" is necessarily a relative word in Noll's current vocabulary. The telescope is one giant step removed from missions that actually visit planets by proxy, the way the Galileo spacecraft is currently exploring the atmosphere and moons of Jupiter. (Recent revelations show closeups of the moon Callisto's cratered surface.) But if planetary scientists don't consider the Hubble a substitute for visitation, they are awfully glad to have it.

"I don't usually think of myself standing on the surface of Ganymede, scooping up a shovel of snow, and seeing all these little bubbles of oxygen in it," Noll says. "But in an abstract way that's what I'm doing, day in and day out." This last was said joyfully, as though Noll couldn't quite believe his good fortune at having found a job that permitted him to live out a childhood dream. Virtually every planetary scientist I've ever interviewed expressed the same sense of awestruck privilege, as though he were pursuing favorite hobbies on company time.

Noll's major research concerns the four largest moons of Jupiter, known as the Galilean satellites, because they were among the first objects Galileo discovered with his homemade telescope, in 1610. Noll relies on an instrument aboard the Hubble called the Faint Object Spectrograph, which allows him to look beyond the realm of visible light into the ultraviolet. Such observations are impossible to conduct from the ground, because Earth's ozone layer blocks out the extremely short wavelengths of ultraviolet radiation. Thanks to the Hubble, however, Noll and his colleagues have identified the presence of ozone around Ganymede, a planet-size Galilean moon. Noll believes that a tenuous oxygen atmosphere surrounds Ganymede. Virtually nothing else about Ganymede's atmosphere seems Earth-like, however, although the grooves and furrows that score its surface recall the linear "canals" of Mars.

"One of the hardest things about being a scientist," Noll says, "is selecting a problem that's small enough for you to actually attack and pursue as a project yet big enough to add something significant to what's already known. One way to fit into the bigger picture is to study systems or phenomena that reflect back to phenomena on Earth. Comparing planets that way can push you ahead or uncover the flaws in your logic. Another way to go, which is a little more interesting to me, is to try to work backward in time and figure out how the planets got the way they are. If you can work your way back to the beginning of the solar system, you're not too big a step away from what you see when you look at other stars that have disks around them, and, presumably, planets forming in the disks. That gives you the connection—the history of how we got from a big blob of gas to a star that has planets, with life on one of them."

While many astronomers routinely spend several days a month travelling, because they have to trek to and from mountaintop telescopes in remote regions of Hawaii, Chile, or Australia, Noll and the other observers using the Hubble don't need to leave their offices. Once the proposals they submit, outlining how and why they want to use the telescope, are approved, the telescope does the rest: it takes the required images or measurements and logs them, digit by digit, onto an onboard tape recorder. Usually within hours the scientific information arrives at the Space Telescope Science Institute, and there it is calibrated, cleaned of background noise, configured, converted into usable units for analysis, and computerized. The observing astronomer receives terse E-mail messages from the institute, the first one saying "We have scheduled your observations" and the last one, ideally, saying "We have taken your observations." A few days later, the data tapes arrive on his or her desk by mail or Federal Express.

The exception so far is a forty-five-year-old planetary scientist named Larry Esposito, who won permission to put the Hubble through its most dangerous mission to date. Last year, he travelled from the University of Colorado at Boulder, where he teaches astronomy, to Baltimore, in order to man the telescope during the crucial nine hours of his Venus observations.

"There were some tricky things that had to do with wiggling the telescope," Esposito explained to me. "Venus is so close to the sun that we faced a risk of damaging the telescope's optics and detectors."

Esposito had made plans to operate Hubble in a Dracula mode—catching quick glimpses of Venus during a five-minute span in each orbit when the telescope still lay hidden in the shadow of Earth but Venus was already visibly risen, and then slewing the delicate optics quickly out of harm's way before sunup. "I definitely didn't want to have to go around saying, 'It was my experiment that fried the space telescope,'" he said.

Esposito submitted his initial application in 1985—five years before the telescope was launched. Nearly a decade passed during which institute review panels first said they would allow Esposito's experiment and then they wouldn't. When the final O.K. came down, Esposito had only a month to get ready instead of the usual yearlong lead time. For a while, it seemed as if he would be followed by misfortune. On the night he arrived, he was told that the Hubble had experienced a malfunction and shut itself down. He flew back West, expecting to wait well over a year

for another chance. But only two weeks later he found himself hurrying back to Baltimore with all systems go.

Esposito continues to analyze the pictures it took him so long to secure. Venus's permanent veiled condition heightens his triumph. For decades, the planet, despite being Earth's closest neighbor and near twin in size, had resisted most efforts at direct exploration. It simply devoured a dozen Russian Venera landers in the sixties; they were all melted or crushed within an hour by nine-hundred-degree heat and by pressures equal to those three thousand feet beneath the sea.

Esposito was promised another look at Venus through Hubble's eyes this past August, but preparations for the next big telescope refurbishment, coming up in March of 1997, have delayed those plans indefinitely.

"In the space business, you have to be very patient," Esposito said. For twelve years, he was able to make daily observations via the Pioneer Venus orbiter, but that ended in October of 1992, when the spacecraft burned up like a meteor falling through Venus's atmosphere. "Hubble is more important now than it used to be," he concluded, with an almost grim determination, "because the missions we sent to Venus have all ended."

FOLLOWING the discovery of one small rock from Mars, a new enthusiasm for visits to planets is building. Scientists and government officials speak of a "return to Mars" as though the twenty-year gap in space missions to that planet were just an oversight, instead of the end of an era. Planetary missions such as Pioneer Venus and its successor Magellan (which spent the early nineties piercing the Venusian clouds with radar to construct detailed maps, and even a globe, of the planet's surface) fit the mold of Big Science. They had followed in the footsteps of the Apollo manned lunar missions, the two Vikings that landed on Mars twenty years ago, and the Voyagers that flew through the environs of the outer planets between 1977 and 1989.

Dan Goldin, the NASA head, described those vehicles to me as "heavy, expensive, multi-decadal spacecraft." They took so long to build, he lamented, that by the time they were launched they were prac-

tically obsolete. His motivational mantra for the modern NASA, "Faster, Better, Cheaper," has apparently sealed the fate of such behemoths. The last planetary mission of its kind, the Cassini mission to Saturn, which is to lift off next October, is currently being made ready in a high-bay clean room, the size of an airplane hangar, at NASA's Jet Propulsion Laboratory, in Pasadena.

Last May, when I visited J.P.L., one of the planetary scientists offered to show me Cassini under construction. Watching the assembly process through a picture window from the scaffold of a visitors' gallery, I tried to pick out the ingredients of the spacecraft from the several garages' worth of instrument components hanging on the walls, stacked on platforms, and freestanding about the floor. Three men dressed in white outfits, much like the one Woody Allen wore when he played the role of a sperm, were fitting pieces together on Cassini's skeletal frame. They moved slowly and deliberately. There was none of the easy swagger one sees at an ordinary construction site, where the guys swing their hammers in a routine rhythm. This is the only machine of its kind anywhere in the world, I found myself thinking. It will take at least another year to build and test all its complex parts. And when they get it finished they will drive it cross-country by truck to Cape Canaveral, load it on a Titan IV rocket, and shoot it on its way to Saturn, nine hundred million miles across the solar system.

Outside the assembly facility, on a sunny Southwest afternoon, the San Gabriel Mountains hovered on the brink of visibility. Their massive shapes faded in and out of sight, reduced to surreality by intervening smog—an eloquent reminder of obscuring effects on the Earth's atmosphere.

As Cassini (named for the seventeenth-century astronomer who detected the dark gap in Saturn's rings) is slowly approaching the launchpad, the Hubble telescope is keeping the best available eye on Saturn. The Hubble's high-resolution images are clear enough to pick up storm systems on the face of the planet, and its ability to observe at infrared wavelengths has allowed researchers to map Saturn's largest moon, Titan, right through the thick orange smog of its atmosphere. Titan, larger than either Mercury or Pluto, has long fostered visions of possible life-forms. When Cassini arrives in the vicinity of Saturn, in 2004, a probe, built by the European Space Agency, will parachute down through Titan's atmosphere, which is predominantly nitrogen, and investigate conditions there.

What Hubble lacks in proximity to Saturn it makes up for in persistence. By virtue of being parked in low Earth orbit, the telescope can react to news reports and weather developments concerning the outer planets. Hubble captured a graceful triple ring-plane crossing on Saturn last year. About every fifteen years, the rings orient themselves more or less edge on to the Earth over a period of several months. At such times the rings become virtually invisible— just a pencil-thin black shadow across Saturn's equator. While the glare of the rings was absent last summer, astronomers using the Hubble went hunting for undiscovered Saturnian moons (in addition to the eighteen already known), and identified two more.

The most memorable of the recent Hubble images were all shot by one instrument: Hubble's Wide Field and Planetary Camera 2, installed during the December, 1993, repair mission. In the eyes of people like Dave Crisp, a member of the team that designed and built the camera at the Jet Propulsion Lab, its work may surpass that of spacecraft like Cassini. "In the beginning, I think people wondered what the Hubble could possibly add to the data collected by spacecraft that had actually flown past or gone into orbit around another planet," Crisp said. "But you have to remember that most of those missions were designed in the late nineteen-sixties and early nineteen-seventies, and they took their images with what amounted to an old television camera. The Voyager instrumentation was state of the art when it was launched, but, boy, by the time it reached Neptune, in 1989, it was the Stone Age. The Hubble at least represents eighties-vintage technology. And the new camera illustrates what you can do with nineties technology."

Which is?

"Whenever we look at an object with an instrument that's ten times better than its predecessor, we almost always learn something new and fundamental about that object."

Crisp has wallpapered his windowless office at J.P.L. with Hubble planet views, giving the most square footage to his two personal favorites, Mars and Neptune.

"Hubble provided an opportunity to observe Mars in a way that we had never had before—not even from the Viking missions that orbited and landed there," he said. "Those spacecraft didn't have instruments that were sensitive at the range of wavelengths Hubble can cover. As a result, Mars has always been portrayed as a barren rock. It's not. It's actually an interesting place." Crisp's travel-brochure-style pinup of Mars shows high, wispy clouds over the afternoon portion of the planet and low-lying ground fog where the Martian morning is breaking. Crisp pointed to a place where a catastrophic flood had occurred perhaps more than three billion years ago, when climate conditions on Mars were wetter—about when the now fossilized forms inside the Mars rock must have gained their foothold there. "This is the basin where the Pathfinder spacecraft will land on July 4, 1997," Crisp said, still pointing.

The Mars Pathfinder, one of the new breed of Discovery missions designed to fit the "Faster, Better, Cheaper" creed, is scheduled for launch on December 2nd. It carries a roving instrument package on wheels that will drive itself around the landing site to monitor the geology there for up to one month. Pathfinder leads a series of more than a dozen planned space probes bound for Mars in the next decade. (One of these, a Russian robot craft, crashed to earth on November 17th. Mars Global Surveyor, launched last month, is expected to begin orbiting Mars in September of 1997.) Within the next seven to nine years, NASA intends to send a mission that will pluck rocks from the Martian surface and ferry them to Earth.

For the Mars Pathfinder mission, scientists will rely on the Hubble telescope to scrutinize the area for them, in preparation for landing. Its resolution is sharp enough to find features as fine as a haze of airborne dust.

"From Hubble observations all through next March, April, and May, we'll be giving daily weather reports," Dave Crisp said, laughing with delight at the prospect. "With Hubble we can monitor physical processes and watch the surfaces of these bodies evolve over time. Planetary science didn't have a way to interpret the effects of change on a planet's atmosphere or surface. And maybe now through such observations we can come to understand these processes a little better, so we can actually start using the larger part of our solar system as a laboratory for studying how planets work."

The hard-rock guys (and girls) have been waiting all their lives for this continuous-run view of solar-system dynamics, where the unexpected occurs every moment.

"I picked planetary astronomy because things change a lot," Heidi Hammel, of M.I.T., an expert on Neptune, told me. "Generally speaking, with galaxies, if you miss it tonight you can look tomorrow night—or next week or next year or ten years from now—and nothing's going to happen. It's going to be the same ten thousand years from now, more or less. But the planets are very active. Any time you look, you don't know what you're going to see. You have to be *on*. You can't screw up. If you miss something, it's over, and it's not going to happen again."

ON June 22nd of this year, the Hubble telescope set a new record for itself by taking its hundred-thousandth exposure after six years in space. The images carry more than scientific import. They excite the interest of schoolchildren and stir enthusiasm in the general public. The Space Telescope Science Institute posts its pretty planet pictures on the World Wide Web, for all to download. It also fills orders, through a photo contractor, for hardcopy prints. And John Trauger, a physicist at the Jet Propulsion Laboratory, and several of his colleagues are compiling a selection of Hubble shots to be published as a book.

"The Hubble results interest people because they push back the darkness," Trauger told me. His own research, on the atmosphere of Jupiter, came from his boyhood interest in the behavior of light. "Astronomers have their own way of looking at things, which is probably not the way everybody does," he conceded. "Scientists do what fascinates them, and what fascinates them is not something you can discover with science. They're interested in investigating where planets come from, say, not because science tells them to do that, but because as human beings they find that interesting. They go after questions they consider worth the investment of a lifetime."

Trauger rummaged among piles of glossy photographs and fished out a picture of Saturn, shimmering in soft light and bisected by the dark line of the rings seen edge on. "This is a thing of beauty, I think," he said. "It's art work. Exquisite, really." He picked up another eight-by-ten print, of an immense region inside the Eagle Nebula where new stars are forming. This photograph, which appeared in press reports all over the world, must be the Hubble Space Telescope's most emotion-laden image yet—an icon to rival the Apollo photograph of the Earth taken from the surface of the moon. It depicts three eerie pillars of dark dust and gas thrusting up into a blue iridescence sprinkled with newborn stars. The pillars glow from the heat of star birth: a deep red fades to halos of gold at their margins. Whorls of interstellar dust alternately billow into cliff-top peaks and trail off in wispy webs of stellar Spanish moss.

When Keith Noll, at the Space Telescope Science Institute, showed me a poster-size blowup of this same spectacle on the wall of a conference room, he had run his forefinger over it, tracing sections that people had compared to a cat, a gargoyle, the erosion-carved needles of Bryce Canyon, the face of Jesus. Then he stepped back to view the whole with me, having said nothing about the towering, celestial-sized phallus at the center of the scene. Its presence seemed to insist that generative forms in nature, whether inorganic or alive, may take only certain well-defined shapes, which repeat themselves from one scale to another across the universe.

Trauger's smaller version of the latter-day creation scene retained all the power of the big picture. Even reduced to the size of a postage stamp, the picture's star-studded pillars would grab you.

Trauger asked me to imagine that I was looking right into a huge dark cloud of cold dust. He said the stellar wind from the newly formed stars had eaten a hole in the side of the cloud, and that the pillars were being sculpted by ultraviolet radiation—"chipping away, like rain coming down." The bright spots, resembling lighted birthday-cake candles, on the dense, dark pillars marked the sites where stars had just begun to burn. And the smallest entities of all—little pointed projections along the pillar walls, and free-floating globules of dust—were really as wide, each of them, as a sun surrounded by a whole solar system.

Dan Goldin also had a large framed print of the Hubble's Eagle Nebula image hanging in his NASA office. "I show that picture all over," Goldin told me as both of us stared at it from the other side of the room.

"What does it say to you?" I asked him.

"It's a question, not a statement," he replied. "You ask fifty questions after you look at that picture." We both kept our eyes riveted on it, waiting for his feelings to take words. "That cloud on the left is six trillion miles high," Goldin said, finally. "That's one light-year. The first thing that comes to my mind is: How, as a species, did we attain the intellect that went into making the tool that could take that picture? Seven thousand light-years from Earth, and look at the clarity we got in that picture. That picture is creation. You're seeing *stars* being formed, if we understand it right." He paused again, then added, "When I showed this picture in Bozeman, Montana, the local merchants stood up and applauded. They were just struck by it. With all the problems of today, people are able to look at that picture and say, 'We need to move out into the future.'"

Goldin returned to his own fond futuristic vision of finding and photographing an Earth-like planet less than a hundred light-years from here, perhaps within the next fifteen or twenty-five years. "*This* picture," he said, nodding appreciatively at the Eagle Nebula on the wall, "is goose-bump material. *That* picture"—and he gestured vaguely toward Earth's undiscovered twin—"is tears."

The Evolution of Life on the Earth

The history of life is not necessarily progressive;
it is certainly not predictable. The earth's creatures have evolved
through a series of contingent and fortuitous events

Stephen Jay Gould

STEPHEN JAY GOULD teaches biology, geology and the history of science at Harvard University, where he has been on the faculty since 1967. He received an A.B. from Antioch College and a Ph.D. in paleontology from Columbia University. Well known for his popular scientific writings, in particular his monthly column in *Natural History* magazine, he is the author of 13 books.

Some creators announce their inventions with grand éclat. God proclaimed, "Fiat lux," and then flooded his new universe with brightness. Others bring forth great discoveries in a modest guise, as did Charles Darwin in defining his new mechanism of evolutionary causality in 1859: "I have called this principle, by which each slight variation, if useful, is preserved, by the term Natural Selection."

Natural selection is an immensely powerful yet beautifully simple theory that has held up remarkably well, under intense and unrelenting scrutiny and testing, for 135 years. In essence, natural selection locates the mechanism of evolutionary change in a "struggle" among organisms for reproductive success, leading to improved fit of populations to changing environments. (Struggle is often a metaphorical description and need not be viewed as overt combat, guns blazing. Tactics for reproductive success include a variety of nonmartial activities such as earlier and more frequent mating or better cooperation with partners in raising offspring.) Natural selection is therefore a principle of local adaptation, not of general advance or progress.

Yet powerful though the principle may be, natural selection is not the only cause of evolutionary change (and may, in many cases, be overshadowed by other forces). This point needs emphasis because the standard misapplication of evolutionary theory assumes that biological explanation may be equated with devising accounts, often speculative and conjectural in practice, about the adaptive value of any given feature in its original environment (human aggression as good for hunting, music and religion as good for tribal cohesion, for example). Darwin himself strongly emphasized the multifactorial nature of evolutionary change and warned against too exclusive a reliance on natural selection, by placing the following statement in a maximally conspicuous place at the very end of his introduction: "I am convinced that Natural Selection has been the most important, but not the exclusive, means of modification."

Natural selection is not fully sufficient to explain evolutionary change for two major reasons. First, many other causes are powerful, particularly at levels of biological organization both above and below the traditional Darwinian focus on organisms and their struggles for reproductive success. At the lowest level of substitution in individual base pairs of DNA, change is often effectively neutral and therefore random. At higher levels, involving entire species or faunas, punctuated equilibrium can produce evolutionary trends by selection of species based on their rates of origin and extirpation, whereas mass extinctions wipe out substantial parts of biotas for reasons unrelated to adaptive struggles of constituent species in "normal" times between such events.

Second, and the focus of this article, no matter how adequate our general theory of evolutionary change, we also yearn to document and understand the actual pathway of life's history. Theory, of course, is relevant to explaining the pathway (nothing about the pathway can be inconsistent with good theory, and theory can predict certain general aspects of life's geologic pattern). But the actual pathway is strongly *underdetermined* by our general theory of life's evolution. This point needs some belaboring as a central yet widely misunderstood aspect of the world's complexity. Webs and chains of historical events are so intricate, so imbued with random and chaotic elements, so unrepeatable in encompassing such a multitude of unique (and uniquely interacting) objects, that standard models of simple prediction and replication do not apply.

History can be explained, with satisfying rigor if evidence be adequate, after a sequence of events unfolds, but it cannot be predicted with any precision beforehand. Pierre-Simon Laplace, echoing the growing and confident determinism of the late 18th century, once said that he could specify all future states if he could know the position and motion of all particles in the cosmos at any moment, but the nature of universal complexity shatters this chimerical dream. History includes too much chaos, or extremely sensitive dependence on minute and unmeasurable differences in initial conditions, leading to massively divergent outcomes based on tiny and unknowable disparities in starting points. And history includes too much contingency, or shaping of present results by long chains of unpredictable antecedent states, rather than immediate determination by timeless laws of nature.

Homo sapiens did not appear on the earth, just a geologic second ago, be-

1. NATURAL HISTORY: THE STAGE FOR HUMAN HISTORY

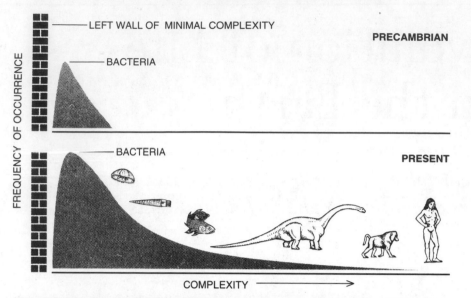

PROGRESS DOES NOT RULE (and is not even a primary thrust of) the evolutionary process. For reasons of chemistry and physics, life arises next to the "left wall" of its simplest conceivable and preservable complexity. This style of life (bacterial) has remained most common and most successful. A few creatures occasionally move to the right, thus extending the right tail in the distribution of complexity. Many always move to the left, but they are absorbed within space already occupied. Note that the bacterial mode has never changed in position, but just grown higher.

cause evolutionary theory predicts such an outcome based on themes of progress and increasing neural complexity. Humans arose, rather, as a fortuitous and contingent outcome of thousands of linked events, any one of which could have occurred differently and sent history on an alternative pathway that would not have led to consciousness. To cite just four among a multitude: (1) If our inconspicuous and fragile lineage had not been among the few survivors of the initial radiation of multicellular animal life in the Cambrian explosion 530 million years ago, then no vertebrates would have inhabited the earth at all. (Only one member of our chordate phylum, the genus *Pikaia*, has been found among these earliest fossils. This small and simple swimming creature, showing its allegiance to us by possessing a notochord, or dorsal stiffening rod, is among the rarest fossils of the Burgess Shale, our best preserved Cambrian fauna.) (2) If a small and unpromising group of lobe-finned fishes had not evolved fin bones with a strong central axis capable of bearing weight on land, then vertebrates might never have become terrestrial. (3) If a large extraterrestrial body had not struck the earth 65 million years ago, then dinosaurs would still be dominant and mammals insignificant (the situation that had prevailed for 100 million years previously). (4) If a small lineage of primates had not evolved upright posture on the drying African savannas just two to four

million years ago, then our ancestry might have ended in a line of apes that, like the chimpanzee and gorilla today, would have become ecologically marginal and probably doomed to extinction despite their remarkable behavioral complexity.

Therefore, to understand the events and generalities of life's pathway, we must go beyond principles of evolutionary theory to a paleontological examination of the contingent pattern of life's history on our planet—the single actualized version among millions of plausible alternatives that happened not to occur. Such a view of life's history is highly contrary both to conventional deterministic models of Western science and to the deepest social traditions and psychological hopes of Western culture for a history culminating in humans as life's highest expression and intended planetary steward.

Science can, and does, strive to grasp nature's factuality, but all science is socially embedded, and all scientists record prevailing "certainties," however hard they may be aiming for pure objectivity. Darwin himself, in the closing lines of *The Origin of Species,* expressed Victorian social preference more than nature's record in writing: "As natural selection works solely by and for the good of each being, all corporeal and mental endowments will tend to progress towards perfection."

Life's pathway certainly includes many features predictable from laws of na-

ture, but these aspects are too broad and general to provide the "rightness" that we seek for validating evolution's particular results—roses, mushrooms, people and so forth. Organisms adapt to, and are constrained by, physical principles. It is, for example, scarcely surprising, given laws of gravity, that the largest vertebrates in the sea (whales) exceed the heaviest animals on land (elephants today, dinosaurs in the past), which, in turn, are far bulkier than the largest vertebrate that ever flew (extinct pterosaurs of the Mesozoic era).

Predictable ecological rules govern the structuring of communities by principles of energy flow and thermodynamics (more biomass in prey than in predators, for example). Evolutionary trends, once started, may have local predictability ("arms races," in which both predators and prey hone their defenses and weapons, for example—a pattern that Geerat J. Vermeij of the University of California at Davis has called "escalation" and documented in increasing strength of both crab claws and shells of their gastropod prey through time). But laws of nature do not tell us why we have crabs and snails at all, why insects rule the multicellular world and why vertebrates rather than persistent algal mats exist as the most complex forms of life on the earth.

Relative to the conventional view of life's history as an at least broadly predictable process of gradually advancing complexity through time, three features of the paleontological record stand out in opposition and shall therefore serve as organizing themes for the rest of this article: the constancy of modal complexity throughout life's history; the concentration of major events in short bursts interspersed with long periods of relative stability; and the role of external impositions, primarily mass extinctions, in disrupting patterns of "normal" times. These three features, combined with more general themes of chaos and contingency, require a new framework for conceptualizing and drawing life's history, and this article therefore closes with suggestions for a different iconography of evolution.

The primary paleontological fact about life's beginnings points to predictability for the onset and very little for the particular pathways thereafter. The earth is 4.6 billion years old, but the oldest rocks date to about 3.9 billion years because the earth's surface became molten early in its history, a result of bombardment by large amounts of cosmic debris during the solar system's coalescence, and of heat generated by radioactive decay of short-lived isotopes. These oldest rocks are too metamorphosed by subsequent heat and pressure to preserve fossils (though some scientists interpret the proportions of carbon isotopes in these rocks as signs of organic production). The oldest rocks sufficiently unaltered to retain cellular fossils—African and Australian sediments dated to 3.5 billion years old—do preserve prokaryotic cells (bacteria and cyanophytes) and stromatolites (mats of sediment trapped and bound by these cells in shallow marine waters). Thus, life on the earth evolved quickly and is as old as it could be. This fact alone seems to indicate an inevitability, or at least a predictability, for life's origin from the original chemical constituents of atmosphere and ocean.

No one can doubt that more complex creatures arose sequentially after this prokaryotic beginning—first eukaryotic cells, perhaps about two billion years ago, then multicellular animals about 600 million years ago, with a relay of highest complexity among animals passing from invertebrates, to marine vertebrates and, finally (if we wish, albeit parochially, to honor neural architecture as a primary criterion), to reptiles, mammals and humans. This is the conventional sequence represented in the old charts and texts as an "age of invertebrates," followed by an "age of fishes," "age of reptiles," "age of mammals," and "age of man" (to add the old gender bias to all the other prejudices implied by this sequence).

I do not deny the facts of the preceding paragraph but wish to argue that our conventional desire to view history as progressive, and to see humans as predictably dominant, has grossly distorted our interpretation of life's pathway by falsely placing in the center of things a relatively minor phenomenon that arises only as a side consequence of a physically constrained starting point. The most salient feature of life has been the stability of its bacterial mode from the beginning of the fossil record until today and, with little doubt, into all future time so long as the earth endures. This is truly the "age of bacteria"—as it was in the beginning, is now and ever shall be.

For reasons related to the chemistry of life's origin and the physics of self-organization, the first living things arose at the lower limit of life's conceivable, preservable complexity. Call this lower limit the "left wall" for an architecture of complexity. Since so little space exists between the left wall and life's initial bacterial mode in the fossil record, only one direction for future increment

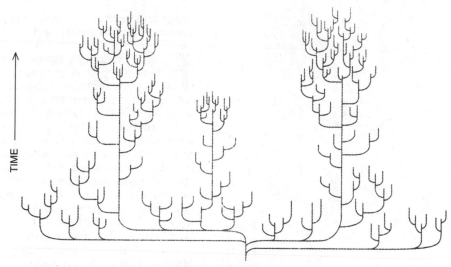

ANATOMICAL DIVERSITY

NEW ICONOGRAPHY OF LIFE'S TREE shows that maximal diversity in anatomical forms (not in number of species) is reached very early in life's multicellular history. Later times feature extinction of most of these initial experiments and enormous success within surviving lines. This success is measured in the proliferation of species but not in the development of new anatomies. Today we have more species than ever before, although they are restricted to fewer basic anatomies.

exists—toward greater complexity at the right. Thus, every once in a while, a more complex creature evolves and extends the range of life's diversity in the only available direction. In technical terms, the distribution of complexity becomes more strongly right skewed through these occasional additions.

But the additions are rare and episodic. They do not even constitute an evolutionary series but form a motley sequence of distantly related taxa, usually depicted as eukaryotic cell, jellyfish, trilobite, nautiloid, eurypterid (a large relative of horseshoe crabs), fish, an amphibian such as *Eryops*, a dinosaur, a mammal and a human being. This sequence cannot be construed as the major thrust or trend of life's history. Think rather of an occasional creature tumbling into the empty right region of complexity's space. Throughout this entire time, the bacterial mode has grown in height and remained constant in position. Bacteria represent the great success story of life's pathway. They occupy a wider domain of environments and span a broader range of biochemistries than any other group. They are adaptable, indestructible and astoundingly diverse. We cannot even imagine how anthropogenic intervention might threaten their extinction, although we worry about our impact on nearly every other form of life. The number of *Escherichia coli* cells in the gut of each human being exceeds the number of humans that has ever lived on this planet. One might grant that complexifica-

tion for life as a whole represents a pseudotrend based on constraint at the left wall but still hold that evolution within particular groups differentially favors complexity when the founding lineage begins far enough from the left wall to permit movement in both directions. Empirical tests of this interesting hypothesis are just beginning (as concern for the subject mounts among paleontologists), and we do not yet have enough cases to advance a generality. But the first two studies—by Daniel W. McShea of the University of Michigan on mammalian vertebrae and by George F. Boyajian of the University of Pennsylvania on ammonite suture lines—show no evolutionary tendencies to favor increased complexity.

Moreover, when we consider that for each mode of life involving greater complexity, there probably exists an equally advantageous style based on greater simplicity of form (as often found in parasites, for example), then preferential evolution toward complexity seems unlikely a priori. Our impression that life evolves toward greater complexity is probably only a bias inspired by parochial focus on ourselves, and consequent overattention to complexifying creatures, while we ignore just as many lineages adapting equally well by becoming simpler in form. The morphologically degenerate parasite, safe within its host, has just as much prospect for evolutionary success as its gorgeously elaborate relative coping with the

slings and arrows of outrageous fortune in a tough external world.

Even if complexity is only a drift away from a constraining left wall, we might view trends in this direction as more predictable and characteristic of life's pathway as a whole if increments of complexity accrued in a persistent and gradually accumulating manner through time. But nothing about life's history is more peculiar with respect to this common (and false) expectation than the actual pattern of extended stability and rapid episodic movement, as revealed by the fossil record.

Life remained almost exclusively unicellular for the first five sixths of its history—from the first recorded fossils at 3.5 billion years to the first well-documented multicellular animals less than 600 million years ago. (Some simple multicellular algae evolved more than a billion years ago, but these organisms belong to the plant kingdom and have no genealogical connection with animals.) This long period of unicellular life does include, to be sure, the vitally important transition from simple prokaryotic cells without organelles to eukaryotic cells with nuclei, mitochondria and other complexities of intracellular architecture—but no recorded attainment of multicellular animal organization for a full three billion years. If complexity is such a good thing, and multicellularity represents its initial phase in our usual view, then life certainly took its time in making this crucial step. Such delays speak strongly against general progress as the major theme of life's history, even if they can be plausibly explained by lack of sufficient atmospheric oxygen for most of Precambrian time or by failure of unicellular life to achieve some structural threshold acting as a prerequisite to multicellularity.

More curiously, all major stages in organizing animal life's multicellular architecture then occurred in a short period beginning less than 600 million years ago and ending by about 530 million years ago—and the steps within this sequence are also discontinuous and episodic, not gradually accumulative. The first fauna, called Ediacaran

1. *Vauxia* (gracile)	11. *Micromitra*	22. *Emeraldella*	34. *Sidneyia*
2. *Branchiocaris*	12. *Echmatocrinus*	23. *Burgessia*	35. *Odaraia*
3. *Opabinia*	13. *Chancelloria*	24. *Leanchoilia*	36. *Eiffelia*
4. *Amiskwia*	14. *Pirania*	25. *Sanctacaris*	37. *Mackenzia*
5. *Vauxia* (robust)	15. *Choia*	26. *Ottoia*	38. *Odontogriphus*
6. *Molaria*	16. *Leptomitus*	27. *Louisella*	39. *Hallucigenia*
7. * Aysheaia*	17. *Dinomischus*	28. *Actaeus*	40. *Elrathia*
8. *Sarotrocercus*	18. *Wiwaxia*	29. *Yohoia*	41. *Anomalocaris*
9. *Nectocaris*	19. *Naraoia*	30. *Peronochaeta*	42. *Lingulella*
10. *Pikaia*	20. *Hyolithes*	31. *Selkirkia*	43. *Scenella*
	21. *Habelia*	32. *Ancalagon*	44. *Canadaspis*
		33. *Burgessochaeta*	45. *Marrella*
			46. *Olenoides*

to honor the Australian locality of its initial discovery but now known from rocks on all continents, consists of highly flattened fronds, sheets and circlets composed of numerous slender segments quilted together. The nature of the Ediacaran fauna is now a subject of intense discussion. These creatures do not seem to be simple precursors of later forms. They may constitute a separate and failed experiment in animal life, or they may represent a full range of diploblastic (two-layered) organization, of which the modern phylum Cnidaria (corals, jellyfishes and their allies) remains as a small and much altered remnant.

In any case, they apparently died out well before the Cambrian biota evolved. The Cambrian then began with an assemblage of bits and pieces, frustratingly difficult to interpret, called the "small shelly fauna." The subsequent main pulse, starting about 530 million years ago, constitutes the famous Cambrian explosion, during which all but one modern phylum of animal life made a first appearance in the fossil record. (Geologists had previously allowed up to 40 million years for this event, but an elegant study, published in 1993, clearly restricts this period of phyletic flowering to a mere five million years.) The Bryozoa, a group of sessile and colonial marine organisms, do not arise until the beginning of the subsequent, Ordovician period, but this apparent

GREAT DIVERSITY quickly evolved at the dawn of multicellular animal life during the Cambrian period (530 million years ago). The creatures shown here are all found in the Middle Cambrian Burgess Shale fauna of Canada. They include some familiar forms (sponges, brachiopods) that have survived. But many creatures (such as the giant *Anomalocaris*, at the lower right, largest of all the Cambrian animals) did not live for long and are so anatomically peculiar (relative to survivors) that we cannot classify them among known phyla.

delay may be an artifact of failure to discover Cambrian representatives.

Although interesting and portentous events have occurred since, from the flowering of dinosaurs to the origin of human consciousness, we do not exaggerate greatly in stating that the subsequent history of animal life amounts to little more than variations on anatomical themes established during the Cambrian explosion within five million years. Three billion years of unicellularity, followed by five million years of intense creativity and then capped by more than 500 million years of variation on set anatomical themes can scarcely be read as a predictable, inexorable or continuous trend toward progress or increasing complexity.

We do not know why the Cambrian explosion could establish all major anatomical designs so quickly. An "external" explanation based on ecology seems attractive: the Cambrian explosion represents an initial filling of the "ecological barrel" of niches for multicellular organisms, and any experiment found a space. The barrel has never emptied since; even the great mass extinctions left a few species in each principal role, and their occupation of ecological space forecloses opportunity for fundamental novelties. But an "internal" explanation based on genetics and development also seems necessary as a complement: the earliest multicellular animals may have maintained a flexibility for genetic change and embryological transformation that became greatly reduced as organisms "locked in" to a set of stable and successful designs.

In any case, this initial period of both internal and external flexibility yielded a range of invertebrate anatomies that may have exceeded (in just a few million years of production) the full scope of animal form in all the earth's environments today (after more than 500 million years of additional time for further expansion). Scientists are divided on this question. Some claim that the anatomical range of this initial explosion exceeded that of modern life, as

many early experiments died out and no new phyla have ever arisen. But scientists most strongly opposed to this view allow that Cambrian diversity at least equaled the modern range—so even the most cautious opinion holds that 500 million subsequent years of opportunity have not expanded the Cambrian range, achieved in just five million years. The Cambrian explosion was the most remarkable and puzzling event in the history of life.

Moreover, we do not know why most of the early experiments died, while a few survived to become our modern phyla. It is tempting to say that the victors won by virtue of greater anatomical complexity, better ecological fit or some other predictable feature of conventional Darwinian struggle. But no recognized traits unite the victors, and the radical alternative must be entertained that each early experiment received little more than the equivalent of a ticket in the largest lottery ever played out on our planet—and that each surviving lineage, including our own phylum of vertebrates, inhabits the earth today more by the luck of the draw than by any predictable struggle for existence. The history of multicellular animal life may be more a story of great reduction in initial possibilities, with stabilization of lucky survivors, than a conventional tale of steady ecological expansion and morphological progress in complexity.

Finally, this pattern of long stasis, with change concentrated in rapid episodes that establish new equilibria, may be quite general at several scales of time and magnitude, forming a kind of fractal pattern in self-similarity. According to the punctuated equilibrium model of speciation, trends within lineages occur by accumulated episodes of geologically instantaneous speciation, rather than by gradual change within continuous populations (like climbing a staircase rather than rolling a ball up an inclined plane).

E ven if evolutionary theory implied a potential internal direction for life's pathway (although previous facts and arguments in this article cast doubt on such a claim), the occasional imposition of a rapid and substantial, perhaps even truly catastrophic, change in environment would have intervened to stymie the pattern. These environmental changes trigger mass extinction of a high percentage of the earth's species and may so derail any internal direction and so reset the pathway that the net pattern of life's history looks

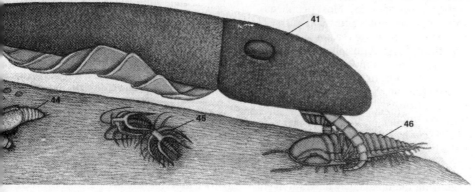

more capricious and concentrated in episodes than steady and directional. Mass extinctions have been recognized since the dawn of paleontology; the major divisions of the geologic time scale were established at boundaries marked by such events. But until the revival of interest that began in the late 1970s, most paleontologists treated mass extinctions only as intensifications of ordinary events, leading (at most) to a speeding up of tendencies that pervaded normal times. In this gradualistic theory of mass extinction, these events really took a few million years to unfold (with the appearance of suddenness interpreted as an artifact of an imperfect fossil record), and they only made the ordinary occur faster (more intense Darwinian competition in tough times, for example, leading to even more efficient replacement of less adapted by superior forms).

The reinterpretation of mass extinctions as central to life's pathway and radically different in effect began with the presentation of data by Luis and Walter Alvarez in 1979, indicating that the impact of a large extraterrestrial object (they suggested an asteroid seven to 10 kilometers in diameter) set off the last great extinction at the Cretaceous-Tertiary boundary 65 million years ago. Although the Alvarez hypothesis initially received very skeptical treatment from scientists (a proper approach to highly unconventional explanations), the case now seems virtually proved by discovery of the "smoking gun," a crater of appropriate size and age located off the Yucatán peninsula in Mexico.

This reawakening of interest also inspired paleontologists to tabulate the data of mass extinction more rigorously. Work by David M. Raup, J. J. Sepkoski, Jr., and David Jablonski of the University of Chicago has established that multicellular animal life experienced five major (end of Ordovician, late Devonian, end of Permian, end of Triassic and end of Cretaceous) and many minor mass extinctions during its 530-million-year history. We have no clear evidence that any but the last of these events was triggered by catastrophic impact, but such careful study leads to the general conclusion that mass extinctions were more frequent, more rapid, more extensive in magnitude and more different in effect than paleontologists had previously realized. These four properties encompass the radical implications of mass extinction for understanding life's pathway as more contingent and chancy than predictable and directional.

Mass extinctions are not random in their impact on life. Some lineages succumb and others survive as sensible outcomes based on presence or absence of evolved features. But especially if the triggering cause of extinction be sudden and catastrophic, the reasons for life or death may be random with respect to the original value of key features when first evolved in Darwinian struggles of normal times. This "different rules" model of mass extinction imparts a quirky and unpredictable character to life's pathway based on the evident claim that lineages cannot anticipate future contingencies of such magnitude and different operation.

To cite two examples from the impact-triggered Cretaceous-Tertiary extinction 65 million years ago: First, an important study published in 1986 noted that diatoms survived the extinction far better than other single-celled plankton (primarily coccoliths and radiolaria). This study found that many diatoms had evolved a strategy of dormancy by encystment, perhaps to survive through seasonal periods of unfavorable conditions (months of darkness in polar species as otherwise fatal to these photosynthesizing cells; sporadic availability of silica needed to construct their skeletons). Other planktonic cells had not evolved any mechanisms for dormancy. If the terminal Cretaceous impact produced a dust cloud that blocked light for several months or longer (one popular idea for a "killing scenario" in the extinction), then diatoms may have survived as a fortuitous result of dormancy mechanisms evolved for the entirely different function of weathering seasonal droughts in ordinary times. Diatoms are not superior to radiolaria or other plankton that succumbed in far greater numbers; they were simply fortunate to possess a favorable feature, evolved for other reasons, that fostered passage through the impact and its sequelae.

Second, we all know that dinosaurs perished in the end Cretaceous event and that mammals therefore rule the vertebrate world today. Most people assume that mammals prevailed in these tough times for some reason of general superiority over dinosaurs. But such a conclusion seems most unlikely. Mammals and dinosaurs had coexisted for 100 million years, and mammals had remained rat-sized or smaller, making no evolutionary "move" to oust dinosaurs. No good argument for mammalian prevalence by general superiority has ever been advanced, and fortuity seems far more likely. As one plausible argument, mammals may have survived partly as a result of their small size (with much larger, and therefore extinction-resistant, populations as a consequence, and less ecological specialization with more places to hide, so to speak). Small size may not have been a positive mammalian adaptation at all, but more a sign of inability ever to penetrate the dominant domain of dinosaurs. Yet this "negative" feature of normal times may be the key reason for mammalian survival and a prerequisite to my writing and your reading this article today.

Sigmund Freud often remarked that great revolutions in the history of science have but one common, and ironic, feature: they knock human arrogance off one pedestal after another of our previous conviction about our own self-importance. In Freud's three examples, Copernicus moved our home from center to periphery; Darwin then relegated us to "descent from an animal world"; and, finally (in one of the least modest statements of intellectual history), Freud himself discovered the unconscious and exploded the myth of a fully rational mind.

In this wise and crucial sense, the Darwinian revolution remains woefully incomplete because, even though thinking humanity accepts the fact of evolution, most of us are still unwilling to abandon the comforting view that evolution means (or at least embodies a central principle of) progress defined to render the appearance of something like human consciousness either virtually inevitable or at least predictable. The pedestal is not smashed until we abandon progress or complexification as a central principle and come to entertain the strong possibility that *H. sapiens* is but a tiny, late-arising twig on life's enormously arborescent bush—a small bud that would almost surely not appear a second time if we could replant the bush from seed and let it grow again.

Primates are visual animals, and the pictures we draw betray our deepest convictions and display our current conceptual limitations. Artists have always painted the history of fossil life as a sequence from invertebrates, to fishes, to early terrestrial amphibians and reptiles, to dinosaurs, to mammals and, finally, to humans. There are no exceptions; all sequences painted since the inception of this genre in the 1850s follow the convention.

Yet we never stop to recognize the almost absurd biases coded into this universal mode. No scene ever shows another invertebrate after fishes evolved, but invertebrates did not go away or stop evolving! After terrestrial reptiles emerge, no subsequent scene ever shows a fish (later oceanic tableaux depict only such returning reptiles as ichthyosaurs and plesiosaurs). But fishes did not stop evolving after one small lineage managed to invade the land. In fact, the major event in the evolution of fishes, the origin and rise to dominance of the teleosts, or modern bony fishes, occurred during the time of the dinosaurs and is therefore never shown at all in any of these sequences—even though teleosts include more than half of all species of vertebrates. Why should humans appear at the end of all sequences? Our order of primates is ancient among mammals, and many other successful lineages arose later than we did.

We will not smash Freud's pedestal and complete Darwin's revolution until we find, grasp and accept another way of drawing life's history. J.B.S. Haldane proclaimed nature "queerer than we can suppose," but these limits may only be socially imposed conceptual locks rather then inherent restrictions of our neurology. New icons might break the locks. Trees—or rather copiously and luxuriantly branching bushes—rather than ladders and sequences hold the key to this conceptual transition.

We must learn to depict the full range of variation, not just our parochial perception of the tiny right tail of most complex creatures. We must recognize that this tree may have contained a maximal number of branches near the beginning of multicellular life and that subsequent history is for the most part a process of elimination and lucky survivorship of a few, rather than continuous flowering, progress and expansion of a growing multitude. We must understand that little twigs are contingent nubbins, not predictable goals of the massive bush beneath. We must remember the greatest of all Biblical statements about wisdom: "She is a tree of life to them that lay hold upon her; and happy is every one that retaineth her."

FURTHER READING

THE BURGESS SHALE. Henry B. Whittington. Yale University Press, 1985.

EXTINCTION: A SCIENTIFIC AMERICAN BOOK. Steven M. Stanley. W. H. Freeman and Company, 1987.

WONDERFUL LIFE: THE BURGESS SHALE AND THE NATURE OF HISTORY. S. J. Gould. W. W. Norton, 1989.

THE BOOK OF LIFE. Edited by Stephen Jay Gould. W. W. Norton, 1993.

Mapping *the* Past

ADAM GOODHEART

Adam Goodheart, an associate editor at CIVILIZATION and author of its Lost Arts column, has also written for *The New York Times, The Washington Post* and other publications.

ANCESTORS HAVE ALWAYS BEEN HARD TO KEEP TRACK OF. We all have them, of course, but most of us can trace our families back only four or five generations. Even the oldest lineages are fairly new on the grand scale of human history; Prince Charles, with his 262,142 recorded ancestors, has a family tree little more than 1,500 years old. (Only one reliable pedigree in the world—that of the Bagratid kings of Georgia—stretches back into classical antiquity, petering out in 326 B.C.) "As each of us looks back into his or her past," wrote E.M. Forster, "doors open upon darkness."

Writing in 1939, Forster was arguing the futility of ever tracing the genetic history of a nation. Indeed, if ancestral accounts are muddled and incomplete at the level of individual families, the genealogies of entire nations and peoples are impossibly confused. Historians who refer to "the Irish" or "the Jews" as though they were well-defined groups have only the vaguest idea of their origins, of how they fit into the family tree of the human race. And when it comes to the origins and fate of long-vanished peoples like the ancient Egyptians, the darkness is almost complete. "A common language, a common religion, a common culture all belong to the present, evidence about them is available, they can be tested," Forster wrote. "But race belongs to the unknown and unknowable past. It depends upon who went to bed with whom in the year 1400 . . . and what historian will ever discover that?"

Yet scientists are now discovering just that—not just who went to bed with whom in 1400, but an entire family history of our species stretching far into the past. It's in an archive we've been carrying with us all along: the coiled molecules of our DNA. "Everybody alive today is a living fossil who contains their own evolutionary history within themselves," says Steve Jones, head of the genetics department at University College, London. Genetics has recently made headlines with the pronouncements of scientists looking ahead, toward medical breakthroughs and moral dilemmas. A far less publicized group of geneticists is looking backward, using new technology to analyze deoxyribonucleic acid, molecule by molecule—and trace the migrations, conquests, expansions and extinctions of ancient peoples.

Genes are often described as a blueprint. That's only a partial analogy. For besides its role in mapping out the makeup of our bodies (and perhaps our personalities), DNA serves as an internal archive handed down from generation to generation. Every individual's genetic code, though unique, contains sequences that have been passed down from parent to child, not just since the beginning of human history, but reaching back over a billion years of evolution.

Picture the human genome, then, not as a blueprint but as an elaborate medieval coat of arms, perhaps the family crest of some inbred princeling of the Holy Roman Empire. To most people, such a heraldic device would look like a mass of meaningless symbols: dots, bars and crosshatchings, rampant lions quartered with screaming eagles. But an expert in heraldry could read in it an entire family history, tracing the prince's forebears as they married Hapsburgs, fathered bastards, conquered duchies, far back through time. Similarly, the genome looks like gibberish: an endless repetition of four chemicals, represented by the letters *A, C, G* and *T*. But geneticists are beginning to recognize sequences that identify specific human lineages, and are using them to reconstruct the family history of the species. Recent technology is also enabling them to unearth fragments of DNA from the remains of our long-dead ancestors. Using these two approaches, one scientist says, researchers are undertaking "the greatest archaeological excavation in history."

Using new genetic techniques, scientists are solving the ancient mysteries of mankind's origins and migrations

EVER SINCE EARLY EXPLORERS OF THE NEW WORLD announced that they had discovered the lost tribes of Israel, the origin of the Native Americans has been the subject of intense debate. Experts now agree that the Indians' ancestors crossed into Alaska over a land bridge from Siberia. Yet no one knows exactly when or how. Even the vaguest legends of that time have been long forgotten, and the land that the hunters crossed, with whatever faint traces their passage left, is hidden beneath the waters of the North Pacific.

Far to the south, Connie Kolman was following the ancient immigrants' track when she drove out into western Panama in the fall of 1991. A molecular biologist with the Smithsonian Institute, Kolman was conducting a study of the genes of some of the New World's most ancient populations. Archaeologists had known for many years that despite Panama's location on a narrow causeway between two continents, many of the tribes who lived there had been isolated from outsiders for many millenniums—perhaps almost since their hunter-gatherer ancestors arrived.

Kolman's scientific team set up their equipment in the small cinder-block schoolhouse that served an entire community of Ngöbé Indian farmers. Just past dawn, the Ngöbé started to arrive: dozens of them, coming down over the hillsides in single file, the traditional ruffled dresses of the women and girls standing out in vivid reds and purples against the tall grass. As the Indians gathered, the visitors explained their mission and asked for volunteers. A medic collected a small vial of blood from each Indian's arm. Over the next few months, back at

---

Genetic historians have begun to read the vast archive in our DNA directly, molecule by molecule

---

their lab in Panama City, Kolman and her colleague Eldredge Bermingham broke down the blood cells in the samples and decoded the ancient historical text that they contained. The text, it turned out, read something like this: TGGGGAG-CACGCTGGC...

The work that genetic historians like Connie Kolman have started to do—reading the DNA archive directly, molecule by molecule—relies on technology that is little more than 10 years old, so their conclusions are often controversial. Like medievalists poring over a newly unearthed manuscript, geneticists argue about every fresh interpretation, every cryptic passage and variant reading.

By the mid-1980s, scientists had begun to identify the specific genetic markers common to all Native Americans, which are similar to sequences found in present-day Asians, as one would expect. What was surprising, however, was that American Indians seemed to be divided into three distinct genetic groups. One lineage included most of the native tribes of North and South America, from northern Canada down to Patagonia. Another comprised the Eskimo and Aleut peoples of the far north. The third group included a number of tribes in northwestern Canada, as well as the Navajos and Apaches of the southwestern United States. These genetic lines corresponded with the three major Indian linguistic groups.

Some scientists, particularly a group from Emory University, have suggested that several different waves of migration crossed the Bering land bridge at different times, not the single migration most scientists envisioned. And in order to account for the genetic differences among modern Indians, these researchers maintain, their ancestors must have begun to arrive around 27,000 B.C.—more than twice as long ago as most archaeologists believe. That would mean that humans were living in North America even before the last ice age, in the days when Neanderthals and woolly rhinoceros still roamed the European continent. "Another migration about 9,000 to 10,000 years ago ... into northwestern North America gave us the Na-Dene speaking peoples, who about 1,000 years ago went down to become the Apaches and the Navajo," says Douglas Wallace, head of the genetics department at Emory. "Finally, there was a recent migration out of Siberia to the northern part of America that gave us the Eskimos and Aleuts."

Could such a radically new version of American history be correct? This is what Kolman hoped to learn from the Ngöbé blood samples. Her research turned up an unanticipated answer: The same kind of separation that existed among the three major Indian genetic groups also divided the Ngöbé from neighboring tribes in Panama. Yet archaeological evidence showed it was impossible that the Panamanian Indians had come over the land bridge in more than one migration. Therefore, she concluded, the genetic difference between Indian groups is the result of their separation from one another over the centuries after their arrival in the New World. Based on her own research, she says, "there doesn't appear to be any support for three waves of migration." The most likely scenario, Kolman argues, is that all of today's Native Americans, from Canada to Patagonia, are the descendants of one hardy group of prehistoric pioneers. In fact, researchers have pinpointed a region of Mongolia where the genetic patterns are similar to those of all three major Indian groups. Some modern Mongolians, then, appear to be remnants of the same population that settled the New World.

Slowly but surely, researchers like Kolman are rewriting history. In the Pacific, scientists are tracing the genetic trail left by the ancient mariners who settled Polynesia, finding evidence of a journey that began in Southeast Asia nearly 4,000 years ago—and sinking for good the widely publicized theories of Thor Heyerdahl, who sailed the balsa raft Kon-Tiki from Peru to the Tuamotu Archipelago to "prove" that American Indians had settled the Pacific. And in disproving Heyerdahl, the geneticists have found evidence of the Polynesians' traditional sagas, which speak of their ancestors' frequent voyages between Hawaii and Tahiti in huge oceangoing canoes. "Archaeologists kept saying it was impossible, that it was just a story people told," says Rebecca Cann, a geneticist at the University of Hawaii. "But by doing a very fine analysis of the DNA, we've seen that there is in fact one very common cosmopolitan lineage that's spread throughout the Pacific, [which] could only have happened if people were in constant physical contact. The idea that these islands were so isolated is really a foreign invention. The Polynesians used the ocean as a superhighway."

THE GREAT ARCHAEOLOGICAL DIG INTO THE HUMAN GEnome began in the villages of northern Italy. In the 1950s, a young Italian geneticist named Luigi Luca Cavalli-Sforza traveled among the towns near Parma, taking blood samples in the sacristies of parish churches after Sunday Mass. He began with the prosperous communities in the river valley, then worked his way up into the smaller towns in the hills until he reached the mountain villages with 100 or fewer inhabitants. As he gathered blood samples, Cavalli-Sforza also began another investigation that, for a geneticist at least, was quite unorthodox: He pored over the parishes' manuscript books of births, marriages and deaths, records dating as far back as the 1500s.

Cavalli-Sforza was investigating the theory of genetic drift, which had never been conclusively proved. Genetic drift proposes that Charles Darwin's law of "survival of the fittest" doesn't suffice to explain all the differences among species, or among peoples. Certain changes just happen naturally over time, independent of the mechanisms of natural selection—especially when populations are isolated from one another for many generations. Sometimes the changes can be quite noticeable, as in the case of remote Alpine valleys where many of the inhabitants are albinos. But more typically the effects of genetic drift are neutral and invisible: For instance, the people in an isolated region will have high percentages of an uncommon blood type. Barring extensive marriage with outsiders, every population will develop a distinctive genetic profile. (This is the same phenomenon that Connie Kolman found among the Panamanian Indians.)

In the 1950s, of course, the technology didn't exist that would allow Cavalli-Sforza to read the DNA directly. But he was able to test for blood type, and what he found confirmed the presence of genetic drift. In the large valley towns, where the parish books recorded many marriages with people from different communities, the blood-group profile was typical of that entire region of Italy. But as Cavalli-Sforza moved up into the small, isolated mountain villages, the genetic "distances" between the various settlements increased. The longer a population had been isolated, the more it differed from its neighbors. If the principle worked for villages in Italy, why shouldn't it work for the rest of the world? "My supposition was this: if enough data on a number of different genes are gathered, we may eventually be able to reconstruct the history of the entire human species," Cavalli-Sforza later wrote. And so he embarked on a decades-long project to study thousands of gene markers in hundreds of indigenous peoples around the world.

Of course, scientists had tried before to establish the relationships among the world's populations, often using methods that they claimed were based on strict Darwinian science. They traveled the world with calipers and charts, measuring the bone structure and skin color of the "natives." (One Victorian geneticist even created a "beauty map" of Britain, grading the women of various regions on a scale of 1 to 5. The low point was Aberdeen.) If you trusted such findings, the Australian aborigines, with their dark skin and flat noses, were closely related to sub-Saharan Africans. Cavalli-Sforza didn't believe it. Those visible similarities, he reasoned, might just be the result of similar adaptation to hot climates. To gauge relationships accurately, one had to measure factors that were genetically neutral, immune to the mechanisms of natural selection.

One of the most elegant aspects of Cavalli-Sforza's approach is that there is no need to sample huge numbers of people in each group under examination. Genetically, after all, each of us represents not only ourself but all of our ancestors. (Long before genome mapping, Henry Adams explained this principle quite well. "If we could go back and live again in all of our two hundred and fifty million arithmetical ancestors of the eleventh century," he wrote, speaking of those with Norman blood, "we should find ourselves . . . ploughing most of the fields of the Cotentin and Calvados; going to mass in every parish church in Normandy; [and] rendering military service to every lord, spiritual or temporal, in all this region.")

In 1994, Cavalli-Sforza, along with Paolo Menozzi and Alberto Piazza, published his magnum opus, *The History and Geography of Human Genes*—a sort of combination atlas and family tree. Cavali-Sforza's genealogy places Africans at the root of the tree, with the Europeans and Asians branching off from them, and American Indians branching off in turn from the Asians. He finds the genetic traces of the Mongol invasions of China, the Bantus' sweep across Africa and the Arabs' spread through the Middle East under the successors of Muhammad.

In his analysis of Europe's genetic landscape, Cavalli-Sforza has shaken the foundations of conventional history. Nine thousand years ago, a technological and cultural revolution swept Europe. From the Balkans to Britain, forests sparsely dotted with the campfires of hunter-gatherers gave way to a patchwork of cultivated fields and burgeoning settlements. In the course of a few thousand years, as the practice of agriculture spread from southeast to northwest, Europeans abandoned the way of life they had led for tens of thousands of years. That much is agreed upon. But Cavalli-Sforza suggests that the agricultural revolution was a genetic revolution as well. It wasn't merely that the Europeans gradually learned about farming from their neighbors to the southeast. Instead, the Middle Eastern farmers actually migrated across Europe, replacing the existing population. This wasn't a case of prehistoric genocide, Cavalli-Sforza emphasizes: The farmers simply multiplied far more rapidly than the hunters, and, as they sought new land to cultivate, they pushed their frontiers to the northwest.

Today's Europeans, Cavalli-Sforza argues, are almost wholly the descendants of these interlopers—with the exception of the Basques, whose gene patterns are so anomalous that he believes they are the last close relatives of the Cro-Magnon hunters. Furthermore, Cavalli-Sforza believes, there was a *second* genetic invasion of Europe around 4000 B.C.—this time from the steppes of Central Asia. His maps show that an important component of the European gene pool spreads out from the area north of the Black Sea like ripples in a pond. Cavalli-Sforza connects this to a controversial archaeological theory: the idea that nomadic herdsmen swept in from the east, bringing with them domesticated horses, bronze weapons and the Indo-European language that would become the basis for all major European tongues.

Cavalli-Sforza's ideas have drawn criticism as well as praise. "All genetic data has a time depth of one generation back from the past," says Erik Trinkaus, an anthropologist at the University of New Mexico: Cavalli-Sforza's maps only prove that present-day Europeans demonstrate genetic divergences that occurred at some point in the past. All the rest is interpretation. Some scholars have argued that these patterns could be explained by more recent migrations, such as the barbarian invasions that toppled the Roman Empire. Even Alberto Piazza, who collaborated with Cavalli-Sforza, admits that "it's important to try to get the dates. If we find that we're talking about 6,000 or 7,000 years ago, as we believe, then it's justifiable to say that we're talking about Indo-Europeans. But if we discover instead that the dates are more recent—2,000 or 3,000 years ago—we could be talking about the Huns."

What was needed, obviously, was a more direct route into the past. As it happened, by the time Cavalli-Sforza's genetic atlas appeared, scientists were already starting to catch glimpses of the DNA in our ancestors' cells.

SINCE THE 19TH CENTURY, SCIENTISTS HAVE BEEN STUDYING fossils to reconstruct our past. But there was no evidence to tell them definitely whether these represented our direct ancestors or were merely dead branches on the family tree. So scientists did the logical thing: They arranged them with the oldest and most dissimilar hominids first, leading up to the most recent and close-to-human types. It was a convenient time line, familiar from textbook illustrations and museum dioramas. And then came Eve.

She debuted before the world in the winter of 1988: a naked woman holding an apple on the cover of *Newsweek*. The article explained that a team of biochemists at Berkeley had discovered the single female ancestor of the entire human race. The scientists, led by Rebecca Cann, had done so by looking at the DNA found in a specific part of the cell called the mitochondria. Unlike other DNA, mitochondrial DNA isn't a combination of both parents' genes; it is inherited only from the mother. This means that the only changes to the mitochondrial genes, as

---

Genetically, each of us represents not only ourself but, in a certain sense, all of our ancestors

---

they pass from generation to generation, are occasional mutations. By calculating the rate of these mutations, and comparing the mitochondrial DNA of people from around the world, the Berkeley researchers had come up with a surprisingly young common ancestress: Eve, as the scientists dubbed her, was only 200,000 years old. "Genetically speaking," writes James Shreeve in *The Neandertal Enigma*, "there was not all that much difference between a [modern] New Guinean highlander, a South African !Kung tribeswoman, and a housewife from the Marin County hills.... Whatever appearances might suggest, they simply hadn't had time enough to diverge."

The Eve discovery shocked evolutionary historians. It meant the hominids that spread out of Africa 1.2 million years ago were not modern humans' direct ancestors. Instead they and their descendants had been supplanted by a far more recent out-of-Africa migration—perhaps only 100,000 years ago. That would mean that all the old standbys of the museum diorama—Peking Man, Java Man, Neanderthal Man—were evolutionary dead ends.

Not surprisingly, traditional paleontologists have attacked Eve with vigor, arguing that Cann's sample was skewed, her computer program flawed, and that even if all humans share a recent female ancestor, it doesn't mean there weren't other contributions to our gene pool. Eve's partisans counterattacked: A number of independent researchers have looked at different parts of the DNA and arrived at similar dates for our divergence from a common ancestor. Last fall, a geneticist at the University of Arizona claimed to have found a common male ancestor who lived 188,000 years ago.

Now scientists are trying to resolve the Eve debate by looking in the most logical place of all: ancient DNA. "If we had even one Neanderthal DNA sample we could be sure of, it would quickly emerge how closely related it was to modern *Homo sapiens*," says Sir Walter Bodmer, former president of the Human Genome Organisation. Just a few years ago, the idea of finding a sample of Neanderthal DNA would have seemed about as probable as the idea of finding a live Neanderthal living deep in some cave, since scientists believed that the fragile DNA molecule decayed rapidly after death. But now geneticists are reading DNA recovered from ancient human remains. Despite skepticism

from many scientists, their results are winning acceptance.

In 1984, a group of Berkeley scientists announced that they had sequenced the DNA of a quagga, an African animal, similar to the zebra, that was hunted to extinction in the late 19th century. They had accomplished this using the polymerase chain reaction (PCR), a chemical method for amplifying tiny DNA sequences. This is the same technique that scientists like Cann and Kolman use on fresh DNA from blood samples; the Berkeley team simply applied it to a fragment of quagga skin that was preserved in a German museum.

Quickly, other researchers began applying PCR to ancient specimens—and reporting spectacular results. Scientists claimed to have cloned DNA from Egyptian mummies, woolly mammoths, even a 120-million-year-old weevil trapped in amber, à la *Jurassic Park*. There was only one problem: The PCR process is extremely vulnerable to contamination, so nearly all these results turned out to be false—the mammoth's DNA, for instance, was that of a lab technician.

However, a few ancient-DNA laboratories have started to produce credible and verifiable work. Last year, two labs independently sequenced genes from the Ice Man, the Stone Age hunter whose frozen body was found high in the Italian Alps in 1991, and both arrived at the same results. Many of the best samples, oddly enough, have come from bones and teeth. "Now people generally accept that you can get DNA from hard tissues," says Oxford geneticist Bryan Sykes, who is generally considered one of the most careful ancient-DNA researchers. "I suppose the oldest we've ever got to was about 15,000 years—that was for some animal bones from a limestone cave in England. But I think most people wouldn't be too surprised if one were to report recovery of

---

Ancient DNA may allow scientists to establish a continuum from very early times to the present

---

DNA from well-preserved bone up to maybe even 100,000 years ago."

That implies that Neanderthal DNA should be waiting to be discovered in the collections of museums around the world. The treasure hunt is now in full swing. No lab yet claims publicly to have sequenced Neanderthal genes (although Sykes, when asked if he has obtained results, hesitates and replies, "Nothing I could reveal to you"). "It's only a matter of time," says Andrew Merriwether of the University of Pittsburgh, who is looking for Neanderthal DNA in some 35,000-year-old teeth from a Croatian cave. "There are a lot of Neanderthal remains around."

Once the treasure hunters find their quarry, they'll use it to put the Eve hypothesis to a powerful test. And that's not all they'll learn. "One particularly burning question just begs to be answered," writes Walter Bodmer in *The Book of Man*. "Exactly what evolutionary advantage did Homo sapiens have over his hominid competitors, and in particular over our nearest evolutionary brothers and sisters, the Neanderthals? What genetic gifts made Homo sapiens so special and allowed us to inherit the Earth, while other hominids conspicuously failed?"

In the meantime, scientists are using more recent ancient DNA to answer less profound questions. Scott Woodward of Brigham Young University is working with the royal mummies of Egypt's 18th dynasty, trying to chart the pharaohs' complex family tree. Sykes is using Neolithic bones from Europe to test Cavalli-Sforza's ideas about the spread of agriculture. Merriwether and Kolman are comparing DNA from ancient American specimens with that of modern Indians, hoping to resolve conclusively the history of the peopling of the New World.

Scientists hope that, bit by bit, ancient DNA samples will allow them to interpret more accurately the history encoded in modern genes. "What ancient DNA will allow us to do is establish a continuum from very early times up to the present," says Woodward. "Right now, all we can look at is a single snapshot. If we go back to 500 years ago, 1,000 years ago, 1,500 years ago, it will give us snapshots of the past. And as we fill in the gaps, soon there will be a motion picture and we'll be able to watch history unfold."

SOUTHWEST OF CAIRO, ON THE EDGE OF THE GREAT fayum oasis, the desert sand teems with thousands upon thousands of graves. Here ancient Egyptians buried their dead, the bodies wrapped in linen cloth, with only a few possessions—a reed mat, a cup, a loaf of bread—to accompany them into the afterlife. For these were common folk, and although they lived in the shadow of the pyramids, the age of the pharaohs was already past. The Fayum cemetery was in use from the middle of the first millennium B.C. to the middle of the first millennium A.D., during the period of Greek and Roman dominion over Egypt.

Still, Scott Woodward is unearthing treasure from the simple burials: clues to the identity of the Egyptian, and to the spread of Christianity. The cemetery's history spans the time when the Egyptians abandoned paganism for the new faith, and the graves reflect the change. Until late in the first century A.D., the dead were buried facing west. Then, suddenly, they were oriented facing east—reflecting the Christian belief that the resurrected Christ would return from the east, according to Woodward and his collaborators. Woodward is analyzing the bodies' DNA to find out just who these early Christians were—native converts or immigrants. "We're [also] trying to answer the question of how much sub-Saharan African influence there was in the ancient Egyptians," Woodward says. "Egypt was probably a very cosmopolitan place, as much of a melting pot as the United States is today. . . . My guess is that we'll see African, we'll see Asian, we'll see Caucasian markers." In time, he says, it will be possible to get a genetic picture of the entire population of the cemetery.

So far, Woodward only has results from a half-dozen burials, none of which shows the typically African DNA marker. Even so, his investigation suggests how DNA research can confirm or question disputes over the identity of a particular people,

like the modern Coptic Christians, who claim that they are the sole descendants of the ancient Egyptians, or those of sub-Saharan African origin, especially in the United States, who derive ethnic pride from the theory that the pharaohs were black.

Sometimes, such research can turn up unwelcome results. "Judaism is without doubt the most genetic of all religions—it depends on descent," says Steve Jones. "Orthodox Jews are very much of the opinion that Judaism is a huge pedigree of individuals who descend from Abraham." Yet studies of Jewish DNA indicate extensive mixing with outsiders. The Yemenite Jews, Jones notes, who have been accepted without question into Israeli society, appear to be almost entirely the descendants of Arab converts. Meanwhile, members of the black Lemba tribe of South Africa, who claim to be one of the lost tribes of Israel, have never been accepted as Jews. But their genes, Jones says, seem to support their claim: They show patterns typical of Middle Eastern origin.

"The genome pushes us to redefine ourselves," says Howard University immunogeneticist Georgia Dunston. Dunston plans a major genetic study to trace the origins of American blacks back to the lands from which their ancestors were taken. "At this point in the history of African-Americans, we are seeking to make connections to roots that extend beyond slavery," she says.

OUR GENES CANNOT WHOLLY ACCOUNT FOR OUR DIVERSITY. In fact, the work of genetic historians would be far easier were it not for the fact that the peoples of the world are so similar under the skin. "It is because they are external that . . . racial differences strike us so forcibly, and we automatically assume that differences of similar magnitude exist below the surface, in the rest of our genetic makeup," Cavalli-Sforza has written. "This is simply not so: the remainder of our genetic makeup hardly differs at all." Indeed, research has shown that culture usually drives the spread of genes and not vice versa. "In the history of human development," Cavalli-Sforza says, "whenever there has been a major expansion geographically or demographically, it has been because one people has had an increase in food or power or transportation. . . . Whenever I see an expansion, I start looking for the innovation that made it." The invention of agriculture or the wheel makes history; genes only reflect it.

Even so, the story that the genes' tiny gradations tell is altering the way we think about the past. "Genetics changed something fundamental about our view of history," says Jones. "It shows us that history is largely the story of love, not war." The genetic historians suggest that it's time we started asking, with E.M. Forster: Who *did* go to bed with whom in the year 1400? And as we consider the possibilities—a Mongol chieftain and his Chinese bride, say; an Aztec woman and her husband; a fumbling pair of teenagers on a French hillside—it is pleasing to think that those ancient acts of love left their mark somewhere within each of us.

Human Presence in Americas Is Pushed Back a Millennium

John Noble Wilford

After long, often bitter debate, archeologists have finally come to a consensus that humans reached southern Chile 12,500 years ago. The date is more than 1,000 years before the previous benchmark for human habitation in the Americas, 11,200-year-old stone spear points first discovered in the 1930's near Clovis, N.M.

The Chilean site, known as Monte Verde, is on the sandy banks of a creek in wooded hills near the Pacific Ocean. Even former skeptics have joined in agreeing that its antiquity is now firmly established and that the bone and stone tools and other materials found there definitely mark the presence of a hunting-and-gathering people.

The new consensus regarding Monte Verde, described in interviews last week and formally announced yesterday, thus represents the first major shift in more than 60 years in the confirmed chronology of human prehistory in what would

much later be called, from the European perspective, the New World.

For American archeologists it is a liberating experience not unlike aviation's breaking of the sound barrier; they have broken the Clovis barrier. Even moving back the date by a little as 1,300 years, archeologists said, would have profound implications on theories about when people first reached America, presumably from northeastern Asia by way of the Bering Strait, and how they migrated south more than 10,000 miles to occupy the length and breadth of two continents.

It could mean that early people, ancestors of the Indians, first arrived in their new world at least 20,000 years before Columbus.

Evidence for the pre-Clovis settlement at Monte Verde was amassed and carefully analyzed over the last two decades by a team of American and Chilean archeologists, led by Dr. Tom D. Dillehay of the University of Kentucky in Lexington.

Remaining doubts were erased by Dr. Dillehay's comprehensive research report, which has been circulated among experts and is to be published next month by the Smithsonian Institution.

And last month, a group of archeologists, including some of Monte Verde's staunchest critics, inspected the artifacts and visited the site, coming away thoroughly convinced. In his report of the site visit, Dr. Alex W. Barker, chief curator of the Dallas Museum of Natural History, said: "While there were very strongly voiced disagreements about different points, it rapidly became clear that everyone was in fundamental agreement about the most important question of all. Monte Verde is real. It's old. And it's a whole new ball game." The archeologists made the site inspection under the auspices of the Dallas museum, where their conclusions were reported yesterday, and with additional support by the National Geographic Society.

The archeologists, all specialists in the early settlement of America, included Dr. C. Vance Haynes of the University of Arizona, Dr. James Adovasio of Mercyhurst College in Erie, Pa., Dr. David J. Meltzer of Southern Methodist University in Dallas, Dr. Dena Dincauze of the University of Massachusetts at Amherst, Dr. Donald K. Grayson of the University of Washington in Seattle and Dr. Dennis Stanford of the Smithsonian Institution in Washington.

Dr. Dincauze, who had expressed serious doubts about the site's antiquity, said the Dr. Dillehay's report made "a convincing case" that the remains of huts, fireplaces and tools showed human occupation by a pre-Clovis culture.

"I'm convinced it's 100 percent solid," Dr. Brian M. Fagan, an anthropologist at the University of California at Santa Barbara, said of the new assessment of Monte Verde. "It's an extraordinary piece of research."

Finally vindicated, Dr. Dillehay said, "Most archeologists had always thought there was a pre-Clovis culture out there somewhere, and I knew that if they would only come to the site and look at the setting and see the artifacts, they would agree that Monte Verde was pre-Clovis."

Monte Verde, on the banks of Chinchihaupi Creek, is in the hills near the town of Puerto Montt, 500 miles south of Santiago. Dr. Dillehay and Dr. Mario Pino of the Southern University of Chile in Valdivia began excavations there in 1976. They found the remains of the ancient camp, even wood and other perishables that archeologists rarely find, remarkably well preserved by the water-saturated peat bog that covered the site, isolating the material from oxygen and thus decay.

As Dr. Dillehay reconstructed the prehistoric scene in his mind, a group of 20 to 30 people occupied Monte Verde for a year or so. They lived in shelters covered in animal hides. They gathered berries in the spring, chestnuts in the fall and also ate potatoes, mushrooms and marsh grasses. They hunted small game

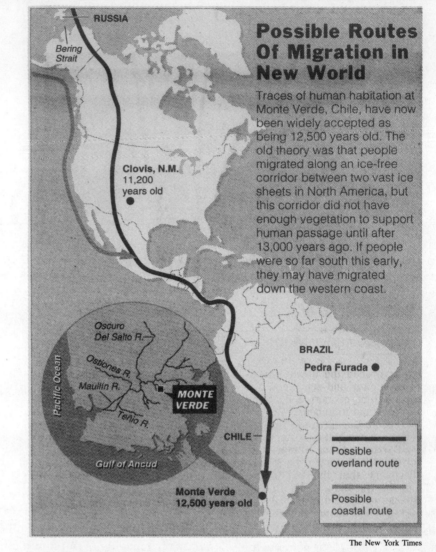

Possible Routes Of Migration in New World

Traces of human habitation at Monte Verde, Chile, have now been widely accepted as being 12,500 years old. The old theory was that people migrated along an ice-free corridor between two vast ice sheets in North America, but this corridor did not have enough vegetation to support human passage until after 13,000 years ago. If people were so far south this early, they may have migrated down the western coast.

The New York Times

and also ancestors of the llama and sometimes went down to the Pacific, 30 miles away, for shellfish. They were hunters and gatherers living far from the presumed home of their remote ancestors, in northeastern Asia.

The evidence to support this picture is extensive. Excavations turned up wooden planks from some of the 12 huts that once stood in the camp, and logs with attached pieces of hide that probably insulated these shelters. Pieces of wooden poles and stakes were still tied with cords made of local grasses, a telling sign that ingenious humans had been there. "That's something nature doesn't do," Dr. Barker said. "Tie overhand knots."

Stone projectile points found there were carefully chipped on both sides, archeologists said. The people

of Monte Verde also made digging sticks, grinding slabs and tools of bone and tusk. Some seeds and nuts were sifted out of the soil. A chunk of meat had managed to survive in the bog, remains of the hunters' last kill; DNA analysis indicates the meat was from a mastodon. The site also yielded several human coprolites, ancient fecal material.

Nothing at Monte Verde was more evocative of its former inhabitants than a single footprint beside a hearth. A child had stood there by the fire 12,500 years ago and left a lasting impression in the soft clay.

Radiocarbon dating of bone and charcoal from the fireplaces established the time of the encampment. The date of 12,500 years ago, said Dr. Meltzer, author of "Search for the First Americans," published in 1993 by the Smithsonian Institution, "could fundamentally change the way we understand the peopling of the Americas."

The research, in particular, shows people living as far south as Chile before it is clear that there existed an ice-free corridor through the vast North American glaciers by which people might have migrated south. In the depths of the most recent ice age, two vast ice sheets converged about 20,000 years ago over what is now Canada and the Northern United States and apparently closed off human traffic there until sometime after 13,000 years ago. Either people migrated through a corridor between the ice sheets and spread remarkably fast to the southern end of America or they came by a differ-

ent route, perhaps along the western coast, by foot and sometimes on small vessels. Otherwise they must have entered the Americas before 20,000 years ago.

Dr. Carol Mandryk, a Harvard University archeologist who has studied the American paleoenvironment, said the concept of an ice-free corridor as the migration route emerged in the 1930's, but her research shows that even after the ice sheets began to open a path, there was not enough vegetation there to support the large animals migrating people would have had to depend on for food.

"It's very clear people couldn't have used this corridor until after 13,000 years ago," Dr. Mandryk said. "They came down the coast. I don't

understand why people see the coast as an odd way. The early people didn't have to be interior big-game hunters, they could have been maritime adapted people."

No archeologists seriously considers the possibility that the first Americans came by sea and landed first in South America, a hypothesis made popular in the 1960's by the Norwegian explorer Thor Heyerdahl. There is no evidence of people's occupying Polynesia that long ago. All linguistic, genetic and geological evidence points to the Bering Strait as the point of entry, especially in the ice age, when lower sea levels created a wide land bridge there between Siberia and Alaska.

The Beginnings of Culture, Agriculture, and Cities

Although the points are debatable, the characteristics of civilization include urbanization; literacy; complex economic, political, and social systems; and an advanced technology. The presence of cities, writing, and metallurgy are indications of this accomplishment. Civilization, it would seem, represents the highest level of human or-ganization, but the definition can ignite arguments. If, for example, a society or tribe cannot write, are they "uncivi-lized"? Since historians embrace written records as the main source of information, moreover, are illiterate people "prehistoric"? This can be a problem since the definition of civilization can imply a judgement about what is best, or valuable. World historians usually avoid such value judgements, but nonetheless use the history of civilizations as an organizing principle.

In the evolution of humankind the tool of writing has been useful as a means to keep permanent, accurate records. It may be that the start of writing came from the Paleolithic pictures and symbols drawn on cave walls such as those found in France. The pictures of horses, bison, sea creatures, and handprints are certainly a form of communication. They are also important as a sign of human creativity. William Allman, in the first article of this unit, points out, however, that the beginning of creativity reaches back to tools and bead making for self-adornment. This came before cave painting. It is reasonable to see this spark of creativity in the development of writing and number systems.

Jared Diamond, in "Writing Right," is analytical about the evolution of writing and finds that there are three main strategies. People have used alphabets, symbols for entire words, and symbols for parts of words. Alphabets offer the most flexible strategy and have undergone 4,000 years of changes. Phonetic qualities are also important so that the written word and the spoken word can be matched. It makes communication easier than having to memorize independent symbols as in the Chinese written language. Although English is now the current *lingua franca*, Diamond argues that it is not as easy as others. This raises a question, therefore, about why English is so widely used and studied.

A further point about such cultural attainment involves how ideas and tools spread. This relates to an old argument about diffusion versus local invention: Do ideas and technology spread from one innovator, or do peoples in different places independently come up with the same thoughts and instruments? There is no definitive answer, but John Noble Wilford, in "Mummies, Textiles Offer Evidence of Europeans in Far East," gives an example of diffusion. Somewhat more controversial, Charles Fenyvesi, in "A Tale of Two Cultures," reviews the idea that the Shang Chinese influenced the culture of the Olmec of Mexico.

The cultivation of corn, one of the principal grains of the world, diffused throughout the Western Hemisphere, but there is controversy about when this happened, as John Noble Wilford explains. There is also a question of which came first—sedentary life or agriculture. In the New World it has long been the assumption, based on old methods of dating, that villages followed agriculture. New dating methods place the cultivation of corn at a later time. This brings into doubt the old assumption of villages following agriculture. In the Old World it has been shown that villages came first and agriculture followed. The beginning of urbanization is explored by John Pfeiffer in "How Man Invented Cities." Urbanization was unplanned, caused by the need to feed increasing populations and plentiful local food sources. Cities were, thus, born independently around the world. That was how civilization began.

Looking Ahead: Challenge Questions

What is creativity? Where does it come from? How has it been used?

What is the argument concerning diffusion and independent origins of ideas and technology? Give examples.

Why would local people in Mexico be upset that the Chinese gave culture to the Olmec?

Which came first—settlement or agriculture?

What were the advantages and disadvantages of living in cities?

What is the role of agriculture in the growth of civilization?

What is the importance of writing in the development of civilization? Can there be civilization without literacy?

Why is English the most important world language at the present time?

THE DAWN OF CREATIVITY

*New discoveries show how humans created art, tools and richly
thriving communities eons ago*

WILLIAM F. ALLMAN

Peering out from the dim past, the cave images still have the power to haunt: Reindeer ford a stream, their necks stretched taut; a massive bison glares, its flanks shimmering; an antler-bedecked half-man, half-beast stares out in expectation of some long lost ritual.

These ancient examples of expression lie at the center of human evolution's deepest mystery: Who were the first "creators"—the toolmakers, craft workers and artisans—who propelled the human species from a run-of-the-mill primate to the tool-wielding, art-making, cultural beings that exist today? At the heart of it lies an evolutionary disconnect. The modern, biological form of Homo sapiens appeared in the fossil record about 100,000 to 130,000 years ago. These were creatures who looked pretty much like us. But as most textbooks still have it, signs of truly human behavior—spirituality, artwork, sophisticated use of the environment and the dense network of family and friends that make up society—did not appear until around 40,000 years ago, when a "cultural explosion" occurred in Europe rather than Africa, where many exerts believe Homo sapiens first arose.

Now several recent archaeological finds hint that the dawning of human creativity may have occurred earlier and was far more widespread than previously thought. In a paper soon to be published in the *Journal of Human Evolution,* Sally McBrearty of the University of Connecticut reports the finding of skillfully crafted stone blades in Africa that date back hundreds of thousands of years before blade tools appear in Europe. In another paper published last year, researchers announced the finding of delicate bone harpoons in Africa that precede the famed cave paintings of Ice Age Europe by more than 40,000 years. Scientists dating newly discovered cave paintings in France report the artwork is 30,000 years old—nearly twice the age of similarly rendered paintings in Lascaux, France. And the recent find of a bizarre structure apparently made by Neanderthals deep within a cavern indicates that "human behavior" might not have been confined to our species.

The new finds suggest that the traditional scenario that says human creativity suddenly burst forth in Europe is wrong. "The beginning of what we call human behavior was far older than 40,000 years ago," says Alison Brooks of George Washington University, who with National Science Foundation anthropologist John Yellen found the harpoons in Zaire. "And it began in Africa, not Europe." More important, the new research suggests that the way our ancestors' minds were most creative was not in their work on tools and cave walls but in the manner in which they created the fabric of society itself.

NEW CANVASES

Dating back tens of thousands of years before the Ice Age paintings in Europe, Brooks and Yellen's ancient harpoons testify to a crucial leap in human creative thinking: looking beyond stone and wood for raw material for tools. To ancient humans, bone, antler and ivory were Paleolithic plastic: tough, flexible, durable and capable of being shaped into everything from deadly spear points to sewing needles to flutes. To make the harpoons, the ancient humans ground the tip of the bone into a point, then cut into the side with a sharp stone to create a triangular "tooth." Circular grooves at the tail end helped fasten the tool to a cord or pole. While not as sophisticated as later harpoon designs, these weapons apparently did the trick: The archaeological site is littered with the remains of a species of giant catfish whose descendants still swim in nearby waters.

The new site suggests that the humans who made the harpoons understood the lives of their prey—and were capable of planning ahead to take advantage of it. The ancient humans, it seems, knew that the catfish spawn at only certain times in the year, during which they are plentiful and easy prey, and they timed their visits to the area accordingly. Brooks notes that there is similar evidence of advanced planning at another site found near a large water hole. The ancient humans apparently staked out the site during the dry season, when they knew that other water holes nearby would be empty, and ambushed animals as they came to drink.

THE NEANDERTHAL ENIGMA

This creative approach to exploiting the environment may have been a crucial divider between ancient humans and their evolutionary cousins, the Neanderthals. These powerfully built, large-brained creatures arose in Europe some 300,000 years ago and disappeared about 30,000 years ago. Scientists long thought Neanderthals were direct ancestors of modern humans, but fossil finds of ancient humans that predate some Neanderthal fossils reveal the two species co-existed for tens of thousands of years. A recent reconstruction of fragments of a 20,000-year-old Neanderthal skull retains the classic features of the species, suggesting they did not interbreed with humans.

Neanderthals have long had an image of being dim-witted, hulking brutes, but recent findings indicate they were capable of sophisticated behaviors such as making complex stone and bone tools, using fire, burying their dead and possibly even speaking. Scientists recently discovered, for instance, a four-walled structure built out of rock by Neanderthals deep within a cave. The ability to create such a structure, which may have had symbolic importance, in the pitch-black cave reveals the Neanderthals had mastered the ability to use torches and to coordinate their activities, perhaps verbally.

For all their intellectual abilities, however, Neanderthals appear to have been subtly different from humans in how they negotiated the world. For instance, scientists have long been puzzled by the fact that in Europe tools used by humans are far more complex than those used by Neanderthals. But in the Near East, the tools of one species are virtually indistinguishable from the other's. New research reveals that *how* these tools were used may have made the difference. Looking at the growth pattern of the teeth of prey found at the sites, which indicates whether the animals were killed during a particular season, Dan Lieberman of Rutgers University and John Shea of the State University of New York at Stony Brook conclude that the Neanderthals stayed at the sites for long periods and at many different times of the year. Humans, on the other hand, were more deliberate and used a site as one of several areas where they took refuge as they followed the weather or their food sources on their migrations. Occupying a single site for a long time inevitably leads to a depletion of the food, argue Lieberman and Shea,

which means Neanderthals had to work harder and harder for each meal.

This way of life seems to have led to severe hardship for Neanderthals. Erik Trinkaus of the University of New Mexico examined the teeth of Neanderthals and humans for telltale defects in the growth of the enamel, which indicate bouts of starvation. He found that more than 70 percent of Neanderthal fossils studied showed at least one defect, whereas "teeth of the ancient humans were clean as a whistle." Equally telling is that defects in Neanderthal teeth dramatically increased after childhood, suggesting that Neanderthals' lives became harder after they had been weaned and had to get food on their own.

The Neanderthals' bones, too, hint of a life that emphasized brawn as much as brain. Trinkaus found that the bones of the Neanderthals, which are thicker and heavier, also are riddled with multiple minor fractures. And these injuries are reflected in the Neanderthals' tool kit: The stone points they made are best suited to being held and thrust, rather than thrown, says Trinkaus. That presumably exposed them to nasty kicks from their prey—and those broken bones.

SOCIAL GLUE

The biggest difference between humans and Neanderthals—one that may have made all the difference in their creative cultures—was how members of each species interacted among themselves. Humans were using long-distance trading networks for the exchange of quality stone and other goods in Africa at least 100,000 years ago, says Brooks. Similar trade networks might have existed among humans in Ice Age Europe, where shells, for instance, are found at sites hundreds of miles from the sea. As people began to live in larger groups, supported by cooperative group hunting, the need for expressing group identity and individuality intensified, argue Steve Kuhn and Mary Stiner of the University of Arizona.

This link between human creativity and sociability is evident in one of the earliest examples of ancient art: bead-

work. As Randall White of New York University points out, the Lascaux cave paintings "are only the midway point of human art history." The dawn of art, he says, began tens of thousands of years earlier and used the human body as a canvas. Ivory beads were sewn into clothing and pierced carnivore teeth were used in belts and headbands.

It probably took about an hour, White says, to make a bead. Such a time-consuming process would never be undertaken unless personal adornment was a vital part of human existence. "We have this image of art being the result of people having lots of free time," says White. "But that's totally contrary to what we see. For these people, art was a necessity." Such an idea should hardly be surprising in a modern culture where wedding bands, high-priced watches and T-shirt slogans all shape how people perceive one another's status and world view.

THE ICE AGE CINEPLEX

Even the magnificent examples of Ice Age cave art—bolstered by the recent discovery in France of two caverns filled with a menagerie of animal paintings—appear to have played a crucial role in the workings of society. Once thought to represent "hunting magic" designed to help get game, the Ice Age galleries may have been part of elaborate ceremonies that perhaps rivaled the best modern-day multimedia displays.

Flutes made of bird bone that play notes in a scale similar to those of today suggest music may have accompanied viewing of the paintings. In one experiment, researchers walked through three ancient caves while whistling through several octaves and mapping where the sounds resonated off the walls best. They found that those places in the caves with the best acoustics nearly always had art nearby, whereas places where sound was dampened typically did not have art. In another experiment, researchers found that near the front of the famed Lascaux cave, where the cave art is dominated by horses, bison and other hoofed animals, a clapping noise gets echoed back and forth among the walls, producing a sound not unlike a stampede. Near the rear of the cave, however, where the images are dominated by panthers and other stealthy creatures, the walls reflect sound in such a way that it is muted.

Nor was the ancient flowering of art confined to Ice Age Europe. Cave paintings also occur in Africa in the same era, and a recent study by Australian archaeologist Rhys Jones suggests that some Australian rock paintings date back 60,000 years. Not only would this be the oldest artwork known, its presence in Australia implies humans could build sophisticated boats 60,000 years ago.

ANCIENT CATHEDRALS

Some of the most mysterious markings in ancient artwork—the strange circles, dots and chevrons on the animals or by themselves—may be the result of the painter being in a hallucinatory trance. South African archaeologist David Lewis-Williams studied the rock art of Africa's !Kung San people, who continue to create rock paintings today. He found the painter in many cases is a shaman using drawing as part of a trancelike state to ward off spirits. The markings reflect the spots and shimmerings that appear to him during the trance.

More evidence that the caves were used in rituals comes from the paintings themselves. In one Ice Age work there are two humanlike figures who seem to be wearing headdresses of antlers. One stares cross-eyed toward the viewer; the other might be playing a musical instrument. In another cave, some bison seem to have been laboriously painted on a

vaulted rock ceiling known as the "Sanctuary." A recent chemical analysis found that although the animals were rendered in a very similar style, the paintings were done hundreds of years apart—in the same way that a modern painting of a cross might reflect art symbolism from the Middle Ages.

Evidence our ancestors were moved by spiritual concerns goes back to the oldest human skeletons: At one Israeli cave site dating back nearly 100,000 years, a man is buried with an antler placed in his hands—an ancient precursor, perhaps, to the tomb offerings of King Tut or rosary beads in modern-day burials. At another ancient site, a woman is buried with her legs deliberately pulled up beneath her and a small child lying at her feet, a pairing that suggests a spiritual concern about being joined after death.

All members in a society appear to have participated in the rituals revealed in Ice Age art. Tiny hand prints of children are found as much as a mile deep within some Ice Age caves, notes NYU's White, and in one cave a side chamber with only a 4-foot-high ceiling is covered with the footprints of children.

CULTURAL EXPLOSION

The social setting implied by the cave art may be what made the so-called cultural explosion 40,000 years ago possible in the first place. Throughout human history, a few people may have worked a piece of bone or done an engraving on a rock. But without that artifact's playing a role in maintaining the func-

tion of a larger group, suggests White, it would have been discarded.

Sophisticated toolmaking and culture became prevalent only when human society grew to the point that such practices became important for survival—and social networks spread each new innovation like wildfire. A similar sea change in human existence occurred some 8,000 years ago, for instance, when humans around the globe abandoned their hunting-and-gathering way of life and settled into farming communities. In that instance, the ancients knew about domesticating plants long before they began to farm, imply recent studies, and only took up agriculture in response to changing climate, a growing population and a dwindling food supply.

The newly discovered examples of sophisticated tools indicate that ancient humans may have always had the capacity for creative thinking, even if they didn't always express it. The University of Connecticut's McBrearty has found stone blades that appear to date back more than 250,000 years, yet examples of more-rudimentary tool-making exist elsewhere up until some 40,000 years ago—suggesting that there wasn't an important social network to perpetuate the tool design or pass it along to others.

Clearly, it was profoundly rich relations that inspired and reinforced creativity among ancient humans. The artists who created the cave images were people of spirituality and grace; they loved painting, music and the beauty as well as the function of their technology. Mostly, they were people whose creativity connected them with the members of their community—those alongside them in the cave or thousands of years in the future.

Mummies, Textiles Offer Evidence of Europeans in Far East

JOHN NOBLE WILFORD

PHILADELPHIA

In the first millennium A.D., people living at oases along the legendary Silk Road in what is now northwest China wrote in a language quite unlike any other in that part of the world. They used one form of the language in formal Buddhist writings, another for everyday religious and commercial affairs, including caravan passes.

Little was known of these desert people, and nothing of their language, until French and German explorers arrived on the scene at the start of this century. They discovered manuscripts in the now-extinct language, which scholars called Tocharian and later were astonished to learn bore striking similarities to Celtic and Germanic tongues. How did a branch of the Indo-European family of languages come to be in use so long ago in such a distant and seemingly isolated enclave of the Eurasian land mass?

More surprises were in store. In the last two decades, Chinese archeologists digging in the same region, the Tarim Basin in Xinjiang Province, have uncovered more than 100 naturally mummified corpses of people who lived there 4,000 to 2,400 years ago. The bodies were amazingly well preserved by the arid climate, and archeologists could hardly believe what they saw. The long noses and skulls, blond or brown hair, thin lips and deep-set eyes of most of the corpses were all unmistakably Caucasian features—more specifically, European.

Who were these people? Could they be ancestors of the later inhabitants who had an Indo-European language? Where did these ancient people come from, and when? By reconstructing some of their history, could scholars finally identify the homeland of the original Indo-European speakers?

East is East, and West is West, but the twain did meet.

Linguists, archeologists, historians, molecular biologists and other scholars have joined forces in search of answers to these questions. They hope that the answers will yield a better understanding of the dynamics of Eurasian prehistory, the early interactions of distant cultures and the spread of kindred tongues that make up Indo-European, the family of languages spoken in nearly all of Europe, much of India and Pakistan and some other parts of Asia—and elsewhere in the world, as a result of Western colonialism.

At a three-day international conference here last month, scholars shared their preliminary findings and hypotheses about how the Tocharian language and the Tarim Basin mummies might contribute to a solution to the Indo-European mysteries. The meeting, held at the University of Pennsylvania Museum, was organized by Dr. Victor H. Mair, a specialist in ancient Asian languages and cultures at the university. Some of the most recent research has been described in the current issue of The Journal of Indo-European Studies.

Dr. Mair, who has spent several seasons in Xinjiang with groups studying the mummies and artifacts, said there was growing optimism that some important revelations might be at hand through genetic studies, a reinterpretation of ancient Chinese texts and art, and a closer

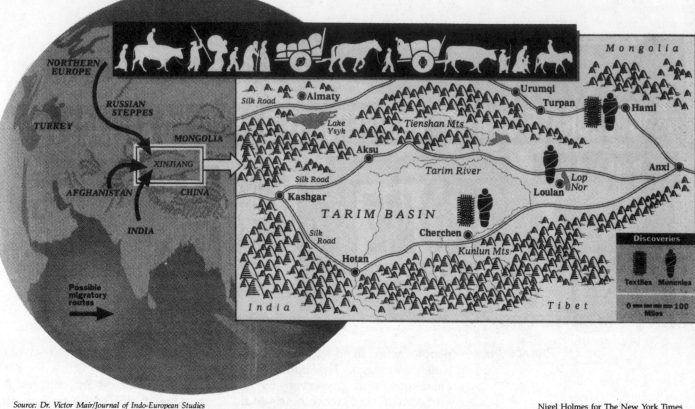

Source: Dr. Victor Mair/Journal of Indo-European Studies

Nigel Holmes for The New York Times

Face to Face With a Mysterious Desert People
Recently found mummified bodies of people who lived 2,400 to 4,000 years ago in the Tarim Basin region of Western China show them to have been strongly European in appearance, some resembling the Irish or Welsh. Their language, the now extinct Tocharian, also shows similarities to Celtic and Germanic tongues.

examination of textiles, pottery and bronze pieces.

The Tocharians were blonds, and they wore plaid.

"Because the Tarim Basin Caucasoid corpses are almost certainly the most easterly representatives of the Indo-European family and because they date from a time period that is early enough to have a bearing on the expansion of the Indo-European people from their homeland," Dr. Mair said, "it is thought they will play a crucial role in determining just where that might have been."

The tenor of discussions at the conference also reflected a critical philosophical shift that could affect attitudes toward other research problems in archeology and prehistory. Most participants invoked without apology the concept of cultural diffusion to explain many discoveries in the Tarim Basin.

For several decades, beginning in the 1960's, cultural diffusion was out of fashion as an explanation for affinities among widely scattered societies. The emphasis, instead, was on independent invention, and archeologists were often rebuked if they strayed from this new orthodoxy, which arose in part as a reaction to the political imperialism that often ignored or belittled the histories and accomplishments of subject lands. The Chinese, moreover, had long discouraged research on outside cultural influences, believing that the

origins of their civilization had been entirely internal and independent.

But Dr. Michael Puett, a historian of East Asian civilizations at Harvard University, said the research on the Tocharians, the mummies and related artifacts revealed clear processes of diffusion. "Diffusionism needs to be taken seriously again," he said. Dr. Colin Renfrew, an influential archeologist at Cambridge University in England, made a point of endorsing this view.

Almost a century of studying the Tocharian manuscripts, dated between the sixth and eighth centuries A.D., has convinced linguists that the language represents an extremely early branching off the original, or proto-Indo-European, language. "That's the working hypothesis, at least for the moment," said Dr. Donald Ringe, a linguist at the University of Pennsylvania.

In that case, the people who came to speak Tocharian might have stemmed from one of the first groups to venture away from the Indo-European homeland, developing a daughter language in isolation. The fact that Tocharian in some respects resembles Celtic and Germanic languages does not necessarily mean that they split off together, scholars said, or that Tocharian speakers originated in northern or western Europe. Tocharian also shares features with Hittite, an extinct Indo-European language that was spoken in what is now Turkey.

One hypothesis gaining favor is that this scattering of Indo-European speakers began with the introduction of wheeled wagons, which gave these herders greater mobility. Working with Russian archeologists, Dr. David W. Anthony, an anthropologist at Hartwick College in Oneonta, N.Y., has discovered traces of wagon wheels in 5,000-year-old burial mounds on the steppes of southern Russia and Kazakhstan. Many scholars suspect that this region is the most likely candidate for the Indo-European homeland, though others argue for places considerably to the east or west or on the Anatolian plain of Turkey.

How did Indo-Europeans get to what is now China?

The possible importance of the wheel in Indo-European diffusion has been supported by evidence that wagons and chariots were introduced into China from the West. Wheels similar to those in use in western Asia and Europe in the third and second millenniums B.C. have been found in graves in the Gobi Desert, northeast of the Tarim Basin, and dated to the late second millennium B.C. Ritual horse burials similar to those in ancient Ukraine have been excavated in the Tarim Basin.

Linguists concede that their analyses of the ancient language will not produce answers to many of the questions about the Tocharians and their ancestors. Archeologists are more hopeful, with the mummy discoveries reviving their interest in the quest.

Early in this century, explorers and archeologists turned up a few mummies in the sands of China's western desert. One reminded them of a Welsh or Irish woman, and another reminded them of a Bohemian burgher. But these mummies, not much more than 2,000 years old, were dismissed as the bodies of isolated Europeans who had happened to stray into the territory and so were of no cultural or historical significance.

But no one could ignore the more recent mummy excavations, from cemeteries ranging over a distance of 500 miles. Not only were they well preserved and from an earlier time, but the mummies were also splendidly attired in colorful robes, trousers, boots, stockings, coats and hats. Some of the hats were conical, like a witch's hat. The grave goods including few weapons and little evidence of social stratification. Could this have been a relatively peaceful and egalitarian society?

One of the most successful excavators of mummies is Dr. Dolkun Kamberi, a visiting scholar at the University of Pennsylvania. He is a member of the dominant Turkic-speaking Muslim ethnic group in the Tarim Basin today, the Uighurs (pronounced WE-gurs). They moved to the area in the eighth century, supplanting the Tocharians, though Dr. Kamberi's fair skin and light brown hair suggests a mixing of Tocharian and Uighur genes.

His most unforgettable discovery, Dr. Kamberi said, came in 1985 at Cherchen on the southern edge of the Taklamakan Desert, an especially forbidding part of the Tarim Basin. The site included several hundred tombs in the salty, sandy terrain. In one tomb, he found the mummified corpse of an infant,

probably no more than three months old at death, wrapped in brown wool and with its eyes covered with small flat stones. Next to the head was a drinking cup made from a bovine horn and an ancient "baby bottle," made from a sheep's teat that had been cut and sewn so it could hold milk.

In a larger tomb, Dr. Kamberi came upon the corpses of three women and one man. The man, about 55 years old at death, was about six feet tall and had yellowish brown hair that was turning white. One of the better-preserved women was close to six feet tall, with yellowish-brown hair dressed in braids. Both were decorated with traces of ocher facial makeup.

Among the other sites of mummy discoveries are cemeteries at Loulan, near the seasonal lake of Lop Nor and outside the modern city of Hami. Dr. Han Kangxin, a physical anthropologist at the Institute of Archeology in Beijing, has examined nearly all the mummies and many other skulls. At the Lop Nor site, he determined that the skulls were definitely of a European type and that some had what appeared to be Nordic features. At Loulan, he observed that the skulls and mummies were primarily Caucasian, though more closely related to Indo-Afghan types.

In nearly all cases, Dr. Han concluded, the earliest inhabitants of the region were almost exclusively Caucasian; only later do mummies and skulls with Mongoloid features begin to show up. At Hami, Caucasian and Mongoloid individuals shared the same burial ground and, judging by their dress and grave goods, many of the same customs.

Scientists have so far been permitted to conduct genetic studies on only one sample, from a 3,200-year-old Hami mummy. Although the recovered DNA samples were badly degraded, Dr. Paolo Francalacci of the University of Sassari in Italy said that he had been able to determine that the individual had belonged to an ancient European genetic group.

He emphasized that the findings were preliminary.

"You can look at the mummy and see it's Caucasoid," Dr. Mair said. "Now we have genetic evidence. This is an important moment in our research."

The graves at Cherchen and Hami also produced the most intriguing textile samples from the late second millennium B.C. One of the Hami fragments was a wool twill woven with a plaid design, which required looms that had never before been associated with China or eastern Central Asia at such an early date. Irene Good, a specialist in textile archeology at the Pennsylvania museum, said that the plaid fabric was "virtually identical stylistically and technically to textile fragments" found in Austria and Germany at sites from a somewhat later period, about 700 B.C.

Dr. Elizabeth J. W. Barber, a linguist and archeologist at Occidental College in Los Angeles and the author of "Prehistoric Textiles" (Princeton University Press, 1991), said that plaid twills had first been discovered in the ruins of Troy, from about 2600 B.C., but had not been common in the Bronze Age. "My impression," she said, "is that weavers from the West came into the Tarim Basin in two waves, first from the west in the early second millennium B.C. and then from the north several centuries later."

Other evidence also seems to point to multiple ancient migrations into the Tarim Basin. "While it is clear that the early inhabitants of the Tarim Basin were primarily Caucasoids," Dr. Mair has written, "it is equally clear that they did not all belong to a single homogeneous group. Rather, they represent a variety of peoples who seem to have connections with many far-flung parts of the Eurasian land mass for more than two millennia."

Whoever they were, scholars said, many of the earlier mummified people were probably ancestors of the Tocharian speakers of the first millennium A.D. But no one knows if those early people spoke Tocharian. As Dr. James Patrick Mallory, an archeologist at Queen's University in Belfast, Northern Ireland, remarked, the mummies did not die "with letters in their pockets."

Wool twills are like those woven on European looms.

With much arm waving in front of maps, scholars speculated on the routes that Indo-European speakers might have followed into the Tarim Basin. Perhaps the earliest migrants, who looked most like Europeans, arrived from the north and northwest, over the mountains from Siberia or Russia. Later migrants, Caucasians but with Indo-Iranian affinities, could have moved in from the west and southwest.

After reviewing the many migration theories, including just about everything short of prehistoric parachute drops, Dr. Mallory sensed the audience's growing perplexity. "If you are not confused now, you have not been paying attention," he said.

One thing seemed clear to the scholars, however. Though East may be East, and West may be West, the twain met often in early times and in places, like the bleak Tarim Basin, that would have surprised Kipling. And these meetings did not begin with the Silk Road, the transcontinental trade route that history books usually describe as opening in the second century B.C. There never was a time, Dr. Mair said, "when people were not traveling back and forth across the whole of Eurasia."

Scholars doubt that these early movements usually took the form of mass migrations over long distances. But after the introduction of wheeled vehicles, pastoral societies could have begun extending their range over generations, coming into contact with others and finding more promising niches far from their linguistic origins.

"For people not in a hurry," said Dr. Denis Sinor, a historian at Indiana University in Bloomington and editor of "The Cambridge History of Early Inner Asia," "the Eurasian continent was a very small world indeed."

In an article on the new research in the Indo-European journal, Dr. Mair wrote, "I do not contend that there were necessarily direct links stretching all the way from northwest Europe to southeast Asia and from northeast Asia to the Mediterranean, but I do believe that there is a growing mountain of hard evidence which indicates indubitably that the whole of Eurasia was culturally and technologically interconnected."

A tale of two cultures

A Beijing scholar links an ancient Chinese
dynasty to the New World's earliest civilization

CHARLES FENYVESI

Abroad for the first time in his life, Han Ping Chen, a scholar of ancient Chinese, landed at Dulles International Airport near Washington, D.C., the night of September 18. Next morning, he paced in front of the National Gallery of Art, waiting for the museum to open so he could visit an Olmec exhibit—works from Mesoamerica's spectacular "mother culture" that emerged suddenly 3,200 years ago, with no apparent local antecedents. After a glance at a 10-ton basalt sculpture of a head, Chen faced the object that prompted his trip: an Olmec sculpture found in La Venta, 10 miles south of the southernmost cove of the Gulf of Mexico.

What the Chinese scholar saw was 15 male figures made of serpentine or jade, each about 6 inches tall. Facing them were a taller sandstone figure and six upright, polished jade blades called celts. The celts bore incised markings, some of them faded. Proceeding from right to left, Chen scrutinized the markings silently, grimacing when he was unable to make out more than a few squiggles on the second and third celts. But the lower half of the fourth blade made him jump. "I can read this easily," he shouted. "Clearly, these are Chinese characters."

For years, scholars have waged a passionate—and often nasty—debate over whether Asian refugees and adventurers might somehow have made their way to the New World long before Columbus, stimulating brilliant achievements in cosmogony, art, astronomy and architecture in a succession of cultures from the Olmec to the Maya and Aztec. On one side are the "diffusionists," who have compiled a long list of links between Asian and Mesoamerican cultures, including similar rules for the Aztec board game of *patolli* and the Asian pachisi (also known as Parcheesi), a theological focus in ancient China and Mesoamerica on tiger-jaguar and dragonlike creatures, and a custom, common both to China's Shang dynasty and the Olmecs, of putting a jade bead in the mouth of a deceased person. "Nativists," on the other hand, dismiss such theories as ridiculous and argue for the autonomous development of pre-Columbian civilizations. They bristle at the suggestion that the indigenous people did not evolve on their own.

Striking resemblances. For diffusionists, Olmec art offers a tempting arena for speculation. Carbon-dating places the Olmec era between 1,000 and 1,200 B.C.,

coinciding with the Shang dynasty's fall in China. American archaeologists unearthed the group sculpture in 1955. Looking at the sculpture displayed in the National Gallery, as well as other Olmec pieces, some Mexican and American scholars have been struck by the resemblances to Chinese artifacts. (In fact, archaeologists initially labeled the first Olmec figures found at the turn of the century as Chinese). Migrations from Asia over the land bridge 10,000–15,000 years ago could account for the Chinese features, such as slanted eyes, but not for the stylized mouths and postures particular to sophisticated Chinese art that emerged in recent millenniums.

Yet until Chen made his pilgrimage to the museum this fall, no Shang specialist had ever studied the Olmec. The scholar emerged from the exhibit with a theory: After the Shang army was routed and the emperor killed, he suggested, some loyalists might have sailed down the Yellow River and taken to the ocean. There, perhaps, they drifted with a current which skirts Japan's coast, heads for California, then peters out near Ecuador. Betty Meggers, a senior Smithsonian archaeologist who has linked pottery dug up in Ecuador to shipwrecked Japanese 5,000 years ago, says such an idea is "plausible" because ancient Asian mariners were far more proficient than they were given credit for.

But Chen's identification of the celt markings is likely to sharpen the controversy over origins even further. For example, Mesoamericanist Michael Coe of Yale University labels Chen's search for Chinese characters as "insulting to the indigenous people of Mexico." And some scholars who share Chen's narrow expertise are equally skeptical. There are only about a dozen experts worldwide in the Shang script, which is largely unrecognizable to readers of modern Chinese. Of the Americans, Profs. William Boltz of the University of Washington and Robert Bagley of Princeton recently looked at a drawing of the celts but dismissed as "rubbish" the notion that the characters could be Chinese. Those looking for a link between the two cultures, Bagley said, are Chinese, and "it no doubt gratifies their ethnic pride to discover that Mesoamerican civilization springs from China."

Others would like to see the celts before taking sides. David Keightley, University of California–Berkeley professor of history, said some characters on the celts "could, of course, be Shang, though I don't at present see it that way." His Chinese colleagues, he said "may just be onto something," and he noted that "it's important that scholars from China examine this material."

Chen, 47, is uninterested in the Mesoamericanists' war. When Prof. Mike Xu, a professor of Chinese history at the University of Central Oklahoma, traveled to Beijing to ask Chen to examine his index of 146 markings from pre-Columbian objects, Chen refused, saying he had no interest in anything outside

China. He relented only after a colleague familiar with Xu's work insisted that Chen, as China's leading authority, take a look. He did and found that all but three of Xu's markings "could have come from China."

Xu was at Chen's side in the National Gallery when the Shang scholar read the text on the Olmec celt in Chinese and translated: "The ruler and his chieftains establish the foundation for a kingdom." Chen located each of the characters on the celt in three well-worn Chinese dictionaries he had with him. Two adjacent characters, usually read as "master and subjects," but Chen decided that in this context they might mean "ruler and his chieftains." The character on the line below he recognized as the symbol for "kingdom" or "country": two peaks for hills, a curving line underneath for river. The next character, Chen said, suggests a bird but means "waterfall," completing the description. The bottom character he read as "foundation" or "establish," implying the act of founding something important. If Chen is right, the celts not only offer the earliest writing in the New World but mark the birth of a Chinese settlement more than 3,000 years ago.

At lunch the next day, Chen said he was awake all night thinking about the sculpture. He talked about how he had studied Chinese script at age 5, tutored by his father, then director of the national archives. But Chen's father did not live to enjoy the honors the son reaped, such as a recent assignment to compile a new dictionary of characters used by the earliest dynasties—the first update since one commissioned by a Han emperor 2,000 years ago.

Color nuances. Chen was so taken with the Olmec sculpture that he ventured beyond scholarly caution. The

group sculpture, he said, might memorialize "a historic event," either a blessing sought from ancestors or the act of founding a new kingdom or both. He was mesmerized by the tallest figure in the sculpture—made from red sandstone as porous as a sponge, in contrast to the others, which are highly polished and green-blue in hue. Red suggests higher status, Chen said. Perhaps the figure was the master of the group, a venerated ancestral spirit. The two dark blue figures to the right might represent the top noblemen, more important than the two others, carved out of pale green serpentine.

The Smithsonian's Meggers says that Chen's analysis of the colors "makes sense. But his reading of the text is the clincher. Writing systems are too arbitrary and complex. They cannot be independently reinvented."

Whether Chen's colleagues ultimately hail him or hang him, his theory yields a tale worthy of Joseph Conrad. And like Conrad, he cannot resist offering yet another footnote from the past: More than 5,000 Shang characters have survived, Chen says, even though the soldiers who defeated the Shang forces murdered the scholars and burned or buried any object with writing on it. In a recent excavation in the Shang capital of Anyang, archaeologists have found a buried library of turtle shells covered with characters. And at the entrance lay the skeleton of the librarian, stabbed in the back and clutching some writings to his breast.

The Olmec sculpture was buried under white sand topped with alternate layers of brown and reddish-brown sand. Perhaps it was hidden to save it from the kind of rage that sought to wipe out the Shang and their memory.

WRITING RIGHT

Some written languages are a precise reflection of a people's speech, while others, like English, are a complete mess. Is this alphabetical evolution? Or the unequal application of logic to literacy?

Jared Diamond

Jared Diamond is a contributing editor of DISCOVER, a professor of physiology at the UCLA School of Medicine, a recipient of a MacArthur genius award, and a research associate in ornithology at the American Museum of Natural History. Expanded versions of many of his DISCOVER articles appear in his book The Third Chimpanzee: The Evolution and Future of the Human Animal.

Do you know how to read and write English? You answer, "Of course, Jared Diamond, you dope. How else would I be reading this magazine?" In that case have you ever tried to *explain* the rules behind written English to someone? The logic, say, of spelling the word *seed* as we do instead of *cede, ceed, or sied*? Or why the sound *sh* can be written as *ce* (as in *ocean*), *ti* (as in *nation*), or *ss* (as in *issue*), to name just a few possibilities?

Innumerable examples like these illustrate the notorious difficulties of written English, even for educated adults. As I am now rediscovering through my twin sons in the first grade, English spelling is so inconsistent that children who have learned the basic rules (insofar as there are any) still can't pronounce many written words or spell words spoken to them. Danish writing is also difficult, Chinese and South Korean harder, and Japanese hardest of all. But it didn't have to be that way. French children can at least pronounce almost any written word, though they often cannot spell spoken words. In Finland and North Korea the fit between spoken sounds and written signs is so nearly perfect that the question "How do you spell it?" is virtually unknown.

"Civilized" people have always considered literacy as the divide between themselves and barbarians. Surely, if we civilized English speakers sat down to devise a writing system, we could do as well as Finns or North Koreans. Why, then, is there such variation in the preci-

sion of writing systems? With thousands of years of literacy now behind us, are today's writing systems—even imperfect ones like our own—at least more precise than ancient ones, such as Eyptian hieroglyphics? Why do we, or any other people, cling to systems that are demonstrably lousy at doing what they're supposed to do?

Before exploring these questions, we need to remind ourselves of the three basic strategies that underlie writing systems. The strategies differ in the size of the speech unit denoted by one written sign: either a single basic sound, or a whole syllable, or a whole word.

The most widespread strategy in the modern world is the alphabet, which ideally would provide a unique sign—a letter—for every basic sound, or phoneme, of the language. Another widespread strategy employs logograms, written signs that stand for whole words. Before the spread of alphabetic writing, systems heavily dependent on logograms were common and included Egyptian hieroglyphs, Mayan glyths, and Sumerian cuneiform. Logograms continue to be used today, notably in Chinese and in kanji, the predominant writing system employed by the Japanese.

The third strategy uses a sign for each syllable. For instance, there could be separate signs for the syllables *fa*, *mi*, and *ly*, which could be strung together to write the word *family*. Such syllabaries were common in ancient times, as exemplified by the Linear B writing of Mycenaean Greece. Some persist today, of which the most important is the kana syllabary, used by the Japanese for telegrams, among other things.

I've intentionally termed these three approaches strategies rather than writing systems because no actual writing system employs one strategy exclusively. Like all "alphabetic" writing systems, English uses many logograms, such as numerals and various arbitrary signs—+, $, %, for example—that are not made up of phonetic elements. "Logographic" Egyptian hieroglyphs included many syllabic signs plus a virtual alphabet of individual letters for each consonant.

Writing systems are still coming into existence, consciously designed by trained linguists. Missionaries, for example, are translating the Bible into native languages of New Guinea, and Chinese government linguists are producing writing materials for their tribal peoples. Most such tailor-made systems modify existing alphabets, although some instead invent syllabaries. But those conscious creations are developed by professional linguists, and linguistics itself is barely a few centuries old. How did writing systems arise before that—also through purposeful design, or by slow evolution? Is there any way we can figure out whether Egyptian hieroglyphs, for example, were a conscious creation?

One way of approaching that question is to look at historical examples of systems that we know were consciously designed by nonprofessionals. A prime example is Korea's remarkable hangul alphabet. By the fifteenth century, when this alphabet was invented, Koreans had been struggling for more than 1,000 years with cumbersome adaptations of already cumbersome Chinese writing—a "gift" from their larger, influential neighbor. The unhappy results were described in 1446 by Korea's King Sejong:

"The sounds of our country's language differ from those of the Middle Kingdom [China] and are not confluent with the sounds of our characters. Therefore, among the ignorant people there have been many who, having something they want to put into words, have in the end been unable to express their feelings. I have been distressed because of this, and have newly designed 28 letters, which I wish to have everyone practice at their ease and make convenient for their daily use."

The King's 28 letters have been described by scholars as "the world's best alphabet" and "the most scientific system of writing." They are an ultrarational system devised from scratch to incorporate three unique features.

First, hangul vowels can be distinguished at a glance from hangul consonants: the vowels are written as long vertical or horizontal lines with small attached marks; consonants, meanwhile, are all compact geometric signs. Related vowels or consonants are further grouped by related shapes. For example, the signs for the round vowels *u* and *o* are similar, as are the signs for the velar consonants *g*, *k*, and *kh*.

Even more remarkable, the shape of each consonant depicts the position in which the lips, mouth, or tongue is held to pronounce that letter. For instance, the signs for *n* and *d* depict the tip of the tongue raised to touch the front of the palate; *k* depicts the outline of the root of the tongue blocking the throat. Twentieth-century scholars were incredulous that those resemblances could really be intentional until 1940, when they discovered the original

draft of King Sejong's 1446 proclamation and found the logic explicitly spelled out.

Finally, hangul letters are grouped vertically and horizontally into square blocks corresponding to syllables, separated by spaces greater than those between letters but less than those between words. That's as if the Declaration of Independence were to contain the sentence:

```
A  me a cr a te e qua
ll   n re e   d    l
```

As a result, the Korean hangul alphabet combines the advantages of a syllabary with those of an alphabet: there are only 28 signs to remember, but the grouping of signs into larger sound bites facilitates rapid scanning and comprehension.

The Korean alphabet provides an excellent example of the cultural phenomenon of "idea diffusion." That phenomenon contrasts with the detailed copying often involved in the spread of technology: we infer that wheels, for example, began to diffuse across Europe around 3500 B.C. because all those early wheels conformed to the same detailed design. However, the Korean alphabet conformed to no existing design; instead it was the *idea* of writing that diffused to Korea. So too did the idea of square blocks, suggested by the block format of Chinese characters; and so did the idea of an alphabet, probably borrowed from Mongol, Tibetan, or Indian Buddhist writing. But the details were invented from the first principles.

There are many other writing systems that we know were deliberately designed by historical individuals. In addition, there are some ancient scripts that are so regularly organized that we can safely infer purposeful design from them as well, even though nothing has come down to us about their origins.

For example, we have documents dating from the fourteenth century B.C., from the ancient Syrian coastal town of Ugarit, that are written in a doubly remarkable 30-letter alphabet. The letters were formed by a technique then widespread in the Near East called cuneiform writing, in which a reed stylus was pressed into a clay tablet. Depending on the stylus's orientation, a sign could be a wedge-tipped vertical line, a wedge-tipped horizontal line, or a broad wedge.

The Ugaritic alphabet's most striking feature is its regularity. The letterforms include one, two, or three parallel or sequential vertical or horizontal lines; one, two, or three horizontal lines crossed by the same number of vertical lines; and so on. Each of the 30 letters requires, on average, barely three strokes to be drawn, yet each is easily distinguished from the others. The overall result is an economy of strokes and consequently, we assume, a speed of writing and ease of reading. The other remarkable feature of the Ugaritic alphabet is that the letters requiring the fewest strokes may have represented the most frequently heard sounds of the Semitic language then spoken at Ugarit. Again, this would make it easier to write fast.

Those two laborsaving devices could hardly have arisen by chance. They imply that some Ugarit genius sat down and used his or her brain to design the Ugaritic alphabet purposefully. As we shall see, by 1400 B.C. the idea of an alphabet was already hundreds of years old in the Near East. And cuneiform writing was by then nearly 2,000 years old. However, as with King Sejong's 28 letters, the Ugarit genius received only those basic ideas by diffusion, then designed the letterforms and the remaining principles independently.

There were other ancient writing systems with such regular organization and for which we can similarly infer tailor-made creation. Furthermore, evidence suggests that even some highly irregular systems were consciously designed. The clearest example of these is the most famous of all ancient writing systems: Egyptian hieroglyphics, a complex mixture of logograms, syllabic signs, unpronounced signs, and a 24-letter consonantal alphabet. Desite this system's complexity, two facts suggest that the underlying principles were quickly designed and did not evolve through a lengthy process of trial and error. The first is that Egyptian hieroglyphic writing appears suddenly around 3050 B.C. in nearly full-blown form, as annotations to scenes carved on ceremonial objects. Even though Egypt's dry climate would have been favorable for preserving any earlier experiments in developing those signs, no such evidence of gradual development has come down to us.

The other fact arguing for the deliberate creation of Egyptian hieroglyphic writing is that it appears suspiciously soon after the appearance of Sumerian cuneiform a couple of centuries earlier, at a time of intense contact and trade linking Egypt and Sumer. It would be incredible if, after millions of years of human illiteracy, two societies in contact happened independently to develop writing systems within a few hundred years of each other. The most likely explanation, again, is idea diffusion. The Egyptians probably learned the idea and some principles of writing from the Sumerians. The other principles and all the specific forms of the letters were then quickly designed by some Egyptian who was clever, but not quite as clever as Korea's King Sejong.

So far, I've been discussing writing systems created by conscious design. In contrast, other systems evolved by a lengthy process of trial and error, with new features added and old features modified or discarded at different stages. Sumerian cuneiform, the oldest known writing system in the world, is one prime example of such an evolved writing system.

Sumerian cuneiform may have begun around 8000 B.C. in the farming villages of the prehistoric Near East, when clay tokens of various simple shapes were developed for accounting purposes, such as recording numbers of sheep. In the last centuries before 3000 B.C., changes in accounting technology and the use of signs rapidly transformed the tokens into the first system of writing. This included a number of innovations, such as the organization of writing into horizontal lines. The most important, however, was the introduction of phonetic representation. The Sumerians figured out how to depict an abstract noun, one that could not be readily drawn as a picture, with another sign that was depictable and that had the same phonetic pronunciation. For instance, it's hard to draw a recognizable picture of *life*, say, but easy to draw a recognizable picture of *arrow*. In Sumerian, both these words are pronounced *ti*. The resulting ambiguity was resolved by adding a silent sign called a determinative to indicate the category of noun the intended object belonged to. Later the Sumerians expanded this phonetic practice, employing it to write syllables or letters constituting grammatical endings.

While revolutionary, the phonetic signs in Sumerian writing nonetheless fell far short of a complete syllabary or alphabet. Some symbols lacked any written sign, while the same sign could be written in different ways or be read as a word, syllable, or letter. The result was a clumsy mess. Eventually, as with the subsequent users of cuneiform writing and along with the 3,000 years of Egyptian hieroglyphics, all passed into oblivion, vanquished by the advantages of more precise alphabetic writing.

Most areas of the modern world write by means of alphabets because they offer the potential advantage of combining precision with simplicity. Alphabets apparently arose only once in history: among speakers of Semitic languages, roughly in the area from modern Syria to the Sinai, during the second millennium B.C. All the hundreds of ancient and modern alphabets were ultimately derived from that ancestral alphabet, either by idea diffusion or by actually copying and modifying letterforms.

There are two likely reasons that alphabets evolved first among Semites. First, Semitic word roots were specified uniquely by their consonants; vowels merely provided grammatical variations on that consonantal root. (An analogy is the English consonantal root *s-ng*, where vowel variations merely distinguish verb tenses—*sing*, *sang*, and *sung*—from one another and from the corresponding noun *song*.) As a result, writing Semitic languages with consonants alone still yields much of the meaning. Consequently, the first Semitic alphabet makers did not yet have to confront the added complication of vowels.

The second reason was the Semites' familiarity with the hieroglyphics used by nearby Egypt. As in Semitic languages, Egyptian word roots also depended mainly on consonants. As I've mentioned, Egyptian hieroglyphics actually included a complete set of 24 signs for the 24 Egyptian consonants. The Egyptians never took what would seem (to us) to be the logical next step of using just their alphabet and discarding all their other beautiful but messy signs. Indeed, probably no one would have noticed that the Egyptians even had a consonantal alphabet lost within their messy writing system had it not been for the rise of a true alphabet. Starting around 1700 B.C., though, the Semites did begin experimenting with that logical step.

Restricting signs to those for single consonants was only one crucial innovation that distinguished alphabets from other writing systems. Another helped users memorize the alphabet by placing the letters in a fixed sequence and giving them easy-to-remember names. Our English names are otherwise-meaningless monosyllables ("a," "bee," "cee," "dee," and so forth). The Greek names are equally meaningless polysyllables ("alpha," "beta," "gamma," "delta"). Those Greek names arose, in turn, as slight modifications, for Greek ears, of the Semitic letter names "aleph," "beth," "gimel," "daleth," and so on. But those Semitic names did possess meaning to Semites: they are the words for familiar objects (aleph = ox, beth = house, gimel = camel, daleth = door). Those Semitic words are related "acrophonically" to the Semitic consonants to which they refer—that is, the first letter of the object is also the letter that is named for the object. In addition, the earliest forms of the Semitic letters appear in many cases to be pictures of those same objects.

A third innovation laying the foundations for modern alphabets was the provision for vowels. While Semitic writing could be figured out even without vowel signs, the inclusion of vowels makes it more comprehensible since vowels carry the grammatical information. For Greek and most other non-Semitic languages, however, reading is scarcely possible without vowel signs. (Try reading the example "ll mn r crtd ql," used earlier in the Korean hangul format.)

The Semites began experimenting in the early days of their alphabet by adding small extra letters to indicate selected vowels (modern Arabic and Hebrew indicate vowels by dots or lines sprinkled above or below the consonantal letters). The Greeks improved on this idea in the eighth century B.C., becoming the first people to indicate all vowels systematically by the same types of letters used for consonants. The Greeks derived the forms of five vowel letters by co-opting letters used in the Phoenician Semitic alphabet for consonantal sounds lacking in Greek.

From those earliest Semitic alphabets, lines of evolutionary modifications lead to the modern Ethiopian, Arabic, Hebrew, Indian, and Southeast Asian alphabets. But the line most familiar to us was the one that led from the Phoenicians to the Greeks, on to the Etruscans, and finally to the Romans, whose alphabet with slight modifications is the one used to print this magazine.

As a group, alphabets have undergone nearly 4,000 years of evolution. Hundreds of alphabets have been adapted for individual languages, and some of those alphabets have now had long separate evolutionary histories. The result is that they differ greatly in how precisely they match signs to sounds, with English, linguists agree, being the worst of all. Even Danish, the second worst, doesn't come close to us in atrocity.

How did English spelling get to be so imprecise? (As a reminder of how bad it is, recall seven fascinating ways we can pronounce the letter o: try horse, on, one, oven, so, to, and woman.) Part of the reason is simply that it has had a long time to deteriorate—the English language has been written since about A.D. 600. Even if a freshly created writing system at first represents a spoken language precisely, pronunciation changes with time, and the writing system must therefore become increasingly imprecise if it is not periodically revised. But German has been written for nearly as long as has English, so that's not the sole answer. Another twist is spelling reforms. As anyone familiar with English and German books printed in the nineteenth century knows, nineteenth-century spelling is essentially identical to modern spelling for English, but not for German. That's the result of a major German spelling reform toward the end of the nineteenth century.

The tragicomic history of English spelling adds to the horror. Those Irish missionaries who adapted the Latin alphabet to Old English did a good job of fitting signs to sounds. But disaster struck with the Norman conquest of England in 1066. Today only about half of English words are of Old English origin; the rest are mostly derived from French and Latin. English words were borrowed from the French using French spellings, according to rules very different from English spelling rules. That was bad enough, but as English borrowings from French continued, French pronunciation itself was changing without much change in French spelling. The result? The French words borrowed by English were spelled according to a whole spectrum of French spelling rules.

English pronunciation itself changed even more radically with time; for example, all written vowels came to sound the same in unstressed syllables. (That is, when pronounced in normal speech, the a in elegant, e in omen, i in raisin, o in kingdom, and u in walrus all sound much the same.) As new words were borrowed from different languages, they were spelled according to the whim of the individual writer or printer. But many English printers were trained in Germany or the Netherlands and brought back still other foreign spelling conventions besides French ones. Not until Samuel Johnson's dictionary of 1755 did English spelling start to become standardized.

While English may have the worst writing system in Europe, it is not the worst in the world. Chinese is even more difficult because of the large number of signs that must be independently memorized. As I said earlier, probably the most gratuitously difficult modern writing system is Japan's kanji. It originated from Chinese writing signs and now has the added difficulty that signs can variously be given Japanese pronunciations or modifications of various past Chinese pronunciations. An attempted remedy that compounds the confusion for Japanese readers is the insertion of spellings in yet another writing system, the kana syllabary, for hard-to-read kanji. As George

Sansom, a leading authority on Japanese, put it, back in the 1920s: "One hesitates for an epithet to describe a writing system which is so complex that it needs the aid of another system to explain it."

Do sub-ideal writing systems really make it harder for adults to read, or for children to learn to read? Many observations make clear that the answer is yes. In 1928 Turkey switched to the Latin alphabet from the Arabic alphabet, which has the twin disadvantages of a complex vowel notation and of changing the forms of letters depending on where they stand within a word. As a result of the switch, Turkish children learned to read in half the time formerly required. Chinese children take at least ten times longer to learn to read traditional Chinese characters than pinyin, a Chinese adaptation of the Latin alphabet. British children similarly learned to read faster and better with a simplified English spelling termed the Initial Teaching Alphabet than with our conventional spelling. Naturally, the educational problems caused by inconsistent spelling can be overcome by increased educational effort. For example, Japan, with the modern world's most difficult spelling system, paradoxically has one of the world's highest literacy rates—thanks to intensive schooling. Nevertheless, for a given educational effort, a simpler spelling system results in more literate adults.

Hebrew provides interesting proof that not only spelling but also letter shapes make a difference. Hebrew writing has several sets of extremely similar letters: only one letter is distinctively tall, and only one letter stands out by dipping below the line (ignoring the special forms of Hebrew letters at the ends of words). As a result, a study suggests that, on the average, readers of Hebrew have to stare at print for longer than do readers of Latin alphabets in order to distinguish those indistinctive letter shapes. That is, distinctive letter shapes permit faster reading.

Since details of writing systems do affect us, why do so many countries refuse to reform their writing systems? There appear to be several reasons for this seeming perverseness: aesthetics, prestige, and just plain conservatism. Chinese writing and Arabic writing are widely acknowledged to be beautiful and are treasured for that reason by their societies; so were ancient Egyptian hieroglyphics. In Japan and Korea, as in China, mastery of Chinese characters implies education and refinement and carries prestige. It's especially striking that Japan and South Korea stick to their fiendishly difficult Chinese-based characters when each country already has available its own superb simple script: kana for the Japanese, and the hangul alphabet for Korea.

Unlike some of these writing systems, our awful English spelling is not considered beautiful or prestigious, yet all efforts to reform it have failed. Our only excuse is conservatism and laziness. If we wanted, we could easily improve our writing to the level of Finland's, so that computer spell-check programs would be unneeded and no child beyond fourth grade would make spelling errors. For example, we should match English spelling consistently to English sounds, as does the Finnish alphabet. We should junk our superfluous letter c (always replaceable by either k or s), and we should coin new letters for sounds now spelled with arbitrary letter combinations (such as sh and th). Granted, spelling is part of our cultural heritage, and English spelling reform could thus be viewed as a cultural loss. But crazy spelling is a part of our culture whose loss would go as unmourned as the loss of our characteristic English medieval torture instruments.

But before you get too excited about those glorious prospects for reform, reflect on what happened to Korea's hangul alphabet. Although it was personally designed by King Sejong, not even a king could persuade his conservative Sinophilic countrymen to abandon their Chinese-derived script. South Korea persists with the resulting mess even today. Only North Korea under Premier Kim Il Sung, a dictator far more powerful than King Sejong ever was, has adopted the wonderful hangul alphabet as the writing norm. Lacking a president with Kim Il Sung's power to ram unwanted blessings down our throats, we Americans shall continue to suffer under spelling rules that become more and more archaic as our pronunciation keeps changing.

Corn in the New World: A Relative Latecomer

John Noble Wilford

A new technique for dating ancient organic matter has upset thinking about the origins of agriculture in the Americas. The earliest known cultivation of corn, it now seems, occurred much more recently than had been thought—4,700 years ago, not 7,000—and scientists are perplexed as they ponder the implications.

The new date means that people in the New World, in the Tehuacán valley of the central Mexican state of Puebla in particular, probably did not begin growing their most important crop until as much as 4,000 or 5,000 years after the beginning of agriculture in the Old World. Hunter-gatherers who settled along the Jordan River valley managed to domesticate wild progenitors of wheat and barley as early as 9,000 to 10,000 years ago, and thus became, as far as anyone knows, the first farmers anywhere. Perhaps such a lengthened time gap could suggest clues to the circumstances favoring the transition to agriculture, one of the foremost innovations in human culture.

Settlement in the Americas preceded cultivation.

The new evidence, said Dr. Gayle J. Fritz, a paleobotanist at Washington University in St. Louis, "makes it necessary to begin building new models for agricultural evolution in the New World."

But reliable as they may be, are the new ages definitive? Because all the ancient corn specimens examined so far were fully domesticated, scientists suspect they have yet to find the intermediate and earliest examples of cultivated corn. They may have been looking in the wrong places.

Dr. Lawrence Kaplan, a botanist at the University of Massachusetts in Boston and a specialist in dating ancient plants, cautioned that it was premature to revise the chronology of New World agriculture. "We ought to reserve judgment on whether the maize for Tehuacán is really as old as it's going to get in Mexico," he said. "Somewhere else, there may be older stuff."

Botanists are urging archeologists to widen their search for evidence of early agriculture in Mexico, the only country where the nearest wild relatives of maize are native. Look in places where the wild teosinte grows, botanists recommend.

In many parts of Mexico, teosinte, an annual plant that shows the greatest biochemical similarity to domesticated corn, is still called Madre de maiz, "mother of maize." The plant thrives in the verdant Balsas River basin, 150 miles west of the Tehuacán valley, but the area has never been systematically surveyed. Rivers and lakes, moreover, are just the places where animals go to drink and are easy prey, where fish can supplement the diet and the soil is moist for planting, all conditions encouraging early settlements and farming.

"The whole issue of origins of agriculture in the Americas is still out there for people to try and figure out," said Dr. Bruce D. Smith, an archeologist at the National Museum of Natural History of the Smithsonian Institution and the author of "The Emergence of Agriculture," a book published last fall by Scientific American Library.

For several decades, archeological research in this field had been somewhat dormant. Archeologists may have been discouraged by the paucity of artifacts among the remains of corncobs in the Tehuacán caves; nothing much to reconstruct the lives of the people who were the corn farmers. Besides, expeditions could count on more fruitful hunting in the ruins of the Olmecs, Maya and Aztecs, whose civilizations afforded more flamboyant discoveries.

Planting in the Old World dates from 5,000 years earlier.

So it was that the timing and pattern of early farming in the New World seemed fixed beyond serious questioning. Corn, or maize, known scientifically as Zea mays, had been established as the first American crop. It was the dietary staple in Mexico and eventually became the

New Theory Of New World

A revised and much later date for the earliest known domesticated corn, based on new dating methods, is making scientists rethink the chronology of Western Hemisphere civilization.

Argentine popcorn, present-day descendant of Tehuacán maize.

Teosinte, closest wild relative of modern corn.

Present — Argentine popcorn is thought to be descended from the first cultivated maize.

— Classic Maya civilization (c. A.D. 200 to A.D. 900).

2,400 years ago — Common beans (Phaseolus vulgaris) first cultivated in Andes and 100 years later at Tehuacán.

3,500 years ago — Lima bean first cultivated in Peru.

4,500-4,700 years ago — **First evidence of cultivated corn from San Marcos cave in Tehuacán Valley. New date is based on accelerator mass spectrometer reading.**

7,000 years ago — Previous estimate of age for San Marcos corn, based on radiocarbon dating.

9,000-10,000 years ago — Domestication of plants and animals in Middle East around Jordan River valley.

12,000 years ago — End of Ice Age. Warmer, moist climate creates conditions favorable to wild plants like teosinte.

Reconstruction of early ear of corn from San Marcos Cave in the Tehuacán Valley.

same throughout most of the two continents.

This decisive cultural step, planting and harvesting, was confidently dated at 7,000 years ago, based on standard radiocarbon analysis of material found in the Tehuacán caves in the 1960's by Dr. Richard S. Mac-Neish of the Andover Foundation for Archeological Research in Andover, Mass. Buried in the dry sediments were two-inch-long ears of corn, each with eight rows of six to nine tiny popcorn-like kernels—a poor foretaste of sweet corn on the cob.

But one thing kept puzzling some scholars. These early New World farmers appeared to be seasonally mobile hunter-gatherers who visited the Tehuacán valley just long enough to plant and harvest a crop, then moved on to where the hunting might be better. Indeed, it has long been a tenet of pre-Columbian anthropology that it was the domestication of corn, providing a steady source of food and thus increasing populations and encouraging a more sedentary life, that cleared the way for complex societies.

In the Old World, though, the sequence was reversed: sedentary life first, then agriculture. People there typically settled into communities near where wild animals and plants were abundant and then over time learned to increase and regularize their food supply through domestication of certain animals and plants, thus making the transition from hunting and gathering to agriculture. The more recent corn date, Dr.

Search for Ancient Agriculture
Archeologists suggest looking for evidence of early farming in places where corn's wild ancestor is still found.

U.S.

Gulf of Mexico

MEXICO

■ Areas of teosinte

Mexico City

Tehuacán

Pacific Ocean

BEL.

GUAT.

0 Miles 200

Fritz thinks, could have given the hunter-gatherers more time to experiment with possible sedentary living before taking up agriculture.

"I would not be at all surprised to find sedentary life before agriculture, probably in river and lake areas," she said. "But we don't have any evidence for it. We haven't really been looking."

In her own research in northeastern Louisiana, Dr. Fritz has already found evidence of other early American societies of hunter-gatherers leading sedentary village life. This way of life was practiced in many places in eastern North America in the centuries before Columbus. The search for evidence of this in Mesoamerica also stands high on the agenda of research into early American farming.

"The problem in Mexico is, the information we have on early sedentary villages is not very good," said Dr. T. Douglas Price, a University of Wisconsin archeologist who specializes in the study of early agriculture. "We've been trying to encourage more people to investigate the archeology of the early farmers."

Many of the old assumptions about New World agriculture are being reexamined in light of the new age estimates for early corn, reported in 1989 by Dr. Austin Long and colleagues at the University of Arizona in Tucson. The scientists applied the new technology of accelerator mass spectrometry, which overcomes a serious limitation of conventional radiocarbon dating: the sample-size barrier.

In the standard method, developed in the 1940's, scientists could determine the age of once-living material, a piece of wood, cloth or corncob, by detecting and counting the decay rate of the radioactive isotope carbon-14 in the material. But this meant destroying a large sample to get the five grams of carbon necessary for the test. In the case of the early Mexican corn, the specimens were too small and too few to part with.

So archeologists had done the next best thing. For the destructive radiocarbon tests, they used large samples of other organic material, usually charcoal found in the same sediments with the corncobs and kernels and thus assumed to be contemporary. It was an indirect measure and not very reliable, as they have found out. Seeds and other small objects have a way of being displaced in sediments, shifting up or down by the actions of burrowing animals, moisture and other disturbances.

With accelerator mass spectrometry, scientists can determine the age of samples as small as one-thousandth the size of those required for the conventional method. Just a pinch of a cob or husk will do; not the whole thing. Rather than counting decay events, the particle accelerator separates and counts directly the carbon-14 atoms. This gives the time elapsed since the material was alive.

In addition to the corn dating, the technique has been used by archeologists to date the skulls of horses found with chariot remains in burial mounds in Kazakhstan, leading them to conclude that the earliest known chariots came from this region 4,000 years ago. This is earlier than Russian scientists had estimated, and several centuries before the best evidence for chariots in the Middle East. Also, French and Spanish scientists recently used the technique to show that painted bison on the ceiling of the Altamira Cave in northern Spain were painted not at the same time but centuries apart.

The earliest Mexican corn samples proved to be 4,700 years old; others were as recent as 1,600 years old. Dr. Kaplan has used the same technology to test the ages of primitive beans in Mexico and South America, once placed at 6,000 to 8,000 years ago. Like corn, domesticated beans, Phaseolus vulgaris, also turn out to be younger than thought—about 2,300 years at Tehuacán and 2,400 years in the Andes. Lima beans from Peru were dated at 3,500 years.

As the new findings undermined the record for a much earlier New World agriculture, Dr. Fritz grew impatient with textbooks and some professors who persisted in using the old corn dates and with re-

---

Which came first: sedentary life or agriculture?

---

searchers doing little to incorporate the new dates in their interpretations of early agriculture.

Writing in the journal Current Anthropology last June, she urged colleagues to "forge ahead with drastic revisions for New World agricultural beginnings based on the earliest good dates available" rather than to cling to chronologies unsupported by solid evidence.

Several scientists, notably Dr. Dolores Piperno of the Smithsonian Institution Tropical Research Institute in Panama, insist that they have pollen and other evidence for domesticated corn and other plants in South America 7,000 years ago. But Dr. Fritz said she remained unconvinced by claims that corn farming had spread into Central America and northern South America before 5,500 years ago. Other botanists familiar with the work tended to side with Dr. Fritz.

Acknowledging that Dr. Fritz was correct to wake up scientists to the new data, Dr. Kaplan of the University of Massachusetts cautioned that the new dates for corn and beans "in no way represent the ultimate answer" concerning the fateful time at which early Americans turned to farming and cultivated a wild plant that became corn. After it was discovered by the rest of the world, corn became the third largest crop, after wheat and rice.

How Man Invented Cities

John Pfeiffer

The most striking mark of man's genius as a species, as the most adaptable of animals, has been his ability to live in cities. From the perspective of all we know about human evolution, nothing could be more unnatural. For over fifteen million years, from the period when members of the family of man first appeared on earth until relatively recent times, our ancestors were nomadic, small-group, wide-open-spaces creatures. They lived on the move among other moving animals in isolated little bands of a few families, roaming across wildernesses that extended like oceans to the horizon and beyond.

Considering that heritage, the wonder is not that man has trouble getting along in cities but that he can do it at all—that he can learn to live in the same place year round, enclosed in sharp-cornered and brightly-lit rectangular spaces, among noises, most of which are made by machines, within shouting distance of hundreds of other people, most of them strangers. Furthermore, such conditions arose so swiftly, practically overnight on the evolutionary time scale, that he has hardly had a chance to get used to them. The transition from a world without cities to our present situation took a mere five or six millenniums.

It is precisely because we are so close to our origins that what happened in prehistory bears directly on current problems. In fact, the expectation is that new studies of pre-cities and early cities will contribute as significantly to an understanding of today's urban complexes as studies of infancy and early childhood have to an understanding of adolescence. Cities are signs, symptoms if you will, of an accelerating and intensive phase of human evolution, a process that we are only beginning to investigate scientifically.

The first stages of the process may be traced back some fifteen thousand years to a rather less hectic era. Homo sapiens, that new breed of restless and intelligent primate, had reached a high point in his career as a hunter-gatherer subsisting predominantly on wild plants and animals. He had developed special tools, special tactics and strategies, for dealing with a wide variety of environments, from savannas and semideserts to tundras and tropical rain forests and mountain regions. Having learned to exploit practically every type of environment, he seemed at last to have found his natural place in the scheme of things—as a hunter living in balance with other species, and with all the world as his hunting ground.

But forces were already at work that would bring an end to this state of equilibrium and ultimately give rise to cities and the state of continuing instability that we are trying to cope with today. New theories, a harder look at the old theories, and an even harder look at our own tendencies to think small have radically changed our ideas about what happened and why.

We used to believe, in effect, that people abandoned hunting and gathering as soon as a reasonable alternative became available to them. It was hardly a safe or reliable way of life. Our ancestors faced sudden death and injury from predators and from prey that fought back, disease from exposure to the elements and from always being on the move, and hunger because the chances were excellent of coming back empty-handed from the hunt. Survival was a full-time struggle. Leisure came only after the invention of agriculture, which brought food surpluses, rising populations, and cities. Such was the accepted picture.

The fact of the matter, supported by studies of living hunter-gatherers as well as by the archaeological record, is that the traditional view is largely melodrama and science fiction. Our preagricultural ancestors were quite healthy, quite safe, and regularly obtained all the food they needed. And they did it with time to burn. As a rule, the job of collecting food, animal and vegetable, required no more than a three-hour day, or a twenty-one-hour week. During that time, collectors brought in enough food for the entire group, which included an appreciable proportion (perhaps 30 per cent or more) of dependents, old persons and children who did little or no work. Leisure is basically a phenomenon of hunting-gathering times, and people have been trying to recover it ever since.

Another assumption ripe for discarding is that civilization first arose in the valleys of the Tigris, Euphrates, and Nile rivers and spread from there to the rest of the world. Accumulating evidence fails to support this notion that civilization is an exclusive product of these regions. To be sure, agriculture and cities may have appeared first in the Near East, but there are powerful arguments for completely independent origins in at least two other widely separated regions, Mesoamerica and Southeast Asia.

In all cases, circumstances forced hunter-gatherers to evolve new ways of surviving. With the decline of the ancient life style, nomadism, problems began piling up. If only people had kept on moving about like sane and respectable primates, life would be a great deal simpler. Instead, they settled down in increasing numbers over wider areas, and society started changing with a vengeance. Although the causes of this settling down remain a mystery, the fact of independent origins calls for an explanation based on worldwide developments.

An important factor, emphasized recently by Lewis Binford of the University of New Mexico, may have been the melting of mile-high glaciers, which was well under way fifteen thousand years ago, and which released enough water to raise the world's oceans 250 to 500 feet, to flood previously exposed coastal plains, and to create shallow bays and estuaries and marshlands. Vast numbers of fish and wild fowl made use of the new environments, and the extra resources permitted people to obtain food without migrating seasonally. In other words, people expended less energy, and life became that much easier, in the beginning anyway.

Yet this sensible and seemingly innocent change was to get mankind into all sorts of difficulties. According to a recent theory, it triggered a chain of events that made cities possible if not inevitable. Apparently, keeping on the move had always served as a natural birth-control mechanism, in part, perhaps, by causing a relatively high incidence of miscarriages. But the population brakes were off as soon as people began settling down.

One clue to what may have happened is provided by contemporary studies of a number of primitive tribes, such as the Bushmen of Africa's Kalahari Desert. Women living in nomadic bands, bands that pick up and move half a dozen or more times a year, have an average of one baby every four years or so, as compared with one baby every two and a half years for Bushman women living in settled communities—an increase of five to eight babies per mother during a twenty-year reproductive period.

The archaeological record suggests that in some places at least, a comparable phenomenon accompanied the melting of glaciers during the last ice age. People settled down and multiplied in the Les Eyzies region of southern France, one of the richest and most-studied centers of prehistory. Great limestone cliffs dominate the countryside, and at the foot of the cliffs are natural shelters, caves and rocky overhangs where people built fires, made tools out of flint and bone and ivory, and planned the next day's hunt. On special occasions artists equipped with torches went deep into certain caves like Lascaux and covered the walls with magnificent images of the animals they hunted.

In some places the cliffs and the shelters extend for hundreds of yards; in other places there are good living sites close to one another on the opposite slopes of river valleys. People in the Les Eyzies region were living not in isolated bands but in full-fledged communities, and populations seem to have been on the rise. During the period from seven thousand to twelve thousand years ago, the total number of sites doubled, and an appreciable proportion of them probably represent year-round settlements located in small river valleys. An analysis of excavated animal remains reveals an increasing dietary reliance on migratory birds and fish (chiefly salmon).

People were also settling down at about the same time in the Near East— for example, not far from the Mediterranean shoreline of Israel and on the border between the coastal plain and the hills to the east. Ofer Bar-Yosef, of the Institute of Archaeology of Hebrew University in Jerusalem, points out that since they were able to exploit both these areas, they did not have to wander widely in search of food. There were herds of deer and gazelle, wild boar, fish and wild fowl, wild cereals and other plants, and limestone caves and shelters like those in the Les Eyzies region. Somewhat later, however, a new land-use pattern emerged. Coastal villages continued to flourish, but in addition to them, new sites began appearing further inland—and in areas that were drier and less abundant.

Only under special pressure will men abandon a good thing, and in this case it was very likely the pressure of rising populations. The evidence suggests that the best coastal lands were supporting about all the hunter-gatherers they could support; and as living space decreased there was a "budding off," an overflow of surplus population into the second-best back country where game was scarcer. These people depended more and more on plants, particularly on wild cereals, as indicated by the larger numbers of flint sickle blades, mortars and pestles, and storage pits found at their sites (and also by an increased wear and pitting of teeth, presumably caused by chewing more coarse and gritty plant foods).

Another sign of the times was the appearance of stone buildings, often with impressively high and massive walls. The structures served a number of purposes. For one thing, they included storage bins where surplus grain could be kept in reserve for bad times, when there was a shortage of game and wild plants. They also imply danger abroad in the countryside, new kinds of violence, and a mounting need for defenses to protect stored goods from the raids of people who had not settled down.

Above all, the walls convey a feeling of increasing permanence, an increasing commitment to places. Although man was still mainly a hunter-gatherer living on wild species, some of the old options no longer existed for him. In the beginning, settling down may have involved a measure of choices, but now man was no longer quite so free to change locales when the land became less fruitful. Even in those days frontiers were vanishing. Man's problem was to develop new options, new ways of working the land more intensively so that it would provide the food that migration had always provided in more mobile times.

The all-important transition to agriculture came in small steps, establishing itself almost before anyone realized what was going on. Settlers in marginal lands took early measures to get more food out of less abundant environments—roughing up the soil a bit with scraping or digging sticks, sowing wheat and barley seeds, weeding, and generally doing their best to promote growth. To start with at least, it was simply a matter of supplementing regular diets of wild foods with some domesticated species, animals as well as plants, and people probably regarded themselves as hunter-gatherers working hard to maintain their way of life rather than as the revolutionaries they were. They were trying to preserve the old self-sufficiency, but it was a losing effort.

The wilderness way of life became more and more remote, more and more nearly irretrievable. Practically every advance in the technology of agriculture committed people to an increasing dependence on domesticated species and on the activities of other people living nearby. Kent Flannery of the University of Michigan emphasizes this point in a study of one part of Greater Mesopotamia, prehistoric Iran, during the period between twelve thousand and six thousand years ago. For the hunter-gatherer, an estimated one-third of the country's total land area was good territory, consisting of grassy plains and high mountain valleys where wild species were abundant; the rest of the land was desert and semidesert.

The coming of agriculture meant that people used a smaller proportion of the countryside. Early farming took advantage of naturally distributed water; the best terrain for that, namely terrain with a high water table and marshy areas, amounted to about a tenth of the land area. But only a tenth of that tenth was suitable for the next major development, irrigation. Meanwhile, food yields were soaring spectacularly, and so was the population of Iran, which increased more than fiftyfold; in other words, fifty times the original population was being supported by food produced on one-hundredth of the land.

A detailed picture of the steps involved in this massing of people is coming from studies of one part of southwest Iran, an 880-square-mile region between the Zagros Mountains and the Iraqi border. The Susiana Plain is mostly flat, sandy semidesert, the only notable features being manmade mounds that loom on the horizon like islands, places where people built in successively high levels on the ruins of their ancestors. During the past decade or so, hundreds of mounds have been mapped and dated (mainly through pottery styles) by Robert Adams of the University of Chicago, Jean Perrot of the French Archaeological Mission in Iran, and Henry Wright and Gregory Johnson of the University of Michigan. Their work provides a general idea of when the mounds were occupied, how they varied in size at different periods and how a city may be born.

Imagine a time-lapse motion picture of the early settling of the Susiana Plain, starting about 6500 B.C, each minute of film representing a century. At first the plain is empty, as it has been since the beginning of time. Then the pioneers arrive; half a dozen families move in and build a cluster of mud-brick homes near a river. Soon another cluster appears and another, until, after about five minutes (it is now 6000 B.C.), there are ten settlements, each covering an area of 1 to 3 hectares (1 hectare = 2.47 acres). Five minutes more (5500 B.C) and we see the start of irrigation, on a small scale, as people dig little ditches to carry water from rivers and tributaries to lands along the banks. Crop yields increase and so do populations, and there are now thirty settlements, all about the same size as the original ten.

This is but a prelude to the main event. Things become really complicated during the next fifteen minutes or so (5500 to 4000 B.C.). Irrigation systems, constructed and maintained by family groups of varying sizes, become more complex. The number of settlements shows a modest increase, from thirty to

forty, but a more significant change takes place—the appearance of a hierarchy. Instead of settlements all about the same size, there are now levels of settlements and a kind of ranking: one town (7 hectares), ten large villages (3 to 4 hectares), and twenty-nine smaller villages of less than 3 hectares. During this period large residential and ceremonial structures appear at Susa, a town on the western edge of the Susiana Plain.

Strange happenings can be observed not long after the middle of this period (about 4600 B.C.). For reasons unknown, the number of settlements decreases rapidly. It is not known whether the population of the area decreased simultaneously. Time passes, and the number of settlements increases to about the same level as before, but great changes have occurred. Three cities have appeared with monumental public buildings, elaborate residential architecture, large workshops, major storage and market facilities, and certainly with administrators and bureaucrats. The settlement hierarchy is more complex, and settlements are no longer located to take advantage solely of good agricultural opportunities. Their location is also influenced by the cities and the services and opportunities available there. By the end of our hypothetical time-lapse film, by the early part of the third millennium B.C., the largest settlement of all is the city of Susa, which covers some thirty hectares and will cover up to a square kilometer (100 hectares) of territory before it collapses in historical times.

All Mesopotamia underwent major transformations during this period. Another city was taking shape 150 miles northwest of Susa in the heartland of Sumer. Within a millennium the site of Uruk near the Euphrates River grew from village dimensions to a city enclosing within its defense walls more than thirty thousand people, four hundred hectares, and at the center a temple built on top of a huge brick platform. Archaeological surveys reveal that this period also saw a massive immigration into the region from places and for reasons as yet undetermined, resulting in a tenfold increase in settlements and in the formation of several new cities.

Similar surveys, requiring months and thousands of miles of walking, are completed or under way in many parts of the world. Little more than a millennium after the establishment of Uruk and Susa, cities began making an independent ap-

pearance in northern China not far from the conflux of the Wei and Yellow rivers, in an area that also saw the beginnings of agriculture. Still later, and also independently as far as we can tell, intensive settlement and land use developed in the New World.

The valley of Oaxaca in Mexico, where Flannery and his associates are working currently, provides another example of a city in the process of being formed. Around 500 B.C., or perhaps a bit earlier, buildings were erected for the first time on the tops of hills. Some of the hills were small, no more than twenty-five or thirty feet high, and the buildings were correspondingly small; they overlooked a few terraces and a river and probably a hamlet or two. Larger structures appeared on higher hills overlooking many villages. About 400 B.C. the most elaborate settlement began to appear on the highest land, 1,500-foot Monte Albán, with a panoramic view of the valley's three arms; and within two centuries it had developed into an urban center including hundreds of terraces, an irrigation system, a great plaza, ceremonial buildings and residences, and an astronomical observatory.

At about the same time, the New World's largest city, Teotihuacán, was evolving some 225 miles to the northwest in the central highlands of Mexico. Starting as a scattering of villages and hamlets, it covered nearly eight square miles at its height (around A.D. 100 to 200) and probably contained some 125,000 people. Archaeologists are now reconstructing the life and times of this great urban center. William Sanders of Pennsylvania State University is concentrating on an analysis of settlement patterns in the area, while Rene Millon of the University of Rochester and his associates have prepared detailed section-by-section maps of the city as a step toward further extensive excavations. Set in a narrow valley among mountains and with its own man-made mountains, the Pyramid of the Sun and the Pyramid of the Moon, the city flourished on a grand scale. It housed local dignitaries and priests, delegations from other parts of Mesoamerica, and workshop neighborhoods where specialists in the manufacture of textiles, pottery, obsidian blades, and other products lived together in early-style apartments.

The biggest center in what is now the United States probably reached its peak about a millennium after Teotihuacán.

But it has not been reconstructed, and archaeologists are just beginning to appreciate the scale of what happened there. Known as Cahokia and located east of the Mississippi near St. Louis, it consists of a cluster of some 125 mounds (including a central mound 100 feet high and covering 15 acres) as well as a line of mounds extending six miles to the west.

So surveys and excavations continue, furnishing the sort of data needed to disprove or prove our theories. Emerging patterns involving the specific locations of different kinds of communities and of buildings and other artifacts within communities can yield information about the forces that shaped and are still shaping cities and the behavior of people in cities. But one trend stands out above all others: the world was becoming more and more stratified. Every development seemed to favor social distinctions, social classes and elites, and to work against the old hunter-gatherer ways.

Among hunter-gatherers all people are equal. Individuals are recognized as exceptional hunters, healers, or storytellers, and they all have the chance to shine upon appropriate occasions. But it would be unthinkable for one of them, for any one man, to take over as full-time leader. That ethic passed when the nomadic life passed. In fact, a literal explosion of differences accompanied the coming of communities where people lived close together in permanent dwellings and under conditions where moving away was not easy.

The change is reflected clearly in observed changes of settlement patterns. Hierarchies of settlements imply hierarchies of people. Emerging social levels are indicated by the appearance of villages and towns and cities where only villages had existed before, by different levels of complexity culminating in such centers as Susa and Monte Albán and Cahokia. Circumstances practically drove people to establish class societies. In Mesopotamia, for instance, increasingly sophisticated agricultural systems and intensive concentrations of populations brought about enormous and irreversible changes within a short period. People were clamped in a demographic vise, more and more of them living and depending on less and less land—an ideal setting for the rapid rise of status differences.

Large-scale irrigation was a highly effective centralizing force, calling for new duties and new regularities and new levels of discipline. People still depended on the seasons; but in addition, canals had to be dug and maintained, and periodic cleaning was required to prevent the artificial waterways from filling up with silt and assorted litter. Workers had to be brought together, assigned tasks, and fed, which meant schedules and storehouses and rationing stations and mass-produced pottery to serve as food containers. It took time to organize such activities efficiently. There were undoubtedly many false starts, many attempts by local people to work things out among themselves and their neighbors at a community or village level. Many small centers, budding institutions, were undoubtedly formed and many collapsed, and we may yet detect traces of them in future excavations and analyses of settlement patterns.

The ultimate outcome was inevitable. Survival demanded organization on a regional rather than a local basis. It also demanded high-level administrators and managers, and most of them had to be educated people, mainly because of the need to prepare detailed records of supplies and transactions. Record-keeping has a long prehistory, perhaps dating back to certain abstract designs engraved on cave walls and bone twenty-five thousand or more years ago. But in Mesopotamia after 4000 B.C. there was a spurt in the art of inventing and utilizing special marks and symbols.

The trend is shown in the stamp and cylinder seals used by officials to place their "signatures" on clay tags and tablets, man's first documents. At first the designs on the stamp seals were uncomplicated, consisting for the most part of single animals or simple geometric motifs. Later, however, there were bigger stamp seals with more elaborate scenes depicting several objects or people or animals. Finally the cylinder seals appeared, which could be rolled to repeat a complex design. These seals indicate the existence of more and more different signatures and more and more officials and record keepers. Similar trends are evident in potters' marks and other symbols. All these developments precede pictographic writing, which appears around 3200 B.C..

Wherever record keepers and populations were on the rise, in the Near East or Mexico or China, we can be reasonably sure that the need for a police force or the prehistoric equivalent thereof was on the increase, too. Conflict, including everything from fisticuffs to homicide, increases sharply with group size, and people have known this for a long time. The Bushmen have a strong feeling about avoiding crowds: "We like to get together, but we fear fights." They are most comfortable in bands of about twenty-five persons and when they have to assemble in larger groups—which happens for a total of only a few months a year, mainly to conduct initiations, arrange marriages, and be near the few permanent water holes during dry seasons—they form separate small groups of about twenty-five, as if they were still living on their own.

Incidentally, twenty-five has been called a "magic number," because it hints at what may be a universal law of group behavior. There have been many counts of hunter-gatherer bands, not only in the Kalahari Desert, but also in such diverse places as the forests of Thailand, the Canadian Northwest, and northern India. Although individual bands may vary from fifteen to seventy-five members, the tendency is to cluster around twenty-five, and in all cases a major reason for keeping groups small is the desire to avoid violence. In other words, the association between large groups and conflict has deep roots and very likely presented law-and-order problems during the early days of cities and pre-cities, as it has ever since.

Along with managers and record keepers and keepers of the peace, there were also specialists in trade. A number of factors besides population growth and intensive land use were involved in the origin of cities, and local and long-distance trade was among the most important. Prehistoric centers in the process of becoming urban were almost always trade centers. They typically occupied favored places, strategic points in developing trade networks, along major waterways and caravan routes or close to supplies of critical raw materials.

Archaeologists are making a renewed attempt to learn more about such developments. Wright's current work in southwest Iran, for example, includes preliminary studies to detect and measure changes in the flow of trade. One site about sixty-five miles from Susa lies close to tar pits, which in prehistoric times served as a source of natural asphalt for fastening stone blades to handles and waterproofing baskets and roofs. By saving all the waste bits of this important raw material preserved in different excavated levels, Wright was able to estimate fluctuations in its production over a period of time. In one level, for example, he found that the amounts of asphalt produced increased far beyond local requirements; in fact, a quantitative analysis indicates that asphalt exports doubled at this time. The material was probably being traded for such things as high-quality flint obtained from quarries more than one hundred miles away, since counts of material recovered at the site indicate that imports of the flint doubled during the same period.

In other words, the site was taking its place in an expanding trade network, and similar evidence from other sites can be used to indicate the extent and structure of that network. Then the problem will be to find out what other things were happening at the same time, such as significant changes in cylinder-seal designs and in agricultural and religious practices. This is the sort of evidence that may be expected to spell out just how the evolution of trade was related to the evolution of cities.

Another central problem is gaining a fresh understanding of the role of religion. Something connected with enormous concentrations of people, with population pressures and tensions of many kinds that started building up five thousand or more years ago, transformed religion from a matter of simple rituals carried out at village shrines to the great systems of temples and priesthoods invariably associated with early cities. Sa-

cred as well as profane institutions arose to keep society from splitting apart.

Strong divisive tendencies had to be counteracted, and the reason may involve yet another magic number, another intriguing regularity that has been observed in hunter-gatherer societies in different parts of the world. The average size of a tribe, defined as a group of bands all speaking the same dialect, turns out to be about five hundred persons, a figure that depends to some extent on the limits of human memory. A tribe is a community of people who can identify closely with one another and engage in repeated face-to-face encounters and recognitions; and it happens that five hundred may represent about the number of persons a hunter-gatherer can remember well enough to approach on what would amount to a first-name basis in our society. Beyond that number the level of familiarity declines, and there is an increasing tendency to regard individuals as "they" rather than "we," which is when trouble usually starts. (Architects recommend that an elementary school should not exceed five hundred pupils if the principal is to maintain personal contact with all of them, and the headmaster of one prominent prep school recently used this argument to keep his student body at or below the five-hundred mark.)

Religion of the sort that evolved with the first cities may have helped to "beat" the magic number five hundred. Certainly there was an urgent need to establish feelings of solidarity among many

thousands of persons rather than a few hundred. Creating allegiances wider than those provided by direct kinship and person-to-person ties became a most important problem, a task for full-time professionals. In this connection Paul Wheatley of the University of Chicago suggests that "specialized priests were among the first persons to be released from the daily round of subsistence labor." Their role was partly to exhort other workers concerned with the building of monuments and temples, workers who probably exerted greater efforts in the belief that they were doing it not for mere men but for the glory of individuals highborn and close to the gods.

The city evolved to meet the needs of societies under pressure. People were being swept up in a process that had been set in motion by their own activities and that they could never have predicted, for the simple reason that they had no insight into what they were doing in the first place. For example, they did not know, and had no way of knowing, that settling down could lead to population explosions.

There is nothing strange about this state of affairs, to be sure. It is the essence of the human condition and involves us just as intensely today. Then as now, people responded by the sheer instinct of survival to forces that they understood vaguely at best—and worked together as well as they could to organize themselves, to preserve order in the face of accelerating change and complexity and the threat of chaos. They could never know that they were creating what we, its beneficiaries and its victims, call civilization.

The Early Civilizations to 500 B.C.E.

Urbanization and agriculture became human destiny. The cycle of more people and more food and more cities has continued to the present. Add to this the Industrial Revolution, when agriculture and the cities both received a boost, and the situation is like that of the current United States where less than 2 percent of the population supplies the food for the rest of the people who live either in or near cities. Projections concerning world population confirm the cycle, and at the year 2000 about half the world's people will be urban dwellers. From the archaeological finds of the earliest city areas, it is apparent that a robust Sumerian urban life spread quickly through Turkey, as John Noble Wilford notes in this unit's first essay. This made possible the first great empire, but prolonged drought brought its downfall, which was marked by abandoned cities and fields.

Natural disaster was not the only hazard for the cities. The fabled city of Troy, which straddled the east-west trade routes, had to be rebuilt at least nine times. It was destroyed in the famous Trojan war, for example, but it was so vital that the city endured for 3,500 years. Herodotus, as reported by Carmine Ampolo, inquired about the stories concerning the abducted Helen and the ensuing war at Troy, but it was adventurer Heinrich Schliemann who located the site in the 1870s and made off with a fabulous treasure. Herodotus, the ancient Greek historian, traveled widely, however, and set a standard of skepticism and inquiry that has served as a foundation for the development of Western historiography.

Herodotus visited Egypt and commented about the pyramids, the tombs of pharaohs. Much of the information about Egypt concerns the upper class and comes from the tombs that survived. Much less is known about the Egyptian people of the time, but excavations at the village of Deir el-Medina near the Valley of the Kings is revealing. This village housed the educated artisans who decorated the rich burial caves in the nearby valley. They were unusually literate and left behind their own letters and messages. There was even information about their system of education for new craftsmen and scribes, as Andrea McDowell explains in the article "Daily Life in Ancient Egypt."

In 1922 the fabulous tomb of King Tutankhamen was uncovered, and in 1995 the most extensive entombment area in the Valley of the Kings was discovered under a proposed parking lot. No treasure has been recovered yet from the new site, but the area is large and likely will take archaeologist Kent Weeks the rest of his career to complete the excavation. The fragments and shards left behind by the ancient grave robbers still make the work worthwhile. It is considered next in importance to the tomb of King Tutankhamen. The essay "All the King's Sons" describes this exciting discovery.

The civilization of ancient Egypt is considered the most developed in Africa, but there is more to be learned about Nubia, an empire south of Egypt on the upper Nile River. The land is now barren, but it flourished in competition with Egypt. The two nations often were at war with each other, and most of our information about Nubians comes from their enemies. Nubian writing has not been deciphered and, thus, historians are at a loss for information. History, therefore, may have been distorted. There is a current argument that the inspiration for Greek culture came from Nubia through Egypt. Most historians are waiting for proof of that assertion, but David Roberts, in "Out of Africa: The Superb Artwork of Ancient Nubia," praises the quality of Nubian artwork, the extant artifacts through which this mysterious civilization is known.

Looking Ahead: Challenge Questions

Explain the role of climate in the success and failure of early civilizations.

What is the significance of archaeology in the study of history?

Compare the archaeological techniques of Heinrich Schliemann, Kent Weeks, and Carl Lumholtz (see unit 6).

Why is Herodotus considered the first Western historian?

Why are the tombs of Egypt of interest today? What sort of society can build such places, and for what reason?

Describe the life of the ancient Egyptian artisan. What are the sources of information?

Why has Nubia been ignored by historians?

Old Tablet From Turkish Site Shows Early Spread of Culture

John Noble Wilford

New discoveries in Turkey and northern Syria, two buried cities and intriguing clay tablets with cuneiform writing, are expanding the known horizons of early urban civilization and literacy well beyond the Sumerian city-states of southern Mesopotamia.

Archeologists say the discoveries are among the most exciting in Mesopotamian studies in recent decades. They are confident that further excavations at the sites will provide answers to one of the most important questions in archeology: how and when did the phenomena of urban living and the first writing spread from their place of origin more than 5,000 years ago in the lower valley of the Tigris and Euphrates rivers far into adjacent regions?

Working in the Balikh River valley of southern Turkey, near the Syrian border, a team of American and Turkish archeologists found traces of a large city that apparently flourished in 2600 B.C. A single tablet with cuneiform inscriptions, the earliest known writing system, was found lying on the surface, prompting hopeful speculation that other, more revealing tablets would eventually be uncovered.

Dr. Patricia Wattenmaker, an archeologist at the University of Virginia and director of the excavations, said the discovery should overturn conventional thinking that confined the development of large urban centers of the period to southern Mesopotamia and dismissed the cultures to the north and west as mere backwaters. Further research, she said, could extend the known range of early literacy.

Preliminary excavations indicate that the site, known as Kazane Hoyuk, holds the remains of a city that spread over at least 250 acres, large for its time and place. One tentative hypothesis is that these are the ruins of Urshu, a northern city mentioned in some Sumerian texts.

"Kazane's a huge place," said Dr. Glenn Schwartz, an archeologist at Johns Hopkins University who is familiar with the discovery, "and has to have been one of the most important political and economic centers of its region."

The other discovery that has excited archeologists is the buried ruins of a smaller city of the third millennium B.C. at Tell Beidar in northern Syria. There European and Syrian archeologists have found a well-preserved temple, administrative buildings and a collection of as many as 70 clay tablets with Sumerian writing and Semitic names, as well as many other tablet fragments. And they have only begun to dig.

"It's the most spectacular find this year in Syria," said Dr. Marc Lebeau, the leader of the discovery team, who is president of the European Center for Upper Mesopotamian Studies in Brussels.

Dating of Tablets

Preliminary analysis places the time of the tablets and other artifacts at about 2400 B.C., during the Sumerian ascendancy in southern Mesopotamia and just before the rise of the Akkadian empire under Sargon the Great. The tablets that have been deciphered appear to be bureaucratic records of a robust economy, including lists of donkeys, oxen and sheep and the names of towns and villages.

Archeologists find traces of Sumerians far north of Mesopotamia.

Dr. Harvey Weiss, a Yale University archeologist, recently visited Tell Beidar and said that it and Kazane Hoyuk "prove everything we've been saying about northern Mesopotamia for many years," namely that the cuneiform archive discovered in 1974 at Ebla, also in Syria, was not an anomaly but strong evidence of the widespread expansion of Sumerian urban civilization, beginning as early as 2600 B.C.

If Ebla, near the city of Aleppo, revealed the civilization's western progression, excavations by Dr. Weiss at Tell Leilan, begun in 1979, produced the first strong evidence of its northern reach. Tell Leilan, identified as the ancient walled city of Shubat Enlil that experienced sudden growth in 2500, lies on the fertile plains of Syria near the borders of Turkey and Iraq. Nearby is the European dig site of Tell Beidar. Farther north is Kazane Hoyuk, at least twice as large as Tell Beidar and the same size as Tell Leilan or larger.

Other scholars had previously failed to recognize this expansion phenomenon mainly because the most thorough excavations had until recently been confined to the Sumerian heartland in the lower Tigris and Euphrates valley.

New View of Mesopotamia

"People used to think of ancient Mesopotamia as small and restricted, but not any longer," said Dr. Elizabeth Stone, an archeologist at the State University of New York at Stony Brook.

The two discoveries were made over the last two summers, but the results have only now become known by word of mouth (and computer mail) to many other archeologists. The details and their implications were discussed in interviews last week.

Dr. Wattenmaker was driving on the road south of the modern Turkish city of Urfa when she saw a prominent mound in the fields near an irrigation canal. In her initial survey last year, pottery shards were found scattered over the ground. Some were as much as 7,000 years old. Others were at least 4,500 years old and in the Sumerian style.

This and other evidence gathered this year indicated that the site had been occupied almost continuously since 5000 B.C., and so should provide evidence of the transition from a simple farming society to an urban culture. It grew to be a large city about 2600 B.C. and was abandoned for an unknown reason around 1800 B.C.

A worker found the baked clay tablet lying on the surface. It is 22 inches by 22, and encrusted in dirt. Cleaning away some of the dirt, archeologists saw the wedge-shaped cuneiform inscriptions typical of early writing, which was first developed by Mesopotamians about 5,000 years ago.

Scholars are especially cautious in their assessment of the tablet because it was a "stray find." It was picked up on the ground, out of context with archeological ruins and in an area that had been disturbed by construction of the canal. Still, they said it appeared to be genuine and from the third millennium B.C.

"It's a tease," said Dr. Piotr Michalowski, a specialist in Sumerian and Babylonian languages at the University of Michigan, who is examining photographs of the tablet inscriptions. "It doesn't tell you much. It is not a connected narrative of any sort, just signs and not very good ones. Somebody might have been practicing writing, and wasn't good at it."

Speculation of Literacy

Since early writing was associated with official record-keeping related to the collection and distribution of grain and goods and since Kazane Hoyuk was a city on known trade routes, Dr. Michalowski said: "I will stick my neck out and say it had to be a literate society. Other tablets may be found there. I've always thought Ebla was only a symptom of a much more widespread literacy in this period."

Although archeologists said they could not yet determine the ancient name of this city, Dr. Michalowski said there was a "good degree of probability" that it was Urshu, which Sumerian inscriptions of 2100 B.C. refer to as a city in the highlands of Ebla; that would put it at some distance to the northwest. The site of Urshu has never been identified. But confirmation of this surmise will have to await the discovery of more and better tablets.

Dr. Wattenmaker plans more excavations, looking for tablets and other evidence regarding the nature of economic and social forces that contributed to the rise of centralized government and urban society. Her research team included archeologists from the Universities of Chicago and Virginia, Istanbul University and the Urfa Museum.

Preliminary study of the tablets at Tell Beidar, Dr. Lebeau said, showed that they are approximately the same age as the Ebla archive, probably a century or two later than the Kazane Hoyuk fluorescence, and that they provide a clear link between this ancient city, Ebla in the west and southern Mesopotamia.

These are the first tablets of this period to be found in northern Syria, and archeologists expect to find more as they dig deeper at the site. The discovery team included archeologists from Belgium, France, Germany, the Netherlands, Spain and Syria.

The new discoveries, Dr. Weiss said, were further evidence for the sudden rise beginning around 2600 B.C. of cities in nearly all directions beyond the bounds of southern Mesopotamia and may help account for this expansion. Was this the consequence of trade among independent people or incipient colonialism and imperialism? If these burning questions in Mesopotamian archeology can be answered, scholars will still be left to ponder the bigger question of how state societies and urban civilization happened to begin then and there in the first place.

Collapse of Earliest Known Empire Is Linked to Long, Harsh Drought

John Noble Wilford

Under the renowned Sargon and his successors, the Akkadians of Mesopotamia forged the world's first empire more than 4,300 years ago. They seized control of cities along the Euphrates River and on the fruitful plains to the north, all in what is now Iraq, Syria and parts of southern Turkey. Then, after only a century of prosperity, the Akkadian empire collapsed abruptly, for reasons that have been lost to history.

The traditional explanation is one of divine retribution. Angered by the hubris of Naram-Sin, Sargon's grandson and most dynamic successor, the gods supposedly unleashed the barbaric Gutians to descend out of the highlands and overwhelm Akkadian towns. More recent and conventional explanations have put the blame on overpopulation, provincial revolt, nomadic incursions or managerial incompetence, though many scholars despaired of ever identifying the root cause of the collapse.

A team of archeologists, geologists and soil scientists has now found evidence that seems to solve the mystery. The Akkadian empire, they suggest, was beset by a 300-year drought and literally dried up. A microscopic analysis of soil moisture at the ruins of Akkadian cities in the northern farmlands disclosed that the onset of the drought was swift and the consequences severe, beginning about 2200 B.C.

"This is the first time an abrupt climate change has been directly linked to the collapse of a thriving civilization," said Dr. Harvey Weiss, a Yale University archeologist and leader of the American-French research team.

Such a devastating drought would explain the abandonment at that time of Akkadian cities across the northern plain, a puzzling phenomenon observed in archeological excavations. It would also account for the sudden migrations of people to the south, as recorded in texts on clay tablets. These migrations doubled the populations of southern cities, overtaxed food and water supplies, and led to fighting and the fall of the Sargon dynasty.

The new findings thus call attention to the role of chance—call it fate, an act of God or simply an unpredictable natural disaster—in the development of human cultures and the rise and fall of civilizations.

Among the drought's refugees were a herding people known as Amorites, characterized by scribes in the city of Ur as "a ravaging people with the instincts of a beast, a people who know not grain"—the ultimate putdown in an economy based on grain agriculture. An 110-mile wall, called the "Repeller of the Amorites," was erected to hold them off. But when the drought finally ended in about 1900 B.C., leadership in the region had passed from Akkad to Ur and then to the Amorites, whose power was centered at the rising city of Babylon. Hammurabi, the great ruler of Babylon in 1800 B.C., was a descendant of Amorites.

The correlation between drastic climate change and the Akkadian downfall also appears to complete the picture of widespread environmental crisis disrupting societies throughout the Middle East in the same centuries. Earlier studies had noted the effects of severe drought, including abandoned towns, migrations and nomad incursions, in Greece, Egypt, Palestine and the Indus Valley. Until now, the connection between chronic drought and unstable social conditions had not been extended to Mesopotamia, the land between the two rivers, the Euphrates and the Tigris, often called "the cradle of civilization."

As to what caused such a persistent dry spell, the scientists said they had no clear ideas, though they suggested that changing wind patterns and ocean currents could have been factors. A tremendous volcanic eruption that occurred in Turkey near the beginning of the drought, the scientists said, almost certainly could not have triggered such a long climate change.

Archeology's Sophistication

"This is a research frontier for climatologists," Dr. Weiss said in an interview.

Dr. Weiss proposed the new theory for the Akkadian collapse at a recent meeting of the Society of American Archeology in St. Louis and then in a report in the current issue of the journal Science. His principal collaborators in the research were Dr. Marie-Agnès Courty, an archeologist and soil scientist at the National Center for Scientific Research in Paris, and Dr. François Guichard, a geologist at the same institution.

Other archeologists said the theory was plausible and appeared to provide the first logical explanation for the Akkadian downfall. Although he had not studied the report, Dr. Robert Biggs, a specialist in Mesopotamian archeology at the University of Chicago, said this was a good example of "archeology's growing sophistication in seeking reasons for serious political changes in the past."

In an article accompanying the report in Science, Dr. Robert McC. Adams, secretary of the Smithsonian Institution and an anthropologist specializing in Mesopotamia, cautioned that Dr. Weiss and his colleagues had not thoroughly established the link between climate and the empire's fall. He questioned whether such widespread and persistent drought could be inferred from local soil conditions at a few sites.

"It will demand of other people in the field to either refute it or replicate it with their own work," Dr. Adams said of the theory. "And the only way to get people to pick up that challenge is for Weiss to stick his neck out. I applaud it."

Dr. Weiss said the conclusions were based on tests of soils mainly at the sites of three Akkadian cities within a 30-mile radius, places now known as Tell Leilan, Tell Mozan and Tell Brak in present-day Syria. Evidence of similar climate change was found in adjacent regions, and the archeologist said further tests of the theory would be conducted with the resumption of field work this week.

Land of Rainy Winters

The most revealing evidence has come from Tell Leilan, where Dr. Weiss has been excavating for 14 years and finding successive layers of ruins going back some 8,000 years. For several millennia, this was a small village established by some of the world's first farmers. Around 2600 B.C., it suddenly expanded six-fold to become the city of Shekhna, with 10,000 to 20,000 inhabitants. They lived in the middle of a land of rainy winters, dry summers and a long growing season for wheat and barley, much as it is today.

All the more reason the kings of Akkad, or Agade, a city-state whose location has never been exactly determined but is assumed to have been near ancient Kish and Babylon, reached out and conquered places like Tell Leilan about 2300 B.C. The region became the breadbasket for the Akkadian empire, which stretched 800 miles from the Persian Gulf to the headwaters of the Euphrates in Turkey.

Ceramics and other artifacts established the Akkadian presence there in Tell Leilan and other northern towns. And for years archeologists puzzled over the 300-year gap in human occupation of Tell Leilan and neighboring towns, beginning in 2200 B.C. It occurred to Dr. Weiss that since no irrigation works had been uncovered there, the region must have relied on rain-fed agriculture, as is the case there today, in contrast to the irrigated farming in southern Mesopotamia. A severe drought, therefore, could be disastrous to life in the north.

This idea was tested by Dr. Courty, using microscopic techniques she pioneered in a scientific specialty, soil micromorphology. By examining in detail the arrangement and nature of sediments at archeological sites, it is possible to reconstruct ancient environmental conditions and human activity.

One of the first discoveries was a half-inch layer of volcanic ash covering the rooftops of buildings at Tell Leilan in 2200 B.C. All ash falls leave distinctive chemical signatures. An analysis by Dr. Guichard traced the likely source of this potassium-rich ash to volcanoes a few hundred miles away in present-day Turkey.

Migration from North

Since the abandonment of Tell Leilan occurred at the same time and the climate suddenly became more arid, volcanic fallout was first suspected as the culprit. Ash and gases from volcanic eruptions can remain suspended in the atmosphere for years, creating sun-blocking hazes and reducing temperatures. But from their knowledge of recent volcanoes, scientists doubted that the eruptions could have perturbed the climate over such a large area for 300 years.

And there seemed no doubt about the drought lasting that long, Dr. Courty said. In the surrounding countryside at Tell Leilan and elsewhere, she examined a layer of soil nearly two feet thick and lying just above the volcanic ash. This layer contained large amounts of fine windblown sand and dust, in contrast to the richer soil in earlier periods. Another telltale sign was the absence of earthworm holes and insect tracks, which are usually present in soils from moister environments.

This was strong evidence, the researchers reported, of a "marked aridity induced by intensification of wind circulation and an apparent increase" of dust storms in the northern plains of Mesopotamia.

It was during the 300-year desertification that archives of the southern cities reported the migration of barbarians from the north and a sharp decline in agricultural production, and showed an increasing number of names of people from the northern tribes, mainly the Amorites.

According to the evidence of the sediments, rain in more abundance returned to northern Mesopotamia in 1900 B.C. and with it the tracks of earthworms and the rebuilding of the deserted cities. Over the ruins of Shekhna, buried in the sands of the drought, rose a new city named Shubat Enlil, which means "dwelling place of Enlil," the paramount Mesopotamian god. The builders were Amorites.

In earlier excavations at Tell Leilan, Dr. Weiss discovered an archive of clay tablets showing that this was the lost capital of a northern Amorite

Akkadians to Babylon

• Sometime before the third millennium B.C.: A tribe of Semitic-speaking herding nomads, perhaps originally from Arabia, gradually settles down in northern Mesopotamia, which comes to be called Akkad.

• Middle of the third millennium B.C.: Akkadian names first appear in Sumerian documents.

• Around 2500 B.C.: Inscriptions written in Akkadian appear.

• 2340–2316 B.C.: Reign of Lugal-zagesi, last of a line of Sumerian kings. It is a time of struggles among city-states for regional supremacy.

• Around 2300 B.C.: Rise of Sargon of Agade or Akkad, a Semitic-speaking ruler; he defeats Lugal-zagesi and reigns for 56 years. The exact location of his city has never been found.

• 2278–2270 B.C.: Reign of his son Rimush, killed in a palace revolt.

• 2270–2254 B.C.: Reign of Rimush's brother Manishtushu, also killed in a palace revolt.

• 2254–2218 B.C.: Reign of Manishtushu's son Naram-Sin, thought to be the first to claim kingship as a divine right. His downfall was traditionally ascribed to divine retribution in the form of invading hordes from the east, called the Gutians. However, new research suggests complex internal problems and the beginning of a 300-year drought as the culprits.

• 2217–2193: Reign of his son Shar-kali-sharri, followed by a period of anarchy.

• 2200 B.C.: Volcanic eruption in Anatolia, after which many Akkadian settlements are abandoned.

• Around 2220–2120: A Gutian dynasty is recorded, among others.

• 2123–2113: Rise of Utu-hegal, who appoints Ur-Nammu as military governor at Ur. Ur-Nammu overthrows his protector, assumes the title of King of Ur and founds a well-organized dynasty. The ziggurat, or stepped tower, prototype of the Tower of Babel, is first recorded in his reign. Ur falls gradually, besieged by invaders like the Amorites and Elamites.

• 2028–2004: Reign of Ibbi-Sin ends with loss of empire. Some years later, a former underling, Ishbi-Erra, expels the Elamites.

• 1984–1975: His son, Shu-ilishu, using the title King of Ur, continues a dynasty noted for peace and prosperity. Amorite influence remains strong and the desert sheiks who lead them are respected. An Amorite dynasty is founded at Larsa. Amorites are gradually assimilated into the Babylonian population.

• 1932–1906 B.C.: An Amorite king, Gungunum, claims titles of King of Sumer and Akkad and of Ur.

• Around 1894 B.C.: Emergence of an Amorite dynasty at Babylon. A city called Shubat-Enlil is built on the ruins of Skekhna, abandoned in the drought.

• 1813–1781: Reign of Shamshi-Adad, a powerful Amorite king.

• 1792–1750 B.C.: Reign of Hammurabi, famous king and lawgiver; toward the end of his reign, Babylon becomes a great military power and the seat of kingship.

• 1595 B.C.: Sack of Babylon by the Hittites, an Indo-European-speaking people from Asia Minor.

kingdom often mentioned in the cuneiform writing of the period. This was the archive of Shamshi-Adad, the Amorite king who reigned from 1813 to 1781 B.C., containing the king's correspondence with neighboring rulers who concluded the ransoming of spies.

By then, the Akkadian kingdom of Sargon and Naram-Sin—the world's first empire—was long lost in the dust, apparently also the first empire to collapse as a result of catastrophic climate change.

"Since this is probably the first abrupt climate change in recorded history that caused major social upheaval," Dr. Weiss said, "it raises some interesting questions about how volatile climate conditions can be and how well civilizations can adapt to abrupt crop failures."

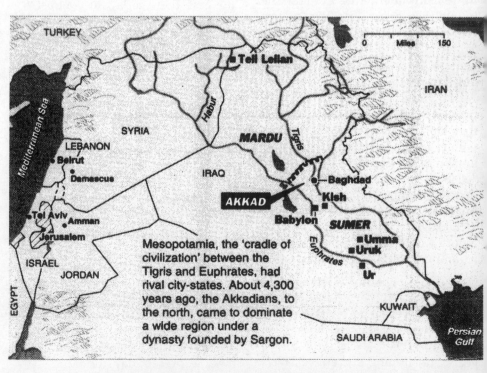

Mesopotamia, the 'cradle of civilization' between the Tigris and Euphrates, had rival city-states. About 4,300 years ago, the Akkadians, to the north, came to dominate a wide region under a dynasty founded by Sargon.

Herodotus

Roving reporter of the Ancient World

Carmine Ampolo

Carmine Ampolo, of Italy, teaches Greek history at the University of Pisa. He has carried out research on the origins of ancient Rome, on Greek politics and society, and on the relationship between myth and history. Among his published works are La citta antica *(1980; "The Ancient City") and, with M. Manfredini,* Le vite di Teseo et di Romolo *(1988; "The Lives of Theseus and Romulus").*

Herodotus of Halicarnassus, his *Researches* are here set down to preserve the memory of the past by putting on record the astonishing achievements both of our own and of other peoples . . . that the great deeds of men may not be forgotten . . . whether Greeks or foreigners: and especially, the causes of the war between them."*

In this introduction to his *Histories,* Herodotus (c. 490–425 BC) provides us with perhaps the earliest definition of the historian's aims and concerns. Some sixty years earlier, his precursor Hecataeus of Miletus, who had sought to inquire rationally into the mythical legends of the Greeks, explained his intentions in the following terms: "Thus speaks Hecataeus of Miletus: I write these things inasmuch as I consider them to be truthful; in fact, the legends of the Greeks are numerous and, to my mind, ridiculous." In this tetchy assertion of the author's role we can already see the two requirements of historiography in the Hellenic world: it must be written and it must be truthful.

With Herodotus the tone changes. He does not seek to give his own personal interpretation of what he relates, and usually he compares the different versions of stories he has collected. He wants to talk about his researches, tell of his inquiries. History as he understands it is at once the gathering of information and the recounting of a story. He thus inaugurated the two main trends in Greek historiography for centuries to come. Sometimes one would be given prominence, sometimes the other, but the prime imperative was always truthfulness, even in the case of historians who attached very great importance to narrative.

THE ART OF STORYTELLING

When Herodotus describes his work as an "exposition of his researches, the narration of an inquiry", these ambivalent terms must be taken to mean both the oral transmission of a story and its written formulation. The blending of oral and written styles in the *Histories* can be explained by the fact that Herodotus would give public readings of the various stories *(logoi)* making up his work. This is confirmed by the allusions in the text to audience reaction, and by the circular structure of the writing.

This practice had a marked effect on the composition of the work, which may seem to be something of a patchwork, with its countless digressions that sometimes fit into one another like Chinese boxes or Russian dolls. More a painter than a sculptor, Herodotus excels in the art of storytelling and possesses the gift of enthralling his audience, whether listener or reader, by his descriptions of a detail, an episode or an individual.

He often tells a story which he has heard at second or third hand. For example, after describing the victory of the Athenians over the Persians at Marathon, he tells what happened to the Athenian soldier Epizelos, who lost his sight while fighting in the battle, though nothing had hit him: "I am told that in speaking about what happened to him he used to say that he fancied he was opposed by a man of great stature in heavy armour, whose beard overshadowed his shield; but the phantom passed him by, and killed the man at his side." It would be a mistake to see this as Herodotus directly reporting what he has heard, but rather as an example of the mirror play that is a common feature of the *Histories:* Epizelos tells his story, others repeat it, Herodotus hears it and tells it in his turn.

This is not simply a taste for the fantastic or the marvellous, for which Herodotus is so often criticized, but a delight in intriguing and surprising his audience. He is able to arouse people's curiosity because his own is so great. He is interested in all kinds of out-of-the-way details, the customs of each people and all the wonders of the world, whether events, inventions or monuments like the pyramids of Egypt, the labyrinth above Lake Moeris and the walls of Babylon. In his quest for knowledge, Herodotus would travel and make inquiries of those who might have information about the countries visited—scholars, priests or people whose names are not recorded: "I learn by inquiry."

The reason for this passion for research emerges clearly in the introduction to the *Histories:* it is the historian's task to combat time, to preserve what he considers to be memorable. In the Greek cities and sanctuaries there were already "memorizers" *(mnemones)* responsible for recollecting and recording divine and human occurrences. But the historian's concerns are much loftier than the purely administrative, legal and religious functions of the *mnemones.* All the illustrious deeds and labours *(erga)* that he relates must retain their *kleos,* their aura of glory, their renown. In some ways Herodotus seems to carry on where the epic

---

*Quotations from *Herodotus: The Histories,* translated by Aubrey de Sélincourt, Penguin Classics, 1954.

Reprinted with permission from *The UNESCO Courier,* March 1990, pp. 16-19.

63

poets left off. They recounted the deeds of heroes, the historian recounts the deeds of men.

The insatiable curiosity shown by Herodotus in his investigations and travels considerably broadened the scope of written history, which ceased to consist solely of myths, genealogical lists and ethno-historical material relating to particular peoples or communities. Although he wanted to preserve as much as possible, he had to select which of the facts to save. For the historian who takes as his subject "great and marvellous actions", not everything is memorable.

Herodotus was aware of the amount of space given in his *Histories* to the long parentheses of the storyteller. On one occasion he even confesses: "I need not apologize for the digression—it has been my plan throughout this work." To understand this attitude, we should not use modern criteria nor even refer to later Greek authors whose works, which were designed exclusively to be read, seem to be better constructed. In a work addressed primarily to listeners and only subsequently to readers, not only the form but the choice of material were determined by the exigencies of spoken communication. It is not enough for details to be historically revealing or admirable; they must also be entertaining and, whether glorious or despicable, arouse the curiosity of the narrator and strike a chord in the minds of his audience.

AN INVESTIGATOR AT WORK

What was Herodotus' raw material? Much of the *Histories* records the history and customs of peoples incorporated in the Persian empire (or those of peoples like the Scythians which were unsuccessfully fought by the empire) as well as facts about the Greek cities in the sixth and fifth centuries BC. The culmination is confrontation between the Greeks and the Persians, which accounts for less than half the work.

Herodotus does not speak of a single people, nor even of a single Greek city, nor of Greece in its entirety. He erects no barriers, shows no scorn. He does not really differentiate between the Greeks and other peoples, the "Barbarians". Born at a time which, under the influence of the Sophists, saw the development of cultural relativism, and originating from a region at the meeting-point of East and West, he showed curiosity, consideration and even respect for other cultures.

He nevertheless viewed them through Greek eyes. In keeping with a typically Hellenic way of seeing the foreigner as a reversed image of oneself, he depicted the behaviour of other peoples as the antithesis of that of the Greeks. Among the "strange practices" of the Egyptians, for example, he mentions that "women attend market and are employed in trade, while men stay at home and do the weaving. . . . Men in Egypt carry loads on their heads, women on their shoulders. . . ." His enumeration of their differences ends as follows: "In writing or calculating, instead of going, like the Greeks, from left to right, the Egyptians go from right to left—and obstinately maintain that theirs is the dexterous method, ours being left-handed and awkward."

This comparative method can be seen as a way of classifying and hence of understanding. But Herodotus also observes similarities, which he scrupulously notes, as in the case of the Spartans. Customs on the death of a king, he reports, "are the same in Sparta as in Asia", and "the Spartans resemble the Egyptians in that they make certain callings hereditary: town-criers (heralds), flute-players and cooks are all, respectively, sons of fathers who followed the same profession."

Although he does not go as far as Thucydides in saying that the Greeks lived formerly in the same way as the Barbarians today, and although he maintains a distance between the two worlds, he does not regard them as two monolithic blocks, one of which is in certain respects inferior to the other or culturally backward. Different though they may be,

he acknowledges the many qualities of the Barbarians, considering, for example, that the Greek gods have Egyptian origins, that Egyptian civilization is older than that of the Greeks, and that the Persians have numerous virtues.

The *Histories* end with a revealing anecdote. To convince his people not to attempt to settle in more fertile lands, the Persian King Cyrus the Great declares to his troops that "soft countries breed soft men", pointing out that the Greeks have preferred to keep their freedom on a harsh land rather than to be slaves cultivating fertile plains for others. It is thus a Persian sovereign who enunciates a truth applying chiefly to the Greeks. Herodotus also sets among the Persians a discussion on the best form of government—democracy, oligarchy or monarchy. They are foreigners, enemies, but not completely different. They could even, in theory at least, be like the Greeks, in the same way that the Greeks in some respects resemble them.

Herodotus does not try to describe a series of mythical or historical events since their origins or even from one of the traditional milestones in Greek history, as other historians were to do after him. His field of study—the Median wars and the events that led up to them—covers a fairly recent period. That which is remote in time is left to poets and genealogists. He displays the same attitude towards Egypt, distinguishing what he has witnessed personally from the information he has collected from the Egyptians. If he consults Persian, Phoenician or Egyptian scholars about mythical episodes, such as the abduction of Helen and the Trojan War, it is mainly in order to retrace and understand the causes of the Median wars.

In choosing as his area of investigation recent history of which he could have direct knowledge, Herodotus had a decisive influence on the development of historiography. Thucydides, half a generation younger, would go even further than his great predecessor, directing his gaze to current events.

Out of Africa: the superb artwork of ancient Nubia

The rich heritage and tradition of this venerable, long-neglected civilization beside the Nile is now celebrated in four great Western museums

David Roberts

David Roberts' latest book, Once They Moved Like the Wind: Cochise, Geronimo and the Apache Wars, *is published by Simon & Schuster.*

To the ancient Greeks and Romans, Nubia was one of the foremost civilizations of the world. Because its domain lay on the edge of the unknown–south of Egypt, along the tortured cataracts of the upper Nile, where few Greek or Roman travelers had ventured–Nubia shimmered with legend. But there was no mistaking the area's might or wealth.

For centuries, exotic goods had flowed north in an inexhaustible stream from this African font: gold, frankincense, ebony, ivory, panther skins, giraffe tails and hippopotamus teeth. Brave mercenary soldiers, virtuosos of the bow and arrow, also traveled north out of the storied land. Herodotus described Nubians as the "tallest and handsomest" people in the world, adding that they reputedly lived to an age of 120, thanks to a diet of boiled meat and milk. Roman chroniclers reported that the southern empire was ruled by queens. From their own artwork, we know that the Nubian ideal of female beauty put a premium on fatness. Indeed, the sardonic Juvenal claimed that the breasts of Nubian women were bigger than their chubbiest babies. Writing in the third century A.D., a romantic biographer of Alexander the Great insisted that in Nubia there were whole temples carved from a single stone, and houses with translucent walls; the queen traveled in a mobile palace on wheels drawn by 20 elephants.

Although these accounts veered into the fabulous, Nubia was no mere phantasm of the poets, no El Dorado. Within Nubia, stretching along the Nile from present-day Aswan in Egypt to Khartoum in the Sudan, at least six distinct, supremely accomplished cultures evolved between 3800 B.C. and A.D. 600. Nubian civilizations lasted far longer than either classical Greece or Rome. Always a rival to the kingdom to its north, Nubia conquered Egypt around 730 B.C. and ruled it for the following 60 years.

Ta-Seti or Yam or Wawat

Why is it, then, that most of us today have barely heard of Nubia?

One reason is semantic. Over millennia, Nubia was known under many different names. To the early Egyptians, it was Ta-Seti or Yam or Wawat. Later it appears as Meroe. The Greeks and Romans called it Aethiopia (today's Ethiopia being Abyssinia to them). In the Bible it appears as Kush.

Another reason has to do with prejudice. Nubia has always been exceedingly remote and difficult of access. From its Christianization in the 6th century A.D. all the way down to the 19th, the kingdom vanished from the European record: only the glowing reports of the classical authors kept its memory alive. This neglect had everything to do with race–for Nubia had been an African empire, and a black African one at that. Even the Greeks perpetrated the prejudice. An early biographer of Alexander the Great records the queen of Nubia responding to an inquisitive letter from the youthful conqueror in the following words: "Do not despise us for the color of our skin. In our souls we are brighter than the whitest of your people."

The first archaeologists to document the glory that was Nubia succumbed to a kindred bias. Even as he dug the remarkable royal cemeteries of El Kurru below the Fourth Cataract, George A. Reisner, working for Harvard University and the Boston Museum of Fine Arts, concluded that the rulers whose tombs he unearthed must have been an offshoot of a dynasty of Libyan (thus, white-skinned) pharaohs. For decades, everything Nubian was regarded as derived from the Egyptian, hence "decadent" and "peripheral."

Only now, perhaps, is the Western world beginning to acknowledge the achievements of ancient Nubia, as signaled by four dazzling new exhibitions at major North American museums. At the Boston Museum of Fine Arts (MFA)–which, thanks to Reisner and his colleagues, owns one of the finest collections of Nubian treasures in the world–a permanent display opened in 1992. Another permanent installation was unveiled the year before at the Royal Ontario Museum in Toronto. Through September 1993, the Oriental Institute Museum in Chicago will host "Vanished Kingdoms of the Nile: The Rediscovery of Ancient Nubia." And at the University of Pennsylvania's Museum of Archaeology and Anthropology, "Ancient Nubia: Egypt's Rival in Africa" recently opened. After closing in Philadelphia in October 1993, the exhibition will travel to seven other museums around the country, through 1996.

The exhibitions have had strong attendance, particularly among African-Americans, many of them in school groups. And there's evidence that awareness of Nubia is seeping into the popular culture. A new comic-book character called "Heru: Son of Ausar," which was created by cartoonist Roger Barnes, is a Nubian hero. A rap band out of New York City calls itself Brand Nubian.

The surge of interest in Nubia did not arise in a vacuum. For the past 30 years, scholars in Europe and the United States have been piecing together a vivid but tantalizing picture of the neglected civilization. Yet it took the building of a dam to stimulate this new appraisal of ancient Nubia.

Reisner, the pioneer of Nubian archaeology, was an Egyptologist working on the lower Nile in 1906 when the Egyptian government decided to raise the dam at Aswan by 16.5 feet. Before the resultant flooding could drown forever many unexcavated sites, Reisner was invited to survey and dig upriver. Thus was launched what one scholar calls the "earliest program of extensive salvage archaeology" in the world.

Close on Reisner's heels came two British archaeologists working for the University of Pennsylvania, David Randall-MacIver and Leonard Woolley. The rich collections existing today in Boston and Philadelphia derive from the seminal fieldwork of these scholars. Yet so strong was the lingering condescension toward Nubia as a kind of second-rate Egypt, that as late as 1960 only one American scholar–Dows Dunham, Reisner's protégé and successor at the MFA–was working in Nubian studies.

In 1959 Egypt announced plans to build a huge new dam at Aswan. The waters of the Nile would create Lake Nasser, stretching 300 miles south to the Second Cataract, just across the border in the Sudan. UNESCO launched an all-out appeal to the archaeologists of the world, who responded with scores of energetic expeditions, sowing the seeds of our current understanding of ancient Nubia.

The disruption wrought by the dam was tragic. Nubians whose ancestors had lived along the middle Nile for as long as the oldest tales could testify gathered their belongings and made their exodus north to the planned villages that would replace their own. They kissed the graves of their ancestors; many filled their pockets with sand, their only keepsake of the lost homeland.

Losing one's way could mean losing one's life

On the face of it, Nubia seems an unlikely place for a major civilization to sprout. It lies in the middle of the hottest and driest area on Earth's surface; in much of Nubia, rain never falls. Farther north, in classical Egypt, the Nile creates a generous floodplain up to 15 miles wide, but in Nubia the fertile land bordering the river comes only in intermittent patches rarely exceeding 1,600 yards in width. The cataracts–canyons seamed with big rapids–as well as long, tormented passages such as Batn el Hajar, the "Belly of Rocks"–make continuous navigation up and down the Nile impossible. In the Sudan, where the river makes two great loops in the shape of an *S*, the ancient trade routes struck off on bold shortcuts across the empty desert. To lose one's way often meant to lose one's life. Even today, travel here remains as difficult and as dangerous as anywhere in Africa.

As Reisner plunged into this archaeologically pristine wilderness, where he worked tirelessly from 1907 to 1932, he slapped provisional names on the various cultures he began to identify. Unfortunately, these temporary labels have stuck. Thus we still allude to some Nubian cultures–each as complex and impressive as, say, that of the Hittites or the Etruscans–as the A-Group, the C-Group and the X-Group.

With the emergence of the A-Group around 3800 B.C., Nubia takes its place on the prehistoric stage. We still know relatively little about this early civilization, which became a serious rival to Pre-Dynastic Egypt. The A-Group's most distinctive artifact is a handsome "eggshell" pottery, named for its thin walls. Crisscross hatches and geometric patterns in red and cream seem to conjure up weaving; it is as if the potters were celebrating the discovery of the vessel that worked better than basketry.

Toward the end of its thousand-year sway, the A-Group emerges also in the written record, as the Egyptians invented their hieroglyphic script. The domain of the blacks in Lower Nubia was known in Egypt as Ta-Seti–the "Land of the Bow." Eventually the pharaohs waged war with Ta-Seti. A great victory around 2600 B.C. was won by the pharaoh Sneferu, who bragged that he took 7,000 Nubians and 200,000 domestic animals captive.

Bruce Williams of Chicago's Oriental Institute believes that the earliest definite evidence anywhere in the world of the institution of kingship may be among the A-Group of Nubia. Williams' argument hinges upon a handful of extraordinary objects found in royal A-Group graves. During my own visit to the Oriental Institute, Williams showed me a beautiful stone incense burner found at Qustul (just north of the Sudanese border), dated to around 3300 B.C. The cylindrical burner is encircled by a frieze of incised figures.

Peering through the display glass, I followed Williams' pointing finger. "The falcon means a god," he said. "That's definitely a representation of a king, and he's wearing a crown. The bound prisoner is going to be bashed in the head in front of the god. The burner is definitely a typical Nubian, not an Egyptian, object."

Other scholars, however, reject Williams' theory. Says David O'Connor of the University of Pennsylvania, "I think there may well have been an elite group in Nubia at the time, in charge of a complex chiefdom. But the objects Williams' argument depends on are almost certainly Egyptian, not Nubian—traded to Nubia in early pharaonic times. The kings he sees were Egyptian kings."

One of the most formidable obstacles to an appreciation of ancient Nubia is that, in terms of the written record, we learn about the civilization almost entirely in the words of its enemies—Egyptians above all, but also Hebrews, Assyrians, Persians and Romans. Thus, for the Egyptians, Nubia is always "vile," "miserable," "wretched." The pharaohs had images of Nubians carved on their footstools and on the bottoms of their sandals so that they could trample on their enemies daily.

The aggression of Egypt throughout the third millennium B.C. seems to have driven A-Group survivors south into the little-known lands above the Second Cataract. Around 2300 B.C., a pair of new cultures springs into view. One, appearing in Lower Nubia, was called by Reisner the C-Group. Elaborate tombs suggest these people were skilled pastoralists, raising huge herds of livestock and perhaps worshiping their gods through a cattle cult.

The C-Group kept peace with the kingdom to the north for centuries, during which time trade flourished and ideas flowed both ways. Then, in the 19th century B.C., the pharaohs turned belligerent again. Their motive may have been to control the gold mines that were being opened in the eastern desert. Thrusting above the Second Cataract, Egyptian armies built a series of colossal fortresses along the tortuous Belly of Rocks. These fortresses were placed so that line-of-sight signals could be flashed from one to the next.

Meanwhile, 170 miles beyond the southernmost Egyptian fortress, the most powerful empire Nubia had yet seen was flourishing. Named the Kerma culture by Reisner, who in 1913 excavated tombs close to the modern town of that name, it was known to the Egyptians as the Kingdom of Kush. An ancillary motive for erecting the Egyptian fortresses, with their intensely defensive character, was no doubt fear of Kush.

A flamboyant and grandiose glory

After 1700 B.C., racked by internal struggles, Egypt retreated from Nubia, abandoning its fortresses along the Belly of Rocks. In the void, Kerma grew magnificently. Nothing declares the flamboyant, even grandiose glory of Kerma more forcefully than its royal tombs. The king was buried under a huge tumulus—a circular mound—with the diameter nearly the length of a football field. He was laid on a gold-covered bed, and the finest objects wrought of gold, bronze, ivory and faience were placed beside him. Into the tomb's central corridor crowded a host of followers and concubines (400 of them in one king's tomb), who, dressed in their best clothes, came willingly to be buried alive in honor of their master.

All through Nubia, from Reisner until the present day, burial sites have monopolized archaeologists' attention. This has been true in part because the remains of habitation sites are so hard to find; houses were made of perishable stuff, but tombs were built to last. Only two large villages from the C-Group, for instance, have ever been excavated. Consequently we know much more about the rulers of Nubia than about the commoners.

At Kerma, however, for the past 28 years an international team under Charles Bonnet, of the University of Geneva, has carried out one of the most ambitious digs in Africa. In the process, they have revealed not only the palaces and cemeteries but the main town of Kerma. When I visited Bonnet in Geneva last fall, he showed me the plan of the settlement. Tapping an outlying area with his pencil, he said, "Just last year we found a whole new section of houses here. It goes on and on!" Bonnet's work documents the oldest city that has ever been found in Africa outside Egypt.

Many of the houses Bonnet's team excavated were rectangles of mud bricks, but the most characteristic domicile was a circular hut made of wood (always a rare substance along the Nile), topped with a thatched roof. Each hut was ingeniously designed to allow the prevailing north wind to blow through it during the desperate heat of summer; in winter, a temporary wall blocked the same breeze. Small neighborhoods of huts were bordered by fields and gardens where crops (chiefly wheat and barley) were raised, and cattle and goats pastured. No general plan governed the shape of the sprawling city, but a defensive palisade surrounded it.

Once more the tides of empire shifted. Around 1550 B.C., a newly invigorated Egypt invaded Nubia. The struggle against Kerma lasted 100 years, but at last the pharaohs conquered all but the southernmost reaches of Nubia. Their sway lasted another 350 years, during which the Nubian upper class became thoroughly Egyptianized, decorating their tombs with images of workers on date palm plantations and with performing dancers and musicians.

But the tides shifted again. At the end of the New Kingdom, about 1080 B.C., Egypt was torn by conflict between the pharaohs and the priesthood. The country began to fragment into city states, among them several in Nubia that became all but autonomous. What happened after 1080 remains a great mystery.

According to Timothy Kendall of the MFA, "the greatest gap in our knowledge of ancient Nubia is the period from 1000 to 850 B.C. We know almost nothing about it. Only one or two sites in Nubia can be dated to this period, and then, only to the latter part of it. Some experts believe Nubia was growing stronger and politically independent; others think that Egyptian enclaves and temple estates persisted. But these are theories spun out of thin air. Nobody really has a clue, except that a series of elaborate tombs began to be built in 850 B.C."

When Nubia emerged from this historical void in the

cighth century B.C., it did so dramatically, achieving the greatest triumph in all its long history. By this time the center of power lay at Napata, which was just below the Fourth Cataract. Here a holy mountain called Jebel Barkal was believed to be the home of the ram-headed god Amun, who spoke oracles through statues and even selected the country's rulers.

Whatever their motive, after 750 B.C. the Napatan kings pushed boldly north. Around 730, a great army under a king named Piye conquered all of Egypt. He and his successors became the pharaohs of the 25th Dynasty, the later kings moving from Napata to Memphis to govern. The Nubian empire now stretched all the way from the junction of the Blue and White Niles to the delta (present-day Alexandria)–1,200 miles as the crow flies.

Although the inscribed victory stela Piye erected to proclaim his triumph alludes to him in Egyptian hieroglyphs as "raging like a panther" and bursting upon his enemies "like a cloudburst," the Nubian pharaohs of the 25th Dynasty ruled with an enlightened benevolence. They were Medicis, rather than Caesars, who awoke Egypt to the artistic and cultural splendor of its own past as they patronized artists, revived lost learning and rebuilt derelict temples.

Piye was also a great lover of horses, the first of four successive pharaohs to have whole chariot teams buried near his grave. The horses, interred in a standing position, were decked with bead nets and brilliant jewelry. When Piye conquered Hermopolis, the defeated King Nemlot opened his harem. But Piye averted his eyes from the women and demanded to see the king's horses instead. These he found nearly starved to death. "That my horses were made to hunger," he thundered at Nemlot (as recorded on Piye's stela), "pains me more than any other crime you committed in your recklessness. Do you not know God's shadow is above me?"

The brilliance of the Napatan empire speaks in many of the objects now on display in Boston, Philadelphia, Chicago and Toronto. In the MFA, I gazed at haunting rows of *shawabtis*, part of a cache of 1,070 found in the tomb of King Taharqo, Piye's son. Figurines carved out of alabaster and gray or black granite, ranging from seven inches to two feet in height, these sober-looking humans with arms crossed were "answerers" who would perform for the deceased king the work the gods commanded of him. (Here, I thought, was a humane alternative to the retainers buried alive at Kerma!)

One of the most exquisite objects ever recovered from Nubia is also on display in Boston. It is a small pendant from the tomb of one of Piye's wives, a gold head of Hathor, goddess of beauty, mounted on a ball of rock crystal, thought to have magical properties.

The Napatan supremacy was short-lived. By 667 B.C. the Nubian pharaohs had abandoned Egypt to another raging panther, King Esarhaddon of Assyria. Once again, we learn of a profoundly pivotal moment in Nubian history only in the contemptuous boasts of its ene-

mies: "I tore up the root of Kush," crowed Esarhaddon, "and not one therein escaped to submit to me."

Gradually through the next four centuries, the Nubian political and cultural center shifted south beyond the Fourth Cataract. In isolation and relative obscurity, the last Nubian empire evolved. Its center was the town of Meroe, halfway between the Fifth Cataract and the junction with the Blue Nile.

Meroe, which flourished from about 270 B.C. to A.D. 350, is in many respects the most intriguing of all the incarnations of Nubian greatness. Cambyses of the Persians, as well as Petronius among the Romans, sent out armies to conquer the distant country, without success. Even Nero contemplated the possibility of an attack. Despite all this contact, the veil of mystery that clung to the legendary southern land never really lifted.

One reason was linguistic. In their isolation from Egypt, the Meroites lost the use of Egyptian hieroglyphs. By 170 B.C. they had developed their own written language, a quasi-cursive script now called Meroitic. Stelae and plaques covered with this writing abound. By 1909 scholars had proved that it was an alphabetic script (unlike the hieroglyphs, which are part ideographic, part phonetic and part alphabetic). Thanks to a few parallel inscriptions, they had learned the sound values for each of the 23 Meroitic letters. Yet more than eight decades later, the language remains undeciphered.

At first, scholars were confident that Meroitic would turn out to be a cognate of the Nubian tongues spoken today along the Nile. That hope faded, and all that the experts can now assert is that Meroitic seems to be related to no other known language. Decipherment must await the discovery of a Nubian Rosetta Stone—a stela with lengthy parallel texts in Meroitic and Egyptian or Meroitic and Greek.

A royal offering to Amun

In the MFA, I walked around and around a five-foot-tall stela found at Jebel Barkal; covered on all sides with writing, the stone bears the longest known inscription in Meroitic. We know the text has something to do with an offering by King Tanyidamani to the god Amun, and we can see places where lines have been deliberately erased. The rest is enigma.

Timothy Kendall tantalized me further by describing the second-longest Meroitic inscription known, found on a stela now in the British Museum. "If we could read it," he sighed, "we'd have the Meroitic version of the war against Petronius and the Romans in 24 B.C."

In its drift away from Egyptian culture over the centuries, Meroitic art developed its own idiosyncratic genius. At the Oriental Institute, Emily Teeter explained to me its quirks. "It becomes a very spontaneous art, full of free-flowing improvisation," she said, pausing before a Meroitic pot. "You see that?" She pointed to a curling snake painted on the vessel, holding in its mouth a drooping flower. "The flower is obviously an *ankh*."

I gasped in sudden recognition. I had seen many an *ankh* on Egyptian objects: a cross-shaped symbol topped with an oval, which is the hieroglyph for the verb "to live." In Egyptian art, the *ankh* appears alone or in rows of declarative rigidity. On the Meroitic pot, the snake stings the world to life with a flower. "The Egyptians are too staid for this," Teeter said. "They don't like loopy things."

At the University of Pennsylvania museum, David O'Connor guided me through several hundred Meroitic objects from the provincial capital of Karanog, excavated by MacIver and Woolley in 1907-08. The same freedom—a set of wild variations on Egyptian themes—graced these priceless objects. In Egypt, O'Connor explained, the *ba* statue, which represents a dead person's spirit, is a formal-looking bird with a human head; in Meroe, the *ba* becomes a human with wings. The pots dance with two-legged crocodiles, with giraffes ranging from the lordly to the comic, with deer darting through shadows. There are abstract designs made of endless waves of draped festoons and floral curlicues.

The sheer exuberance of Meroitic art proclaims a civilization that believed in pleasure and playfulness. The pots were largely used for wine drinking. At certain Meroitic sites, whole barrooms have been excavated.

At the end of the fourth century A.D., Meroe declined. The distinctive script fell out of use, and no new temples were built. It has long been the fashion to regard the 250-year interim before Christianity, whose culture Reisner called the X-Group, as a Nubian Dark Age; but recent scholars point to the continued excellence of pottery and jewelry, to a flowering of brilliant work in bronze and iron, as well as to the magnificent royal tombs at Ballana and Qustul, as signs of a healthy culture, original in its own right.

Although the Meroitic language seems to have been lost forever, scholars who travel in the Sudan have been struck by the remarkable survival in living cultures of traits and belongings they know also from archaeology. The wood-and-palm-fiber bed a Sudanese sleeps on today looks very much like ones found in royal tombs in Kerma. The throwstick, a proto-boomerang still used for hunting today, is identical to ones retrieved by Reisner from a Kerma tomb. Even current Sudanese fashions in hairstyle and facial scarification find their counterparts in ancient paintings of Nubians.

Thus the discipline of ethnoarchaeology, still in its infancy, may yield new insights into Nubia, as scholars ask living informants to comment on ancient relics. Emily Teeter told me of a pair of small revelations. Shortly after the Oriental Institute's exhibition opened, she met Awad Abdel Gadir, a Sudanese teaching in Texas. He took her aside, pointed to a stone object and said politely, "That's not an incense burner. We have those in our village. It's a receptacle for a liquid offering." Teeter changed the label. He paused before a "thorn-removal kit" from the X-Group—a kind of Swiss Army Knife of iron tools on a chain, including tweezers, picks and scrapers. "I remember," said Abdel Gadir, "my grandmother used to wear a set like that on her belt."

Meanwhile, the archaeological surface of ancient Nubia has barely been scratched. The sites that lie in lower Nubia, north of the Egypt-Sudan border, are gone forever, swallowed by Lake Nasser. In the Sudan, the 1989 coup that brought Islamic fundamentalists to power, as well as the civil war that continues to rage in the country's south, have made it harder than ever for Western archaeologists to work there.

Yet, in the Sudan, a French survey has counted one million ancient mounds, only a fraction of which have been excavated. There are more royal pyramids in the Sudan than in all of Egypt. I asked Timothy Kendall, who has done breakthrough work at Jebel Barkal, where he would dig if he had carte blanche to choose among the Sudan's best Nubian sites.

He leaned back in his chair, put his hands behind his head and smiled. "I'd go to Naga," he said, "although it's just a pipe dream, because the Sudanese Antiquities Service is saving it for themselves."

I knew Naga as a Meroitic site that, uncharacteristically, lay inland in the Butana Desert, some 25 miles south of the Nile. "Why Naga?"

"It's a complete Meroitic city founded about the first century A.D., with important temples, a settlement and a cemetery," Kendall answered. "The residents built an artificial reservoir of water. Not a single spadeful of earth has ever been turned there.

"Of course," he added, gazing off into space at the eternal dilemma that bedevils archaeologists, "you'd need a lot of money, a big team, a lot of cooperation, extreme physical endurance." He paused. "And a very, very long life."

Additional reading

Nubia: Corridor to Africa by William Y. Adams, Princeton University press, 1977

Meroe by Peter L. Shinnie, Praeger (New York), 1967

Nubia Under the Pharaohs by Bruce G. Trigger, Westview Press (Boulder, Colorado), 1983

The African Origin of Civilization: Myth or Reality by Cheikh Anta Diop, Lawrence Hill, 1974

Daily Life in Ancient Egypt

Workmen and their families lived some 3,000 years ago in the village now known as Deir el-Medina. Written records from the unusually well educated community offer fascinating descriptions of everyday activities

Andrea G. McDowell

During the period known as the New Kingdom (1539–1075 B.C.), Egypt's southern capital city of Thebes developed into one of the great urban centers of the ancient world. The massive temple complexes of Karnak and Luxor were built during this time, and the two monuments still dominate the east bank of the Nile in the modern city, now called Luxor. The nearby Valley of the Kings, on the west bank of the Nile, contains some 60 tombs, including that of the pharaoh Tutankhamen. Hundreds of private tombs, some of them magnificently painted, also dot the landscape along the base of the cliffs on the Nile's west bank.

Although some of the paintings in the private monuments preserve tantalizing pictures of the luxurious life of the nobility, on the whole, the remaining temples and tombs tell us more about religious experience and beliefs concerning the afterworld than about the experiences of the living. Daily life is less well documented because, unlike the stone monuments we see today, the majority of homes, which were made of sun-dried brick, have succumbed to the damp of the floodplain, along with the furnishings and any written material that would have documented the lives of the literate few. On the westernmost edge of the sprawling ancient city, however, the remains of one small community escaped the general disintegration. This is the village now called Deir el-Medina, the home of the craftsmen who cut and decorated the royal tombs in the Valley of the Kings.

Lying in an arid and relatively isolated region, the site remains remarkably well preserved: houses and chapels are still standing to a height of up to two meters in some places. Archaeologists in the first half of this century found a wealth of religious monuments and household possessions among the effects, as well as intact tombs containing coffins, furniture and clothing. And across the entire site but especially in the town's garbage dumps, researchers recovered tens of thousands of written documents, most of them dating from the period between 1275 and 1075 B.C. Some of the texts are on sheets of papyrus, but most are on shards of pottery or smooth, white flakes of limestone, known as ostraca, that served as a sort of scrap paper for the community.

These writings bring the villagers to life. In them, one finds government records, love poems and private letters describing family strife, health concerns and legal disputes. The documents also offer some insight into the education system of ancient Egypt—a topic I have been investigating for some time. The wealth of texts from the site suggests that in some periods of its history, most men in the town could read and write. (Scholars do not know whether many women in Deir el-Medina were literate.

Women in the village did exchange letters, but they may have dictated their thoughts to men.) This high literacy rate stands in stark contrast to the situation throughout the rest of ancient Egyptian society, which during the New Kingdom period had a total literacy rate hovering around only 1 or 2 percent. The ostraca illuminate how the villagers achieved such an impressive level of education.

"Bring Some Honey for My Eyes"

Before we look more closely at the educational system in Deir el-Medina, however, a quick survey of some of the recovered ostraca will help reconstruct life in the village and the context in which this extraordinary rate of literacy developed. As the large number of administrative documents suggests, the Egyptians of this period were obsessive bureaucrats, keeping careful records of the tools issued to the men laboring on the tombs, the rations delivered to the gang, the overall progress of the work and almost every other detail that could be quantified.

The residents' private jottings are even more varied. Many are purely practical: receipts for purchases or records of legal battles (the villagers were avid litigators). The most intriguing texts are perhaps the personal letters, which take the reader straight into the world of New Kingdom Egypt. In one such missive, a father, Pay, writes to his son about his eye

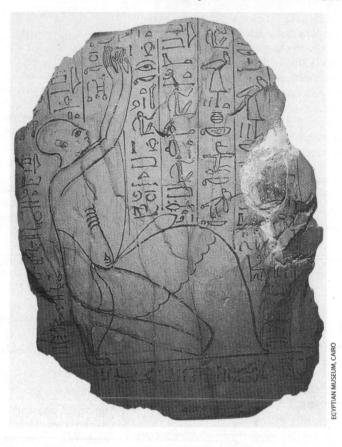

PORTRAITS of a stonecutter (*left*) and a scribe (*right*) demonstrate two distinct styles of drawing found on ostraca in Deir el-Medina. The rather informal sketch of the stonecutter with his chisel and mallet shows a bulbous nose, stubbled chin and open mouth, no doubt exaggerated for comic effect. The self-portrait of the scribe Amenhotep adoring the god Thoth adheres to the formal canons of Egyptian art.

disease—apparently one of the hazards of tomb building because of the dust, bad lighting and flying splinters of stone associated with the task:

The draftsman Pay says to his son the draftsman Pre[emhab?]: Do not turn your back on me; I am not well. Do not c[ease] weeping for me, because I am in the [darkness(?) since] my lord Amon [has turned] his back on me.

May you bring me some honey for my eyes, and also some ocher which is made into bricks again, and real black eye paint. [Hurry!] Look to it! Am I not your father? Now, I am wretched; I am searching for my sight and it is not there.

Pay's lament is not surprising: blindness would have completely incapacitated a draftsman, who painted the figures and hieroglyphs inside the tombs. Descriptions of the mixture of honey, ocher and black eye-paint that Pay requested appear in specialized medical papyri, suggesting that it was a common remedy. Indeed, honey does have antiseptic properties, and ocher, an in-

gredient in many other prescriptions of the day, feels cool on the eyelids and was thought to reduce swelling. Because so many workmen suffered from this type of eye disease, this treatment may have been well known, and Pay was ordering it for himself. Alternatively, Pay could have been asking his son to fill a doctor's prescription.

Roughly half the texts found at Deir el-Medina are religious or literary pieces. Copies of most of the "classics" from ancient Egyptian literature have been found at the site; in some cases, ostraca from the village provide the only surviving example of a work. These classics were a fundamental part of a student's education: thousands of school texts bear extracts from the masterpieces of Middle Kingdom (roughly 2000–1640 B.C.) literature, composed in a language as remote from the vernacular of the students as the English of Chaucer is from ours. Furthermore, many of the villagers were authors in their own right, composing instruction texts, hymns and letters. For example, the scribe Amennakhte wrote a poem in praise of the cosmopolitan city of Thebes, located just across the Nile:

What do they say to themselves
   in their hearts every day,
   those who are far from Thebes?
They spend the day
   dreaming [?] of its name, [saying]
   "If only its light were ours!" ...
The bread which is in it is more tasty
   than cakes made of goose fat.
Its [water] is sweeter than honey;
   one drinks of it to drunkenness.
Behold, this is how one lives
   in Thebes!
The heaven has doubled [fresh] wind
   for it.

The villagers held knowledge of and ability in the literary arts in high esteem, as indicated on a papyrus found in the archives of a resident scribe. In this extract, the writer presents an unusual tribute to learning: whereas other documents tend to emphasize primarily writing skills and familiarity with classical literature, this description of the profession of scribe emphasizes authorship, the creation of texts and the fame that can come after death. In short, the writer appeals to the great Egyptian aspiration for immortality:

As for the learned scribes from the time that came after the gods—those who foretold the things to come—their names endure forever, although they have gone, having completed their lifetimes, and their relatives are forgotten.

They did not make for themselves pyramids of copper with tombstones of iron. They were unable to leave an heir in the form of children [who would] pronounce their name, but they made for themselves an heir of the writings and instructions they had made.

The Importance of Being Educated

The exceptional rate of literacy among the workmen at Deir el-Medina no doubt developed because the many skilled artisans needed an understanding of hieroglyphs for their job in the royal tombs. Early in the history of the village, the pharaohs' tombs contained only simple copies of the guides to the afterworld, written in cursive script with accompanying vignettes drawn in stick figures. But at the end of the 14th century B.C., elaborately carved and painted scenes began to appear in tombs. At the same time, the literacy rate in the town rose sharply, as evidenced by the increase in the number of texts written after this period.

The king Horemheb, who ruled from 1319 to 1292 B.C., introduced these painted reliefs to the Valley of the Kings. The more elaborate projects of Horemheb and later kings required a team of draftsmen to do the initial drawings and the final paint job; because the tomb paintings included large amounts of hieroglyphic texts, these workers had to be literate.

Perhaps more surprising was that at least some of the men responsible for the grueling task of carving the tomb out of the mountainside were also literate, even though their job did not call on such skills. Ambition may have motivated these laborers: education and literacy offered the keys to a good career in Egypt, separating the artisan class from the peasants, and the skills would have stood the workers in good stead had there been no job for them among the tomb builders. In addition, the culture of learning in the village may have also been a powerful stimulus, encour-

A Lesson in Egyptian Literature

The ostracon shown here bears an excerpt from the poem "Satire on the Trades," a classic of Middle Egyptian literature. The poem describes a variety of occupations, such as weaver, arrow maker and courier, that the author considered inferior to the laudable profession of scribe. The student who made this copy was apparently unfamiliar with the archaic language of the poem—written more than 700 years earlier—and garbled the original text. At the end of the lesson, the student wrote the date in red ink. —A.G.McD.

Original excerpt

The courier goes into the desert,
Leaving his goods to his children;
Fearful of lions and Asiatics,
He knows himself [only] when
  he's in Egypt.
When he reaches home at night,
The march has worn him out;
Be his home of cloth or brick,
His return is joyless.
  Translation by Miriam Lichtheim, from
  Ancient Egyptian Literature I
  (University of California Press, 1973)

Student's copy of excerpt

The courier goes into the desert,
Leaving his goods to his children;
Fearful [of] lions and Asiatics,
What is it when he's in Egypt?
When he reaches home distressed,
The journey has divided him.
While he comes forth [from] his
  cloth [or] brick,
He will not come it in joy.
  —*Third month of winter
  season, day 1*

aging young people to study to keep up with their peers.

Egyptologists can glean numerous details from the ostraca found in Deir el-Medina, but unfortunately, we still know little of how the residents actually learned to read and write. Egyptian texts of the New Kingdom refer to schools only incidentally, indicating that they existed and that relatively young children attended them. For example, a short story found in the village describes the experiences at school of its young hero, a boy whose mother is not married:

He was sent to school and learned to write very well. He practiced all the arts of war and he surpassed his older companions who were at school with him. Then his companions said to him: "Whose son are you? You don't have a father!" And they reviled

him and mocked him: "Hey, you don't have a father!"

But scholars have no evidence for an actual school at Deir el-Medina—no textual references to a school building, no structure that looks like a schoolroom, and no concentrations of student exercises that might signify a teaching area. In fact, we have no clues about how the workmen's children learned their primary skills of reading and writing.

Some of the ostraca left behind do give a somewhat more complete picture of what could be called secondary education—additional training in reading, writing and culture. Many of the documents found in the village are obviously exercises for advanced students, occasionally signed with the names of the student and teacher. Some of the writings bear a date marking the end of a

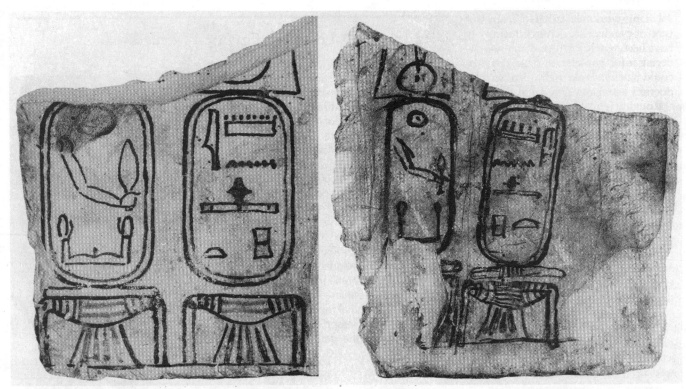

TEACHER'S EXAMPLE of the cartouches of King Amenhotep I was drawn with a confident hand on one side of this ostracon (*left*). A student then turned over the ostracon and made a copy (*right*), in the process reversing some of the signs.

day's lesson; some texts include several such dates, suggesting that a student used a single ostracon for several lessons.

From the various signatures on the ostraca, it is clear that fathers or grandfathers often supervised their sons' or grandsons' education, although on some occasions, fathers—even literate ones— might send their sons to someone of a higher rank for advanced training. (One signature, unfortunately badly preserved, may be a female student's, so at least one woman might have received her education in this fashion.) Pupils would have been from any station in life, including not only the future leaders of the community but also some boys who would never rise above the rank of stonecutter. Teachers consistently came from higher classes, however: the instructors mentioned in the ostraca were primarily scribes, draftsmen or chief workmen.

The students seem to have fit their lessons around their jobs at the tomb, as indicated by the dates in the ostraca— for example, texts often contain multiple dates separated by several days, indicating that there was usually time between lessons when both the instructor and pupil were presumably at work. Nevertheless, there was plenty of time for learning. Workers had many days off, especially as the tomb neared completion toward the end of a pharaoh's reign. During the final stages of construction, they might spend no more than one day out of four in the Valley of the Kings.

The education system in Deir el-Medina differed from that in other cities and towns around Egypt, most notably in who learned to read and write. Furthermore, the writing materials used

OVENS for baking stood in the kitchen areas behind the houses in Deir el-Medina. In this sketch, the words "blowing into the oven" can be seen in the text to the left of the woman.

and the time available for instruction also stand in contrast to practices elsewhere. Student exercises found in other locations were composed on reused papyrus—readily available to those in official positions—and appear to be the handiwork of young apprentices who were being groomed for government service. These students pursued their studies daily and managed to complete several pages of papyrus a day.

Although some aspects of the schooling system in Deir el-Medina diverged from the typical approach to education, the residents of the village apparently agreed with widespread notions about what should be taught and why. Teachers in this workmen's village might train stonecutters in between days on the job, writing on flakes of limestone (the material most available to them), but they still instructed their students in the great classics of Egyptian literature, with the goals of passing on wisdom and ensuring a successful career. As one village scribe wrote to a young pupil: "Set your heart very firmly on writing, a useful profession for the one who does it. Your father had hieroglyphs, and he was honored in the streets."

FRENCH INSTITUTE OF EASTERN ARCHAEOLOGY, CAIRO

STUDENT'S DRAWING of a royal portrait on this ostracon has been corrected in white by his teacher. In Deir el-Medina, young men had individual tutors who educated them in reading, writing and culture.

The Author

ANDREA G. McDOWELL began her study of Deir el-Medina while working on her Ph.D. in ancient history at the University of Pennsylvania. She was a lecturer at Leiden University, junior research fellow at Somerville College at the University of Oxford and an assistant professor of Egyptology at Johns Hopkins University before moving to Yale University, where she is now a student in the law school. McDowell is also working on a book about Deir el-Medina, tentatively scheduled for release next fall.

Further Reading

A COMMUNITY OF WORKMEN AT THEBES IN THE RAMESSIDE PERIOD. Jaroslav Černý. French Institute of Eastern Archaeology, Cairo, 1973.
COMMODITY PRICES FROM THE RAMESSID PERIOD: AN ECONOMIC STUDY OF THE VILLAGE OF NECROPOLIS WORKMEN AT THEBES. Jac. J. Janssen. E. J. Brill, Leiden, 1975.
THE TOMB-BUILDERS OF THE PHARAOHS. Morris Bierbrier. British Museum Publications, London, 1982.
LETTERS FROM ANCIENT EGYPT. Translated by Edward F. Wente. Edited by Edmund S. Meltzer. Scholars Press, 1990.

ALL THE KING'S SONS

*The biggest archeological find in Egypt since King Tut's tomb is also the most unusual: it may explain
the fate of most of Ramesses II's fifty-two sons, New Kingdom funerary practices, and pharaonic sex.
What does it feel like to be the first person to enter such a place in three thousand years?*

BY DOUGLAS PRESTON

On February 2, 1995, at ten in the morning, the archeologist Kent R. Weeks found himself a hundred feet inside a mountain in Egypt's Valley of the Kings, on his belly in the dust of a tomb. He was crawling toward a long-buried doorway that no one had entered for at least thirty-one hundred years. There were two people with him, a graduate student and an Egyptian workman; among them they had one flashlight.

To get through the doorway, Weeks had to remove his hard hat and force his large frame under the lintel with his toes and fingers. He expected to enter a small, plain room marking the end of the tomb. Instead, he found himself in a vast corridor, half full of debris, with doorways lining either side and marching off into the darkness. "When I looked around with the flashlight," Weeks recalled later, "we realized that the corridor was tremendous. I didn't know *what* to think." The air was dead, with a temperature in excess of a hundred degrees and a humidity of one hundred per cent. Weeks, whose glasses had immediately steamed up, was finding it hard to breathe. With every moment, clouds of powder arose, and turned to mud on the skin.

The three people explored the corridor, stooping, and sometimes crawling over piles of rock that had fallen from the ceiling. Weeks counted twenty doorways lining the hundred-foot hallway, some opening into whole suites of rooms with vaulted ceilings carved out of the solid rock of the mountain. At the corridor's end, the feeble flashlight beam revealed a statue of Osiris, the god of resurrection: he was wearing a crown and holding crossed flails and sceptres; his body was bound like that of a mummy. In front of Osiris, the corridor came to a T, branching into two transverse passageways, each of them eighty feet long and ending in what looked like a descending staircase blocked with debris. Weeks counted thirty-two additional rooms off those two corridors.

The tomb was of an entirely new type, never seen by archeologists before. "The architecture didn't fit any known pattern," Weeks told me. "And it was so *big*. I just couldn't make sense of it." The largest pharaonic tombs in the Valley contain ten or fifteen rooms at most. This tomb, with its T shape, had a warren of side chambers, suites, and descending passageways. Weeks knew from earlier excavations that the tomb was the resting place for at least four sons of Ramesses II, the pharaoh also known as Ramesses the Great—and, traditionally, as simply Pharaoh in the Book of Exodus. Because of the tomb's size and complexity, Weeks had to consider the possibility that it was a catacomb for as many as fifty of Ramesses' fifty-two sons—the first example of a royal family mausoleum in ancient Egypt. This one had at least sixty-seven—the total making it not only the biggest tomb in the Valley but possibly the biggest in all Egypt. Most tombs in the Valley of the Kings follow a standard architectural plan—a series of consecutive chambers and corridors like a string of boxcars shot at an angle into the bedrock, and ending with the burial vault.

Weeks had discovered the tomb's entrance eight years earlier, after the Egyptian government announced plans to widen the entrance to the Valley to create a bus turnaround at the end of an asphalt road. From reading old maps and reports, he had recalled that the entrance to a lost tomb lay in the area that was to be paved over. Napoleon's expedition to Egypt had noted a tomb there, and a rather feckless Englishman named James Burton had crawled partway inside it in 1825. A few years later, the archeologist Sir John Gardner Wilkinson had given it the designation KV5, for Kings' Valley Tomb No. 5, when he numbered eighteen tombs there. Howard Carter—the archeologist who discovered King Tutankhamun's tomb in 1922, two hundred feet farther on—dug two feet in, decided that KV5's entrance looked unimportant, and used it as a dumping ground for debris from his other excavations, thus burying it under ten feet of stone and dirt. The location of the tomb's entrance was quickly forgotten.

It took about ten days of channelling through Carter's heaps of debris for Weeks and his men to find the ancient doorway of KV5, and it proved to be directly across the path from the tomb of Ramesses the Great. The entrance lay at the edge of the asphalt road, about ten feet below grade and behind the rickety booths of T-shirt venders and fake-scarab-beetle sellers.

Plans for the bus turnaround were cancelled, and, over a period of seven years, Weeks and his workmen cleared half of the first two chambers and briefly explored a third one. The tomb was packed from floor to ceiling with dirt and rocks that had been washed in by flash floods. He uncovered finely carved reliefs on the walls, which showed Ramesses presenting various sons to the gods, with their names and titles recorded in hieroglyphics. When he reached floor level, he found thousands of objects: pieces of faience jewelry, fragments of furniture, a wooden fist from a coffin, human and animal bones, mummified body parts, chunks of sarcophagi, and fragments of the canopic jars used to hold the mummified organs of the deceased—all detritus left by ancient tomb robbers.

The third chamber was anything but modest. It was about sixty feet square, one of the largest rooms in the Valley, and was supported by sixteen massive stone pillars arranged in four rows. Debris filled the room to within about two feet of the ceiling, allowing just enough space for Weeks to wriggle around. At the back of the chamber, in the axis of the tomb, Weeks noticed an almost buried doorway. Still believing that the tomb was like others in the Valley, he assumed that the doorway merely led to a small, dead-end annex, so he didn't bother with it for several years—not until last February, when he decided to have a look.

Immediately after the discovery, Weeks went back to a four-dollar-a-night pension he shared with his wife, Susan, in the mud village of Gezira Bairat, showered off the tomb dust, and took a motorboat across the Nile to the small city of Luxor. He faxed a short message to Cairo, three hundred miles downriver. It was directed to his major financial supporter, Bruce Ludwig, who was attending a board meeting at the American University in Cairo, where Weeks is a professor. It read, simply, "Have made wonderful discovery in Valley of the

University in Cairo, under whose aegis Weeks was working. It became the biggest archeological story of the decade, making the front page of the *Times* and the cover of *Time*. Television reporters descended on the site. Weeks had to shut down the tomb to make the talk-show circuit. The London newspapers had a field day: the *Daily Mail* headlined its story "PHARAOH'S 50 SONS IN MUMMY OF ALL TOMBS," and one tabloid informed its readers that texts in the tomb gave a date for the Second Coming and the end of the world, and also revealed cures for AIDS and cancer.

The media also wondered whether the tomb would prove that Ramesses II

first, dismissing inquiries with a wave of the hand. "It's all *kalam fadi*," he said, using the Arabic phrase for empty talk. Eventually, however, so many offers poured in that he engaged an agent at William Morris to handle them; a book proposal will be submitted to publishers later this month.

In the fall, Weeks and his crew decided to impose a partial media blackout on the excavation site—the only way they could get any work done, they felt—but they agreed to let me accompany them near the end of the digging season. Just before I arrived, in mid-November, two mysterious descending corridors, with dozens of new cham-

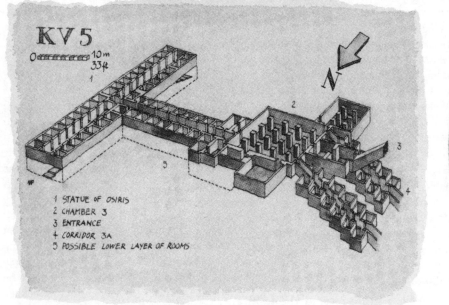

A floor plan of KV5, which may be the largest tomb in Egypt and the only royal mausoleum. Ramesses II, the master builder of Thebes, now rests in the Cairo Museum.

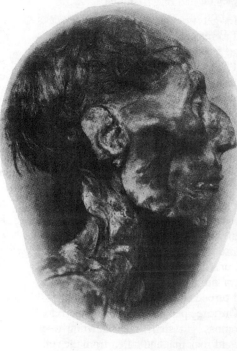

Kings. Await your arrival." Ludwig instantly recognized the significance of the fax and the inside joke it represented: it was a close paraphrase of the telegram that Howard Carter had sent to the Earl of Carnarvon, his financial supporter, when he discovered Tutankhamun's tomb. Ludwig booked a flight to Luxor.

"That night, the enormousness of the discovery began to sink in," Weeks recalled. At about two o'clock in the morning, he turned to his wife and said, "Susan, I think our lives have changed forever."

The discovery was announced jointly by Egypt's Supreme Council of Antiquities, which oversees all archeological work in the country, and the American

was indeed the pharaoh referred to in Exodus. The speculation centered on Amun-her-khopshef, Ramesses' firstborn son, whose name is prominent on KV5's walls. According to the Bible, in order to force Egypt to free the Hebrews from bondage the Lord visited a number of disasters on the land, including the killing of all firstborn Egyptians from the pharaoh's son on down. Some scholars believe that if Amun-her-khopshef's remains are found it may be possible to show at what age and how he died.

Book publishers and Hollywood producers showed great interest in Weeks's story. He didn't respond at

bers, unexpectedly came to light, and I had the good fortune to be the only journalist to see them.

THE Valley of the Kings was the burial ground for the pharaohs of the New Kingdom, the last glorious period of Egyptian history. It began around 1550 B.C., when the Egyptians expelled the foreign Hyksos rulers from Lower Egypt and reëstablished a vast empire, stretching across the Middle East to Syria. It lasted half a millennium. Sixty years before Ramesses, the pharaoh Akhenaten overthrew much of the Egyptian religion and decreed that thenceforth Egyptians should worship only one god—Light, whose visible symbol was Aten, the disk of the sun. Akhenaten's revolution came to a halt at his death. Ramesses represented the culmination of the return to tradition. He was an exceedingly conservative man, who saw himself as the guardian of the ancient customs, and he was particularly zealous in erasing the heretic pharaoh's name from his temples and stelae, a task begun by his father, Seti I. Because Ramesses disliked innovation, his monuments were notable not for their architectural brilliance but for their monstrous size. The New Kingdom began a slow decline following his rule, and finally sputtered to an end with Ramesses XI, the last pharaoh buried in the Valley of the Kings.

The discovery of KV5 will eventually open for us a marvellous window on this period. We know almost nothing about the offspring of the New Kingdom pharaohs or what roles they played. After each eldest prince ascended the throne, the younger sons disappeared so abruptly from the record that it was once thought they were routinely executed. The burial chambers' hieroglyphics, if they still survive, may give us an invaluable account of each son's life and accomplishments. There is a remote possibility—it was suggested to me by the secretary-general of the Supreme Council of Antiquities, Professor Abdel-Halim Nur el-Din, who is an authority on women in ancient Egypt—that Ramesses' daughters might be buried in KV5 as well. (Weeks thinks the possibility highly unlikely.) Before Weeks is done, he will probably find sarcophagi, pieces of funerary offerings, identifiable pieces of mummies, and many items with hieroglyphics on them. The tomb will add a new chapter to our understanding of Egyptian funerary traditions. And there is always a possibility of finding an intact chamber packed with treasure.

Ramesses the Great's reign lasted an unprecedented sixty-seven years, from 1279 to 1213 B.C. He covered the Nile Valley from Nubia to the delta with magnificent temples, statuary, and stelae, which are some of the grandest monuments the world has ever seen. Among his projects were the enormous forecourt at Luxor Temple; the Ramesseum; the cliffside temples of

Abu Simbel; the great Hall of Columns at Karnak; and the city of Pi-Ramesse. The two "vast and trunkless legs of stone" with a "shattered visage" in Shelley's poem "Ozymandias" were those of Ramesses—fragments of the largest statue in pharaonic history. Ramesses outlived twelve of his heirs, dying in his early nineties. The thirteenth crown prince, Merneptah, became pharaoh only in his sixties.

By the time Ramesses ascended the throne, at twenty-five, he had fathered perhaps ten sons and as many daughters. His father had started him out with a harem while he was still a teenager, and he had two principal wives, Nefertari and Istnofret. He later added several Hittite princesses to his harem, and probably his sister and two daughters. It is still debated whether the incestuous marriages of the pharaohs were merely ceremonial or actually consummated. If identifiable remains of Ramesses' sons are found in KV5, it is conceivable that DNA testing might resolve this vexing question.

In most pharaonic monuments we find little about wives and children, but Ramesses showed an unusual affection for his family, extolling the accomplishments of his sons and listing their names on numerous temple walls. All over Egypt, he commissioned statues of Nefertari (not to be confused with the more famous Nefertiti, who was Akhenaten's wife), "for whose sake the very sun does shine." When she died, in Year 24 of his reign, Ramesses interred her in the most beautiful tomb yet discovered in the Valley of the Queens, just south of the Valley of the Kings. The tomb survived intact, and its incised and painted walls are nearly as fresh as the day they were fashioned. The rendering of Nefertari's face and figure perhaps speaks most eloquently of Ramesses' love for her. She is shown making her afterlife journey dressed in a diaphanous linen gown, with her slender figure emerging beneath the gossamer fabric. Her face was painted using the technique of chiaroscuro—perhaps the first known example in the history of art of a human face being treated as a three-dimensional volume. The Getty Conservation Institute recently spent millions restoring the tomb. The Getty recommended that

access to the tomb be restricted, in order to preserve it, but the Egyptian government has opened it to tourists, at thirty-five dollars a head.

The design of royal tombs was so fixed by tradition that they had no architect, at least as we use that term today. The tombs were laid out and chiselled from ceiling to floor, resulting in ceiling dimensions that are precise and floor dimensions that can vary considerably. All the rooms and corridors in a typical royal tomb had names, many of which we still do not fully understand: the First God's Passage, Hall of Hindering, Sanctuaries in Which the Gods Repose. The burial chamber was often called the House of Gold. Some tombs had a Hall of Truth, whose murals showed the pharaoh's heart being weighed in judgment by Osiris, with the loathsome god Ammut squatting nearby, waiting to devour it if it was found wanting. Many of the reliefs were so formulaic that they were probably taken from copybooks. Yet even within this rigid tradition breathtaking flights of creativity and artistic expression can be found.

Most of the tombs in the Valley were never finished: they took decades to cut, and the plans usually called for something more elaborate than the pharaoh could achieve during his rule. As a result, the burial of the pharaoh was often a panicky, ad-hoc affair, with various rooms in the tomb being adapted for other purposes, and decorations and texts painted in haste or omitted completely. (Some of the most beautiful inscriptions were those painted swiftly; they have a spontaneity and freshness of line rivalling Japanese calligraphy.)

From the time of Ramesses II on, the tombs were not hidden: their great doorways, which were made of wood, could be opened. It is likely that the front rooms of many tombs were regularly visited by priests to make offerings. This may have been particularly true of KV5, where the many side chambers perhaps served such a purpose. The burial chambers containing treasure, however, were always sealed.

Despite all the monuments and inscriptions that Ramesses left us, it is still difficult to bridge the gap of thirty-one hundred years and see Ramesses as a person. One thing we do know: the standard image of the pharaoh, embodied in Shelley's "frown, and wrinkled lip, and sneer of cold command," is a misconception. One of the finest works from Ramesses' reign is a statue of the young king now in the Museo Egizio, in Turin. The expression on his face is at once compassionate and otherworldly, not unlike that of a Giotto Madonna; his head is slightly bowed, as if to acknowledge his role as both leader and servant. This is not the face of a tyrant-pharaoh who press-ganged his people into building monuments to his greater glory. Rather, it is the portrait of a ruler who had his subjects' interests at heart, and this is precisely what the archeological and historical records suggest about Ramesses. Most of the Egyptians who labored on the pharaoh's monuments did so proudly and were, by and large, well compensated. There is a lovely stela on which Ramesses boasts about how much he has given his workers, "so that they work for me with their full hearts." Dorothea Arnold, the head curator of the Egyptian Department at the Metropolitan Museum, told me, "The pharaoh was *believed* in. As to whether he was beloved, that is beside the point: he was *necessary*. He was life itself. He represented everything good. Without him there would be nothing."

Final proof of the essential humanity of the pharaonic system is that it survived for more than three thousand years. (When Ramesses ascended the throne, the pyramids at Giza were already thirteen hundred years old.) Egypt produced one of the most stable cultural and religious traditions the world has ever seen.

Very little lives in the Valley of the Kings now. It is a wilderness of stone and light—a silent, roofless sepulchre. Rainfall averages a quarter inch per year, and one of the hottest natural air temperatures on earth was recorded in the surrounding mountains. And yet the Valley is a surprisingly intimate place. Most of the tombs lie within a mere forty acres, and the screen of cliffs gives the area a feeling of privacy. Dusty paths and sun-bleached, misspelled signs add a pleasant, ramshackle air.

The Valley lies on the outskirts of the ancient city of Thebes, now in ruins. In a six-mile stretch of riverbank around the city, there are as many temples, palaces, and monuments as anywhere else on earth, and the hills are so pockmarked with the yawning pits and doorways of ancient tombs that they resemble a First World War battlefield. It is dangerous to walk or ride anywhere alone. Howard Carter discovered an important tomb when the horse he was riding broke through and fell into it. Recently, a Canadian woman fell into a tomb while hiking and fractured her leg; no one could hear her screams, and she spent the days leading up to her death writing postcards. One archeologist had to clear a tomb that contained a dead cow and twenty-one dead dogs that had gone in to eat it.

Almost all the tombs lying open have been pillaged. A papyrus now in Italy records the trial of someone who robbed KV5 itself in 1150 B.C. The robber confessed under torture to plundering the tomb of Ramesses the Great and then going "across the path" to rob the tomb of his sons. Ancient plunderers often vandalized the tombs they robbed, possibly in an attempt to destroy the magic that supposedly protected them. They smashed everything, levered open sarcophagi, ripped apart mummies to get at the jewelry hidden in the wrappings, and sometimes threw objects against the walls with such force that they left dents and smudges of pure gold.

Nobody is sure why this particular valley, three hundred miles up the Nile from the pyramids, was chosen as the final resting place of the New Kingdom pharaohs. Egyptologists theorize that the sacred pyramidal shape of el-Qurn, the mountain at the head of the Valley of the Kings, may have been one factor. Another was clearly security: the Valley is essentially a small box canyon carved out of the barren heart of a desert mountain range; it has only one entrance, through a narrow gorge, and the surrounding cliffs echo and magnify any sounds of human activity, such as the tapping of a robber's pick on stone.

Contrary to popular belief, the tombs in the Valley are not marked with curses. King Tut's curse was invented by Arthur Weigall, an Egyptologist and journalist at the *Daily Mail*, who was furious that Carnarvon had given the London *Times* the exclusive on the discovery. Royal tombs did not need curses to protect them. Priests guarded the Valley night and day, and thieves knew exactly what awaited them if they were caught: no curse could compete with the fear of being impaled alive. "There are a few curses on some private tombs and in some legal documents," James Allen, an Egyptologist with the Metropolitan Museum, told me. "The most extreme I know of is on a legal document of the Ramesside Period. It reads, 'As for the one who will violate it, he shall be seized for Amun-Ra. He shall be for the flame of Sekhmet. He is an enemy of Osiris, lord of Abydos, and so is his son, for ever and ever. May donkeys f . . . him, may donkeys f . . . his wife, may his wife f. . . . his son.' "

Some scholars today, looking back over the past two hundred years of archeological activity, think a curse might have been a good idea: most of the archeology done in the Valley has been indistinguishable from looting. Until the nineteen-sixties, those who had concessions to excavate there were allowed to keep a percentage of the spoils as "payment" for their work. In the fever of the treasure hunt, tombs were emptied without anyone bothering to photograph the objects found or to record their positions in situ, or even to note which tomb they came from. Items that had no market value were trashed. Wilkinson, the man who gave the tombs their numbers, burned three-thousand-year-old wooden coffins and artifacts to heat his house. Murals and reliefs were chopped out of walls. At dinner parties, the American lawyer Theodore M. Davis, who financed many digs in the Valley, used to tear up necklaces woven of ancient flowers and fabric to show how strong they were after three thousand years in a tomb. Pyramids were blasted open with explosives, and one tomb door was bashed in with a battering ram. Even Carter never published a proper scientific report on Tut's tomb. It is only in the last twenty-five years that real archeology has come to Egypt, and KV5 will be one of the first tombs in the Valley of the Kings to be entirely excavated and documented according to proper archeological techniques.

Fortunately, other great archeological projects remain to be carried out with the new techniques. The Theban Necropolis is believed to contain between four thousand and five thousand tombs, of which only four hundred have been given numbers. More than half of the royal tombs in the Valley of the Kings have not been fully excavated, and of these only five have been properly documented. There are mysterious blocked passageways, hollow floors, chambers packed with debris, and caved-in rooms. King Tut's was by no means the last undiscovered pharaonic tomb in Egypt. In the New Kingdom alone, the tombs of Amosis, Amenhotep I, Tuthmosis II, and Ramesses VIII have never been identified. The site of the burial ground for the pharaohs of the entire Twenty-first Dynasty is unknown. And the richness and the size of KV5 offer the tantalizing suggestion that other princely tombs of its kind are lying undiscovered beneath the Egyptian sands; Ramesses would surely not have been the only pharaoh to bury his sons in such style.

WORK at KV5 in the fall season proceeds from six-thirty in the morning until one-thirty in the afternoon. Every day, to get to KV5 from my hotel in Luxor, I cross the Nile on the public ferry, riding with a great mass of fellaheen—men carrying goats slung around their necks, children lugging sacks of eggplants, old men squatting in their djellabas and smoking cigarettes or eating *leb* nuts—while the ancient diesel boat wheezes and blubs across the river. I am usually on the river in time to catch the sun rising over the shattered columns of Luxor Temple, along the riverbank. The Nile is still magical—crowded with feluccas, lined with date palms, and bearing on its current many clumps of blooming water hyacinths.

The ferry empties its crowds into a chaos of taxis, camels, donkeys, children begging for baksheesh, and hopeful guides greeting every tourist with a hearty "Welcome to Egypt!" In contrast to the grand hotels and boulevards of Luxor, the west bank consists of clusters of mud villages scattered among impossibly green fields of cane and clover, where the air is heavy with smoke and the droning prayers of the muezzin. Disembarkation is followed by a harrowing high-speed taxi ride to the Valley, the driver weaving past donkey carts and herds of goats, his sweaty fist pounding the horn.

On the first day of my visit, I find Kent Weeks sitting in a green canvas tent at the entrance to KV5 and trying to fit together pieces of a human skull. It is a cool Saturday morning in November. From the outside, KV5 looks like all the other tombs—a mere doorway in a hillside. Workmen in a bucket brigade are passing baskets filled with dirt out of the tomb's entrance and dumping them in a nearby pile, on which two men are squatting and sifting through the debris with small gardening tools. "Hmm," Weeks says, still fiddling with the skull. "I had this together a moment ago. You'll have to wait for our expert. He can put it together just like that." He snaps his fingers.

"Whose skull is it?"

"One of Ramesses' sons, I hope. The brown staining on it—here—shows that it might have come from a mummified body. We'll eventually do DNA comparisons with Ramesses and other members of his family."

Relaxing in the tent, Weeks does not cut the dapper, pugnacious figure of a Howard Carter, nor does he resemble the sickly, elegant Lord Carnarvon in waistcoat and watch chain. But because he is the first person to have made a major discovery in the Valley of the Kings since Carter, he is surely in their class. At fifty-four, he is handsome and fit, his ruddy face peering at the world through thick square glasses from underneath a Tilley hat. His once crisp shirt and khakis look like hell after an hour in the tomb's stifling atmosphere, and his Timberland shoes have reached a state of indescribable lividity from tomb dust.

Weeks has the smug air of a man who is doing the most interesting thing he could possibly do in life. He launches into his subject with such enthusiasm that one's first impulse is to flee. But as he settles back in his rickety chair with the skull in one hand and a glass of *yansoon* tea in the other, and yarns on about lost tombs, crazy Egyptologists, graverobbers, jackal-headed gods, mummies, secret passageways, and the mysteries of the Underworld, you begin to succumb. His conversation is laced with obscene sallies delivered with a schoolboy's relish, and you can tell he has not been to any gender-sensitivity training seminars. He can be disconcertingly blunt. He characterized one

archeologist as "ineffectual, ridiculously inept, and a wonderful source of comic relief," another as "a raving psychopath," and a third as "a dork, totally off the wall." When I asked if KV5 would prove that Ramesses was the Biblical Pharaoh, he responded with irritation: "I can almost guarantee you that we will *not* find anything in KV5 bearing on the Exodus question. All the speculation in the press assumed there *was* an exodus and that it was described accurately in the Bible. I don't believe it. There may have been Israelites in Egypt, but I sincerely doubt Exodus is an exact account of what occurred. At least I *hope* it wasn't—with the Lord striking down the firstborn of Egypt and turning the rivers to blood."

His is a rarefied profession: there are only about four hundred Egyptologists in the world, and only a fraction of them are archeologists. (Most are art historians and philologists.) Egyptology is a difficult profession to break into; in a good year, there might be two job openings in the United States. It is the kind of field where the untimely death of a tenured figure sets the photocopying machines running all night.

"From the age of eight, I had no doubt: I wanted to be an Egyptologist," Weeks told me. His parents—one a policeman, the other a medical librarian—did not try to steer him into a sensible profession, and a string of teachers encouraged his interest. When Weeks was in high school, in Longview, Washington, he met the Egyptologist Ahmed Fakhry in Seattle, and Fakhry was so charmed by the young man that he invited him to lunch and mapped out his college career.

In 1963, Weeks's senior year at the University of Washington, one of the most important events in the history of Egyptology took place. Because of the construction of the High Dam at Aswan, the rising waters of the Nile began to flood Nubia; they would soon inundate countless archeological sites, including the incomparable temples of Abu Simbel. UNESCO and the Egyptian and Sudanese governments issued an international plea for help. Weeks immediately wrote to William Kelly Simpson, a prominent Egyptologist at Yale who was helping to coördinate the salvage project, and offered his services.

He received plane tickets by return mail.

"The farthest I'd been away from home was Disneyland, and here I was going to Nubia," Weeks said. "The work had to be done fast: the lake waters were already rising. I got there and suddenly found myself being told, 'Take these eighty workmen and go dig that ancient village.' The nearest settlement was Wadi Halfa, ninety miles away. The first words of Arabic I learned were 'Dig no deeper' and 'Carry the baskets faster.' "

Weeks thereafter made a number of trips to Nubia, and just before he set out on one of them he invited along as artist a young woman he had met near the mummy case at the University of Washington museum— Susan Howe, a solemn college senior with red hair and a deadpan sense of humor.

"We lived on the river on an old rat-infested dahabeah," Susan told me. "My first night on the Nile, we were anchored directly in front of Ramesses' knees. It was all lit up, because work was going on day and night." An emergency labor force was cutting the temple into enormous blocks and reassembling it on higher ground. "After five months, the beer ran out, the cigarettes ran out, the water was really hot, the temperature was a hundred and fifteen degrees in the shade, and there were terrible windstorms. My parents were just *desperate* to know when I was coming home. But I thought, Ah! This is the life! It was so romantic. The workmen sang songs and clapped every morning when we arrived. So we wrote home and gave our parents ten days' notice that we were going to get married."

They have now been married twenty-nine years. Susan is the artist and illustrator for many of Kent's projects, and has also worked for other archeologists in Egypt. She spends much of her day in front of KV5, in the green tent, wearing a scarf and peach-colored Keds, while she makes precise scale drawings of pottery and artifacts. In her spare time, she wanders around Gezira Bairat, painting exquisite watercolors of doorways and donkeys.

Weeks eventually returned to Washington to get his M.A., and in 1971 he received a Ph.D. from Yale; his dissertation dealt with ancient Egyptian anatomical terminology. He landed a plum job as a curator in the Metropolitan Museum's Egyptian Department. Two years later, bored by museum work, he quit and went back to Egypt, and was shortly offered the directorship of Chicago House, the University of Chicago's research center in Luxor. The Weekses have two children, whom they reared partly in Egypt, sending them to a local Luxor school. After four years at Chicago House, Weeks took a professorship at Berkeley, but again the lure of Egypt was too strong. In 1987, he renounced tenure at Berkeley, took a large pay cut, and went back to Egypt as a professor of Egyptology at the American University in Cairo, where he has been ever since.

While in Nubia, Weeks excavated an ancient working-class cemetery, pulling some seven thousand naturally desiccated bodies out of the ground. In a study of diet and health, he and a professor of orthodontics named James Harris X-rayed many of these bodies. Then Weeks and Harris persuaded the Egyptian government to allow them to X-ray the mummies of the pharaohs, by way of comparison. A team of physicians, orthodontists, and pathologists studied the royal X-rays, hoping to determine such things as age at death, cause of death, diet, and medical problems. They learned that there was surprisingly little difference between the two classes in diet and health.

One finding caused an uproar among Egyptologists. The medical team had been able to determine ages at death for most of the pharaohs, and in some cases these starkly contradicted the standard chronologies of the Egyptologists. The mystery was eventually solved when the team consulted additional ancient papyri, which told how, in the late New Kingdom, the high priests realized that many of the tombs in the Valley of the Kings had been robbed. To prevent further desecration, they gathered up almost all the royal mummies (missing only King Tut) and reburied them in two caches, both of which were discovered intact in the nineteenth century. "What we think happened is that the priests let the name dockets with some of the mummies fall off and put them back wrong," Weeks told me. It is also possible that the mixup occurred when the mummies were moved down the river to Cairo in the nineteenth century.

The team members analyzed the craniofacial characteristics of each mummy and figured out which ones looked most like which others. (Most of the pharaohs were related.) By combining these findings with age-at-death information, they were able to restore six of the mummies' proper names.

Weeks's second project led directly to the discovery of KV5. In 1979, he began mapping the entire Theban Necropolis. After an overview, he started with the Valley of the Kings. No such map had ever been done before. (That explains how KV5 came to be found and then lost several times in its history.) The Theban Mapping Project is to include the topography of the Valley and the three-dimensional placement of each tomb within the rock. The data are being computerized, and eventually Weeks will re-create the Valley on CD-ROM, which will allow a person to "fly" into any tomb and view in detail the murals and reliefs on its walls and ceilings.

Some Egyptologists I spoke with consider the mapping of the Theban Necropolis to be the most important archeological project in Egypt, KV5 notwithstanding. A map of the Valley of the Kings is desperately needed. Some tombs are deteriorating rapidly, with murals cracking and falling to the floors, and ceilings, too, collapsing. Damage has been done by the opening of the tombs to outside air. (When Carter opened King Tut's tomb, he could actually hear "strange rustling, murmuring, whispering sounds" of objects as the new air began its insidious work of destruction. In other tombs, wooden objects turned into "cigar-ash.") Greek, Roman, and early European tourists explored the tombs with burning torches—and even lived in some tombs—leaving an oily soot on the paintings. Rapid changes in temperature and humidity generated by the daily influx of modern-day tourists have caused even greater damage, some of it catastrophic.

The gravest danger of all comes from flooding. Most of the tombs are now wide open. Modern alterations in the topography, such as the raising of the valley floor in order to build paths for the tourists, have created a highway directing floodwaters straight into the mouths of the tombs. A brief rain in November of 1994 generated a small flash flood that tore through the Valley at thirty miles an hour and damaged several tombs. It burst into the tomb of Bay, a vizier of the New Kingdom, with such force that it churned through the decorated chambers and completely ruined them. Layers of debris in KV5 indicate that a major flash flood occurs about once every three hundred years. If such a flood occurred tomorrow, the Valley of the Kings could be largely destroyed.

There is no master plan for preserving the Valley. The most basic element in such a plan is the completion of Week's map. Only then can preservationists monitor changes in the tombs and begin channelling and redirecting flood-waters. For this reason, some archeologists privately panicked when Weeks found KV5. "When I first heard about it," one told me, "I thought, Oh, my God, that's it, Kent will never finish the mapping project."

Weeks promises that KV5 will not interfere with the Theban Mapping Project. "Having found the tomb, we've got an obligation to leave it in a good, stable, safe condition," he says. "And we have an obligation to publish. Public interest in KV5 has actually increased funding for the Theban Mapping Project."

At 9 A.M., the workmen laboring in KV5—there are forty-two of them—begin to file out and perch in groups on the hillside, to eat a breakfast of bread, tomatoes, green onions, and a foul cheese called *misht*. Weeks rises from his chair, nods to me, and asks, "Are you ready?"

We descend a new wooden staircase into the mountain and enter Chamber 1, where we exchange our sun hats for hard hats. The room is small and only half cleared. Visible tendrils of humid, dusty air waft in from the dim recesses of the tomb. The first impression I have of the tomb is one of shocking devastation. The ceilings are shot through with cracks, and in places they have caved in, dropping automobile-size pieces of rock. A forest of screw jacks and timbers holds up what is left, and many of the cracks are plastered with "telltales"—small seals that show if any more movement of the rock occurs.

The reliefs in Chamber 1 are barely visible, a mere palimpsest of what were once superbly carved and painted scenes of Ramesses and his sons adoring the gods, and panels of hieroglyphics. Most of the damage here was the result of a leaky sewer pipe that was laid over the tomb about forty years ago from an old rest house in the Valley. The leak caused salt crystals to grow and eat away the limestone walls. Here and there, however, one can still see traces of the original paint.

The decorations on the walls of the first two rooms show various sons being presented to the gods by Ramesses, in the classic Egyptian pose: head in profile, shoulders in frontal view, and torso in three-quarters view. There are also reliefs of tables laden with offerings of food for the gods, and hieroglyphic texts spelling out the names and titles of several sons and including the royal cartouche of Ramesses.

A doorway from Chamber 2 opens into Chamber 3—the Pillared Hall. It is filled with dirt and rock almost to the ceiling, giving one a simultaneous impression of grandeur and claustrophobia. Two narrow channels have been cut through the debris to allow for the passage of the workmen. Many of the pillars are split and shattered, and only fragments of decorations remain—a few hieroglyphic characters, an upraised arm, part of a leg. Crazed light from several randomly placed bulbs throws shadows around the room.

I follow Weeks down one of the channels. "This room is in such dangerous condition that we decided not to clear it," he says. "We call this channel the Mubarak trench. It was dug so that President Mubarak could visit the tomb without having to creep around on his hands and knees." He laughs.

When we are halfway across the room, he points out the words "James Burton 1825" smoked on the ceiling with the flame of a candle: it represents the Englishman's farthest point of penetration. Not far away is another graffito—this one in hieratic, the cursive form of hieroglyphic writing. It reads "Year 19"—the nineteenth year of Ramesses' reign. "This date gives us a *terminus ante quem* for the presence of Ramesses' workmen in this chamber," Weeks says.

He stops at one of the massive pillars. "And here's a mystery," he says,

"Fifteen of the pillars in this room were cut from the native rock, but this one is a fake. The rock was carefully cut away—you can see chisel marks on the ceiling—and then the pillar was rebuilt out of stone and plastered to look like the others. Why?" He gives the pillar a sly pat. "Was something very large moved in here?"

I follow Weeks to the end of the trench—the site of the doorway that he crawled through in February. The door has been cleared, and we descend a short wooden staircase to the bottom of the great central corridor. It is illuminated by a string of naked light bulbs, which cast a yellow glow through a pall of dust. The many doors lining both sides of the corridor are still blocked with debris, and the stone floor is covered with an inch of dust.

At the far end of the corridor, a hundred feet away, stands the mummiform statue of Osiris. It is carved from the native rock, and only its face is missing. Lit from below, the statue casts a dramatic shadow on the ceiling. I try to take notes, but my glasses have fogged up, and sweat is dripping onto my notebook, making the ink run off the page. I can only stand and blink.

Nothing in twenty years of writing about archeology has prepared me for this great wrecked corridor chiselled out of the living rock, with rows of shattered doorways opening into darkness, and ending in the faceless mummy of Osiris. I feel like a trespasser, a voyeur, gazing into the sacred precincts of the dead. As I stare at the walls, patterns and lines begin to emerge from the shattered stone: ghostly figures and faint hieroglyphics; animal-headed gods performing mysterious rites. Through doorways I catch glimpses of more rooms and more doorways beyond. There is a presence of death in this wrecked tomb that goes beyond those who were buried here; it is the death of a civilization.

With most of the texts on the walls destroyed or still buried under debris, it is not yet possible to determine what function was served by the dozens of side chambers. Weeks feels it likely, however, that they were *not* burial chambers, because the doorways are too narrow to admit a sarcophagus. Instead, he speculates they were chapels where the Theban priests could make offerings to the dead sons. Because the tomb departs so radically from the standard design, it is impossible even to speculate what the mysterious Pillared Hall or many of the other antechambers were for.

Weeks proudly displays some reliefs on the walls, tracing with his hand the figure of Isis and her husband, Osiris, and pointing out the ibis-headed god Thoth. "Ah!" he cries. "And here is a *wonderful* figure of Anubis and Hathor!" Anubis is the jackal-headed god of mummification, and Hathor a goddess associated with the Theban Necropolis. These were scenes to help guide Ramesses' sons through the rituals, spells, and incantations that would insure them a safe journey through the realm of death. The reliefs are exceedingly difficult to see; Susan Weeks told me later that she has sometimes had to stare at a wall for long periods—days, even—before she could pick out the shadow of a design. She is now in the process of copying these fragmentary reliefs on Mylar film, to help experts who will attempt to reconstruct the entire wall sequence and its accompanying text, and so reveal to us the purpose of the room or the corridor. KV5 will only yield up its secrets slowly, and with great effort.

"Here's Ramesses and one of his sons," Weeks says, indicating two figures standing hand in hand. "But, alas, the name is gone. Very disappointing!" He charges off down the corridor, raising a trail of dust, and comes to a halt at the statue of Osiris, poking his glasses back up his sweating nose. "Look at this. Spectacular! A three-dimensional statue of Osiris is very rare. Most tombs depict him painted only. We dug around the base here trying to find the face, but instead we found a lovely offering of nineteen clay figs."

He makes a ninety-degree turn down the left transverse corridor, snaking around a cave-in. The corridor runs level for some distance and then plunges down a double staircase with a ramp in the middle, cut from the bedrock, and ends in a wall of bedrock. Along the sides of this corridor we have

passed sixteen more partly blocked doors.

"Now, here is something new," Weeks says. "You're the first outsider to see this. I hoped that this staircase would lead to the burial chambers. This kind of ramp was usually built to slide the sarcophagi down. But look! The corridor just ends in a blank wall. Why in the world would they build a staircase and ramp going nowhere? So I decided to clear the two lowest side chambers. We just finished last week."

He ushers me into one of the rooms. There is no light; the room is large and very hot.

"They were empty," Weeks says.

"Too bad."

"Take a look at this floor."

"Nice." Floors do not particularly excite me.

"It happens to be the finest plastered floor in the Valley of the Kings. They went to enormous trouble with this floor, laying down three coats of plaster at different times, in different colors. Why?" He pauses. "Now stamp on the floor."

I thump the floor. There is a hollow reverberation that shakes not only the floor but the entire room. "Oh, my God, there's something underneath there!" I exclaim.

"*Maybe*," Weeks says, a large smile gathering on his face. "Who knows? It could be a natural cavity or crack, or it might be a passageway to a lower level."

"You mean there might be sealed burial chambers below?"

Weeks smiles again. "Let's not get ahead of ourselves. Next June, we'll drill some test holes and do it properly."

We scramble back to the Osiris statue.

"Now I'm going to take you to our latest discovery," Weeks says. "This is intriguing. *Very* fascinating."

We make our way through several turns back to the Pillared Hall. Weeks leads me down the other trench, which ends at the southwest corner of the hall. Here, earlier in the month, the workmen discovered a buried doorway that opened onto a steep descending passageway, again packed solid with debris. The workmen have now cleared the passageway down some sixty feet, exposing twelve more side chambers, and are still at work.

We pause at the top of the newly ex-

cavated passageway. A dozen screw jacks with timbers hold up its cracked ceiling. The men have finished breakfast and are back at work, one man picking away at the wall of debris at the bottom of the passageway while another scoops the debris into a basket made out of old tires. A line of workmen then pass the basket up the corridor and out of the tomb.

"I've called this passageway 3A," Weeks says. He drops his voice. "The incredible thing is that this corridor is heading toward the tomb of Ramesses himself. If it connects, that will be extraordinary. No two tombs were ever deliberately connected. This tomb just gets curiouser and curiouser."

Ramesses' tomb, lying a hundred feet across the Valley, was also wrecked by flooding and is now being excavated by a French team. "I would dearly love to surprise them," Weeks says. "To pop out one day and say '*Bonjour! C'est moi!*' I'd love to beat the French into their own tomb."

I follow him down the newly discovered corridor, slipping and sliding on the pitched floor. "Of course," he shouts over his shoulder, "the sons might also be buried *underneath* their father! We clearly haven't found the burial chambers yet, and it is my profound hope that one way or another this passageway will take us there."

We come to the end, where the workmen are picking away at the massive wall of dirt that blocks the passage. The forty-two men can remove about nine tons of dirt a day.

At the bottom, Weeks introduces me to a tall, handsome Egyptian with a black mustache and wearing a baseball cap on backward. "This is Muhammad Mahmud," Weeks says. "One of the senior workmen."

I shake his hand. "What do you hope to find down here?"

"Something very nice, *inshallah.*"

"What's in these side rooms?" I ask Weeks. All the doorways are blocked with dirt.

Weeks shrugs. "We haven't been in those rooms yet."

"Would it be possible . . ." I start to ask.

He grins. "You mean, would you like to be the first human being in three thousand years to enter a chamber in an ancient Egyptian tomb? Maybe Saturday."

As we are leaving the tomb, I am struck by the amount of work still unfinished. Weeks has managed to dig out only three rooms completely and clear eight others partway—leaving more than eighty rooms entirely untouched. What treasures lie under five or ten feet of debris in those rooms is anyone's guess. It will take from six to ten more years to clear and stabilize the tomb, and then many more years to publish the findings from it. As we emerge from the darkness, Weeks says, "I know what I'll be doing for the rest of my life."

ONE morning, I find a pudgy, bearded man sitting in the green tent and examining, Hamlet-like, the now assembled skull. He is the paleontologist Elwyn Simons, who has spent decades searching the sands of the Faiyum for primate ancestors of human beings. Susan Weeks once worked for him, and now he is a close friend of the couple, dropping in on occasion to look over bones from the tomb. Kent and Susan are both present, waiting to hear his opinions about the skull's sex. (Only DNA testing can confirm whether it's an actual son of Ramesses, of course.)

Simons rotates the skull, pursing his lips. "Probably a male, because it has fairly pronounced brow ridges," he says. "This"—he points to a hole punched in the top of the cranium—"was made post mortem. You can tell because the edges are sharp and there are no suppressed fractures."

Simons laughs, and sets the skull down. "You can grind this up and put it in your soup, Kent."

When the laughter has died down, I venture that I didn't get the joke.

"In the Middle Ages, people filled bottles with powdered mummies and sold it as medicine," Simons explains.

"Or mummies were burned to power the railroad," Weeks adds. "I don't know how many miles you get per mummy, do you, Elwyn?"

While talk of mummies proceeds, a worker brings a tray of tea. Susan Weeks takes the skull away and puts another bone in front of Simons.

"That's the scapula of an artiodactyl. Probably a cow. The camel hadn't reached Egypt by the Nineteenth Dynasty."

The next item is a tooth.

"Artiodactyl again," he says, sipping his tea. "Goat or gazelle."

The identification process goes on.

The many animal bones found in KV5 were probably from offerings for the dead: valley tombs often contained sacrificed bulls, mummified baboons, birds, and cats, as well as steaks and veal chops.

Suddenly, Muhammad appears at the mouth of the tomb. "Please, Dr. Kent," he says, and starts telling Weeks in Arabic that the workers have uncovered something for him to see. Weeks motions for me to follow him into the dim interior. We put on our hard hats and duck through the first chambers into Corridor 3A. A beautiful set of carved limestone steps has appeared where I saw only rubble a few days before. Weeks kneels and brushes the dirt away, excited about the fine workmanship.

Muhammad and Weeks go to inspect another area of the tomb, where fragments of painted and carved plaster are being uncovered. I stay to watch the workmen digging in 3A. After a while, they forget I am there and begin singing, handing the baskets up the long corridor, their bare feet white with dust. A dark hole begins to appear between the top of the debris and the ceiling. It looks as if one could crawl inside and perhaps look farther down the corridor.

"May I take a look in there?" I ask.

One of the workmen hoists me up the wall of dirt, and I lie on my stomach and wriggle into the gap. I recall that archeologists sometimes sent small boys into tombs through holes just like this.

Unfortunately, I am not a small boy, and in my eagerness I find myself thoroughly wedged. It is pitch-black, and I wonder why I thought this would be exciting.

"Pull me out!" I yell.

The Egyptians heave on my legs, and I come sliding down with a shower of dirt. After the laughter subsides, a skinny man named Nubie crawls into the hole. In a moment, he is back out, feet first. He cannot see anything; they need to dig more.

The workmen redouble their efforts, laughing, joking, and singing. Working in KV5 is a coveted job in the surrounding villages; Weeks pays his workmen four hundred Egyptian pounds a month (about a hundred and twenty-

five dollars), four times what a junior inspector of antiquities makes and perhaps three times the average monthly income of an Egyptian family. Weeks is well liked by his Egyptian workers, and is constantly bombarded with dinner invitations from even his poorest laborers. While I was there, I attended three of these dinners. The flow of food was limitless, and the conversation competed with the bellowing of a water buffalo in an adjacent room or the braying of a donkey tethered at the door.

After the hole has been widened a bit, Nubie goes up again with a light and comes back down. There is great disappointment: it looks as though the passageway might come to an end. Another step is exposed in the staircase, along with a great deal of broken pottery. Weeks returns and examines the hole himself, without comment.

AS the week goes by, more of Corridor 3A is cleared, foot by foot. The staircase in 3A levels out to a finely made floor, more evidence that the corridor merely ends in a small chamber. On Wednesday, however, Weeks emerges from the tomb smiling. "Come," he says.

The hole in 3A has now been enlarged to about two feet in diameter. I scramble up the dirt and peer inside with a light, choking on the dust. As before, the chiselled ceiling comes to an abrupt end, but below it lies what looks like a shattered door lintel.

"It's got to be a door," Weeks says, excited. "I'm afraid we're going to have to halt for the season at that doorway. We'll break through next June."

Later, outdoors, I find myself coughing up flecks of mud.

"Tomb cough," Weeks says cheerfully.

ON Thursday morning, Weeks is away on business, and I go down into the tomb with Susan. At the bottom of 3A, we stop to watch Ahmed Mahmud Hassan, the chief supervisor of the crew, sorting through some loose dirt at floor level. Suddenly, he straightens up, holding a perfect alabaster statuette of a mummy.

"Madame," he says, holding it out.

Susan begins to laugh. "Ahmed,

that's beautiful. Did you get that at one of the souvenir stalls?"

"No," he says. "I just found it." He points to the spot. "Here."

She turns to me. "They once put a rubber cobra in here. Everyone was terrified, and Muhammad began beating it with a rock."

"Madame," Ahmed says. "Look, please." By now, he is laughing, too.

"I see it," Susan says. "I hope it wasn't too expensive."

"Madame, please."

Susan takes it, and there is a sudden silence. "It's real," she says quietly.

"This is what I was telling Madame," Ahmed says, still laughing.

Susan slowly turns it over in her hands. "It's beautiful. Let's take it outside."

In the sunlight, the statuette glows. The head and shoulders still have clear traces of black paint, and the eyes look slightly crossed. It is an *ushabti*, a statuette that was buried only with the dead, meant to spare the deceased toil in the afterlife: whenever the deceased was called upon to do work, he would send the *ushabti* in his place.

That morning, the workmen also find in 3A a chunk of stone. Weeks hefts it. "This is very important," he says.

"How?"

"It's a piece of a sidewall of a sarcophagus that probably held one of Ramesses' sons. It's made out of serpentine, a valuable stone in ancient Egypt." He pulls out a tape measure and marks off the thickness of the rim. "It's eight-point-five centimetres, which, doubled, gives seventeen centimetres. Add to that the width of an average pair of human shoulders, and perhaps an inner coffin, and you could not have fitted this sarcophagus through any door to any of the sixty side chambers in that tomb." He pauses. "So, you see, this piece of stone is one more piece of evidence that we have yet to find the burial chambers."

Setting the stone down with a thud on a specimen mat, he dabs his forehead. He proceeds to lay out a theory about KV5. Ramesses had an accomplished son named Khaemwaset, who became the high priest of an important cult that worshipped a god represented by a sacred bull. In Year 16, Khaemwaset began construction of the Serapeum, a vast catacomb for the bulls, in Saqqara. The original design of the Serapeum is

the only one that remotely resembles KV5's layout, and it might have been started around the same time. In the Serapeum, there are two levels: an upper level of offering chapels and a lower level for burials. "But," Weeks adds, throwing open his arms, "until we find the burial chambers it's *all* speculation."

ON Friday, Bruce Ludwig arrives—a great bear of a man with white hair and a white beard. Dressed like an explorer, he is lugging a backpack full of French wine for the team.

Unlike Lord Carnarvon and other wealthy patrons who funded digs in the Valley of the Kings, Ludwig is a self-made man. His father owned a grocery store in South Dakota called Ludwig's Superette. Bruce Ludwig made his money in California real estate and is now a partner in a firm managing four billion dollars in pension funds. He has been supporting Weeks and the Theban Mapping Project for twelve years.

Over the past three, he has sunk a good deal of his own money into the project and has raised much more among his friends. Nevertheless, the cost of excavation continually threatens to outstrip the funds at hand. "The thing is, it doesn't take a Rockefeller or a Getty to be involved," he told me over a bottle of Château Lynch-Bages. "What I like to do is show other successful people that it won't cost a fortune and that it's just hugely rewarding. Buildings crumble and fall down, but when you put something in the books, it's there forever."

Ludwig's long-term support paid off last February, when he became one of the first people to crawl into the recesses of KV5. There may be better moments to come. "When I discover that door covered with unbroken Nineteenth Dynasty seals," Weeks told me, joking, "you bet I'll hold off until Bruce can get here."

SATURDAY, the workers' taxi picks the Weekses and me up before sunrise and then winds through a number of small villages, collecting workers as it goes along.

The season is drawing to a close, and Susan and Kent Weeks are both subdued. In the last few weeks, the prob-

able number of rooms in the tomb has increased from sixty-seven to ninety-two, with no end in sight. Everyone is frustrated at having to lock up the tomb now, leaving the doorway at the bottom of 3A sealed, the plaster floor unplumbed, the burial chambers still not found, and so many rooms unexcavated.

Weeks plans to tour the United States lecturing and raising more funds. He estimates that he will need a quarter of a million dollars per year for the indefinite future in order to do the job right.

As we drive alongside sugarcane fields, the sun boils up over the Nile Valley through a screen of palms, burning into the mists lying on the fields. We pass a man driving a donkey cart loaded with tires, and whizz by the Colossi of Memnon, two enormous wrecked statues standing alone in a farmer's field. The taxi begins the climb to a village once famous for tomb robbing, some of whose younger residents now work for Weeks. The houses are completely surrounded by the black pits of tombs. The fragrant smell of dung fires drifts through the rocky streets.

Along the way, I talk with Ahmed, the chief supervisor. A young man with a handsome, aristocratic face, who comes from a prominent family in Gezira Bairat, he has worked for Weeks for about eight years. I ask him how he feels about working in the tomb.

Ahmed thinks for a moment, then says, "I forget myself in this tomb. It is so vast inside."

"How so?"

"I feel at home there. I know this thing. I can't express the feeling, but it's not so strange for me to be in this tomb. I feel something in there about myself. I am descended from these people who built this tomb. I can feel their blood is in me."

When we arrive in the Valley of the Kings, an inspector unlocks the metal gate in front of the tomb, and the workers file in, with Weeks leading the way. I wait outside to watch the sunrise. The tourists have not yet arrived, and if you screen out some signs you can imagine the Valley as it might have appeared when the pharaohs were buried here three thousand years ago. (The venders and rest house were moved last year.) As dawn strikes el-Qurn and invades the upper reaches of the canyon walls, a soft, peach-colored light fills the air. The encircling cliffs lock out the sounds of the world; the black doorways of the tombs are like dead eyes staring out; and one of the guard huts of the ancient priests can still be seen perched at the cliff edge. The whole Valley becomes a slowly changing play of light and color, mountain and sky, unfolding in absolute stillness. I am given a brief, shivery insight into the sacredness of this landscape.

At seven, the tourists begin to arrive, and the spell is dispersed. The Valley rumbles to life with the grinding of diesel engines, the frantic expostulations of venders, and the shouting of guides leading groups of tourists. KV5 is the first tomb in the Valley, and the tourists begin gathering at the rope, pointing and taking pictures, while the guides impart the most preposterous misinformation about the tomb: that Ramesses had four hundred sons by only two wives, that there are eight hundred rooms in the tomb, that the greedy Americans are digging for gold but won't find any. Two thousand tourists a day stand outside the entrance to KV5.

I go inside and find Weeks in 3A, supervising the placement of more screw jacks and timbers. When he has finished, he turns to me. "You ready?" He points to the lowest room in 3A. "This looks like a good one for you to explore."

One of the workmen clears away a hole at the top of the blocked door for me to crawl through, and then Muhammad gives me a leg up. I shove a caged light bulb into the hole ahead of me and wriggle through. I can barely fit.

In a moment, I am inside. I sit up and look around, the light throwing my distorted shadow against the wall. There is three feet of space between the top of the debris and the ceiling, just enough for me to crawl around on my hands and knees. The room is about nine feet square, the walls finely chiselled from the bedrock. Coils of dust drift past the light. The air is just breathable.

I run my fingers along the ancient chisel marks, which are as fresh as if they were made yesterday, and I think of the workmen who carved out this room, three millennia ago. Their only source of light would have been the dim illumination from wicks burning in a bowl of oil salted to reduce smoke.

There was no way to tell the passage of time in the tomb: the wicks were cut to last eight hours, and when they guttered it meant that the day's work was done. The tombs were carved from the ceiling downward, the workers whacking off flakes of limestone with flint choppers, and then finishing the walls and ceilings with copper chisels and sandstone abrasive. Crouching in the hot stone chamber, I suddenly get a powerful sense of the enormous religious faith of the Egyptians. Nothing less could have motivated an entire society to pound these tombs out of rock.

Much of the Egyptian religion remains a mystery to us. It is full of contradictions, inexplicable rituals, and impenetrable texts. Amid the complexity, one simple fact stands out: it was a great human bargain with death. Almost everything that ancient Egypt has left us—the pyramids, the tombs, the temples—represents an attempt to overcome that awful mystery at the center of all our lives.

A shout brings me back to my senses.

"Find anything?" Weeks calls out.

"The room's empty," I say. "There's nothing in here but dust."

The Later Civilizations to 500 C.E.

Life in the ancient world was likely to be short and brutal. Poor nutrition, disease, hazards of childbirth, warfare, and violence all took their toll. In the Roman Empire, for example, only one child in eight could be expected to reach 40 years of age. Since people were often judged by their usefulness, long life was not necessarily a blessing. Women were often subservient and mistreated, criminals and slaves were publicly slaughtered, and unwanted children were abandoned to die. Yet, at the same time, humankind built splendid cities, formed empires, wrote history, invented sports, and created art treasures. Aspects of this growing diversity is examined in this section.

In the New World, civilization evolved later than in the Old World, perhaps due to the pattern of migration to that hemisphere and the later development of agriculture. The Aztecs, Maya, and Inca, nonetheless, constructed stone cities and developed complex social and economic institutions. Unfortunately, much of these accomplishments were destroyed during the Spanish invasion. Forerunners of these groups have been discovered at Teotihuacán in Mexico and along the western coast of Peru. Funeral art from the Moche culture, rescued from modern looters, gives an indication of the rich life and skill of these prehistoric peoples in the New World. Interestingly, it may have been climatic changes that led to the Moche downfall.

Athens, in the Old World, developed into one of the most interesting of the ancient Greek city-states and was important for the origin of modern ideas about government, art, and sport. At the center of the city was the agora, a plaza surrounded by civic and religious buildings. The modern word "agoraphobia," fear of open places, comes from this place in Greek cities. In Athens the agora served as a meeting place for merchants and scholars, as John Fleischman points out. Persepolis in ancient Persia was a more ceremonial city, a place of palaces for the empire. It was destroyed by Alexander the Great even though it surrendered its buildings and treasure without a fight. The viciousness of the assault is part of the brutality of the age.

Life was precarious in ancient Rome. The average lifespan of a female was 25 years, and for a male, it was only 23 years. There were numerous hazards, such as the smallpox pandemic that struck in 165 C.E. Some 2,000 people a day died in Rome. Life was short also for one of the most famous women of the ancient world, Cleopatra. She died at age 39 after enrapturing the most powerful men of her time. Her story has been told by others, not in her own words, with the result that her history may never reach any sort of objectivity. Barbara Holland, with a certain wry skepticism, however, tells what has happened to Cleopatra's history at the hands of Hollywood producers as well as playwrights and historians.

In spite of such mortality, the ancient world produced the earliest sports events for entertainment. Allen Guttmann, a leading sports historian, notes the murals of wrestling found in Egypt, Minoan frescoes of boxing, and Etruscan pictures of chariot racing. The most important development, however, were the Olympic Games of Greece that lasted 1,100 years, from the eighth century B.C.E. until the fourth century C.E. Even with the Greek emphasis on the harmony of body and mind, most of these early sports had a basis in military or survival skills. It was these old competitions of throwing, running, and wrestling, however, that inspired the Olympics of the present time.

Looking Ahead: Challenge Questions

Compare the artifacts found in the tombs of the Moche with those of Egypt. Is there evidence of interest in art and religion? What effect has looting had on the study of these people?

Are there places in modern life that serve the purpose of an agora?

Why did Alexander the Great permit the destruction of Persepolis while other cities were spared?

What do the sports of a society tell you about the culture of the society?

What was the purpose of sports in the ancient world?

Why have people through time been interested in Cleopatra?

What are the historical problems in finding out the truth about Cleopatra? What would Herodotus have done to find the "real" Cleopatra?

Tales from a Peruvian Crypt

The looting of a prehistoric pyramid stimulates an operation in salvage archeology, with unexpected scientific dividends

Walter Alva and Christopher B. Donnan

Walter Alva, a native of Peru, has participated in numerous excavations on that country's north coast and is the director of the Museo Brüning at Lambayeque. Coauthor Christopher B. Donnan is a professor of anthropology and director of the Fowler Museum of Cultural History at the University of California, Los Angeles. They are the coauthors of Royal Tombs of Sipán *(Los Angeles: Fowler Museum of Cultural History, University of California, 1993).*

In the fertile river valleys that relieve Peru's arid coastal plain, mud-brick pyramids stand as the most visible evidence of the prehistoric Moche civilization, which flourished between the first and eighth centuries A.D. Rising out of agricultural fields in the Moche River valley, the massive Pyramid of the Sun was the largest structure ever built in South America. With a ramp that led up to small buildings on its flat summit, it stood about 135 feet high and sprawled over 12.5 acres at its base. It once contained more than 130 million sun-dried bricks. Some of it has eroded away naturally, while part was demolished in the seventeenth century by Spanish entrepreneurs in search of rich burials or other treasures.

About ninety-five miles north of the Pyramid of the Sun, in the Lambayeque River valley, the Moche cemeteries and three pyramids near the village of Sipán have long been the target of looters. Over the years they have dug many deep holes with picks and shovels in hopes of locating intact tombs containing ceramic vessels, shell and stone beads, and rarer ornaments of silver and gold. By November 1986, they had nearly exhausted the cemeteries, and one group of treasure seekers decided to focus on the smallest pyramid. Working at night to avoid police detection, they dug a series of holes, but found little of value. Then, on the night of February 16, 1987, at a depth of about twenty-three feet, they suddenly broke into one of the richest funerary chambers ever looted, the tomb of an ancient Moche ruler.

The looters removed several sacks of gold, silver, and gilded copper artifacts. They also took some ceramic vessels, but they broke and scattered many others in their haste. Almost immediately, the looters quarreled over the division of the spoils, and one of them tipped off the police. The authorities were able to seize some of the plundered artifacts, but only a pitiful amount was salvaged from the find. The rest disappeared into the hands of Peruvian collectors or was illegally exported for sale in Europe, Japan, and the United States.

Building on civilizations that preceded them in coastal Peru, the Moche developed their own elaborate society, based on the cultivation of such crops as corn and beans, the harvesting of fish and shellfish, and the exploitation of other wild and domestic resources. They had a dense, socially stratified population, with large numbers of workers devoted to the construction and maintenance of irrigation canals, pyramids, palaces, and temples. Their lords apparently received food and commodities from their subjects and distributed them to lesser nobles and to the potters, weavers, metalworkers, and other artisans who created luxury objects for the elite. In sculptures, decorated ceramics, and murals, archeologists have glimpsed many complex scenes of Moche life, including hunting, combat, and ceremonial practices.

The luxury items from Sipán that were confiscated by the police, including hollow gold beads of various shapes and sizes, hinted at the magnificence of the plundered burial, which must have belonged to one of the Moche elite. More fortune-hunters descended on the site in search of overlooked valuables. They hacked at the tomb walls and sifted through the excavated dirt. By the time the police secured the area, little was left except a boot-shaped hole. Nevertheless, with armed guards stationed around the clock, we hastily organized an archeological survey to learn everything possible of scientific value (author Walter Alva directed the project; coauthor Christopher B. Donnan was one of the many participants.)

We began by making a contour map of the three pyramids and what remained of their ramps and adjacent plazas. The small pyramid, where the

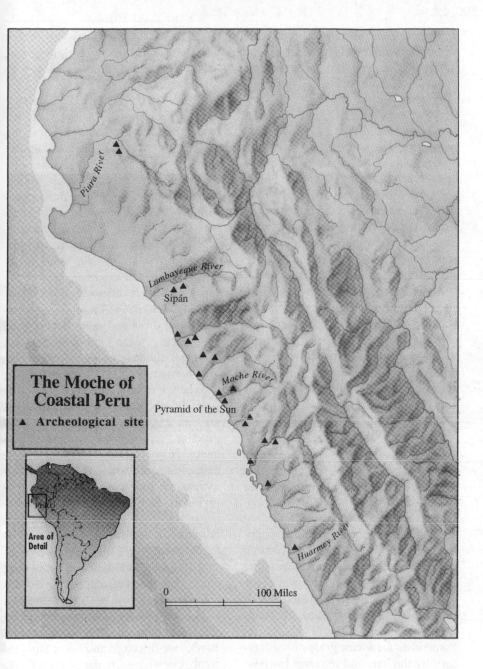

The Moche of Coastal Peru

▲ Archeological site

Area of Detail

0   100 Miles

platform with a balustrade, surrounding an open-front building with one back wall and a peaked roof supported by posts. Seventeen double-faced human heads decorated the roof ridge, while depicted in relief on the wall was a supernatural creature, half feline and half reptile, copulating with a woman on a crescent moon.

Knowing that the pyramid would be further plundered once we left, we decided to open up a new section to methodical excavation, choosing a ten-by-ten meter (1,076-square-foot) area near the summit. Here we came upon a place where the mud brick had been carved out and refilled in ancient times. Digging down, we found eight decomposed wood beams, similar to those that had roofed the looted burial chamber. Buried beneath these, in the debris of what had been a small rectagular chamber, we found 1,137 ceramic bowls, jars, and bottles. They portrayed a variety of human figures: warriors holding war clubs and shields, nude prisoners with leashlike ropes around their necks, musicians with drums, and seated figures wearing beaded pectorals (biblike coverings). Some were arranged in symbolic tableaux, for example, musicians and prisoners ringing and facing noble personages.

As we removed the ceramics, we found several pieces of copper and, finally, a man's skeleton lying jackknifed on its back, with chin, knees, and arms pulled in toward the torso. Since the Moche customarily buried their dead in a fully extended position, we interpreted this individual to be a sacrificial victim, whose body had been shoved into the small chamber as part of the ritual offering.

Even as these offerings were being excavated, we discovered a second, larger rectangular area that appeared to have been carved into the pyramid and refilled. As we carefully excavated this, we found, about thirteen feet below the original surface of the pyramid, the skeleton of a man wrapped in a cotton shroud. He lay stretched out on his back and wore a gilded copper helmet. Over the right forearm, which rested on his chest, was a round copper shield. A little below we found the

tomb had been found, was riddled with looters' tunnels, but in some places, the piles of dirt they had excavated helped preserve the original contours. The tunnels also enabled us to examine the internal construction. The pyramid and the rest of the complex evidently had been built and rebuilt over a long period of time, undergoing many changes as the various parts were enlarged. The small pyramid seems to have gone through six phases, beginning in the first century A.D. and ending about 300.

Although the burial chamber had been gouged out of shape, we were able to determine that it had originally

been roofed with large wood beams, which had decomposed. To our great surprise, we were able to uncover some of the tomb's contents that had been missed by the original looters and the subsequent gleaners. Clearing along one side of the chamber, we found the remains of a large, gilded copper crown decorated with metal disks; four ceramic jars modeled in the shape of human figures; and a copper mask with inlaid turquoise eyes. In excavating these, we also discovered a heavy copper scepter forty inches long, pointed at one end and bearing a three-dimensional architectural model on the other. The model depicted a remains of seventeen parallel beams that, we dared hope, lay over a major, undisturbed burial chamber.

The discoveries that subsequently emerged surpassed our dreams. Buried in the chamber were the remains of a wood coffin that contained the richest grave offerings ever to be excavated scientifically in the Western Hemisphere. The body of a man between thirty-five and forty-five years of age had been laid to rest with a feathered headdress, banners of cloth with gilded copper decorations, beaded pectorals, nose ornaments and necklaces of gold and silver, ear ornaments of gold and turquoise, face coverings of gold, a gold backflap and a silver backflap that would have been hung from the belt, and countless other precious objects. In his right hand the deceased had held a gold and silver scepter topped with a large rattle, and in his left hand, a smaller scepter of cast silver. In relief on the rattle, which was shaped like an inverted pyramid, were scenes of an elaborately dressed warrior subjugating a vanquished opponent. The sculpted head of the smaller scepter echoed this theme.

Working six days a week, it took us four months to document and safely empty the delicate contents of the tomb. As our original budget became exhausted, we received some partial funding from a brewery and a truckload of noodles donated by a pasta manufacturer. At one point we were paying the fieldworkers with a combination of cash and noodles. We eventually secured new support from the Research Committee of the National Geographic Society and were able to proceed with further excavation.

All the while we had been working and moving equipment around the coffin burial, we had been walking only inches above hundreds of ceramic vessels, two sacrificed llamas, a dog, and the burials of two men, three women, and a child of nine or ten. Although we do not know this for sure, the men and the child might have been buried as sacrifices to accompany the principal figures. The remains of the females, however, were partly decomposed at the time they were placed in the tomb,

as evident from the way the bones were somewhat jumbled. They had probably died years earlier and their remains maintained elsewhere until this final interment.

As we excavated the tomb and cataloged its contents, we couldn't help wondering who was the important personage buried there. The key to the answer was a major photographic archive of Moche sculpture and drawings at the University of California at Los Angeles. As the tomb was being excavated, photographs of the objects were sent to UCLA for comparative study.

Many of the objects in the coffin suggested the man buried there was a warrior. The archive of Moche art contains hundreds of depictions from which we can reconstruct a sequence of Moche militarism and ceremonial activity. We can see processions of warriors carrying war clubs, spears, and spear throwers, perhaps on their way to battle. We can see warriors in combat, apparently away from settled areas. The essence of Moche combat appears to have been the expression of individual valor, in which warriors engaged in one-on-one combat, seeking to vanquish, rather than kill, an opponent. The victor is often shown hitting his opponent on the head or upper body with the war club, while the defeated individual is depicted bleeding from his nose or losing his headdress or other parts of his attire. Sometimes the victor grasps his adversary by the hair and removes his nose ornament or slaps his face.

As far as we can tell, the Moche warriors fought with one another, not against some foreign enemy. Once an opponent was defeated, he was stripped of some or all of his clothing and a rope was placed around his neck. The victor made a bundle of the prisoner's clothing and weapons and tied it to his own war club as a trophy. After a public parading of the spoils, the prisoners were arraigned before a high-status individual and finally brought back to the Moche settlements or ceremonial precincts. There the priests and their attendants sacrificed them, cutting their throats and drinking the

blood from tall goblets. The bodies were then dismembered and the heads, hands, and feet tied individually with ropes to create trophies.

Many representations of the sacrifice ceremony exist in Moche art. Although they vary, not always depicting all personages in the ceremony, apparently three principal priests and one priestess were involved, each associated with specific garments and ritual paraphernalia. The most important was the "warrior priest," generally depicted with a crescent-shaped nose ornament, large circular ear ornaments, a warrior backflap, a scepter, and a conical helmet with a crescent-shaped ornament at its peak. A comparison of these and other details with the contents of the tomb convinced us that the individual buried there was just such a warrior priest.

When the sacrifice ceremony was first identified in Moche art, in 1974, no one could be sure it was a real practice, as opposed to a mythical event. Now we had archeological evidence that this was an actual part of Moche life. Here was one of the individuals who presided over the sacrifices. Further, because the limited numbers of objects salvaged from the looted tomb were similar to some of those we had excavated, we could conclude that the looted tomb also must have belonged to a warrior priest.

As if this were not enough, during the excavation of the warrior priest's tomb, we located another suspected tomb elsewhere on the pyramid. We held off excavation until work on the earlier find was nearly complete. The knowledge we gained made it easier to anticipate the sequence of excavation. Again we found the residue of a plank coffin containing the rich burial of a man between thirty-five and forty-five years old. Among his grave goods was a spectacular headdress ornament of gilded copper, in the form of the head and body of an owl from which arched long banks with suspended bangles, representing the feathered wings. Nearby we found the remains of four other individuals: a male between fourteen and seventeen years of age, two females in their late teens or early twenties, and an eight- to ten-year-old child. Buried with the child were a dog and a snake.

The contents of this tomb were only a little less lavish than those of the warrior priest. They suggest that the principal individual was another of the priests depicted in the sacrifice ceremony—one we call the "bird priest." The major clue was the large owl headdress. He was also buried with a copper cup near his right hand, similar in proportion to the cups portrayed in pictures of the sacrifice ceremony.

Having identified these individuals as participants in the sacrifice ceremony, we began to wonder if such ceremonies took place in Sipán itself. The answer was soon revealed when, about eleven yards from the bird priest's tomb, we found several small rooms that contained hundreds of ceramic vessels, human and llama bones, and miniature ornaments and implements, mixed with ash and organic

residues. Among the human remains were hands and feet, quite possibly the trophies taken from dismembered sacrificial victims. Altogether these looked to be the residue of sacrifice ceremonies, which the Moche apparently carried out at Sipán, as no doubt they did at their other centers.

The looted tomb, the two excavated tombs, and the sacrificial offerings all seem to date to about A.D. 290. While excavating the offerings, we found a fourth, somewhat earlier tomb containing the remains of a man between forty-five and fifty-five years old, also richly endowed with grave goods, including a necklace of gold beads in the form of spiders on their webs, anthropomorphic figures of a crab and a feline, scepters, an octopus pectoral with gilded copper tentacles, and numerous other ornaments and objects. Nearby we found the body of a young, sixteen- to eighteen-year-old woman next to a sacrificed llama. This tomb

may also have belonged to a warrior priest, but not all the identifying elements are there. Possibly, this is simply because it dates to an earlier period than the depictions we have of the sacrifice ceremony, which are all from after A.D. 300.

Moche civilization collapsed suddenly, probably as a result of one or more of the natural cataclysms that periodically devastate coastal Peru—earthquake, flooding, or drought. The Moche had no writing system, so they left no records we can hope to decipher. They disappeared before Europeans reached the New World and could leave us eyewitness accounts. Yet with the scientific excavation of these royal tombs, we have gained an intimate portrait of some of their most powerful lords. Work at Sipán continues, now at a promising location near the tomb of the bird priest. As we dig more deeply, we look forward to our next encounter.

In Classical Athens, a market trading in the currency of ideas

For 60 years, archaeologists have pursued secrets of the Agora, where Socrates' society trafficked in wares from figs to philosophy

John Fleischman

John Fleischman, who wrote about the excavation of the legendary site of Troy in Smithsonian *last year, braved Athens' summer heat on the trail of his story.*

Athens on an August afternoon: the clear radiant light of Greece suffuses every stone and walkway. From my vantage point, I squint upward to the outcropping of the Acropolis, crowned by Athena's temple, the Parthenon; hordes of tourists lay constant siege to the site. Standing at the base of that fabled rampart, I begin to traverse a quiet, heat-baked square, crisscrossed by gravel paths, dotted with the stubs of ancient walls and scrubby pomegranate and plane trees.

This dusty archaeological park, a sanctuary amid the roar of overmotorized Athens, is in fact one of the most remarkable sites in Classical archaeology. I am crossing the Agora—or central marketplace—of ancient Athens. That this place still exists seems nothing short of miraculous. I am walking in Socrates' footsteps.

The gadfly philosopher frequented this very square— as did his compatriots in the extraordinary experiment that was Classical Athens. Shades of Pericles, Thucydides, Aristophanes, Plato. They all strolled in this place—the Agora, where philosophy and gossip were retailed along with olive oil. And where Classical Athens actually lived, traded, voted and, of course, argued. The Agora was the city's living heart. Here, politics, democracy and philosophy (their names, after all, are Greek) were born.

For every ten tourists who climb to the Parthenon, only one discovers the precincts of the serene archaeological site at its base. Those visitors are in fact missing an excursion into history made palpable, as well as a glimpse into what must be acclaimed as one of this century's most triumphant urban archaeology undertakings.

Since 1931, the American School of Classical Studies has been digging here, unearthing a dazzling array of artifacts from the layers of history compacted under this earth: Neolithic, Mycenaean, Geometric, Classical, Hellenistic, Roman, Byzantine and more—all collected from this 30-acre site. Still, it is the objects from Classical Athens that seem to speak with greatest resonance.

And fortunately for those of us unable to make it to Athens anytime soon, we have a chance to see for ourselves some of the Agora's most celebrated artifacts. The occasion of this opportunity is a striking anniversary: 2,500 years ago, the Athenian reformer Cleisthenes renounced tyranny and proclaimed the birth of a radically new form of government, democracy. His genius was to offer a straightforward plan. To diffuse powerful political factions, Cleisthenes reshuffled the Athenian city-state into ten arbitrary tribes and called 50 representatives from each to a senate, or boule, of 500. This, then, was the beginning of democracy, however imperfect and subject to subversion and strife it might have been.

Hence the arrival of the exhibition "The Birth of Democracy," which opened recently in the rotunda of the National Archives in Washington, D.C. and continues there through January 2, 1994. A few steps from our own Declaration of Independence, Constitution and Bill of Rights lie the humble tools of Athenian self-government, nearly all of them unearthed in the Agora over the past 60 years by American excavators.

You can look upon actual fourth century B.C. Athenian jurors' ballots, discovered still inside a terra-cotta ballot box. The ballots, stamped "official ballot," look like metal tops. Each juror was handed two; the spindle shafts designated the vote, solid for acquittal and hollow for guilty. Taking the spindle ends between thumb and forefinger, an Athenian juror was assured that no one could see which spindle he deposited in the ballot box.

For the too powerful, a decree of exile

Also on view are ostraca, pottery fragments on which Athenians inscribed the names of persons they felt too powerful for the good of the city and deserving of ostracism, or ten years' exile, a procedure formalized by Cleisthenes. More than 1,300 ostraca, condemning many famous figures—Pericles, for instance, and Aristides and Themistocles—have been found in the Agora. Looking closely at the sherds, you can spell out the names straight from the history books and realize that these ostraca were written out by contemporaries who knew these men personally. And in some cases hated them.

Ostracism was not the worst punishment the democracy could decree. The National Archives also displays a set of distinctive pottery vials uncovered from the fifth-century B.C. Athenian state prison. These tiny vials were used to hold powerful drugs, such as lethal doses of hemlock. Socrates swallowed just such a dose, voted for him in 399 B.C. by his fearful fellow citizens. Archaeologists say the death scene of Socrates described in Plato's *Phaedo* fits the layout of a precise location in the Agora—a building near the southwest corner of the market square.

Plato recounts that after Socrates took the poison, he walked about, then lay down, telling his friends to stop weeping "for I have heard that one ought to die in peace." When the numbness spread from his legs upward to his abdomen, he covered his face. His last words were, as always, ironic. Socrates claimed he had a debt to the god of medicine. "I owe a cock to Asclepius," he informed a companion, "do not forget, but pay it."

The exhibition contains several other objects associated with Socrates, including part of a small marble statue, thought to be of the philosopher, that was also recovered from the prison. Visitors can find, as well, actual hobnails and bone eyelets from the Agora shop of one Simon the cobbler. Socrates is known to have met at such a shop with young students and prominent Athenians alike.

The boundaries of the Agora were clearly marked, and entrance was forbidden to Athenian citizens who had avoided military service, disgraced themselves in the field—or mistreated their parents. Around the open square, but outside its actual boundaries, lay the key civic buildings—courts, assembly halls, military headquarters, the mint, the keepers of the weights and measures, commercial buildings and shrines to the city gods. One such shrine, the Altar of the Twelve Gods, stood within the Agora and marked the city's center.

On business days, the square was filled with temporary wicker market stalls, grouped into rings where similar wares were offered. There was a ring for perfume, for money changing, for pickled fish, for slaves. The Agora was a constantly changing mix of the mundane and the momentous—pickled fish and the world's first democracy. The comic poet Eubulus described the scene: "You will find everything sold together in the same place at Athens: figs, witnesses to summonses, bunches of grapes, turnips, pears, apples, givers of evidence, roses, medlars, porridge, honeycombs, chickpeas, lawsuits, beestings-puddings, myrtle, allotment machines, irises, lambs, water clocks, laws, indictments."

"The Agora was a place for hanging out," according to archaeologist John M. Camp, who is my patient guide this afternoon. "You'd have men of affairs doing a little business, conducting a little politics and stirring up a little trouble." Camp has spent most of his adult life digging here, and he's tireless even in the heat. (He's also the author of *The Athenian Agora*, an erudite and delightful guide to the site, written for a general audience.) The real pleasure of studying this site, he says, is the shock of recognition. "Our own ideas, our own concepts originated right *here*," he told me, gesturing toward the bright open square of the Agora. "It's not only democracy, it's virtually all of Western drama, law—you name it. Over and over again, you find the only thing that's really changed is the technology. Everything else, they thought of it before. They did it before, and it all happened *here*."

In the beginning, archaeologists banked on hope

The open Agora at midday is suited only for mad tourists and foreign archaeologists, both on tight schedules. The tourists can see the Agora today because American archaeologists (funded in large part by American philanthropists—principally John D. Rockefeller jr. and the David and Lucile Packard Foundation) saved the site from total obliteration. At the outset, the archaeologists who began nosing around here in the late 1920s were banking on educated hope. Although the memory of the Agora was preserved by sources such as Plato and the historian Xenophon, tantalizing description was all that remained. That celebrated site had vanished at least 1,400 years before, lost to waves of pillaging barbarians, buried under layers of settlement from medieval times on.

In short, no one knew for sure where the ancient Agora really was. (Greek and German archaeologists had made some tentative beginnings in the 19th century, but their efforts had shed little light on the actual location.) The most likely site, authorities agreed, was at the foot of the northwestern slopes of the Acropolis. That area, however, was buried beneath a dense neighborhood of 19th-century houses and shops.

The debate remained largely academic until 1929, when the Greek government offered to the American School of Classical Studies a dig-now-or-forever-hold-your-peace deal. The Americans would have to demolish 300 houses and relocate 5,000 occupants. The Greek government required that a permanent museum be built for any finds and that the Agora be landscaped as a park.

The American School finally commenced excavations in 1931. As archaeologists have labored here for more than 60 years, we can read the life and times of Classical Athens in the spaces they have cleared and excavated.

Take the Panathenaic Way, for example, a diagonal street running uphill to the Acropolis. The roadway is packed gravel today, as it was in the days of the Panathenaia, the city's great religious festival. The celebrations began with the Athenian cavalry leading a procession of priests, sacrificial animals, chariots, athletes and maidens across the Agora to the temples of the gods above. All of Athens would have gathered along this route to witness the splendid parade wending across the marketplace. One Panathenaic event, the *apobates* race, in which a contestant in full armor leapt on and off a moving chariot, continued in the Agora well into the second century B.C.

With or without armor, walking uphill is not a recommended Athenian summer-afternoon activity. But taking your time and picking your shade, you can cut across the square to the base of a sharply inclined hill and look upward at a large Doric temple just beyond the western limit of the Agora. This is the Hephaisteion—a temple dedicated to Hephaestus, the god of the forge, and to Athena, patron deity of the city and of arts and crafts. Excavations have shown that it was once surrounded by shops where bronze sculpture, armor and fine pottery were made. Today the world's best-preserved Classical temple, it is a marvel unto itself. Somehow it has survived from Pericles' time onward, a marble monument to the miracle of Athens.

The temple's friezes are carved with scenes that spoke to the imagination of every Athenian. Theseus battling the Minotaur, the labors of Hercules, the Battle of the Centaurs—all images from a world where gods and men resided in a kind of rarefied complicity.

Below the Hephaisteion stood the most important buildings of the Athenian city-state. Here was the Bouleuterion where the 500 representatives of the tribes met. (An older assembly hall stood next door.) Nearby was the round, beehive-shaped Tholos where the 50 members of the executive committee of the Boule served 35- or 36-day terms of continuous duty, living and dining in the Tholos at state expense. (Those early practitioners of democracy apparently subsisted on simple fare—cheese, olives, leeks, barley, bread and wine. No lavish state dinners yet.)

In front of the Bouleuterion stood the statues of the Eponymous Heroes, the ten tribal namesakes chosen by the Delphic Oracle (and the source of our word for a group or thing named after a real or mythical person). Athenians tended to throng before this monument—not out of piety but because this was the site of the city's public notice board, a kind of proto-daily-paper for ancient news junkies. Nearby lay the Strategeion where the ten military leaders of the tribes made their headquarters (and gave us a Greek word for military planning).

North of the Bouleuterion complex rose the Stoa, or covered colonnade, of Zeus, a religious shrine but apparently an excellent place to practice philosophy. Both Plato and Xenophon said that the Stoa of Zeus was a favorite teaching post of Socrates. No one is more closely associated with the Agora than Socrates. He lived his life here. He met his death here. Xenophon remembered his former teacher moving among the market tables and stoas: "he was always on public view; for early in the morning he used to go to the walkways and gymnasia, to appear in the agora as it filled up, and to be present wherever he would meet with the most people."

As much as Socrates enjoyed the public scene in the Agora, he made it clear, according to Plato, that he was not a "public" person, that is, he was not interested in politics. This was a scandalous opinion to hold in Athens, where the real work of every Athenian citizen was just that—being a citizen. In Plato's *Apology*, Socrates rounded on his critics: "Now do you really imagine that I could have survived all those years, if I had led a public life, supposing that . . . I had always supported the right and had made justice, as I ought, the first thing?"

He had learned the hard way. Allotted to a turn in the Bouleuterion in 406-05 B.C., he was assigned to the Tholos as a member of the executive committee. And thus it fell to Socrates to preside over a wild meeting of the mass Athenian Assembly when word arrived of the sea battle at Arginusae. It was an Athenian win, but the victorious generals were accused of leaving their own dead and dying behind. The majority moved to condemn the generals to death as a group without individual trials. Socrates resisted. "Serving in the Boule and having sworn the bouleutic oath [to serve in accordance with the law], and being in charge of the Assembly, when the People wished to put all nine [actually eight of the ten] generals to death by a single vote, contrary to the laws, he refused to put the vote," according to Xenophon. "He considered it more important to keep his oath than to please the People by doing wrong."

That was the sort of behavior that could earn you a great many enemies. Eventually, three citizens brought charges against Socrates for mocking the gods and corrupting Athenian youth. The exact location of the courtroom where Socrates stood trial still eludes identification, but the place of his indictment, the Royal Stoa, has been excavated. As for the place of his death, if you hunt carefully on the rising slope beyond the Tholos, you can find the low precinct of exposed stones that archaeologists believe was the site of his demise.

The precise forces and circumstances that led to the jury's death sentence have never been elucidated completely. What is clear is that the questions raised by that trial so long ago are not dead letters. Dissent versus consent, public good versus private conscience, they still buzz about the ears of modern democracies. "I am the gadfly which the god has given the state," Socrates told his jury in the *Apology*, "and all day long and in all places am always fastening upon you, arousing and persuading and reproaching you."

The Athenian Agora still buzzes with surprises and mysteries. In 1981, on the northern edge of the Agora, Princeton archaeologist T. Leslie Shear jr. hit the corner of one of the most famous buildings of ancient Athens, the Poikile, or Painted, Stoa. This discovery was stunning good news for Agora archaeology. The structure had been renowned throughout the ancient world for its spectacular wall paintings. The glowing images, covering enormous wooden panels, lionized Athenian victories both mythological (over the Amazons, for instance) and historical (over the Persians at Marathon).

The fabled paintings were removed by the Romans in the fourth century A.D. but survived long enough to have been described by the second-century A.D. chronicler Pausanias. "The last part of the painting," he recorded, "consists of those who fought at Marathon. . . . In the inner part of the fight the barbarians are fleeing and pushing one another into the marsh; at the extreme end of the painting are the Phoenician ships and the Greeks killing the barbarians who are tumbling into them."

For Athenians, the Painted Stoa was the arena of their triumphs made visible. It was also a hotbed of philosophical speculation, eventually turning up as the gathering place of the third-century B.C. followers of Zeno of Citium. Zeno preached that the wise man should remain indifferent to the vanities of the transient world. The people of Athens associated the school of thought with the building, calling Zeno's disciples Stoics and their philosophy Stoicism. And 2,300 years later, so do we.

Stoicism is a necessity in Agora archaeology. As Leslie Shear explains, his father had, in some ways, an easier time of it here. The elder Shear supervised the original excavations during the 1930s. He had a squad of colleagues and 200 paid workmen to take down a whole neighborhood at a time. This summer, Shear has John Camp, his coinvestigator and colleague of 25 years, a nine-week season, and 33 student volunteers (American, Canadian and British) in addition to a small crew of Greek workmen who handle the heavy machinery and earthmoving. And he has his wife, Ione, a highly trained archaeologist in her own right, who has also worked at the site for 25 years.

Pursuing the Agora in the present Athens real estate market is tedious and expensive. It is house-to-house archaeology—negotiation, demolition and then excavation. While he has been busy elsewhere on the site, Shear is still waiting patiently to acquire the five-story building that is standing on the rest of the Painted Stoa.

Meanwhile, every water jug, bone or loom weight excavated anywhere in the Agora must receive a numbered tag. Every number goes into the dig's records, meticulously kept in special 4-by-6-inch clothbound notebooks. When in use in the field, these notebooks reside in an old, cheap suitcase that sits on a rough wooden desk that looks even older and cheaper. With a folding umbrella for shade, this is the nerve center for the dig. The senior archaeologists sit here, drawing tiny diagrams of the strata and the find location for every tagged item.

May 28, 1931: "H. A. Thompson commenced . . ."

It is, as Camp puts it, "dinosaur-age" archaeology in the era of field computers, but it works. Completed notebooks go into filing cabinets in offices inside the Stoa of Attalos. (This colonnade, originally a great commercial arcade in the second century B.C., was completely reconstructed in the 1950s to house the excavation's museum, laboratories, offices and storage vaults.) There the records march back in unbroken order through the decades to May 28, 1931, and the very first entry: "In the afternoon, H. A. Thompson commenced the supervision of Section A."

Looking back over more than 60 years, from the other side of the Atlantic, Homer Thompson smiled when he heard again that clipped description of the first day. He was a young, relatively inexperienced archaeologist then. Today he is a vigorous professor emeritus at the Institute for Advanced Study in Princeton, New Jersey. He oversaw the Agora excavations from 1947 to 1967.

Back in the '30s, he recalls, it took seven years to find the first boundary stone that used the word "Agora." It wasn't a thrill so much as a relief, says Thompson, who was in charge of the crew that uncovered the marker, wedged in by the wall of Simon the cobbler's shop. "We believed we were working in the Agora, but we had so little to show for it—in inscriptions—that some of our colleagues would come by and ask 'How do you know that you're in the Agora?' Well, this settled it."

Finding the second boundary stone took another 30 years. The marker lies on the southwest corner of the square. Ione Shear uncovered it one afternoon in 1967.

It is a very ordinary marble block. The faintly visible lettering runs across the top and then down one side. The important thing, says Leslie Shear, is that this block and the one found near Simon's shop have not been moved in 2,500 years. Other boundary stones have been found uprooted, buried in rubble fill. "But these two stand where they've stood since the sixth century B.C.," he observes. "They were set out at about the time the democracy was founded. In a very real sense, democracy as we understand it was invented in the Agora of Athens." He leaned down to trace the letters.

Stones can speak, although they rarely speak in the first person. This one spoke loud and clear: "I am the boundary of the Agora." There was no dispute after that. This was the word. This was the place.

Additional reading

The Athenian Agora: Excavations in the Heart of Classical Athens by John M. Camp, Thames and Hudson (London), 1986

The Birth of Democracy: An Exhibition Celebrating the 2500th Anniversary of Democracy, edited by Josiah Ober and Charles W. Hedrick, American School of Classical Studies at Athens (Princeton, New Jersey), 1993

The Athenian Agora: A Guide to the Excavation and Museum, American School of Classical Studies at Athens, 1990

The Agora of Athens, The Athenian Agora, Volume XIV by H. A. Thompson and R. E. Wycherley, American School of Classical Studies at Athens, 1972

The mystery of Persepolis

Charles-Emmanuel Doxuan

CHARLES-EMMANUEL DOXUAN
is a French dramatist and screenwriter with a special interest in ancient history.

"Just as Persepolis had surpassed other cities in prosperity, so too it surpassed them in misfortune!" With these words the Greek historian Diodorus Siculus commented on the destruction of the Achaemenid holy city in 330 B.C., two centuries after its foundation by Darius the Great. The fall of Persepolis symbolized the end of the immense Persian empire that Cyrus the Great and his successors had carved out from the Nile to the Indus.

The city fell without a fight to Alexander the Great's cavalry, who found there an amazing treasure trove: 40,000 silver talents and such a profusion of riches that, according the Greek historian Plutarch, at least 10,000 pairs of mules and 5,000 camels were needed to carry them away. Darius III, the last Achaemenid king, had taken refuge in Ecbatana after suffering a bloody defeat at Alexander's hands at Gaugamela, close by the ruins of the ancient Nineveh. At least for the time being his forces presented no serious threat to the conquerors. So why did Alexander raze Persepolis?

Had not Babylon, which had also opened its gates to the young emperor, been spared? And at Susa Alexander had sat on Darius's throne without spilling a drop of blood. . . .

FIRE AND SWORD

It is true that Alexander's army had had to fight a hard battle at the pass of the Persian Gates, which was defended by 40,000 men under the command of Ariobarzanes, the satrap of Persia. Later, as the troops marched across the plain, they saw straggling towards them a raggamuffin band of 800 old Greek prisoners, most of them horribly mutilated. They had been left with only their "useful" limbs, i.e. those needed to carry out the tasks assigned to them. Feelings had run high in the Greek ranks.

When most of the army joined Alexander in Persepolis, a council of war was held at which the conqueror came out in favour of looting the city and destroying it. Parmenio, one of his lieutenants, tried to dissuade him. Why should he destroy something that now belonged to him? And why run the risk of rekindling local resistance by a wanton act of cruelty? Alexander rejected his arguments but agreed to spare the royal buildings. Thus the residential part of the city was abandoned to the ferocity of the Greek soldiers. The Roman historian Quintius Curtius Rufus, author of *The History of Alexander*, tells how the Persian leaders, dressed in their finest robes, threw themselves from the tops of their walls or burned themselves alive in their houses rather than fall into the hands of their enemies. Bands of soldiers ran in every direction, slitting the throats of their prisoners or killing one another when they fought over the plunder. The carnage lasted several days.

Persepolis's misfortunes were not yet over, however. Back in the city after a swift expedition against a mountain people, the Mardi, Alexander decided to march against the remnants of the Persian army. Before sending his phalanxes onto the road to the northwest, he offered his entourage a magnificent banquet. It was held on the very spot where the Great Kings of Persia had entertained their guests, on the vast stone terrace where stood the palaces and gardens that had been saved by Parmenio's supplications. Wine flowed in rivers, and it was not long before everyone was drunk. Suddenly Thaïs, an Athenian courtesan famed for her beauty and quick wit, began to harangue the crowd, urging them to burn the palace of Xerxes, who had once destroyed her native city, and thus avenge Greece. Her words were greeted with a roar of approval, and Alexander, swept along in the general enthusiasm, grabbed a torch and led the crowd on its way. The revellers made their way to all the palaces of the royal city and, to the sound of flutes and pipes, set fire to anything that would burn.

Reprinted with permission from *The UNESCO Courier*, May 1995, pp. 40-43.

It is a moot point whether or not Alexander really intended to go so far. Although Plutarch seems to suggest that an outburst of orgiastic madness took place, he does not say so categorically. The historians of antiquity each give their own version. What is certain is that on the following day Alexander ordered the fires to be put out and, when a few days later the body of Darius was discovered where he had been left to die by traitors, ordered that the Persian leader be buried with due honours.

The flames of a single night did not destroy the whole of royal Persepolis. Only the superstructures of the buildings, mostly made of cedarwood, perished immediately. What fire began, however, time and neglect concluded. The walls of Persepolis, like those of Mesopotamian cities, were of mud brick, and the centuries eventually got the better of them. Persepolis (meaning the "city in ruin" in Greek) sank into oblivion. Its destiny had been both short-lived and improbable.

A MONUMENTAL BLEND

Darius I, the city's founder, was probably not of royal blood. His seizure of the throne marked a break in the dynasty and was fraught with dangers for his future reign. In order to highlight the refoundation of the empire he ordered two new capitals to be built, one at Susa, the other at Parsâ, the site of an important temple in the heart of Persis, 80 kilometres from present-day Shiraz (Iran).

At Parsa, against the side of Kuh-i Rahmat, the Mount of Mercy, Darius laid the foundations of a vast terrace 18 metres high, 530 metres long and 330 metres wide, and then began to build on it. First he built a monumental double stairway leading up to it, and then, on another terrace, a grand audience hall whose cedarwood ceiling was supported by 36 columns almost 20 metres high. This state chamber, which could hold thousands of people, was known as the Apadana. It opened out onto three porticoes, one of which looked out over the plain below. Behind the Apadana Darius built a smaller palace, the Tachara, which was used for state banquets. His successors, especially his son Xerxes (486-465 B.C.) and his grandson Artaxerxes (465-424 B.C.) continued the construction work. Persepolis never entirely ceased to be a building site. The terrace was

Royal residence and spiritual capital of the Persian empire, Persepolis (Takht-e Jamshid in present-day Iran) came to a tragic end when it was destroyed by Alexander the Great. Excavations on the site, which was abandoned for many centuries, have yielded a mass of information about Achaemenid Persia. Persepolis was placed on UNESCO's World Heritage List in 1979.

gradually covered by buildings: porticoes, a council hall, and a throne room, a harem and a treasury. The Achaemenid kings intended Persepolis to be an architectural expression of their greatness.

They brought in workmen and foremen from all the provinces of their empire: Achaemenid royal art borrowed styles from the different peoples under Persian domination. These influences, which are clearly visible, produce an overall effect that is undeniably original. A striking example of this blending is to be found in the columns which, with the plant motifs at their base, their tall shafts and their zoomorphic capitals, simultaneously recall Egypt, Ionian Greece and Assyria, while remaining typically Persian.

The blend owes much, it is true, to the personality of the first master-builder. After Darius, Achaemenid art veered towards the colossal. At the head of the great staircase Xerxes built a massive portal defended by two huge human-headed bulls. In the recesses of his hall of a hundred columns, he had himself depicted as a giant killing equally gigantic monsters. Artaxerxes, on the other hand, did not follow his father's example and opted for greater refinement. This was the time when Phidias was supervising the construction of the Parthenon in Athens, and the flowering of Greek art probably had an influence in the Great King's court. The successors of Artaxerxes, with the exception of Artaxerxes III, who added a building to the terrace, simply embellished buildings that existed already.

What did Persepolis stand for in the Persian empire? It was neither a political capital nor a centre of economic activity. Nor did it have any great strategic importance. The king spent only a small part of the year there. In autumn and winter he was usually in residence at Susa; when the warm weather returned, he and his retinue went up to Ecbatana. These were

the two cities from which the Achaemenid sovereigns promulgated their decrees, dispensed justice and conducted diplomacy. Persepolis became a kind of spiritual capital of Persia.

A SPIRITUAL CAPITAL

Each spring, at the vernal equinox, the King presided over a great celebration to mark the New Year, the Noruz. No foreign envoys were ever invited, which probably explains why neither the festival nor the city where it was held are ever mentioned in western sources. The perpetuation of an ancient Persian feast, Noruz was a religious celebration held under the auspices of Ahura Mazda, the supreme god of the empire, whose winged symbol was everywhere to be seen, but it was also a great political communion to which the King of Kings invited his subjects. Everything in Persepolis seems to have been designed to celebrate Noruz, and the ruling dynasty visited the city each year to re-establish its power symbolically by receiving tribute from the Persian and Mede nobility and submission from the empire's twenty-three nations. The ceremony ended with a magnificent banquet at which guests were offered all kinds of meat, from camel to ostrich, before leaving with the silver dishes from which they had eaten.

Today, twenty-five centuries later, only the barest of bones remain of Persepolis. A strange army of ruins, of empty door frames and the bases of stone columns, seems to gaze out over the immense plain, eternally expectant. These vestiges provoke speculation, as they have done for centuries. Since the 1930s, excavations at Persepolis have yielded a mass of precious data about the civilization of ancient Persia. But the city's mystery remains. It is not hard to imagine Darius emerging from his tomb in Naqsh-e Rustam a few kilometres away to review the Immortal Ten Thousand of his praetorian guard.

Old Sports

The Olympic Games were not the earliest athletic rituals in the eastern Mediterranean

Allen Guttmann

Guttman recently completed an English translation of Sports and Games of Ancient Egypt, *by Wolfgang Decker. A professor of English and American studies at Amherst College, he now plans to examine the diffusion of modern sports from England and America as a case of cultural imperialism.*

Every four years at Olympia, the athletes of ancient Greece paid homage to Zeus by demonstrating their *arete,* their excellence of mind and body. According to Hippias of Elis, the nearby city-state that organized the competitions, the Olympic Games began in 776 B.C. with a simple footrace, and other events were subsequently added. But the list of victors Hippias compiled, sometime about 400 B.C., exaggerated the age of the games, apparently to aggrandize the glory of his native city. Plutarch admonished that Hippias "had no fully authoritative basis for his work," and historians now believe that the games began, with as many as five different sports, about 600 B.C., more or less at the same time as the sacred games at Delphi, Corinth, and Nemea, which rounded out the four-year cycle of Greek athletics. (Isaac Newton anticipated modern scholars, estimating the games' later origin by recalculating the duration of royal reigns and accurately dating eclipses referred to by ancient astronomers.)

The true precursors of the sixth-century games remain elusive, but we do know that the Greeks were not the only people of the eastern Mediterranean to emphasize athletic ritual as a religious and political statement. In ancient Egypt, for example, from at least 3000 B.C., physical prowess was a necessary sign of a pharaoh's fitness to rule. As a representative of divinity on earth, his role required him to maintain order against the forces of chaos. A pharaoh commemorating the thirtieth anniversary of his enthronement would formally prove his fitness by executing a ceremonial run in the jubilee known as the Festival of Sed. The course, from one mark to another and back, symbolized the boundaries of the kingdom he protected. The earliest known turn markers, at the pyramid of Djoser (ca. 2600 B.C.), lie about sixty yards apart.

There were numerous other occasions for a pharaoh to display his strength and stamina. Inscriptions and reliefs testify to almost superhuman demonstrations of hunting skill, events that may or may not have actually occurred. Tuthmosis III, for example, one of the monarchs of the Eighteenth Dynasty (1552–1306 B.C.), boasted, "In an instant I killed seven lions with my arrows." Similarly, he and several other monarchs of that dynasty were said to have so mastered the composite bow (made of hardwood, softwood, and horn) that their arrows were able to transfix sheets of copper "three fingers thick."

(Modern attempts to replicate this feat have failed.) The pharaoh had to be seen as the mightiest archer, most successful hunter, and swiftest runner. An American president can lose a tennis match without unleashing the forces of chaos, but Tuthmosis III was required to surpass all mortal achievements.

In the biography of Cheti, prince of Siut, who lived during the Eleventh Dynasty (2134–1991 B.C.), we read that "he learned to swim together with the children of the pharaoh." But despite the central role of the Nile in Egyptian life, there is no evidence that the pharaoh was expected to demonstrate his prowess at swimming. Or perhaps Egyptian artists considered the physical movements too undignified to show in a representation of divinity. There is, however, an inscription telling of the amazing boating exploits of the Eighteenth Dynasty monarch Amenophis II, who was said to have steered his "falcon ship" for three *itrw* (about 18.6 miles), when others gave up in exhaustion after a mere half *itrw*. And according to Egyptian legend, the gods Horus and Seth, both of whom claimed the right to rule the universe, agreed to settle their dispute with a diving contest.

If the quantity of visual evidence is any indication, wrestling was among the most popular Egyptian sports. Murals discovered in the eleventh-century tombs at Beni Hasan depict nearly every hold known to modern wrestlers. Although the sport has a religious character in many cultures, including those of Africa south of the Sahara, for the ancient Egyptians it seems to have been a purely secular contest. A pharaoh thrown roughly to the ground would have been a terrifying portent of disaster.

The pharaohs most celebrated for their athletic achievements were the martial monarchs of the Eighteenth Dynasty, especially Tuthmosis III, Amenophis II, Tuthmosis IV, and Amenophis III. These were the immediate successors of the Hyksos, a seminomadic people whose warriors swept from the northeast into the valley of the Nile about 1650 B.C. Their war chariots spread terror among the Egyptians of the time, for whom this was an unknown weapon. For more than a century, the Hyksos usurpers ruled Egypt; once they were expelled, more emphasis than ever was placed on the pharaoh's physical prowess. Even Queen Hatshepsut, an Eighteenth Dynasty monarch who ruled as if she were a man, had to prove her fitness with the time-honored ceremonial run. A relief discovered at Karnak depicts her in the middle of the ceremony, accompanied by the bull-god Apis. The great exception was the pacific Amenophis IV (who ruled as Akheneten), best remembered for his heretical monotheistic religious views.

The Hyksos were expelled; the chariot remained. It was used for hunting as well as for waging war, and pharaohs were often portrayed wielding spears or drawing bows from the basket of a chariot. Chariot races as such were not part of ancient Egyptian culture, despite the suitability of the terrain. But later, during the Hellenistic age (fourth to first centuries B.C.), when Alexander the Great and his successors spread Greek culture throughout the eastern Mediterranean, chariot races became immensely popular in Alexandria and elsewhere in Egypt.

The Egyptians seem never to have been as passionate about horses as were the Hyksos, the Hittites (of what is now central Turkey), the Assyrians of Mesopotamia (modern Iraq), and other peoples of the Near East, who devoted enormous amounts of time and energy to their care and breeding. An obscure fourteenth-century Hittite named Kikkuli has left us a detailed account of these matters in writings sometimes referred to as *The Book of Horses*. The later Persian empire, which came close to overwhelming Greek civi-

lization in 490 B.C., had similar roots. As Xenophon and other Greek historians made clear, equestrianism was an essential aspect of the education of a Persian prince, whose skill as a rider and hunter was a warranty of fitness to rule.

We know little about the role of sports in the great Minoan civilization, which reached its height on the island of Crete between 2200 and 1400 B.C. The written language remains mostly a mystery. But few frescoes have engendered more speculation than the one excavated at the Palace of Minos in Knossos, which shows adolescents, a boy and two girls, seizing the horns of a charging bull and somersaulting over its back. Ever since Arthur Evans discovered the image in 1900, scholars have wondered whether people really performed this dangerous stunt and, if so, what it signified. Was it a contest in which youths competed against each other, like modern gymnasts, or was the bull their adversary, as in a Spanish *corrida de toros?* Another fresco from Knossos, now at the National Museum in Athens, depicts a group of male and female spectators arranged on terraces, or tiers. Whether the audience consists of assembled worshipers or sports enthusiasts is not clear, but some scholars believe they are attending a bull-vaulting performance.

Vases, statuettes, coins, and other remains of Minoan culture attest to the popularity of hunting, boxing, and wrestling. Among the most tantalizing discoveries is a fresco from the island of Thera, a Minoan outpost, that shows two boys wearing some kind of boxing gloves, squaring off as if in a modern ring. The guides in Thera call them the "boxing princes," but whether they really were princes proving their fitness for rule or merely two boys at play remains the artist's secret.

The Etruscans, whose civilization flourished during the seventh century B.C. in the region north and west of Rome, were enthusiastic about sports, perhaps as a result of Greek influence. The murals inside the so-called Tomb of the Monkey and other burial sites feature Etruscan wrestling and boxing, while chariots race across the walls of the Tomb of the Olympics, Tomb of the Two-Horse Chariots, and others. The murals of the chariot races include the spectators and perhaps the officials, at least one of whom seems to have been female. Jean-Paul Thuillier, the leading authority on Etruscan sports, argues that these types of murals represented fu-

neral games, traditionally held to honor the dead. This is plausible for many sports, but one wonders about the scenes in the Tomb of Hunting and Fishing, which include a fine picture of a man diving.

A mysterious Etruscan sport appears in the Tomb of the Augurs and Tomb of the Olympics. Known as the Phersu combat, from a word inscribed in the latter tomb, it pitted a masked man against a dog held on a leash by a second man. It may have inspired the later Roman combats of men and animals (*venationes*).

Scholars once believed that the Etruscans also gave the Romans the idea for their *munera,* combats between pairs of armed gladiators. An origin in Campania, south of Rome, or Samnia, east of Rome, now seems more likely. The precedent may have been a deadly funeral contest that had evolved from a still earlier ritual of human sacrifice. Such sacrifices would have been made to provide dead heroes with an entourage and appease the gods of the underworld. Eventually, death in combat might have been deemed a better offering than the less thrilling sacrifice of a passive victim. The Romans took the ultimate step of making a fight to the death a gruesome form of entertainment. (The religious trappings of Rome's pagan games, incidentally, were what horrified Christian theologians like Tertullian, who deplored idolatry more than the martyrdom of his fellow believers.)

Funeral games may also have been the chief precursors of the Greek Olympics. Our best early source is not visual art or archeology but literature: Homer's *Iliad*, a ninth-century account of the Trojan War, which probably occurred in the thirteenth century B.C. In Book XXIII, the Greeks, who have not yet captured the city of Troy, celebrate funeral games for Patroklos, who has been slain by the Trojan hero Hektor. Lavish prizes are offered by the great Achilles, Patroklos's bosom friend.

The first event of the games is a chariot race, for which Achilles offers five prizes, chief of which is "a woman skilled in fair handiwork." Although Greece was not the ideal place to breed horses, chariot races were apparently common in Attica, Thessaly, and other places where the terrain was not too forbidding. The plain before "the topless towers of Ilium" provides a suitable course, but the race is a rough one, with the goddess Athene intervening to assure victory for her favorite, Diomedes. (Fair play, which requires that everyone compete under the same rules, is as much a nineteenth-century concept as the nearly defunct amateur rule of the modern Olympics.)

The chariot race is followed by the boxing and wrestling contests. The first is won by Epeius, who fells his opponent with a mighty blow to the cheek. The second is declared a draw when neither Odysseus nor Ajax can throw the other. Then comes the footrace, in which Athene again intervenes, this time to favor Odysseus, whose limbs she lightens. The oafish Ajax she causes to slip and fall on offal left from the ritual slaughter of oxen.

When Ajax recovers, he is matched against Diomedes in potentially deadly armed combat, but the spectators stop the fight when Diomedes thrusts fiercely at Ajax's throat. Ajax has apparently suffered enough for a single day. The games conclude with the hurtling of the discus and with an archery contest in which the target is a dove tethered to a ship's mast. (The javelin contest, which was supposed to end the games, is canceled when Achilles, deciding that Agamemnon is

certain to win anyway, gives him the prize.)

In Homer's dramatization, we can see that the games were a form of religious ritual, an appropriate way to worship the gods and to honor a fallen warrior. The contests also emphasized the skills and accomplishments of warriors. Both themes were eventually incorporated in the Greek Olympics, although the nature of the contestants changed somewhat. At first they were aristocratic warriors, but later, ordinary Greek men also competed and the role of the full-time athlete grew.

Pelops, a local hero said to be buried at Olympia, may have been honored by funeral games, and subsequent commemorative contests may explain why the site was chosen when the official games were instituted about 600 B.C. Originally, the Olympics probably consisted of a number of events, foremost of which was the short-distance race, or stade, from one end of the field to the other (a stadium for the footrace built later at Olympia may still be visited). The other events may have included a chariot race and the pentathlon or its constituents—a footrace, the discus,

long jump, javelin, and wrestling. Other contests added over the years included longer footraces, a race in armor, and boys' events.

Neither the *Iliad*'s archery contest nor its armed combat were a part of the Olympic Games. Nor, despite the location of most Greek cities on the shores of the Aegean or on the banks of a river, were there swimming events at Olympia or any of the other sacred games. This was true even of the Isthmian Games, held at Corinth in honor of Poseidon, god of the sea.

Although the Greek athletic festivals were not the only, or even the earliest, ritualized sports of antiquity, they, more than any others, characterized an entire culture and embodied many of its people's highest aspirations. When, nearly a century ago, Pierre de Coubertin championed ancient Greece as an inspiration for modern games, he chose his model wisely. Amenophis II proved his divinity by his superhuman (and probably imaginary) athletic performance. Olympic victors, true exemplars of human physical excellence, won their immortality the hard way.

Cleopatra: what kind of a woman was she, anyway?

Serpent of the Nile? Learned ruler? Sex kitten?
Ambitious mom? African queen? History
is still toying with the poor lady's reputation

Barbara Holland

Barbara Holland, who often writes wryly about history and politics for the magazine, is the author of several books, including Endangered Pleasures *(Little, Brown).*

Until now, everyone has had pretty much the same fix on Cleopatra: passion's plaything, sultry queen, a woman so beautiful she turned the very air around her sick with desire, a tragic figure whose bared bosom made an asp gasp when she died for love. Inevitably, the best-known incarnation of her is Hollywood's: Theda Bara, Claudette Colbert, Elizabeth Taylor, telling us what fun it was to be filthy rich in the first century B.C., spending days in enormous bathtubs and nights in scented sheets. Drinking pearls dissolved in vinegar. (Do not try this at home; it doesn't work.) Lounging around on a barge, being waited on hand and foot. Sometimes the asp looks like a small price to pay.

Hollywood's queen rests less on George Bernard Shaw's Cleopatra, who is a clever sex kitten, than on William Shakespeare's; in the Bard's *Antony and Cleopatra* she's a fiercer soul, downright unhinged by love for Mark Antony. Of course, they both had to leave out her children. Everyone does. It's tough being the world's top tragic lover with four kids underfoot. Even if you can get a sitter, it doesn't look right.

The latest version, part of the current debate about the possible influences of Africa on Greek and Roman culture, suggests that she was black. The last time we looked she was a Macedonian Greek, but the black-Cleopatra advocates like to point out that since nobody knows anything about her paternal grandmother except that she wasn't legally married to Ptolemy IX, it is possible that she was black.

Most classical scholars disagree. Some note that though Ptolemy II, more than a century earlier, had an Egyptian mistress, the Ptolemies were wicked snobs, so proud of their bloodline, not to mention the line of suc-cession to their throne, that they tended to marry their brothers and sisters to keep it untainted. When they picked mistresses, they customarily chose upper-class Greeks. They felt so superior to the Egyptians, in fact, that after 300 years in Alexandria, they couldn't say much more than "good morning" to the locals in their native tongue; Cleopatra was the first in her family to learn the language.

Nobody should be surprised at such claims, however. For the fact is that for purposes political and otherwise, people have been fooling around with Cleopatra's image to suit themselves for centuries. In *All for Love* John Dryden gives us a traditional Cleo less a queen and a ruler than an addictive substance. Shaw made her stand for everything unBritish and thus deplorable. In the course of his *Caesar and Cleopatra* she evolves from a superstitious, cowardly little girl into a vengeful, blood-thirsty little girl. To underline his point he lops five years off her actual age and leaves her under the thumb of a sturdy Roman governor, forerunner of the wise and kindly British administrators of later colonies full of childish foreigners.

Of course, nearly everyone's story goes back to Plutarch, the first-century Greek biographer, who included two versions of Cleo. He knew the writings and stories of people in her part of the world who remembered her as a scholar in their own refined tradition, so unlike the ignorant, loutish Romans; a mothering goddess; a messiah sent to liberate the East from under the jackboots of Rome. On the other hand, he had the Roman story, largely attributed to her enemy in war, and conqueror, Octavian (who later became the emperor Augustus—portrayed as the clueless husband of the evil Livia in the television series *I, Claudius*). Octavian worked hard to set her up as everything scheming, treacherous, female, foreign and, most of all, sexually rapacious. His Queen Cleopatra was a drunken harlot, the wickedest woman in the world.

 From *Smithsonian* magazine, February 1997, pp. 57-62, 64.

Actually, where we can reasonably deduce them, the facts are more interesting than these exotic scenarios.

Cleopatra VII was born in 69 B.C., the third child of Ptolemy XII, called Auletes, known as the Flute Player. Egypt was still rich, then, but its ancient empire had been nibbled away, and the natives, unfond of their Macedonian masters, were restless. The Flute Player kept going to Rome to get help in holding onto his throne. He may have taken Cleopatra along when she was 12; she may have watched the Roman loan sharks charge him 10,000 talents, or nearly twice Egypt's annual revenue, for services to be rendered.

Not only couldn't he control his subjects, he couldn't do a thing with his children. While he was away his eldest daughter, Tryphaena, grabbed the throne. After she got assassinated, second daughter Berenice grabbed it next—until Ptolemy came back with Roman help and executed her. Cleopatra, now the eldest, had cause to ponder. She knew Egypt needed Roman help, but paying cash for help was beggaring the state. She knew she had to watch her back around her family. I suppose you could call it dysfunctional.

She seems to have found herself an education. Cicero, like most Romans, couldn't stand her, but he grudgingly admits she was literary and involved like him in "things that had to do with learning." The Arab historian Al-Masudi tells us she was the author of learned works, "a princess well versed in the sciences, disposed to the study of philosophy." According to Plutarch she spoke at least seven languages.

In 51 B.C., when Cleopatra was 18, the Flute Player died and left the kingdom to her and her 10-year-old brother (and fiancé) Ptolemy XIII. The reign got off on the wrong foot because the Nile refused to flood its banks to irrigate the yearly harvest. A court eunuch named Pothinus reared his ugly head; he'd got himself appointed regent for little Ptolemy, squeezed Cleopatra clear out of town and began giving orders himself.

Rome, meanwhile, was in the process of shedding its republican privileges to become an empire. An early phase involved the uneasy power-sharing device called the First Triumvirate, with Caesar, Pompey and Crassus (a money man) jointly in charge. It wasn't Rome's brightest idea. Caesar and Pompey quarreled, Caesar defeated Pompey in Greece, Pompey took refuge in Egypt. Not wanting to harbor a loser, the Egyptians had him murdered and cut off his head and presented it to victorious Caesar when he sailed into Alexandria to collect the defunct Flute Player's debts. Pothinus had reason to hate and fear Rome. He was very likely plotting to do in Caesar, too, who took over the palace and stayed on with a guard of 3,000 Roman soldiers. He couldn't take his ships and go home; the winds were unfavorable.

Cleopatra needed a secret word with him, so as we've all heard, she got herself rolled up in some bedding and had herself delivered to Caesar as merchandise. According to Plutarch, Caesar was first captivated by this proof of Cleopatra's bold wit, and afterward so overcome by the charm of her society that he made a reconciliation between her and her brother. Then he killed Pothinus. So there was Cleopatra, at the price of being briefly half-smothered in bedding, with her throne back. And of course, sleeping with Caesar, who was in his 50s and losing his hair.

How did she do it? Cleopatra's looks are one of the burning issues of the ages. European painters tend to see her as a languishing blue-eyed blonde with nothing to wear but that asp. However, there's a coin in the British Museum with her profile on it, and she looks more like Abraham Lincoln than a voluptuous queen. Most people who have written about her agree that she commissioned the coins herself and, being a woman, was vain of her looks, so even this profile could have been downright flattering. In any case, it launched a lot of cracks about her proboscis. Had Cleopatra's nose been shorter, according to 17th-century French writer Blaise Pascal, the whole face of the world would have been changed. However, there's no evidence that Antony was unhappy with her nose the way it was.

Or maybe it wasn't so long. Maybe she thought more of her kingdom than her vanity and wanted to scare off possible enemies by looking fierce. Considering the speed with which she corrupted Rome's top commanders—both of them widely traveled, experienced married men—it's possible she looked more like a woman and less like Mount Rushmore than she does on the coins. Besides, the second-century Greek historian Dio Cassius says Cleopatra seduced Caesar because she was "brilliant to look upon . . . with the power to subjugate everyone." (She knew a few things about fixing herself up, too, and wrote a book on cosmetics full of ingredients unknown to Estee Lauder, like burnt mice.) And Plutarch reports that "It was a pleasure merely to hear the sound of her voice, with which, like an instrument of many strings, she could pass from one language to another. . . ."

She bowled Caesar over, anyway, and when reinforcements came he squelched the rebellious Egyptian army for her. In the process he had to burn his own ships, and the fire spread and took out part of Alexandria's famous library, which housed most of what had been learned up to the time—Shaw called it "the memory of mankind." When the smoke cleared they found Ptolemy XIII drowned in the Nile in a full suit of golden armor, but as far as we know, his sister hadn't pushed him. Caesar then married her to her youngest brother, Ptolemy XIV, age 12, whom she ignored. When Caesar left, she was pregnant. Anti-Cleopatrans scoff at the notion that Caesar was the father, claiming he never admitted it himself, but there was plenty he never admitted, including his whole Egyptian fling, and somehow it seems likely. Giving the childless Caesar a son was a much shrewder move than getting pregnant by your 12-year-old brother; as policy it might have done wonders for Egypt. She named her son Ptolemy Caesar, always referred to him as Caesarion, and took him with her to Rome in 46 B.C. Mindful of her father's mistake, she took Ptolemy XIV, too, so she could keep an eye on him.

In Rome she was Caesar's guest. They gave fabulous parties together. He put up a golden statue of her in the temple of Venus Genetrix, causing a scandal that made him more vulnerable to the people who were plotting to kill him, as they did in March of 44. After he got stabbed, it turned out that he hadn't named Caesarion as his heir, but his great-nephew Octavian, so Cleopatra had to pack up and go home. When brother Ptolemy XIV conveniently died, she appointed the toddler Caesarion as coruler.

Here the record loses interest in her for several years, between lovers, but she must have been busy. She'd inherited a country plagued by civil wars, Egypt was broke, and twice more the Nile floods misfired. Somehow, though, by the time the West began to notice her again, peace reigned even in fractious Alexandria. She'd played her cards deftly with Rome and her subjects loved her. According to the first-century A.D. Jewish historian Josephus, she'd negotiated a sweetheart real estate deal with the Arabs and in general managed the economy so well that Egypt was the richest state in the eastern Mediterranean. So rich that Mark Antony came calling in 41 B.C. in search of funds to finance an attack on the Parthians.

By then the Romans were pigheadedly pursuing the triumvirate notion again, this time with Octavian, Lepidus and Antony. If you believe Plutarch, Antony was simple, generous and easygoing, though a bit of a slob. Cicero says his orgies made him "odious," and there's a story that, after an all-night party, he rose to give a speech and threw up into the skirt of his toga while a kindly friend held it for him. Still, he was doing all right until Cleopatra came along, when he was, as Dryden laments, "unbent, unsinewed, made a woman's toy."

Plutarch's description of their meeting on her barge makes poets and movie producers salivate. Who could resist those silver oars and purple sails, those flutes and harps, the wafting perfumes, the costumed maidens, and the queen herself dressed as Venus under a canopy spangled with gold? Not Antony, certainly. She knew what he'd come for and planned to drive a hard bargain. Naturally, they became lovers; they also sat down to deal; she would pay for his Parthian campaign, he would help fight her enemies and, for good measure, kill her sister Arsinoe, her last ambitious sibling.

Antony came for money and stayed to play. A sound relationship with Rome was tops on the whole world's agenda at the time. So, like a perfect hostess, Cleopatra lowered her standards of decorum and encouraged her guest in rowdy revels that have shocked the ages. The ages feel that all that froliving means she was a frivolous woman, and not that, like any Washington lobbyist with a pocketful of Redskins tickets, she was putting her time and money where they mattered most.

She drank and gambled and hunted and fished with him. Sometimes they dressed as servants and roamed the town teasing the natives. Plutarch's grandfather knew a man who knew one of her cooks and reported that each night a series of banquets was prepared. If Antony wanted another round of drinks before dinner, the first banquet was thrown out and a second was served up, and so on. Anyone standing outside the kitchen door must have been half-buried in delicacies.

Back in Rome, Antony's third wife, Fulvia, and his brother raised an army against Octavian. (Lepidus, like Crassus, fizzled out early.) She got whipped, and Antony had to bid the fleshpots farewell and go patch things up. Then Fulvia died, and Antony sealed a temporary peace by marrying Octavian's sister, Octavia. Within weeks of that ceremony in Rome, Cleopatra had twins, Alexander Helios and Cleopatra Selene.

At the news of Antony's marriage, Shakespeare's queen has hysterics and tries to stab the messenger, but the Bard is guessing. The real queen probably took it in stride. She could recognize a political move when she saw it; she had Antony's alliance and a son to prove it, and a country to run besides.

She had no time to loll in ass's milk

No one suggests she had a prime minister, and after Pothinus, who would? No one denies, either, that Egypt was in apple-pie order. So there sits our drunken harlot, with Caesarion and the twins in bed, working late by oil light, signing papyri, meeting with advisers, approving plans for aqueducts, adjusting taxes. Distributing free grain during hard times. Receiving ambassadors and haggling over trade agreements. She may hardly have had time to put eyeliner on, let alone loll in ass's milk, and apparently she slept alone.

Antony finally got it together enough to invade Parthia. He needed help again, so he sent for Cleopatra to meet him at Antioch and she brought the children. Some see this as strictly business, but Plutarch insists his passion had "gathered strength again, and broke out into a flame." Anyway, they were rapturously reunited, and she agreed to build him a Mediterranean fleet and feed his army in exchange for a good deal of what is now Lebanon, Syria, Jordan and southern Turkey.

Did she really love him, or was it pure ambition? Ambition certainly didn't hurt, but it seems she was fond of him, though he probably snored after parties. Sources say she tried to introduce him to the finer things in life and dragged him to learned discussions, which at least sounds affectionate.

After a happy winter in Antioch, he went off to attack Parthia and she was pregnant again. The Parthian campaign was a disaster, ending with the loss or surrender of nearly half his army.

But for Cleopatra it was another boy, Ptolemy Philadelphus. When she'd recovered, she went to Antony's rescue with pay and warm clothes for the survivors. Presently Octavia announced that she, too, was coming to bring supplies. Antony told her to forget it and stay home. Octavian felt his sister had been dissed and suggested to the Romans that Antony was a deserter who planned to move the capital of the empire to Alexandria and rule jointly with his queen from there.

You could see it that way. In a public ceremony in Alexandria, Antony assembled the children, dressed to the teeth and sitting on thrones, and proclaimed Cleopatra "Queen of Kings" and Caesarion "King of Kings." He made his own three kids royalty, too, and gave them considerable realms that weren't, strictly speaking, his to give. Worst of all, he announced that Caesarion, not Octavian, was Julius Caesar's real son and the real heir to Rome.

Then he divorced Octavia.

All hands prepared for war. If the lovers had been quick off the mark, they might have invaded Italy at once and won, but instead they retired to Greece to assemble their forces, including Cleopatra's fleet. She insisted on sailing with it, too; her national treasury was stowed in the flagship. The upshot was that in 31 B.C. they found themselves bottled up at Actium, facing Octavian across the Ambracian Gulf. The standard version of the Battle of Actium is that while the fight hung in the balance, Cleopatra took her ships and left, because, being a woman, she was a coward and deserted in battle. The besotted Antony, we're told, followed her like a dog, and the fight turned into a rout.

With battles, the winner gets to tell the tale. Octavian was the winner, and he saw Cleopatra as a threat to Rome, a lascivious creature, and himself as a noble Roman able to resist her Eastern blandishments. All we really know is that it was a bloody mess, from which she managed to retreat with the treasury intact, enough to build another fleet with change left over. Octavian wanted that money to pay his troops. She wanted Egypt for her children. Perhaps deals could be made. Antony even suggested killing himself in trade for Cleopatra's life, but Octavian was bound for Egypt and he wouldn't deal.

Thus threatened, the queen swiftly stuffed a big mausoleum with treasure, along with fuel enough to burn it down if all else failed, and locked herself in with her serving maids. It's unclear whether Antony was told she was dead or he just felt depressed, but anyway he disemboweled himself. He botched the job—it's harder than you'd think—and lingered long enough to be hauled to the mausoleum and hoisted through the upstairs window, where presumably he expired in Cleopatra's arms. Victorious Octavian marched into town. He sent his henchmen to the queen, and they tricked their way in, snatched away her dagger, taking her—and her treasure—prisoner.

According to Plutarch, at 39 "her old charm, and the boldness of her youthful beauty had not wholly left her

and, in spite of her present condition, still sparkled from within." It didn't help, so she and her ladies dressed up in their best finery and killed themselves. Octavian did the handsome thing and had her buried with Antony. Then he tracked down and killed Caesarion and annexed Egypt as his own personal colony.

The best-remembered Cleo story is the asp smuggled in with the basket of figs. Plutarch, who saw the medical record, mentions it as a rumor, wrestles with the evidence and concludes that "what really took place is known to no one, since it was also said that she carried poison in a hollow comb . . . yet there was not so much as a spot found, or any symptom of poison upon her body, nor was the asp seen within the monument. . . ."

Later it was suggested—probably by Octavian—that she'd tried various substances on her slaves and, so the story usually goes, opted for the asp, but in truth its bite is even less fun than disemboweling. Maybe she used a cobra, whose effects are less visible. But where did it go? Some people claimed there were two faint marks on her arm, but they sound like mosquito bites to me. Others insist they saw a snake's trail on the sand outside; fat chance, with all those guards and soldiers and distressed citizens milling around shouting and trampling the evidence.

It looks likelier that she'd brewed up a little something to keep handy. She was clever that way; remember the second brother. Octavian's men had patted her down—"shook out her dress," Plutarch says—but she was smarter than they were. And why gamble on the availability of snakes and smugglers when you could bring your own stuff in your suitcase? When Octavian led his triumph through Rome, lacking the actual queen, he paraded an effigy of her with her arm wreathed in snakes, and the asp theory slithered into history. Maybe he'd heard the rumor and believed it, or maybe he started it himself. It would have played well in Rome. In Egypt the snake was a symbol of royalty and a pet of the goddess Isis, but in Rome it was strictly a sinuous, sinister reptile, typical of those Easterners, compared with a forthright Roman whacking out his innards.

History has always mixed itself with politics and advertising, and in all three the best story always carries the day. But why did the man who was now undisputed ruler of the known world work so hard to ruin a dead lady's reputation? Maybe she'd been more formidable than any of our surviving stories tell. We do know she was the last great power of the Hellenistic world, "sovereign queen of many nations" and the last major threat to Rome for a long time. She might have ruled half the known world or even, through her children, the whole thing, and ushered in the golden age of peace that she believed the gods had sent her to bring to the Mediterranean.

At least she would have left us her own version of who she was, and maybe it would be closer to the truth than the others. And then again, given the human urge to tell good stories, maybe not.

The Great Religions

At the moment there are about 1.9 billion Christians, 1 billion Muslims, 751 million Hindus, 334 million Buddhists, 19 million Jews, and 6 million Confucians in the world. Most people profess some sort of religion. Although it is often difficult to ascribe religious motivation to people and events, the world religions, nonetheless, provide a moral foundation for human interaction. In some instances the role of religion is obvious, such as in the conflict between Jews and Muslims in Israel, Protestants and Catholics in Ireland, and Muslims and Hindus in India. In other situations the role of religion is not so obvious, but in any historical analysis the religious motivation should not be ignored.

Despite the various subdivisions and numerous denominations today, the great religions originated in premodern times. In the story of their development there are common themes—the relationship of one person to another and the relationship of people to a higher entity. Since development happened so long ago, there are unsolved historical questions. North of Mexico City at Teotihuacán, for example, an imposing pyramid dedicated to a goddess, apparently, was the center of a thriving city-state that led the cultural development of Mesoamerica. The culture disappeared suddenly for unknown reasons in the eighth century.

The influence of religion can also be seen entwined in the history of India. "Ancient Jewel" by T. R. Sundaram outlines the significant religious ideas of Indian civilization. This civilization, among the oldest in the world, created not only Hinduism, but also Buddhism. The religion of the Buddha, however, left India and migrated into Asian civilization. Curious Buddhist monks have since returned to India on pilgrimages to seek out the roots of their belief, as described in "Messengers of Light." The idea of a pilgrimage to a religious site is a common phenomenon of religions, and today many such seekers head toward the same place, Jerusalem.

Jerusalem, the "Thrice-Holy City," is sacred for Jews, Muslims, and Christians. All have historical claims to the city and it is no wonder that it is often a point of conflict between the rival religions. The reopening of a historic tunnel that came close to the Muslim's Dome of the Rock, for example, was a reason for riots between Muslims and Jews in 1996. Christians make pilgrimages to the city to celebrate Easter, the resurrection of Christ. Jews visit the "Wailing Wall," the remaining stone wall of their ancient temple, to pray.

As a focal point of major religions, there is also interest in the archaeology of the region in order to confirm the stories in the ancient texts. The search for Jesus as a person in history is part of an effort by current scholars to confirm or deny Bible stories, since the resurrection of Christ is fundamental to Christianity. Is there scientific proof of this event? "Rethinking the Resurrection" summarizes the current thought about the question. The role of women in the Bible is also of contemporary interest, especially for feminist scholars. "Women and the Bible" explores that concern.

Much more is known about Muhammad and the founding of Islam than about Jesus and Christianity. Islam emerged from the same background and geographic area, but the religions are much different in respect to politics. Jesus advocated a separate church with his advice to give to Caesar what belonged to Caesar. In the Muslim world religion and politics are fused. There is no separation of church and state, as explained by Bernard Lewis, one of the great scholars of the Middle East. Confucius likewise was vitally concerned about politics, but was much less spiritual. His thought from the fifth century B.C.E., however, endures as an influence in Chinese thinking. Jonathan Spence, a fine Chinese scholar, comments on why Confucius is worthy of study.

Comparisons between faiths are not easy, and the three holy books discussed by Thomas Coburn are not alike. Yet, spiritual matters have long been of interest to humankind and they cannot be lightly dismissed or cynically disregarded in the study of world history. Even in nations that profess religious freedom and emphasize the separation of religion from government, such as the United States, religion has a permeating influence. Therefore, in evaluating any nation or society, this dimension of human existence merits consideration.

Looking Ahead: Challenge Questions

What is the purpose of religion in human life?

Why is there concern about the historical Jesus, the historical Mohammed, the historical Confucius, or the historical Buddha?

What is the message of the various religions about the treatment of fellow human beings?

Why do people of one religion often mistrust people of another?

On what points are the major religions alike and different? What do they say about life after death? What do they say about relationships to government? How have they treated women?

Why is it difficult to study religion in a scientific manner?

Mysterious Mexican Culture Yields Its Secrets

Scientists explore the ancient enigma of Teotihuacan.

John Noble Wilford

SAN FRANCISCO

The brooding pyramids that rise from the high basin north of Mexico City have long mystified archeologists. Even the Aztecs, awestruck at their first sight of the monuments seven centuries ago, could not come up with an earthly explanation. Deciding that something so grand could only have been built by the gods, they called the site Teotihuacan, "the place of the gods" in their language.

The culture of Teotihuacan (pronounced Tay-oh-tee-wha-KAHN) flourished from the first century A.D. until its abrupt collapse, for as yet unknown reasons, in A.D. 750. But almost nothing has been known about the people, their origins, the language they spoke or what they called themselves. Compared to them, the other large civilizations of the region—the Olmecs before them, the Zapotec and Maya who were contemporaries, and the Toltecs and Aztecs who followed—are an open book.

Only now, after decades of plodding research and excavation, have American and Mexican archeologists begun to crack the enigma of Teotihuacan and develop an image of the first urban state in the Americas.

A thorough survey of buried ruins surrounding the monuments has revealed that this was not just a religious ceremonial center, as had been thought, but a densely populated, multi-ethnic city. At its zenith in A.D. 600, Teotihuacan was one of the largest cities in the world, with possibly as many as 200,000 people. Constantinople, with half a million people, was the largest.

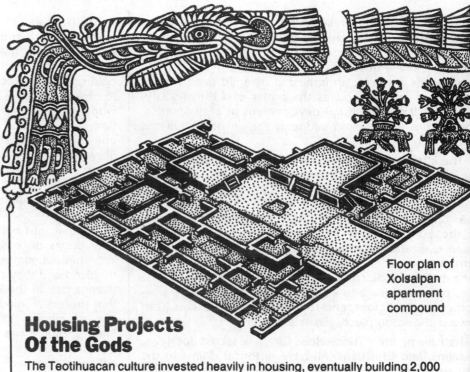

Floor plan of Xolsalpan apartment compound

Housing Projects Of the Gods

The Teotihuacan culture invested heavily in housing, eventually building 2,000 stone and adobe compounds, with apartments of several rooms arranged around open courtyards. The compounds may have housed groups of related families or people with similar occupations or ranks. The images above the floor plan are detail of a mural depicting a feathered serpent and flowering trees, from a compound believed to have housed military leaders.

Sources: "Teotihuacan," (Fine Arts Museums of San Francisco); "Feathered Serpents and Flowering Trees," (Fine Arts Museums of San Francisco)

The New York Times; Illustration by Patricia J. Wynne

Most of the Teotihuacanos lived in elaborate apartment compounds built of stone and adobe, some of which appeared to be so spacious and comfortable that archeologists at first mistook them for small palaces. More than 2,000 such multifamily compounds have been mapped, and recently several have been excavated in work that has been going on continuously since the early 1960's. No other ancient culture in Mesoamerica is known to have invested so much in the housing of its population.

Another aspect setting the civilization apart from most other prehistoric American cultures is the fact that its supreme deity was a goddess. In mural paintings and other art, the goddess is always shown with her face either missing or covered with a mask and her hands giv-

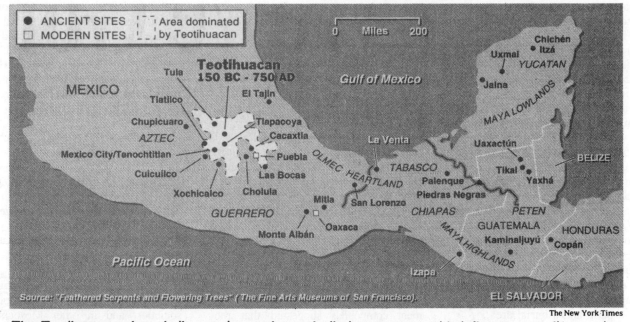

Source: "Feathered Serpents and Flowering Trees" (The Fine Arts Museums of San Francisco).

The New York Times

The Teotihuacan culture built a major market and pilgrimage center with influence extending to sites throughout Mesoamerica. It had trading colonies as far south as what is now Guatemala.

ing, in various versions, water, seeds or treasures.

In some less beneficent poses, the supreme goddess is associated with military imagery, heart sacrifice and destruction. Evidence of the mass sacrifice of more than 200 young soldiers has been discovered at the Temple of the Feathered Serpent. So much for earlier ideas of Teotihuacan as a peaceful theocracy run by priests.

A notable absence in the ruins may also be revealing. So far no lavish tomb or burial has been found that could be attributed to a powerful ruler. Nor does the art glorify any specific rulers; power is represented in mythic beings, like the supreme goddess, a storm god and the feathered serpent, a symbol of wealth and fertility. The celebration of the larger society in art and the construction of substantial housing for the general population, scholars say, could mean that Teotihuacan was guided by an ideology of collective power, with rulers subject to checks and balances—quite a contrast to the dynastic rule of other Mesoamerican societies.

"It's increasingly clear that there was no other early city like Teotihuacan anywhere," said Dr. René Millon, professor emeritus of anthropology at the University of Rochester and leader of the three-decades-long mapping project.

Dr. Esther Pasztory, an art historian at Columbia University and authority on the Teotihuacan culture, said, "It was

probably one of the most fascinating and unique civilizations that ever existed."

While the Maya, Aztecs and Incas continue to dominate most pre-Columbian studies, the nature and importance of Teotihuacan have emerged slowly from the new archeological findings. A dramatic expression of this new knowledge is the collection of stone sculptures and masks, colorful ceramics and mural paintings being exhibited here at the M. H. De Young Memorial Museum. The exhibition, "Teotihuacan: City of the Gods," will run through Oct. 31. Dr. Pasztory and Kathleen Berrin, an art historian at the museum, are co-curators of the exhibition.

At a symposium in connection with the exhibition, scholars said the new research has produced a revised chronology for Teotihuacan, showing the culture to have been older than once thought and divided into at least two periods architecturally and perhaps politically.

As early as the first or second century B.C., scholars say, some charismatic leaders probably drew together various clans to establish a religious center. The largest monument, the Pyramid of the Sun, was erected at about that time over a natural cave, probably the focus of a creation myth and the dwelling place of the supreme goddess. There is a ritual cave inside the pyramid.

"I imagine that the rulers of Teotihuacan created a powerful religious cult that

either attracted, urged or forced people to move to Teotihuacan and build its monuments," Dr. Pasztory said, adding that the people were probably promised that they were "finding and creating paradise on earth."

By the first century A.D., Dr. Millon said, this city was on its way to being a major market and pilgrimage center with influence extending throughout Mesoamerica. The city appeared to have a few trading colonies as far south as what is now Guatemala.

Teotihuacan's splendor and power would eventually be enhanced by the addition of two other imposing monuments—the Pyramid of the Moon and the Temple of the Feathered Serpent. This mythic creature carved in stone, a serpent covered with the feathers of the quetzal bird, is familiar in many Mexican cultures, scholars point out, but may have been largely a creation of Teotihuacan.

ELABORATE APARTMENT COMPLEXES

Dr. Millon attributed Teotihuacan's enduring success in Mesoamerica to "the instrumental way its leaders used the attraction of its holy places and the prestige of its religion to make it so significant to so many for so long a time."

A great change came over the culture in the third century A.D. The construction of religious architecture on a grand scale came to an end. Nearly all effort began to be directed at building permanent living quarters for the people. Since there are no archeological remains of the previous housing, it is assumed that it consisted of huts made of thatch and other perishable materials, as was the case with many other prehistoric cultures.

From A.D. 250 on, as the ruins indicate, dwellings of stone and adobe clustered in compounds behind high walls were built along avenues laid out in a grid pattern. The apartment compounds were alike in concept. As Dr. Linda Manzanilla, an archeologist at the National University of Mexico, said, each compound enclosed several apartments, each of which presumably was occupied by a nuclear family. Each apartment included an area for food preparation and consumption, sleeping quarters, storage rooms, a patio and a burial area.

A religious shrine, with decorative incense burners and sometimes mural paintings, would occupy a courtyard used by all the families. The compounds varied in size to accommodate from 50 to 100 people, usually related families. Noting that there were about 230 temple complexes and 2,000 apartment compounds, Dr. Pasztory suggested that the city was organized so that there was a temple complex for every 100 compounds.

Other archeological research suggests that in some cases the compounds were organized along occupational lines, with obsidian knappers, potters and lapidaries concentrated in certain sections. Other compounds were reserved for foreigners, one barrio in the south of the city for people from Oaxaca and one in the east for people from Vera Cruz.

In the last six months, Rubén Cabrera Castro, an archeologist with the National Institute of Archeology and History in Mexico City, has excavated an older section of the city, known as La Ventilla, situated near the civic and religious center. He reported finding evidence of a sewer system with drains running from the apartment compounds to the streets, where bigger drains gather water and

channeled it to a river. He also found traces of canals that brought drinking water to the compounds.

AVOIDANCE OF HERO WORSHIP

Many of the buildings in La Ventilla, Mr. Cabrera said, were decorated with red borders on the floors, in moldings, on stairways and at doorways. Even the murals emphasize red hues. The significance of this has so far eluded archeologists. But in a religious-civic compound, he noted, buildings were crowned with roof ornaments made of clay from which project clay simulations of three drops of liquid, possibly blood.

The layout of the city implied effective centralized control of growth and construction, and the similarities of the apartment compounds suggested that they were part of a planned state endeavor.

Gertrude Stein once wrote, "Every civilization insisted in its own way before it went away." That is, each society has its own character and approach to life, qualities she called "insistence" because they are so often repeated.

According to Dr. Pasztory, the Teotihuacan insistence can be inferred from the city's art and architecture. The early colossal architecture was created without any accompanying images of gods or rulers. When the people began to express themselves in sculpture, murals and figurines, from A.D. 250 on, much of the art was abstract or included human figures all dressed alike.

In the book "Feathered Serpents and Flowering Trees: Reconstructing the Murals of Teotihuacan," edited by Ms. Berrin, Dr. Pasztory wrote that the art expresses values that are impersonal, corporate and communal. The art, she said, "suggests that the ideology that held Teotihuacan together for 700 years as a state and a city was one that stressed the relationship of various groups to one another and avoided dynastic personality cults with a fervor comparable to the American democratic abhorrence of monarchy."

But the society was probably not egalitarian, Dr. Pasztory said. In all likelihood, it had powerful rulers and social stratification, though, she added, "Teotihuacan must have maintained a delicate balance between power, control, hierarchy and a sense of collective belonging."

MYSTERIOUS MASKS AND FIGURES

The insistence on a communal ideology may also be reflected in the culture's apparent lack of writing on a large scale. Only a few murals contained glyphs, archeologists said, and their nonstandardized forms suggest that they were too idiosyncratic to be writing.

The development of writing usually went hand in hand with the rise of urban societies, and in other Mesoamerican cultures like the Maya it was employed on pottery and stone as a form of political propaganda, describing and celebrating the exploits of warrior kings. Since nothing like this has been found at Teotihuacan, scholars take this as another indication that the culture had a different system of government from most Mesoamerican dynastic kingships.

Another defining characteristic of the Teotihuacanos may have been their stone masks. Mr. Cabrera recently excavated several of these masks in temple complexes rather than in burials, and none have been found in the apartment compounds. For this reason, it is assumed that their use was restricted to the elite or in political or religious ceremonies.

Archeologists have also been intrigued by what Dr. Warren Barbour of the State University of New York at Buffalo calls "host figures," so called because the ceramic hollow figures had "guests" inside them.

Some scholars are beginning to think of the host figures, unlike anything in other early American cultures, as representing the Teotihuacan view of the world: a sheltering deity protecting and nourishing the diverse society of Teotihuacan.

Ancient Jewel

From early Greece to the modern civil rights movement, Indian thought and philosophy have had a wide-ranging influence on Western culture.

T.R. (Joe) Sundaram

T.R. (Joe) Sundaram is the owner of an engineering research firm in Columbia, Maryland, and has written extensively on Indian history, culture, and science.

The very word *India* conjures up exotic images in one's mind. Yet this name for the south Asian subcontinent is of Western making, mediated by the Persians and the Arabs. The name used in ancient Sanskrit texts is *Bharat* (for the land of Bharatha, a legendary king), which is also the official name of the modern republic. Other familiar Western words such as *Hindu, caste,* and *curry* are also totally foreign to India. The general knowledge that exists in the West about India, its early history, philosophy, and culture is, at best, superficial. Nevertheless, since it would be impossible in a brief article to do justice to even one of these topics, I shall provide a brief, accurate glimpse into each.

India covers about 1.2 million square miles and is home to a population of 895 million; in comparison, the United States covers 3.6 million square miles and has 258 million residents. Thus, the population density of India is nearly 10 times that of the United States. (The size of classical India—which includes modern-day India, Pakistan, Bangladesh, and parts of Afghanistan—is about two-thirds that of the continental United States.)

But statistics about India can be misleading. For example, while only about one-quarter of the population is "literate," able to read and write, this has to be viewed in light of the strong oral traditions present in India since antiquity. Therefore, while a "literate" American may often be unaware of the collective name of the first 10 amendments to the U.S. Constitution, an "illiterate" Indian peasant would be aware of the history of his ancestors from antiquity to the present day.

Not only is India one of the oldest civilizations in the world, being more than 6,000 years old, but also it may be the oldest continuing civilization in existence; that is, one without any major "gaps" in its history. As the renowned historian A.L. Basham has pointed out,

Until the advent of archeologists, the peasant of Egypt or Iraq had no knowl-

This article originally appeared in *The World & I,* October 1996, pp. 24-31. Reprinted by permission of *The World & I,* a publication of The Washington Times Corporation. © 1996.

edge of the culture of his forefathers, and it is doubtful whether his Greek counterpart had any but the vaguest ideas about the glory of Periclean Athens. In each case there had been an almost complete break with the past. On the other hand, the earliest Europeans to visit India found a culture fully conscious of its own antiquity.

India is a land of many ancient "living" cities, such as, for example, Varanasi. Even at sites like Delhi, many successive cities have been built over thousands of years. Among old buried cities that have been unearthed in modern times by archaeologists are Mohenjo-Daro and Harappa.

Of these cities, the renowned archaeologist Sir John Marshall writes that they establish the existence

in the fourth and third millennium B.C., of a highly developed city life; and the presence in many houses, of wells and bathrooms as well as an elaborate drainage system, betoken a social condition of the citizens at least equal to that found in Sumer, and superior to that prevailing in contemporary Babylonia and Egypt.

Thus, India was the "jewel of the world" long before the Greek and Roman civilizations.

Nor was classical India isolated from developing civilizations in other parts of the world. Clay seals from Mohenjo-Daro have been found in Babylonia and vice versa. Ancient Indian artifacts such as beads and bangles have been found in many parts of the Middle East and Africa. India and Indian culture were known to the Greeks even before the time of Alexander the Great. The Greek historian Herodotus wrote extensively about India during the sixth century B.C. Also, during this period many Greeks, including Pythagoras, are known to have traveled to India.

Sixth century B.C. was a period of great religious and philosophical upheaval in India. Hinduism was already an established, "old" religion, and reform movements were beginning to appear, such as one by a prince known as Siddhartha Gautama, who later came to be known as the Buddha. The religion that was founded based on his teachings spread not only throughout Asia but also to many parts of the world, including Greece, and it helped spread Indian culture in the process.

In Alexander the Great's campaign to conquer the world, his ultimate goal was India; he died without achieving that objective. When Seleucus Nicator, Alexander's successor, tried to follow in Alexander's footsteps, he was soundly defeated by Indian emperor Chandragupta Maurya. A peace treaty was signed between the two, and Seleucus sent an ambassador, Megasthenes, to the court of Chandragupta. Megasthenes sent glowing reports back to Greece about India, and he pronounced Indian culture to be equal or superior to his own, a high compliment indeed, since Greece was then near its zenith.

For the next 1,500 years or so, India—being rich in material wealth, scientific knowledge, and spiritual wisdom—enjoyed the reputation of being at the pinnacle of world civilizations. Arab writers of the Middle Ages routinely referred to mathematics as *hindsat,* the "Indian science."

And as is well known now, it was Columbus' desire to reach India that led to the discovery of America. Indeed, the explorer died thinking that he had discovered a new sea route to India, while he had merely landed on a Caribbean island. Columbus' mistake also led to the

Crucible of Learning

⚜ *India's may be the oldest continuing civilization in existence.*

⚜ *To avoid misunderstanding India, it is essential to appreciate three central tenets of Indian thinking: assimilating ideas and experiences, a belief in cycles, and the coexistence of opposites.*

⚜ *India has made numerous contributions to contemporary Western understanding of mathematics, science, and philosophy.*

❖ *Continuous civilization:* Excavations at Mohenjo-Daro (*right*) and Harappa reveal well-planned towns and a sophisticated urban culture dating back to 2500 B.C.

EMBASSY OF INDIA

mislabeling of the natives of the land as "Indians," a label that survived even after the mistake had been discovered.

The Upanishads

Indian philosophy is almost as old as Indian civilization, and its zenith was reached nearly 3,000 years ago with the compilation, by unknown sages, of 108 ancient philosophical texts known as the Upanishads. These texts reflect even older wisdom, which was passed down from generation to generation through oral transmission. A Western commentator has remarked that in the Upanishads the Indian mind moved from cosmology to psychology, and that while most other contemporary civilizations were still asking the question "What am I?" the Indian mind was already asking, "Who am I?"

When translations of the Upanishads first became available in the West in the nineteenth century, the impact on European philosophers such as Goethe and Schopenhauer and on American writers such as Emerson and Whitman was profound. "In the whole world," wrote Schopenhauer emotionally, "there is no study as beneficial and as elevating as the Upanishads." Emerson wrote poems based on the texts.

One of the principal underlying themes in the Upanishads is the quest for a "personal reality." This quest began with the conviction that the limitations of our sensory perceptions give us an imperfect model to comprehend the real world around us; this is known as the concept of *maya.* Since individual perceptions can be different, different people can also have different "realities."

For example, a happy event for one individual may be an unhappy one for another. Recognition and perfection of our personal reality is the quintessential goal of Indian philosophy and is also the basic principle behind yoga. Indeed, the literal meaning of the Sanskrit word *yoga* is "union," and the union that is sought is not with any external entity but with one's self. This is, of course, also the principal tenet of modern psychoanalysis.

From a Western perspective, to avoid misunderstanding India in general, and Indian philosophy in particular, it is essential to appreciate three central tenets of the Indian way of thinking. These are:

Assimilation. In the Indian way of thinking, new experiences and ideas never replace old ones but are simply absorbed into, and made a part of, old experiences. Although some have characterized such thinking as static, in reality such thinking is both dynamic and conservative, since old experiences are preserved and new experiences are continually accumulated.

Belief in cycles. Another central tenet of the Indian character is the belief that all changes in the world take place through cycles, there being cycles superimposed on other cycles, cycles within cycles, and so on. Inherent in the concept of cycles is alternation, and the Upanishads speak of the two alternating states of all things being "potentiality" and "expression."

Acceptance of the coexistence of opposites. Early Western readers of the Upanishads were puzzled by the apparent inherent ability of the Indian mind to accept the coexistence of seemingly diametrically opposite concepts. Belief in, and acceptance of, contradictory ideas is a natural part of the Indian way of life, and the logical complement to the tenets already mentioned. It is an indisputable fact that birth (creation) must necessarily be eventually followed by death (destruction). Creation and destruction are inseparable alternations. Even concepts such as "good" and "evil" are complementary, as each of us may have within us the most lofty and divine qualities and at the same time the basest qualities. We ourselves and the whole world can be whatever we want to make of them.

These three tenets are responsible for the amazing continuity of the Indian civilization, its reverence for the elderly, and the acceptance of the aging process without a morbid fear of death.

Ironically, the culture that taught of the need to renounce materialistic desires also produced some of the most pleasurable things in life. The intricacies and highly developed nature of Indian art, music, dance, and cuisine are examples. And the Kama Sutra is perhaps the oldest, and best known, manual on the pleasures of love and sex.

From Pythagoras to King

Throughout history, India's contributions to the Western world have been considerable, albeit during the Middle Ages they were often felt only indirectly,

❖ *A terra-cotta toy cow:* **Ancient Indian civilizations featured highly talented artisans and craftsmen.**

EMBASSY OF INDIA

❖ *Melodic inpiration:* **Performing traditional dance and music in Orissa (*opposite*). Indian music has influenced Western artists, particularly in modern times. The beat of the tabla (*right*) can be heard in pop music ranging from the Beatles to Michael Jackson.**

KHORRUM OMER / THE WORLD & I

having been mediated by the Middle Eastern cultures.

After the early contacts between Greece and India in the sixth and fifth centuries B.C., many concepts that had been in use in India centuries earlier made their appearance in Greek literature, although no source was ever acknowledged. For example, consider the so-called Pythagorean theorem of a right triangle and the Pythagorean school's theory of the "transmigration of souls"; the former was in use in India (for temple construction) centuries earlier, and the latter is merely "reincarnation," a concept of Vedic antiquity. There was also a flourishing trade between the Roman Empire and the kingdoms in southern India, through which not only Indian goods but also ideas made their journey westward.

During the Middle Ages, the Arabs translated many classical Indian works into Arabic, and the ideas contained in them eventually made their way to Europe. A principal mission of the "House of Wisdom" that was established by the caliph in Baghdad in the eighth century was the translation of Indian works.

Among the major Indian ideas that entered Europe through the Arabs are the mathematical concept of zero (for which there was no equivalent in Greek or Roman mathematics) and the modern numerical system we use today. Until the twelfth century, Europe was shackled by the unwieldy Roman numerals. The famous French mathematician Laplace has written: "It is India that gave us the ingenious method of expressing all numbers by ten symbols, each receiving a value of position as well as an absolute value, a profound and important idea which appears so simple to us now that we ignore its true merit."

India's contributions to other areas of science and mathematics were equally important. The seventh-century Syrian astronomer Severus Sebokht wrote that "the subtle theories" of Indian astronomers were "even more ingenious than those of the Greeks and the Babylonians."

The scientific approach permeated other aspects of Indian life as well. For example, classical Indian music has a highly mathematical structure, based on divisions of musical scales into tones and microtones.

In modern times, Indian music has had a considerable influence on Western music. Starting in the 1960s, the famous Indian sitar virtuoso Ravi Shankar popularized sitar music in the West, and now the melodic strains of the sitar, as well as the beat of the Indian drum known as tabla, can be heard in the works of many pop-music artists, ranging from the Beatles to Michael Jackson. The movies of the Indian filmmaker Satyajit Ray have also made a significant impact on the West.

The contributions of many modern Indian scientists have been important to the overall development of Western science. The mathematical genius Srinivasa Ramanujan, who died in 1920, has been called "the greatest mathematician of the century" and "the man who knew infinity." The discovery by the Nobel Prize–winning Indian physicist Chandrasekhara Venkata Raman of the effect (which bears his name) by which light diffusing through a transparent material changes

KHORRUM OMER / THE WORLD & I

in wavelength has revolutionized laser technology. The theoretical predictions by the Nobel Prize–winning astrophysicist Subrahmanyan Chandrasekhar on the life and death of white-dwarf stars led to the concept of "black holes."

In the literary area, the poetry of Nobel laureate Rabindranath Tagore and the philosophical interpretations of the scholar (and a former president of India) Sarvepalli Radhakrishnan have inspired the West. Albert Einstein was one of the admirers of the former and corresponded with him on the meaning of "truth."

In terms of our daily dietary habits, many vegetables such as cucumber, eggplant, okra, squash, carrots, many types of beans, and lentils were first domesticated in India. Rice, sugarcane, and tea, as well as fruits such as bananas and oranges, are of Indian origin. The name *orange* is derived from the Sanskrit word *narangi*. Chicken and cattle were also first domesticated in India, albeit the latter for milk production and not for meat consumption. Cotton was first domesticated in India. The process of dying fabrics also was invented in India. Indian fabrics (both cotton and silk) have been world renowned for their quality since antiquity. The game of chess was invented in India, and the name itself derives from the Sanskrit name Chaturanga.

India's most popular modern exports have been yoga and meditation. Hatha yoga, the exercise system that is a part of yoga, is now taught widely in America, in institutions ranging from colleges to hospitals. Many scientific studies on the beneficial effects of yoga practice are now under way. A similar state of affairs is true of Indian meditation techniques, which people under stress use for mental relaxation.

Finally, the Rev. Martin Luther King, Jr., repeatedly acknowledged his debt to Mahatma Gandhi for the technique of nonviolent civil disobedience, which he used in the civil rights movement. For all India's material contributions to the world, it is its spiritual legacy that has had the widest impact. The ancient sages who wrote the Upanishads would have been pleased.

Additional Reading

A.L. Basham, *The Wonder That Was India*, Grove Press, New York, 1959.

———, *Ancient India: Land of Mystery*, Time-Life Books, Alexandria, Virginia, 1994.

Will Durant, *The Story of Civilization: Part I, Our Oriental Heritage*, Simon and Schuster, New York, 1954.

Messengers of light: Chinese Buddhist pilgrims in India

Chinese monks embarked on a long and arduous journey when they sought instruction at the wellsprings of Buddhism

Paul Magnin

PAUL MAGNIN, of France, is a research director at his country's National Centre for Scientific Research (CNRS) in Paris. He is a specialist in Chinese Buddhism and the history of Chinese thought and has published many studies and articles in these fields.

When Chinese Buddhist pilgrims set out for India on the "Western journey"—the title many of them gave to the record they kept of their travels—they could choose between three overland routes and a sea-route. Two of the overland routes passed through central Asia and corresponded to what since the nineteenth century has been widely known as the Silk Road, a portmanteau term used to describe the east-west trade routes that traversed the region. After crossing part of the arid Gobi Desert, the pilgrims had to choose between a northern and a southern route in order to avoid crossing the vast basin formed by the swampy regions of Lobnor, the Tarim Basin and the Taklamakan desert, which was notorious for its shifting sands.

The northern route skirted the Celestial Mountains (Tianshan) whose highest peaks were some 7,000 metres above sea level. This route took the pilgrims through staging-points and oases as far as Kashgar, which controlled access to the routes leading westwards to Ferghana and thence to Samarkand or the southwest. After leaving Kashgar, the pilgrims had to cross the Pamir mountains, the steep passes of the Karakoram range, Gilgit and the high valley of the Indus, before crossing the Burzil pass (over 4,000 metres high) on the road to what is now Srinagar, or skirting the Indus gorges and the Kagan valley to the city now known as Islamabad. Next they travelled through Kashmir into northern India and the central basin of the Ganges where most of the great Buddhist sites associated with the life of the Buddha and the first Buddhist communities are situated.

For the sake of simplicity, let us follow each of the major routes through central Asia by retracing the steps of a famous Chinese pilgrim: Huanzang for the northern route, Faxian for the southern route, and Yijing for the sea route.

Reprinted with permission from *The UNESCO Courier,* May 1995, pp. 24-27.

Judging by their respective travel diaries, the principal mission of the three monks was to collect all the written and oral traditions, canonical or legendary, which could add to their knowledge of the Buddha's teachings and Buddhist religious practices, with a view to their use in China. This primary concern did not prevent them from observing the geography, the customs and behaviour of the many kingdoms through which they passed. Wishing to serve Buddha with the greatest possible detachment, they also became historians, geographers and sociologists.

Faxian's fifteen-year journey

Faxian (334-420) made a journey that marked the high point of the first wave of Chinese pilgrims in India. He left China in 399 and returned in 414. At this time Chinese Buddhists were searching for their identity. No longer satisfied with the incomplete and ambiguous texts which often came into their hands during the first centuries of the spreading of the "new religion", they felt a growing need to set out in search of texts that formed part of the Buddhist canon recognized by monks living in the land of the Buddha's birthplace.

Familiar with all the mysteries of the Buddhist doctrine, Faxian discovered that the texts belonging to the monks and faithful scholars had been scattered and mutilated as a result of quarrels between the small kingdoms of central Asia, the inevitable route which ideas circulating between the West and China had to take. Most of Faxian's journal, entitled *Foguo ji* ("An account of Buddhist Kingdoms"), described Buddhist rituals and ethics as he saw them. He also interpreted the basic notions of Buddhist teaching. Most of all Faxian wished to obtain a complete set of the Buddhist rules of discipline, or *vinayas,* which were sorely missing in China when he began his journey.

Thanks to the efforts of Faxian and other foreign pilgrims and monks who arrived in China around the same time as he returned there, at the beginning of the fifth century Chinese monks had access to *vinayas* of all the main schools of Indian Buddhism, to the founding sutras—the Lotus, Vimalakirti and Nirvana sutras—and also to the Amitabha Sutra, the fundamental scripture of the Pure Land Buddhist faith, and the Perfection of Wisdom sutra, from which the whole of Chinese Buddhism would draw inspiration.

Huanzang, the prodigal monk

Huanzang (596-664), who went to India in 629 by the route running north of the Taklamakan desert, is the best-known of all Chinese pilgrims. His fame is not only due to his great record of his travels, which has been translated into several Western languages, but also to Wu Cheng'en's novel, published around 1570 in the Ming Dynasty under the title *Hiyou Ji* ("Journey to the West"), which recounted the imaginary adventures of Huanzang and his strange companion, the monkey king Sun Wukong.

A native of Henan province, Huanzang took the vows at a monastery in Luoyang when he was thirteen years old. Famed for his erudition, he was extremely aware of the ambiguities and contradictions in the Buddhist texts used in the monasteries. To solve the problems involved in understanding these texts, he decided to go to India. In 629, without a travel permit from the Emperor, he left Chang'an by stealth and set out on the longest route that a pilgrim had hitherto taken.

Between 635 and 641, Huanzang travelled through India, visiting all the great Buddhist sanctuaries and teaching the doctrine of Mahayana (or "Great Vehicle") Buddhism. In 643, he decided to return to China by way of the Pamir mountains and the route running south of the Taklamakan desert. In 645 he arrived at the gates of Chang'an, the T'ang capital, where he received a tumultuous welcome from the population. With him was a twenty-horse caravan laden with texts, relics and icons destined to enlighten the minds of his contemporaries and to increase their faith.

Not only did Emperor Taizong of the Tang Dynasty forgive Huanzang for having left the country without a travel permit, he assigned him a team of collaborators, including the prime minister and several high officials, with instructions to translate the mass of Sanskrit Buddhist texts the pilgrim had brought back. The emperor appointed him Grand Master of the Temple of Benevolence *(Ci'en si),* which was inaugurated in 648, and organized a magnificent ceremony at court to celebrate the event. It was on Huanzang's advice that the famous Pagoda of the Wild Goose was built in 652 to house all the Buddhist texts.

An influential figure in the history of Chinese Buddhism (he was responsible for around a quarter of all the translations of Sanskrit texts into Chinese), Huanzang was also the author of an important book, "Memoirs on the western regions during the period of the great Tang dynasty", which presented a wealth of detailed and precise data about the regions he had visited—their physical and human geography, their customs and economic life, and the situation of the Buddhist communities there. Huanzang also bequeathed to the Chinese the manuscript of a fine metaphysical and epistemological treatise, *Yogacaryabhumisastra* ("The Lands of the Yoga Masters").

Yijing's passage to India

The third great Chinese pilgrim to India was Yijing (635-713), who travelled there by boat. His journal is interesting for other reasons than those of his eminent predecessors in that he described the practical rules and institutions of Buddhist communities not only in India (although he went no further westward than Benares), but above all in southeast Asia, part of which was under the domination of the Sailendra dynasty based at Srivijaya. It was this dynasty which produced the magnificent sculptures of Borobudur in Java.

Yijing recorded all his observations in his *Nanhai jigui neifa zhuan* ("Account of Buddhism, sent from the South Seas"). This book and his "Memoirs" (see box below) should not make us forget that Yijing is also credited with the translation of more than fifty texts and that he introduced to the Chinese the longest and most detailed of the codes of discipline, the *vinaya* of the Mulasarvastivadin.

Yijing seems to have wanted to clear away any ambiguities that may have surrounded the pilgrims' intentions. "We are not looking for personal gratification," he wrote, "nor are we asking Heaven for posthumous glory. We have sworn to sacrifice this body exposed to dangers in order to search for the victorious doctrine. We all hope to satisfy our passion for spreading the Light."

Indifferent to honours and high living though they were, pilgrims still needed basic provisions. They took with them objects and food products that could be exchanged en route. Many received substantial allowances from generous donors. Once equipped, they had to be prepared to face up to many natural hazards, difficult situations arising from revolts and wars between the different regions and kingdoms through which they traveled, as well as sickness, which claimed the lives of many of them and to which the youngest were not always the most immune. All these difficulties and risks were well known. The pressures on potential pilgrims were so great that some gave up at the last minute before setting out, while others dropped out before reaching their destination.

Places of worship and study

Chinese pilgrims stayed in India for a long period because they had so much to do and so many sites to visit as they followed in the Buddha's footsteps. Four holy places held particularly strong claims to their veneration.

They visited the Buddha's birthplace, in the Lumbini Park at Kapilavastu, where the celebration of his birth took place on the eighth day of the fourth month. Kapilavastu was also associated with the memory of the departure of the future Buddha when he stealthily left his family in order to seek the Way, an event celebrated on the eighth day of the second month. The third celebration was held on the 15th of the

---

PILGRIMS IN PERIL

In the time that elapsed between Faxian and Huanzang, there were pilgrims who passed through the purple barrier (the Great Wall) and walked on alone; others crossed the great sea and travelled companionless. Not one of them failed to devote all his thoughts to the sacred vestiges of the Buddha or to prostrate himself to pay the ritual honours. All were intent on returning to express their gratitude to their father, their mother, the Tathagata (the Buddha) and their master in the law by spreading hope.

However the triumphal Way was hedged with difficulties; the holy places were faraway and vast. For the dozens who grew and flourished, and for several who dared, there was hardly one who bore fruits and gave real results. And there were few who completed their task!

The real cause was the immensities of the rocky deserts [leading to] the Land of the Elephant (Buddha and India), the great rivers and the brilliance of the sun which spits out its ardour; or the mass of water of the waves raised by the *makara*, a gigantic fish; the enormous gulfs and the waves which rise and swell up to the sky. Walking alone beyond the Iron Gates [a narrow path bordered by steep cliffs between Samarkand and Balkh], they travelled among ten thousand mountains and fell over precipices; navigating alone beyond the Copper Columns [erected by the Chinese General Ma Yuan in the year 42 at the border of China and the former Tonkin], they crossed the thousand rivers [an allusion to what are now Thailand and Cambodia] and some lost their lives. Others had no food for several days or ceased to drink for several mornings.

This is what it means to deny the principle of one's existence, to discard good health because of pain and weariness. This is why those who left were more than fifty in number; only a handful of men survived.

YIJING

Da Tang xiyu qiufa gaoseng zhuan (689-692, "Memoirs written at the time of the Great Tang Dynasty on eminent religious men who went in search of the Law in the countries of the West").

first month to venerate "Setting in Motion the Wheel of the Truth" in the Deer Park, Mgrdava, northwest of Benares and now called Sarnath. It was there that the Buddha, shortly after his Enlightenment at Uruvela under the Bodhi tree, presented the essence of his experience of the Four Noble Truths to the five companions who had followed him in his life as a wandering ascetic. The fourth event, celebrated on the 15th of the second month, marked the Buddha's entry into complete extinction, *parinirvana,* in the woods of Sala.

Many Chinese monks also visited Nalanda, the chief centre for training in monastic life and the study of Buddhist texts. Yijing gave the Chinese a detailed description of it and suggested that they should build an imitation.

When they reached these sites associated with so many historical and sacred events, the pilgrims performed all kinds of rituals to express their veneration. Yijing's own conduct was an example of what the pilgrims achieved as they followed in the Buddha's footsteps.

One highly important aspect of the pilgrimage of Chinese monks to India that should not be forgotten is their quest for instruction by the best teachers, who could help them to achieve perfect understanding of the texts of the different schools of Buddhism. In order to derive as much benefit as possible from this teaching, many of the pilgrims studied Sanskrit so successfully that they won the acclaim of the Indian monks. After they had been in India for a time, many Chinese pilgrims were invited to preach and expound the great Buddhist texts in the local language. Kings, princes and the superiors of large monasteries organized important ceremonies at which the pilgrims preached.

The thrice-holy city

Jerusalem is a magnet for Jewish, Christian and Muslim pilgrims from all over the world

Annie Laurent

ANNIE LAURENT is a French writer and journalist who specializes in the Middle East. She is the author (with Antoine Basbous) of *Guerres secrètes au Liban* ("Secret Wars in Lebanon") published by Gallimard, Paris, 1987.

Jerusalem enjoys the unique privilege of being holy three times over—for Jews, Christians and Muslims.

The Jews learn in the Torah (a Hebrew translation of the Greek word "Pentateuch", designating the first five books of the Bible) that at the end of time the Messiah announced by the prophets will appear on Mount Zion—one of the seven hills of Jerusalem, once the "City of David"—and that all peoples will become one. In order to be as near to the fulfilment of this prediction as possible, believing Jews the world over dream of being buried in the cemetery on the side of this sacred hill. Until then, it is written that Jews must remain "a holy nation and a people of priests", and not merge into other nations. This is one of the underlying reasons for the foundation of the state of Israel as both a temporal and a spiritual kingdom with Jerusalem as its "eternal" capital.

Christians refer to the Revelation of St. John the Divine in the New Testament and believe that the earthly Jerusalem will be transformed into a heavenly city. Except for the short-lived "Kingdom of Jerusalem" in the eleventh and twelfth centuries, which was established after the city was taken by the Crusaders, Christians have never placed the city on a political footing. They venerate Jerusalem only for its role in the coming of Christianity and for the memories associated with this. It is there that Jesus Christ, the Son of God, took on human form to redeem the world and experienced the most painful and the most glorious moments of his earthly existence, notably the crucifixion and the resurrection.

According to Muslim tradition, the faithful await the coming of Muhammad on the Temple esplanade, where he will meet Abraham, Moses and Jesus (in the Qur'an Jesus is only referred to as a prophet) and pray with them as a harbinger of the last judgment and the resurrection. But Jerusalem means something more to Muslims. As Muhammad's destination on the night of the mystic journey during which he was carried to heaven on his mare, it is the third most holy site in Islam after Mecca and Medina. Because it is recorded in the Qur'an, this episode is accepted as an absolute truth: "Glory be to Him, who carried His servant by night from the Holy Mosque to the Further Mosque the precincts of which We have blessed, that We might show him some of Our signs." (Surah XVII).

Tens of thousands of faithful pilgrims belonging to the three major monotheistic religions flock to Jerusalem all the year round, transforming the city into an astonishingly colourful canvas of human diversity. The effect is intensified by the fact that the main holy sites are concentrated in the Old City, a relatively small area surrounded by four kilometres of ramparts. The Old City (East Jerusalem) has four districts (Jewish, Muslim, Christian and Armenian), and was under Jordanian rule between 1948, when the state of Israel was created and the first Israelo-Arab war took place, and 1967, when it was conquered by the Israelis during the Six-Day War. Since 1967 the Israelis have controlled the pilgrimage process.

The Wailing Wall

Temple Mount is a site of supreme importance for the Jews. The famous edifice that protected the Holy of Holies was rebuilt by Herod I the Great in 37 B.C. on the ruins of the First Temple built by Solomon. All that remains of Herod's temple, which was destroyed by the Roman legions of Titus in 70 A.D., is a twelve-metre-high foundation wall familiarly known as the "Wailing Wall", which the Israelites had sworn never to abandon.

The dilapidated quarter in which the Wall stood until 1967 has been torn down and replaced by a broad paved esplanade. Pious Jews fervently wish for the Temple to be rebuilt, but this is impossible since it would mean demolishing Muslim sanctuaries that have since been built on the site. A synagogue and a rabbinical school have also been built near the foundations of the Temple.

The Noble Holy Place

The raised platform once occupied by the Jewish Temple became the Muslims' *al-Haram ash-Sharif* ("The Noble Holy Place"). In 636 Jerusalem was captured by Caliph Umar, one of whose successors, Abd al-Malik, built an octagonal-shaped mosque on the site to house the rock where Muhammad is reputed to have had his dream. This is why the building is known as the "Dome of the Rock". As the French writer René de Chateaubriand noted in his *Itinéraire de Paris à Jérusalem* ("Journey from Paris to Jerusalem"), only Muslims were allowed access to the platform, and if the nineteenth-century French traveler Pierre Loti was privileged to walk beneath the Dome of the Rock, it was because he received a special dispensation from the Pasha of Jerusalem.

Today the "Noble Holy Place" is open to everyone except on Fridays, the Muslim day of special congregational prayer, and on Islam's great feast days (the Mawlid, which commemorates Muhammad's birthday, and the Id-al-Fitr, which marks the end of Ramadan). The gatherings do not, however, take place at the Dome but at the nearby al-Aqsa mosque, which was built around the same time.

Al-Aqsa draws from all over the East a growing number of the faithful, who mingle with the early morning crowds of Palestinians who ride in from the outlying villages of the West Bank and Gaza in hired coaches. On most mornings the atmosphere is fairly relaxed, but on Fridays it is tense because entrance into the "Noble Holy Place" is carefully screened by Israeli soldiers posted in front of the wooden gate leading into it. Many of the faithful are not admitted either because they are suspected of being activists or because there are too many of them. The excluded have to be content to pray packed together in the nearby streets.

The Holy Sepulchre

Christian pilgrims flow into Jerusalem during the main Christian festivals, Easter being the most popular because of the importance of the events remembered at that moment in the Christian year. Their first destination is the Church of the Holy Sepulchre which was begun by St.

Helena, the mother of the Emperor Constantine. This huge, dark building covers Calvary, the small outcrop where Christ was crucified, and the tomb fifty paces away where he was buried and from which he arose on the third day. Chateaubriand noted that the church, "consisting of several churches built on uneven ground and lit by a multitude of lamps, is par-ticularly mystical. A darkness reigns there that fosters piety and inner reflection."

For centuries, the hierarchies of different denominations have disputed the guardianship of the Christian holy places. Unable to reach agreement, they have made ad hoc arrangements about the occupation of time and space. Franciscan "Custodians of the Holy Land" rub shoulders with Greek and Russian patriarchs, Coptic and Abyssinian monks from Egypt and Ethiopia, Maronites and Melchites from Lebanon, Armenians and Nestorian priests from Syria and Iraq. To add to this mosaic of Christianity are Christians from the English-speaking world, including Mormons, Anglicans and other Protestants, who do not actually have any rights over the holy places but possess a historical, cultural and liturgical heritage in the Old City which they jealously protect.

The Way of the Cross, a Good Friday procession through narrow streets (the *Via Dolorosa*) whose shops remain open, takes place in an atmosphere of indescribable confusion. In reaction to such difficulties a growing number of Christian pilgrims prefer to visit Jerusalem "out of season" when they can fully benefit from the silence of the holy places that are so dear to them.

THE ROADS OF FAITH

As part of the World Decade for Cultural Development, UNESCO has launched a "Roads of Faith" project as a tribute to Jerusalem's international, intercultural and inter-religious importance and to make the city a centre of peace and understanding among people.

Launched in 1991, the project has acquired new significance in the light of the peace talks between Israel and the Arab countries. Mr. Doudou Diène, UNESCO's Director for Intercultural Projects, notes that it could open up new possibilities for UNESCO to contribute to the peace process through an attempt to rediscover the network of relationships woven in the past between the three monotheistic religions.

Rethinking the Resurrection

KENNETH L. WOODWARD

F CHRIST IS NOT RAISED, SAINT Paul wrote in his first letter to the Corinthians, "then our preaching is in vain and so is your faith." This is the week Christians round the world gather to remember the passion and death of Jesus on a criminal's cross. Once again, the familiar story will be relived in liturgy, sermon and song: the somberness of Good Friday, the tomblike silence of Holy Saturday, followed by the radiance of Easter Sunday proclaiming Christ's resurrection to a new life by the power of God. As the Apostle Paul insisted, the Risen Christ is the center of the Christian faith, the mystery without which there would be no church, no hope of eternal life, no living Christ to encounter in eucharistic bread and wine. By any measure, the resurrection of Jesus is the most radical of Christian doctrines. His teachings, his compassion for others, even his martyr's death—all find parallels in other stories and religious traditions. But of no other historical figure has the claim been made persistently that God has raised him from the dead.

From the very beginning, the resurrection of Jesus was met by doubt and disbelief. To the Jews of Biblical Jerusalem, it was simply blasphemous for the renegade Christians to claim that a crucified criminal was the Messiah. To the cultivated Greeks, who believed in the soul's immortality, the very idea of a resurrected body was repugnant. Even among Gnostic Christians of the second cen-

> *When they reached the place called The Skull, there they crucified him and the two criminals, one on his right, the other on his left. Jesus said, 'Father, forgive them; they do not know what they are doing.'*
>
> LUKE 23: 33-34

tury, the preferred view was that Jesus was an immortal spirit who merely discarded his mortal cloak. And yet, if the New Testament is to be believed, it was the appearance of the resurrected Christ that lit the flame of Christian faith, and the power of the Holy Spirit that fired a motley band of fearful disciples to proclaim the Risen Jesus throughout the Greco-Roman world. According to the late German Marxist philosopher, Ernst Bloch, "It wasn't the morality of the Sermon on the Mount which enabled Christianity to conquer Roman paganism, but the belief that Jesus had been raised from the dead. In an age when Roman senators vied to see who could get the most blood of a steer on their togas—thinking that would prevent death—Christianity was in competition for eternal life, not morality."

Christianity won, but the battle for the spiritual imagination is never ending. Every generation reinterprets for itself the meaning of Jesus; it's one way to keep faith—and its traditions—alive. While believers head for church and even lapsed Christians prepare holiday lambs, this season academics, most of them committed Christians, do battle. Over the past five years, scholars have published more than two dozen books and scores of footnoted articles, initiating a fierce debate over the Risen Jesus. In their relentless search for "the historical Jesus," various Biblical scholars argue that the Gospel stories of the empty tomb and Jesus' post-resurrection appearances are fictions devised long after his death to justify claims of his divinity. To hear them tell it, the Resurrection is an embarrassment to the modern mind and a disservice to the itinerant Jewish preacher from rural Galilee.

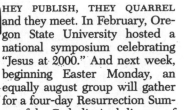

THEY PUBLISH, THEY QUARREL and they meet. In February, Oregon State University hosted a national symposium celebrating "Jesus at 2000." And next week, beginning Easter Monday, an equally august group will gather for a four-day Resurrection Summit at the seminary of the Catholic Archdiocese of New York. They will present an assortment of theological and philosophical papers. At St. Patrick's Cathedral they will listen to two sopranos from the Metropolitan Opera. And they will publish yet another book.

Now as before, Jesus lives in controversy. The questioning could not be more basic, more subversive, or more relevant to believers and professional critics alike. What can be known about the real Jesus? Can the historical Jesus be separated from the Risen Christ of faith? Does Christianity owe its origins to the Resurrection? What do Christians mean when they claim that Jesus rose from the dead and ascended into heaven? Must a Christian believe in Jesus' bodily resurrection?

For answers, the scholars deploy the tools at hand. They search for traces of a historical figure who did not leave behind contemporaneous accounts. They apply the critical tools of today: text chopping, psychological speculation and colleague-bashing. And then they take leaps of faith, often of their own creation. Of the dozens of recent books denying the resurrection stories, many are written by liberal scholars who think the time has come to replace the "cultic" Jesus of Christian worship with the "real" Jesus unearthed by academic research. Theirs is not disinterested historical investigation but scholarship with a frankly missionary purpose: by reconstructing the life of Jesus they hope to show that belief in the bodily resurrection of Jesus is a burden to the Christian faith and deflects attention from his role as social reformer.

Most Christians still believe in the Risen Jesus. For fundamentalists, the Bible is as good as its word, whichever translation happens to be in use. Since the Scriptures say Jesus returned physically from the dead, then that's what happened. But very few Christians are literalists on this point, and among Christians there is a range of opinion on what the Resurrection means. For example, a Harris poll taken in 1994 found that 87 percent of Americans believe that Jesus was raised from the dead. But a survey conducted last month by the Barna Research Group, a conservative Christian organization in Glendale, Calif., finds that 30 percent of "born again" Christians do not believe that Jesus "came back to physical life after he was crucified."

Nor does German New Testament scholar Gerd Ludemann, a visiting professor at Vanderbilt Divinity School. To him, the Resurrection is "an empty formula" that must be rejected by anyone holding a "scientific world view." In his latest book, "What Really Happened to Jesus: A Historical Approach to the Resurrection" *(147 pages. Westminster John Knox Press),* Ludemann argues that Jesus' body "rotted away" in the tomb. The Risen Christ that appeared to the Apostle Peter, according to Ludemann, whose book evoked a roar of protest from German Christians, was a subjective "vision" produced by Peter's overwhelming grief and "guilt" for having denied Jesus when he was arrested. For the Apostle Paul, who had previously persecuted Christians, his vision of the Risen Jesus was the resolution of an unconscious "Christ complex." And what the New Testament describes as Jesus' appearance to "more than 500" followers was a "mass ecstasy." In short, modern psychology reduces the Risen Christ to a series of interpsychic experiences that produced in the disciples a renewed sense of missionary zeal and spiritual self-confidence.

For John Dominic Crossan, a prolific Biblical scholar at DePaul University in Chicago and a former Roman Catholic priest, the tomb of Jesus was indeed empty. The reason: his body had been already been devoured by wild dogs—a fate, claims Crossan, typical of crucified Roman criminals. There were no post-Resurrection appearances either, not even visions or ecstacies; Crossan does not believe that any of these stories from the New Testament have historical roots. In his most recent book, "Who Killed Jesus?" *(238 pages. Harper-Collins),* Crossan argues that "the Easter faith . . . did not begin on Easter Sunday." Rather, it began during Jesus' lifetime in rural Galilee. According to Crossan's historical reconstruction, Jesus was a peasant philosopher preaching an inclusive kingdom of God among Israel's outcasts. Although Jesus' revolutionary agenda challenged the Jewish religious establishment of his day, Crossan insists that only the Romans were responsible for his death. Eventually, the original Jesus movement died, too, the victim of a developing Christian establishment that transformed the human Jesus into a divine son of God.

Sound familiar? In many of their basic conclusions, contemporary questers for the historical Jesus echo the findings of earlier generations of Biblical skeptics. More than 150 years ago, David Friedrich Strauss published "The Life of Jesus Critically Examined," which argued that the early Christians applied to Jesus all the myths that had accumulated about the expected Messiah. Today, scholars in search of the Jesus behind the "myths" have more exacting historical-critical tools for dis-

---

MARK 15: 44-46 *Pilate, astonished that he should have died so soon, summoned the centurion and enquired if he had been dead for some time. Having been assured of this by the centurion, he granted the corpse to Joseph who bought a shroud, took Jesus down from the cross, wrapped him in the shroud and laid him in a tomb which had been hewn out of the rock. He then rolled a stone against the entrance to the tomb.*

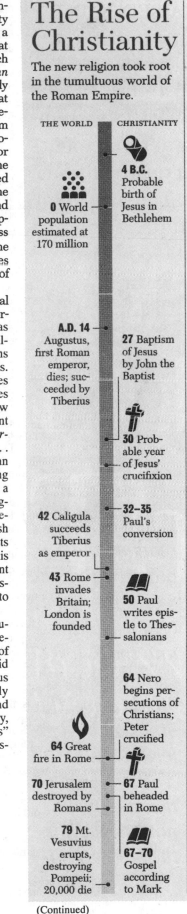

The Rise of Christianity

The new religion took root in the tumultuous world of the Roman Empire.

THE WORLD	CHRISTIANITY
	4 B.C. Probable birth of Jesus in Bethlehem
0 World population estimated at 170 million	
A.D. 14 Augustus, first Roman emperor, dies; succeeded by Tiberius	**27** Baptism of Jesus by John the Baptist
	30 Probable year of Jesus' crucifixion
42 Caligula succeeds Tiberius as emperor	**32–35** Paul's conversion
43 Rome invades Britain; London is founded	**50** Paul writes epistle to Thessalonians
	64 Nero begins persecutions of Christians; Peter crucified
64 Great fire in Rome	
70 Jerusalem destroyed by Romans	**67** Paul beheaded in Rome
79 Mt. Vesuvius erupts, destroying Pompeii; 20,000 die	**67–70** Gospel according to Mark

(Continued)

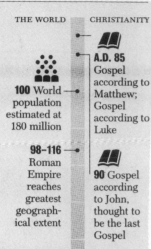

THE WORLD	CHRISTIANITY

A.D. 85
Gospel according to Matthew; Gospel according to Luke

100 World population estimated at 180 million

98–116 Roman Empire reaches greatest geographical extent

90 Gospel according to John, thought to be the last Gospel

164–180 The Roman army carries the Great Plague from Parthia (Iraq) into the empire

190 By this time, Catholic bishops' power is established and a new testament canon is formulated

200 World population estimated at 190 million

202 Roman Emperor Septimus Severus makes baptism a criminal act

220 Goths invade Asia Minor and Balkan peninsula

248 Rome celebrates its 1,000th anniversary

250 Emperor Decius increases persecutions of Christians

286 Roman Empire splits, with eastern capital in Byzantium

312 Constantine accepts Christianity; reunites empire

SOURCES: THE OXFORD HISTORY OF CHRISTIANITY, THE ENCYCLOPEDIA OF WORLD FACTS AND DATES

RESEARCH BY BRAD STONE

313 Constantine mandates tolerance of Christianity

secting sacred texts. They also rely on recently discovered texts, such as Gnostic Gospels and the Dead Sea scrolls. From these, critics fashion rather different biographies of Jesus than those found in the Gospels of Matthew, Mark, Luke and John.

According to one international best seller, "Jesus and the Riddle of the Dead Sea Scrolls" *(451 pages. HarperCollins)*, the historical Jesus was really "the wicked priest" mentioned in the scrolls of the Essene sect at Qumran. Australian author Barbara Thiering uses the scrolls to unlock what she considers the secret story encoded in the canonical Christian Scriptures. What they reveal is that Jesus was actually crucified at Qumran and buried in a cave by the Dead Sea. But he only appeared to be dead, thanks to a slow-acting poison administered to him on the cross. Later, Simon Magus, a magician mentioned in the New Testament, gave Jesus a purgative and some myrrh to soothe his mucous membranes. Thus revived, Jesus went on to marry Mary Magdalene, father three children, divorce her and marry Lydia, another minor New Testament figure. Eventually, he died in Rome.

However fanciful, all these efforts at recovering the historical Jesus share certain assumptions that even more traditional scholars readily accept. All agree that the New Testament was created by believers whose main concern was to preach the "good news" of Jesus Christ. All recognize that the Gospel narratives were composed from oral traditions at least 40 years after the death of Jesus, each with its own theological bent. All accept the fact that the Gospel stories—like the Epistles and Luke's Acts of the Apostles—reflect controversies within the early church. All acknowledge that the New Testament authors interpreted Jesus in light of various images and beliefs from the Hebrew Scriptures. And all are trained in the intricate historical-critical method of placing specific scriptural passages in their historical context.

According to this elaborate academic protocol, the Resurrection is ruled a priori out of court because it transcends time and space. Historians then have to find another reason to explain the origins of Christianity. Thus the Gospel's narrative frame is discarded and the pieces of Scripture are reshuffled to reveal the scholar's own "historical" Jesus. In some ways, this is what the Gospels do themselves. Each of them is a written composition that brings together parables and stories, events and theological assertions, that existed earlier only in

oral form. Each offers different facets and insights into a figure who otherwise slips into the crevices of first-century Palestine. What holds these pieces together is the belief that the Risen Christ is living yet—a belief that many contemporary reconstructors do not share.

Even the most orthodox Scripture scholars recognize that the brief, almost enigmatic accounts of Jesus' resurrection and its aftermath are fraught with special problems for the historian. For one thing, there were no witnesses to the Resurrection. As Ignatius of Antioch aptly put less than a century later, "Jesus rose in the silence of God," and no New Testament writer describes what happened. For another, the post-resurrection stories contain a variety of factual discrepancies about the main characters, places, times and the messages attributed to the Risen Jesus. For example, the Gospel of Matthew has Jesus appearing first to Mary Magdalene and other women. Luke gives the first appearance to Peter, and (with the exception of a later addition to his Gospel) Mark contains no post-Resurrection appearances at all. Luke's Gospel says that Jesus appeared to the apostles in the Jerusalem area; Matthew says it was in Galilee. In short, the post-Resurrection narratives are ambiguous stories allowing ample room for historians to imagine what really took place.

But there is little doubt that God's raising of Jesus to new life was an early Christian conviction. The New Testament offers two sets of signs that point to the resurrection: the empty tomb and the various appearances of the Risen Christ. Some scholars think the story of the empty tomb was invented by Mark, the earliest Gospel, as a way of saying that Jesus had risen. In itself, however, the empty tomb merely indicates that the body was not there. Matthew's Resurrection story even anticipates that doubters would immediately claim the corpse had been stolen. In Matthew's account, the empty tomb is discovered by Mary Magdalene and another woman who are told by an angel that Jesus is risen. They then meet Jesus, who instructs them to tell the apostles that he will meet them later in Galilee. What is significant here is that the first witnesses to the Risen Christ were women, not men. Had the story been invented solely for propaganda purposes, the early Christians would have made men the first witnesses, since the testimony of women carried far less authority in the patriarchal Jewish society.

Paul's first letter to the Corinthians, which pre-

MATTHEW 28: 1-6 *After the Sabbath, and towards dawn on the first day of the week, Mary of Magdala and the other Mary went to visit the sepulchre. And suddenly there was a violent earthquake, for an angel of the Lord, descending from heaven, came and rolled away the stone and sat on it . . . The angel said to the women, 'There is no need for you to be afraid. I know you are looking for Jesus . . . He is not here, for he has risen . . .*

dates all the Gospels, reports that Jesus made several post-resurrection appearances: to Cephas (Peter); then to the 12 apostles; to a group "of more than 500 brethren at one time"; to James; to "all the apostles," and finally to the convert Paul himself. But what was it that they saw? What did they hear? What was the character of the Resurrection experience? These are some of the questions scholars will take up next week in New York at the Resurrection Summit.

On one point scholars are unanimous: resurrection does not mean the resuscitation of a corpse. It is not as if "the soul of Jesus left his body and then returned to it like someone going out of the house at night and coming back in the morning," says Father Gerald O'Collins, a specialist on the Resurrection at the Jesuits' Gregorian University in Rome and cochairman of the summit. "We are talking about a glorified body, one that has been transformed by the power of God, and something none of us have ever seen." The Gospels themselves admit of various interpretations. On the one hand, they describe the Risen Jesus eating with his disciples. In John's Gospel, the apostle known as "doubting" Thomas refuses to believe that Jesus has returned from the dead until Christ allows him to put his finger into the hole in his side, where a soldier's lance had pierced him during his slow death on the cross.

On the other hand, several Gospel stories clearly indicate that Jesus' resurrected body was not at all like normal human flesh. He mysteriously appears and disappears, passes through closed doors and, as in his appearance (in Luke's account) to two disciples on the road to Emmaus, often goes unrecognized by his own close companions. To some theologians, this suggests that only those of deep faith actually saw Jesus, and then only in a God-given vision. Indeed, most scholars believe that in Paul's case, that is exactly what happened. But Stephen T. Davis, a philosopher at Claremont McKenna College in California and cochair of the Resurrection Summit, takes the minority view that even a nonbeliever with a 20th-century camera could have captured the Risen Jesus on film. "A glorified body is still a body," he writes in a paper for the Resurrection Summit, "still a material object that can be seen."

For most believing Christians, what matters is not only what the apostles experienced 2,000 years ago, but what they meant when they preached that God raised Jesus from the dead. "A resuscitation is excellent news for the patient and family," observes Luke Timothy Johnson, professor of Christian Origins at Emory University's Candler School of Theology in Atlanta. "But it is not 'good news' that affects everyone else. It does not begin a religion. It does not transform the lives of others across the ages. It is not what is being claimed by the first Christians." Indeed, what was most distinctive about the claims made for Jesus was not that he was the Messiah or that he was "King of the Jews," as the Romans mockingly suggested. Rather, in proclaiming that Jesus had been resurrected, they were asserting something profoundly new about God as well as about Jesus himself.

AS JEWS THEMSELVES, JESUS' apostles knew only one God— the Yahweh of Hebrew Scriptures. From those Scriptures they could hardly have expected that they would ever see their disgraced and executed master again. According to those Scriptures, even Moses died, and of the other Hebrew prophets, only two—Elijah and Enoch— had ascended to heaven. But neither rose from the dead. "The Hebrew Bible is very reticent to talk about life after death," says Alan Segal, professor of religion at Barnard College in New York, a Jew who is the only non-Christian participant in the Resurrection Summit. "There must have been beliefs in life after death, but the people who edited the Bible kept them out."

But during the Maccabean revolt (circa 167 B.C.), the idea of bodily resurrection began to surface among the Jews. In a nationalist revolt against Greek rulers, young Jewish men were dying as martyrs in defense of what they considered the laws of God. A just God, it was believed, would eventually restore them to life. Early Christianity was born in a climate of apocalyptic expectation created by the Maccabees' revolt, Segal believes. In Jesus' 33-year lifetime there were Pharisees who thought that the just would be resurrected by God at the end of secular time. "But they didn't speculate about how it would take place," says Segal.

Against this background, the resurrection of Jesus was a provocative claim for anyone to make. In a highly original paper prepared for next week's summit, New Testament scholar Carey C. Newman points to another tradition in the Hebrew Scriptures that helps explain what the first Christians saw in Christ's resurrection. According to

LUKE 24: 30-34 *Now while he was with them at table, he took the bread and said the blessing; then he broke it and handed it to them. And their eyes were opened and they recognised him; but he had vanished from their sight . . . They set out that instant and returned to Jerusalem. There they found the Eleven assembled together with their companions, who said to them, 'The Lord has indeed risen . . .'*

JOHN 20: 24-27 *Thomas . . . who was one of the Twelve, was not with them when Jesus came . . . 'Unless I can see the holes that the nails have made in his hands and can put my finger into the holes they made . . . I refuse to believe.' Eight days later the disciples were in the house again. The doors were closed, but Jesus came in and stood among them . . . he spoke to Thomas. 'Put your finger here . . . Give me your hand; put it into my side. Do not be unbelieving any more but believe.'*

that tradition, "The Glory of Yahweh"—meaning the divine presence—appeared at key moments and places in Jewish history: in the Exodus cloud, at Mount Sinai and over the temple, among others. Those moments, says Newman, who teaches at Southern Baptist Seminary in Louisville, Ky., also signal major changes in Yahweh's dealings with his people. For the early Christians the Resurrection was another of those moments, Newman argues. It brought them together as a new religious community and immediately distinguished them from other apocalyptic Jewish movements. The early Christians claimed that in the Risen Christ, the Glory of Yahweh was made manifest in a new and unexpected way. It revealed the dawn of a "new creation"—the church—and a new hope, that "in Christ" everyone could reliably expect his or her own resurrection from the dead.

From the very beginning of Christianity, Christ's "victory" over death, as Paul put it, was not his alone. It was also a victory promised to those who were baptized into his body, the church. Throughout two centuries of Roman persecution, countless Christian martyrs went to their deaths convinced that in God's coming kingdom they would rise again with a new, glorified body. In her magisterial new study, "The Resurrection of the Body in Western Christianity, 200-1336" *(368 pages. Columbia University Press)*, medieval historian Caroline Walker Bynum traces the persistent Christian conviction that the body as well as the soul would inherit eternal life. It wasn't easy. "Right through the Middle Ages," says Bynum, "you find spiritual and material interpretations of both the resurrected body of Christ and of our own resurrected bodies." But time and again in contention with neo-Platonists, Gnostics and other spiritualizers, advocates of the more physical interpretation win out over the more vaporous explanations. Why? "They saw the body as the carrier of particularity, including gender and race," Bynum says. "Choosing for the body was choosing for individual identity for all eternity."

For as long as death remains a mystery, so, too, will resurrection. That Jesus rose from the dead is a statement of Christian faith and of human hope—and implies a bond of trust between those who live in the presence of Christ today and those who first carried the Easter message 2,000 years ago. Bonds like these sustain all religious traditions. "If we can dismiss as 'unhistorical' most of the Gospels' Jesus of Christianity, what can we of faithful Israel save of our rabbi, Moses, for Judaism?" asks Rabbi Jacob Neusner, a distinguished Talmudist at the University of South Florida in Tampa. "Religion does not merely recite secular facts about what happened in ordinary affairs on a particular day. Religion speaks of God's intervention into the world, and that claim does not come before the court of secular history, to be judged true or false by historians' ways of validating or falsifying ordinary facts."

AFTER 150 YEARS OF SCHOLARLY search, there are signs that the quest for the "historical" Jesus has reached a dead end. There have been no new data on the person of Jesus since the Gospels were written. And though scholars continue to piece together information from archeology and other disciplines, these are valuable chiefly for fashioning a better understanding of Christian origins and how the Gospels, in particular, were composed. In the best of the recent flow of books, "The Real Jesus" *(182 pages. HarperCollins)*, Emory's Luke Timothy Johnson offers a devastating critique of those scholars who prefer their own reconstructed Jesuses to the one attested to in the New Testament. As Johnson demonstrates, truth is not always historical, and what seems warranted by historical evidence does not always turn out to be true. Unfortunately, apart from what is found in Scripture, there is little that one can say about the identity of Jesus. Like Socrates, Jesus is inscribed in the words of those who wrote about him. And all of them proclaimed his Resurrection from the dead.

The Resurrection is not all that they proclaimed. They also claimed "that after his death [Jesus] entered into an entirely new form of existence, one in which he shared the power of God and in which he could share that power with others," Johnson writes. In the New Testament, Jesus' death and resurrection are united with his ascension and the apostles' Pentecost experience. As Johnson puts it, "The sharing in Jesus' new life through the power of the Holy Spirit is an essential dimension of the resurrection." Not everyone can or will accept that belief. But without it there is no Easter.

ACTS 1: 9-10 *. . . He was lifted up while they looked on, and a cloud took him from their sight. They were still staring into the sky as he went . . .*

Women and the Bible

*Motivated variously by historical, theological, and personal concerns,
a rapidly growing cadre of scholars, most of them women, is exploring
one of the great overlooked subjects in scholarship: the domain of Jewish
and Christian women in ancient times*

Cullen Murphy

Cullen Murphy is the managing editor of The Atlantic Monthly. *He writes the comic strip* Prince Valiant *and is the author, with William Rathje, of* Rubbish!: The Archaeology of Garbage *(1992). Murphy's article "Who Do Men Say That I Am?", about research on Jesus, was* The Atlantic*'s cover story in December of 1986.*

Perhaps a rumor of impending persecution lay behind it, as several scholars have speculated. Perhaps the reason for concealment was something else entirely. We can never know why twelve ancient codices and a fragment of a thirteenth came to rest where they were found. The place was a rugged curtain of cliffs rising above the valley of the Nile River, near where today there is a village called Nag Hammadi. The time was the late fourth century or early fifth century A.D. For whatever reason, someone, perhaps a monk from the local monastery of St. Pachomius, took steps to preserve some holy books—Coptic translations of works that had originally been written in Greek, works of the kind that had been denounced as heretical by Athanasius, the archbishop of Alexandria. The words of the prophet Jeremiah may have played through the mind of the person hiding the codices: "Put them in an earthenware jar, that they may last for a long time." For it was in an earthen jar, hidden in a cavity under a rock at the base of the cliffs, that the papyrus manuscripts were eventually discovered.

The Nag Hammadi library, as these texts have come to be called, was brought to light in 1945. By the early 1950s, after

feuds and transactions of Levantine complexity, almost all of the Nag Hammadi collection was in the safe but jealous hands of the Coptic Museum, in Cairo, which for many years proved exceedingly particular about whom it would allow to study the documents. It was clear very early, however, that the codices, which contained forty previously unknown works, would offer unprecedented access to the world of the Gnostics, a variegated group of Christian communities, active as early as a century after the time of Jesus, that diverged sharply from the emerging Christian orthodoxy in many ways—one of them frequently being the prominence, both in theology and in community life, of women.

Elaine Pagels was a doctoral student in religion at Harvard University during the late 1960s, when mimeographed transcriptions of the Nag Hammadi library were circulating among American and European scholars. Her area of interest was the history of early Christianity. There were no women then on the faculty of Harvard's program in religion, and the dean who accepted Pagels as a doctoral candidate had turned her down the first time she applied. In this field, he explained in a letter, women didn't last. But now, after applying again, here she was, with the working knowledge of Latin and Greek that anyone dealing with early Christian texts requires, and the Nag Hammadi mimeographs caught her attention. Because the transcriptions were in Coptic, which is Egyptian written with the Greek alphabet and a few other characters, Pagels added Coptic to her repertoire (and also Hebrew) and got to work.

Sitting one afternoon recently in her office at the Institute for Advanced Study,

in Princeton, I spoke with Pagels about her Harvard years and other matters. Pagels, who is a professor in the religion department at Princeton University, works at certain times at the institute, which offers scholars a chance to pursue research without the distraction of teaching. It is a modern and spacious place, set impersonally among vast lawns. In Pagels's office a photograph of her late husband sat upon the sill. A girl's bicycle was propped against a wall. Pagels has two young children, and a demeanor that somehow manages to be calmer than her circumstances are.

"I discovered," Pagels said, thinking back to her initial encounter with the Nag Hammadi materials, "as did the other graduate students, that our professors had file folders full of Gnostic texts of secret Gospels that many of them told us were absurd and blasphemous and heretical—but interesting. And I *did* find these texts interesting. And exciting. I think that perhaps my empathy for them had something to do with being a woman in an environment that was almost exclusively male. I found things among the heretics that were startlingly congenial." Pagels became part of the team that would translate the Nag Hammadi texts into English and provide a critical apparatus for them.

Not until 1975, five years after completing a doctoral dissertation on certain aspects of the Nag Hammadi library, did Pagels have an opportunity to inspect the documents themselves. At various times during a stay in Egypt, Pagels would visit the small, unprepossessing room in the Coptic Museum where the Nag Hammadi library is kept, one day perhaps to examine The Interpretation of Knowledge, another to examine A Valentinian Exposition or The Gospel of Mary. The documents looked, she remembers thinking, like tobacco leaves. Each fragile page, each fragment, lies flat between sheets of hard plastic, the black lettering stark against a mottled golden background, the underlying weave of the crushed papyrus fronds plainly visible. The Coptic Museum was a place of columns and courtyards and quiet. The only interruption was caused by the cleaning woman, and Pagels and any other scholars present would continue working at their desks when she came in, lifting their legs as soapy water was spilled and spread beneath them over the stone floors.

In a book called *The Gnostic Gospels* (1979), which received wide attention when it was published and occasioned a sometimes bitter scholarly debate, Pagels took some of those fragments that lie flat between plastic and sought to give them dimension, set them in history, bring ancient sensibilities back to life. She described Gnostic groups who saw God as a "dyad" embodying both masculine and feminine aspects, and who explicitly invoked the feminine aspect in their prayers: "May She who is before all things, the incomprehensible and indescribable Grace, fill you within, and increase in you her own knowledge." Some groups conceived of the third person in Christianity's trinitarian God—a God consisting of Father, Son, and Holy Spirit—to be female, and so rendered the Trinity, logically enough, as Father, Son, and Mother. Powerful feminine imagery and ideology suffuse many Gnostic texts, and this found parallels in the practice of a number of Gnostic groups, which permitted women to hold priestly office. Gnostic thought was disorderly and fantastical, and for a variety of reasons was spurned by Christian polemicists (although some elements seem to find echoes in the Gospel of John). But it preserves some early Christian traditions, and is valuable for its reflection of currents in popular religion that are only dimly reflected in the canon of sanctioned Christian works—currents important to an understanding of Christianity's unruly beginnings.

Some of the Gnostics were much intrigued by the Creation stories in the Book of Genesis. Pagels, too, became intrigued, and in 1988 she produced *Adam, Eve, and the Serpent* a book more ambitious than *The Gnostic Gospels*. The Bible's Creation stories—or, perhaps more precisely, the interpretation of the Cre-

ation stories that came to be accepted—form the basis for a view of humanity as existing in a fallen state, of woman as having led humanity astray, of man as being ordained to be the master of woman, and of sexuality as a corrupting aspect of human nature. And yet, as Pagels shows, this is not how the Creation stories were interpreted by many Jews and early Christians, and it is sometimes difficult to see how such conclusions came to be drawn. Pagels points to other traditions in Jewish and Christian thought: of the Creation stories as parables of human equality, men and women both being formed in the image and likeness of God of the stories as evocations of God's gift of moral freedom. *Adam, Eve, and the Serpent* traces the clashes of interpretation in the early Church, which culminated in the triumph of Augustine, whose harsh views on the subject would become those of much of the Western world—would help define Western consciousness—for a millennium and a half.

> *The Creation stories form the basis for a view of humanity as existing in a fallen state, of woman as having led humanity astray, of man as being ordained to be the master of woman.*

The point is, Pagels told me, early Christianity was a remarkably diverse and fractious religious movement. There were traditions within it that the evolution of a stronger, more institutionalized tradition would largely destroy. Acknowledging this fact has implications for our own time and for people who have often felt excluded or even oppressed by the dominant tradition. It has implications in particular for women. "The history of Christianity has been told from a single point of view," Pagels said. "If that point of view is no longer tenable historically then it enables people to develop other perceptions."

The work of Elaine Pagels is but one manifestation of a larger phenomenon: the rapidly expanding influence of feminist scholars in the study of Jewish and Christian history, and the reassessment of certain issues

that has ensued as a result. The body of work that these scholars have produced is by now substantial. Virtually all of it has been published within the past fifteen years. Most has been published within the past ten. While the writing can at times be difficult—some scholars don methodology like chain mail—a strikingly large proportion, whether in specialized journals or in books, is written so as to be broadly accessible to readers outside academe.

The motivations, besides simple intellectual curiosity, that lie behind this work are not difficult to discern. There is the perception that the Hebrew Bible and the New Testament deal with women unfairly in many spheres; the need to understand why they do; the suspicion that an alternative past awaits recovery. Among some scholars there is a conviction, too, that recovering the past could help change the present—for example, could help make the case for giving women access to positions in religious ministry and religious leadership from which they are now barred. Although half of all Christian denominations permit the ordination of women, as do Reform and Conservative Judaism, the issue remains a matter of strongly felt conflict. The work of feminist scholars, both individually and collectively, has been greeted in some quarters with impatience, irritation, dismissiveness, even contempt. But it has also established women's issues as a permanent focus of biblical studies. That it has done so is one important element of the broader engagement of feminism with every aspect of organized religion.

A few years ago I set out to explore this branch of scholarship—to meet some of its practitioners and become familiar with some of their work. My focus was not on politics but on research. The people whose work is touched on here are drawn not from the sometimes airy or angry outskirts of the feminist biblical enterprise but from its solid scholarly core. They come from several religious backgrounds, represent several scholarly disciplines, and, as feminists, display a range of stances toward religion in general and the Bible in particular. Their work thus defies easy summary. My intention is to let it speak for itself.

THE PATRIARCHY PROBLEM

The women's movement has as yet had meager impact on some academic realms, but the realm of religion is not among the scarcely affected. Even if the convergence of feminism and religion has prompted developments on the fringes of popular culture which would strike some as bizarre (the proliferation of neo-pagan "goddess" movements comes to mind), the truly significant consequences have occurred closer to the mainstream of ministry and scholarship. Walk into the department of religion or the divinity school at any major university today and the bulletin board will paint the same picture: seminar after workshop after lecture on almost any conceivable matter involving women and religion. The influx of women into divinity-school programs has by now received considerable attention. So has the movement to adopt "inclusive" language, when appropriate, in translations of Scripture, and to correct mistranslations of Scripture that have served to obscure feminine references and imagery. This movement saw its most important victory in 1990, with the publication by the National Council of Churches of the New Revised Standard version of the Bible. But much of the work being done by women in biblical scholarship and related fields—work that demands immense erudition—remains far less well known.

The Bible has always been a compelling object of study, both because questions of religious faith are inextricably involved and because it is a window—albeit one whose refractions may distort and occlude—onto much of human history. With respect to issues of gender the Bible is also, of course, highly problematic, to use a word that no feminist scholar I've spoken with can help uttering in a tone of ironic politeness. It is a central tenet of contemporary feminism that a patriarchal template governs the way people have come to think and behave as individuals and as societies. The Bible is no stranger to patriarchy. It is an androcentric document in the extreme. It was written mostly if not entirely by men. It was edited by men. It describes a succession of societies over a period of roughly 1,200 years whose public life was dominated by men. And because the Bible's focus is predominantly on public rather than private life, it talks almost only about men. In the Hebrew Bible as a whole, only 111 of the 1,426 people who are given names are women. The proportion of women in the New Testament is about twice as great, which still leaves them a small minority.

As a prescriptive text, moreover, the Bible has been interpreted as justifying the subordination of women to men: "In pain you shall bring forth children, yet your desire shall be for your husband, and he shall rule over you." "Wives, be subject to your husbands as you are to the Lord." "Indeed, man was not made from woman, but woman from man. Neither was man created for the sake of woman, but woman for the sake of man." As a text that has been presumed by hundreds of millions of people to speak with authority, moreover, the Bible has helped enforce what it prescribes. There is no getting around the disturbing character, for women, of much of the Bible, short of an interpretive reading (a "hermeneutic," to use the term of art) that may represent something of a stretch—short of what one biblical scholar has called an act of "hermeneutical ventriloquism."

The subjection of the Bible to historical and critical scrutiny, a revolution in scholarship that began during the latter half of the nineteenth century, was undertaken almost entirely by men. It did not occur to these men that the way the Bible treats women—or, just as important, fails to treat women—might be a fit matter for study. The Society of Biblical Literature, which remains to this day the leading professional group in the field, was founded in 1880, and inducted its first woman member in 1894. But the relative handful of women who embarked on careers in biblical studies in the nineteenth century and the first half of the twentieth showed virtually no interest in women's issues. As the historian Dorothy Bass, of the Chicago Theological Seminary, has shown, it was women outside academe who first pursued the matter: women like the abolitionist Sarah Grimké, in the 1830s, and, later, Frances Willard, of the Women's Christian Temperance Union.

Their aims, initially, were two. The first was to identify and critically confront passages and stories about women which they deemed objectionable—the stories, for example, of Delilah, in the Book of Judges, and of Jezebel, in I Kings. The second aim was to seek out and elevate to greater prominence passages and stories about women which are positive and ennobling—for example, the remarkable image of Wisdom personified as a woman, in Proverbs, and the stories of Deborah, in Judges, and of the prophetess Huldah, in II Kings. Both these strands of the early feminist re-

sponse to the Bible have survived, in increasingly sophisticated forms, down to the present.

The suffragist leader Elizabeth Cady Stanton made a contribution by means of that remarkable fin-de-siècle document *The Woman's Bible,* the first volume of which was published in 1895. Though well into her eighties, Stanton oversaw a committee of female editors who scrutinized and critically glossed every passage in the Bible having to do with women. She came to the conclusion that little could be salvaged from Scripture which was fully compatible with the belief system of a rational modern feminist. None of the women who worked on *The Woman's Bible* was a biblical scholar. Female biblical scholars refused to participate in the project, afraid, Stanton believed, "that their high reputation and scholarly attainments might be compromised by taking part in an enterprise that for a time may prove very unpopular."

Female biblical scholars did not face up to issues of gender—did not, as Frances Willard had urged, "make a specialty of Hebrew and New Testament Greek in the interest of their sex"—in any significant way until the 1960s. One call to action came from a professor of biblical literature at Smith College, Margaret Brackenbury Crook, who in a book called *Women and Religion* (1964) took aim at the "masculine monopoly" on all important matters in all the world's great faiths. She repeated the plaintive question of the biblical figure Miriam: "Has the Lord spoken only through Moses?" By the 1970s, of course, a generalized version of that question could be sensed almost everywhere in the culture. Departments of religion and divinity schools were merely two among the crowd of institutions that saw more and more women seeking access, bringing with them unfamiliar questions and ways of thinking.

Biblical scholarship is still a predominantly male endeavor, but inroads by women have been substantial. The female membership of the Society of Biblical Literature amounted to three percent of the total in 1970. It now exceeds 16 percent. The share of the student membership that is female—a harbinger, surely—is 30 percent. In 1987 the society elected its first woman president, Elisabeth Schüssler Fiorenza, a theologian who at the time was a professor at Episcopal Divinity School, and who now teaches at Harvard. The joint annual meeting of the SBL and the American Academy of Religion today features a large number of sessions on women's issues, chiefly by women but sometimes by men. "Prostitutes and Penitents in the Early Christian Church." "Redeeming the Unredeemable: Genesis 22—A Jewish Feminist Perspective." "Rape as a Military Metaphor in the Hebrew Bible." The opening address at the AAR portion of last year's joint meeting was given by Mary Daly, whose first two books, *The Church and the Second Sex* (1968) and *Beyond God the Father* (1973), were a source of inspiration to many women with an interest in religion. (Daly herself has ventured not only beyond God the Father but also beyond Christianity, and is by now well off the beaten track; she maintains an uneasy professorship in the department of theology at Boston College, a school run by Jesuit priests.) At the next joint meeting, this coming November, the SBL will install its second woman president: Phyllis Trible, of Union Theological Seminary.

It was Schüssler Fiorenza's work—most notably her book *In Memory of Her* (1983), to which I was introduced almost a decade ago in the course of research on a related subject—that drew me into the world of women whose academic lives revolve, one way or another, around the central texts of the Jewish and Christian traditions. Schüssler Fiorenza, a soft-spoken native of Germany, is the Krister Stendahl Professor of Divinity at the Harvard Divinity School. She is also a founder and a co-editor of the *Journal of Feminist Studies in Religion,* one of several academic journals in the field with a focus on women. Schüssler Fiorenza is quick to acknowledge that coming to the United States, as she did in 1970, with a fresh doctorate in New Testament studies from the University of Münster, marked a turning point in her interests. The United States offered what Germany at the time did not: a strong and active feminist movement and a university system whose faculties—crucially, whose theology-department faculties—were open to women. Schüssler Fiorenza, in her own words, "began doing theology as a woman and for women." Her writing has focused primarily on the role played by women during the conception, birth, and infancy of Christianity.

Historical reconstruction of the Jesus movement is risky and fraught. Among other things, as Schüssler Fiorenza reminded me during a conversation one afternoon, "within both Judaism and Christianity the patriarchal side won"—thus determining the lens through which interpretation would look. One must approach the texts with a "hermeneutic of suspicion," to use a phrase that is by now a cliché in feminist biblical circles. The references to women that do exist in Christian works, Schüssler Fiorenza said, surely represent the tip of the iceberg, though unfortunately much of the part that is submerged now is likely to remain submerged forever.

And yet, she went on, there is some significant material about women to work with, if only we are not blind to it. The Gospels, she noted, are unequivocal in placing women prominently among the marginalized people who made up so much of Jesus' circle. Women are shown as having been instrumental in opening up the Jesus community to non-Jews. After the Crucifixion it was the women of Galilee who helped hold together the Jesus movement in Jerusalem as other disciples fled. Women were the first to discover the empty tomb and the first to experience a vision of a resurrected Jesus. Jesus' message was in part a radical attack on the traditional social structures of the Greco-Roman world—structures that limited the participation of women in the public sphere, and that the Jesus movement sought to replace with what Schüssler Fiorenza calls "a discipleship of equals."

After the crucifixion it was women who helped hold together the Jesus movement. Women were the first to discover the empty tomb, the first to experience a vision of a resurrected Jesus.

And after Jesus was gone? Christianity's penumbral first centuries can be difficult to apprehend. The texts that would make up the New Testament—not to mention the many other texts that survive from Christian communities—were at this time being written, edited, and re-edited, each text created in the context of certain communities and to fulfill certain purposes. What emerges from Schüssler Fiorenza's reading is a Christian missionary movement that in its initial stages "allowed for the full participation and leadership of women." She notes in *In Memory of Her* that in the authentic letters of Paul, women are singled out by name and given titles the same as or comparable to those held by male leaders. Prisca, a traveling missionary, is described by Paul as a peer, a "co-worker." Phoebe, in Cenchreae, is called a *diakonos,* a title Paul also gives himself.

Some scholars have in the past tried to explain away evidence like this, Schüssler Fiorenza writes, by arguing that when held by women such titles must have been mere honorifics. Or they have translated the titles differently. *Diakonos,* for example, which is usually translated as "minister," "missionary," or "deacon" when associated with men, has usually been downplayed as "deaconess" or even "helper" when associated with women. Scholars have also argued that people whose names are apparently female must actually have been men. Schüssler Fiorenza observes that the social mores of the time left ample room for women to wield authority in early Christianity. For one thing, the rituals of Christianity evolved in a network of churches based in homes, and within the home, women could claim important rights and responsibilities. Schüssler Fiorenza argues, finally, that early Christianity was built around a theology of equality; that Paul's famous reiteration in Galatians 3:28 of the ancient baptismal formula—"There is no longer Jew or Greek, there is no longer slave or free, there is no longer male and female; for all of you are one in Christ Jesus"—represents not a radical and temporary breakthrough in Paul's thinking but an expression of broad and ordinary Christian belief. In Schüssler Fiorenza's view, Galatians 3:28 is "the magna carta of Christian feminism."

Schüssler Fiorenza is a theologian, and she has an explicitly theological agenda. In her approach to Scripture she aims to highlight themes of unfolding liberation and emancipation. But large portions of her work exemplify a strategy pursued by non-theologians as well: the attempt to pierce the veil of the sources, to discern what was social and religious reality in a distant time. This may involve textual scholarship—trainng attention on vocabulary, on rhetorical style, on whatever can be inferred about the editing process. It may involve the disciplines of archaeology and anthropology—coming at early Jewish and Christian life from the outside, and looking at what the physical record has to say. All this work presupposes a broad grounding in some very obscure aspects of history. The work can be frustrating in the extreme. The materials available are often meager, and the conclusions drawn sometimes precarious and insubstantial.

Elaine Pagels spoke about some of the endeavor's hazards and intricacies and opportunities in one of our conversations. We had been talking about the issue of an author's point of view. Pagels observed that in some instances the documentary record of certain suppressed opinions consists only of the surviving criticisms of those opinions. Before the discovery of the Nag Hammadi library, Gnostic thinking was a prime example: many Gnostic beliefs had been scathingly summarized in the writings of Irenaeus of Lyons, a second-century theologian and foe of heretics. Images of women can sometimes be made out in the same way. "We have to read the texts aware that the point of view may not reflect the whole social reality," Pagels told me. "It will reflect the point of view of the people writing the texts, and the groups they represent. And generally women were not doing the writing. So we have to make a lot out of the few clues that are found."

She reached for a comparison to bring home the nature of this situation. "Imagine," she said after a moment's reflection, "having to re-create the thinking of Karl Marx on the basis of a handful of anti-communist tracts from the 1950s."

SALVAGE OPERATIONS

Union Theological Seminary, in New York, occupies two city blocks along Broadway, in a neighborhood that might be thought of as upper Manhattan's religion district. The Jewish Theological Seminary of America lies across the street to the northeast, taking up much of a third city block. Across the street to the southwest, taking up a fourth city block, lies The Interchurch Center, which houses scores of religious organizations: groups devoted to social work, missionary work, publishing, broadcasting. (The square, clunky structure is known as "the God box.") And across the street directly to the west, occupying a fifth city block, is Riverside Church, long a bulwark of social activism with a mildly hallowed cast. Union is an example of the kind of liberal, nondenominational seminary whose student body in recent years has become increasingly female: almost 55 percent of its more than 300 students are women. It is a comfortable, reassuring place. The architecture is monastic, preserving outwardly in cool stone a way of life that no longer prevails inside. In the library's reading room, whose shelves hold the leather-bound classics required for exegetic work, and from around whose perimeter gleam the marbled pates of learned men, it is perhaps possible to believe that this is still the Union Seminary of Paul Tillich and Reinhold Niebuhr. But in the hallways of the living quarters the tricycles and toys betray a changed demography. The omnipresent flyers announcing meetings also tell a story. "Hunger Strike Demanding Action for Peace and Reunification in Korea." "Feminists for Animal Rights." "Lesbian-Gay Caucus Sez Howdy." These people, one senses, are busy, committed. They do not lack up-to-date agendas.

Phyllis Trible is the Baldwin Professor of Sacred Literature. Her office at Union sits high above the quadrangle, under the eaves, and in it one can occupy a certain chair at a certain angle and almost be persuaded that the world outside the window is the world of Oxford or Cambridge. On a wall of Trible's office hangs a photograph of a white-haired man in a dark suit and tie—James Muilenburg, who was a professor at Union when Trible was a student here, in the late 1950s and early 1960s, and who taught the first class she attended at the seminary. "I'll never forget that class," Trible recalled one day. She speaks with precision in an accent shaped by her native Virginia. "He walked in with a stack of syllabi under his arm and he put them down on the table and started quoting Hebrew poetry: the 'Sword of Lamech,' in Genesis. And he dramatized the whole thing—took the sword and plunged it in. He asked us where that sword reappeared, and jumped to Peter in the New Testament. I was utterly captivated, and have never gotten over it to this day." Trible is but one of several female biblical scholars I've met who, whatever problems being a woman may have caused them in academe, warmly acknowledge a close intellectual relationship with a male mentor.

Trible believes that the Bible can be "reclaimed" as a spiritual resource for women. The Bible, she said, is sometimes not as patriarchal as translations would make it seem.

Trible is the author of two books, *God and the Rhetoric of Sexuality* (1978) and *Texts of Terror: Literary-Feminist Readings of Biblical Narratives* (1984), that would appear in anyone's canon of feminist biblical studies. Even colleagues who have no affinity with Trible's work—who differ radically in outlook—may acknowledge a debt. Ask graduate students in their twenties or established scholars in their thirties or forties how an interest was awakened in women's issues and biblical studies, and the answer will often turn out to involve an article or a book by Trible.

It is important to recognize where Trible stands in a spectrum that ranges, as she explained to me, "from some fundamentalists who claim that they are feminists but say they have no problem with the Bible to those at the other extreme who are unwilling to concede the Bible any authority at all." Trible is in the middle. She doesn't forget for a minute, she said, that the Bible is a thoroughly patriarchal text. But she is hardly a member of the rejectionist camp. She believes that the Bible can be "reclaimed" as a spiritual resource for women. And in all fairness, she said, it must be pointed out that the Bible is sometimes not as patriarchal as translations would make it seem. This is not just a matter of exclusive language. Trible pulled down a copy of the Revised Standard Version of the Bible, opened it to Deuteronomy 32:18, and read this passage: "You were unmindful of the Rock that begot you, and you forgot the God who gave you birth." She said, "Those words 'gave you birth' are from a Hebrew term for 'writhing in labor,' so the translation, if accurate, is tame. But here is how the Jerusalem Bible translates it: 'fathered you.'"

133

The work that initially brought Trible to prominence was a pair of journal articles in the 1970s on the two Creation stories in the Book of Genesis. These articles—the first ones written on the subject from a feminist perspective—were an attempt at reclamation. Trible argued that properly understood, the Creation stories, including the story of Adam and Eve, did not actually say what centuries of interpretation have made them say. For example, is woman to be considered subordinate to man, as some traditional interpretations would have it, simply because she was created after he was? If that is the case, Trible argued, then why are human beings not regarded as subordinate to animals, since Genesis 1:27 plainly declares that human beings were created after the animals were?

But that is almost beside the point, because it is a mistake, in Trible's view, to think of the first human being, Adam, as male. She points out that the Hebrew word 'adham, from which "Adam" derives, is a generic term for humankind—it denotes a being created from the earth—and is used to describe a creature of undifferentiated sex. Only when the Lord takes a rib from 'adham to make a companion are the sexes differentiated, and the change is signaled by the terminology. The creature from whom the rib was taken is now referred to not as 'adham but as 'ish ("man"), and the creature fashioned from the rib is called 'ishshah ("woman"). In Trible's reading, the sexes begin in equality. It is only after the act of disobedience occasioned by the serpent's temptation, and the departure of 'ish and 'ishshah from their initial and intended condition, that the sexes fall out of equality. It is only then, in this disobedient state, that the man establishes his dominance. Oppression of women by men, then, is not what was meant for humanity, even if it is what we have come to. "Rather than legitimating the patriarchal culture from which it comes," Trible concluded, "the myth places that culture under judgment."

Much as one hears the polite word "problematic" applied to material in the Bible which some feminist scholars deem to be negative, so also one hears the polite word "optimistic" applied to interpretations that some feminist scholars deem to be too positive. Trible is not unfamiliar with the latter charge. Her response would be that "optimistic" is a term that makes sense only if one assumes that the relationship people have with the Bible is as with something dead. She thinks of the Bible differently—as if it were a pilgrim forging new relationships over time. There are ways, she believes, of articulating a conversation between feminism and the Bible in which each critiques the other.

I was familiar, of course, with how feminism might critique the Bible. I asked Trible what critique the Bible offers of feminism. She replied that there was sometimes a tendency to make too 'much of feminism, to put it on a pedestal, and that the Bible calls attention to that kind of propensity. "It warns," she said, "against idolatry."

Trible's specialty is a form of criticism known as rhetorical criticism, which pays particular attention to a document's literary architecture. During one conversation Trible walked me through some passages that, together, may offer an instance of a biblical woman's falling victim to editorial manhandling. The passages tell the story of Miriam—the sister of Moses and Aaron, a woman who was perhaps considered by the Israelites to be the equal of her brothers, but of whom few traces survive in the Bible as it has finally come down to us.

We meet Miriam in the Book of Exodus. It is she who persuades Pharaoh's daughter to raise the infant Moses—left in a basket among the rushes on the banks of the Nile—as her own, and to bring along Moses' mother as nurse. Miriam is not at this point given a name; the woman who saves the infant's life is identified only as his sister. And as the story of Moses proceeds, Miriam disappears—until the crossing of the Red Sea. Then, when the Israelites reach the far shore, Pharaoh's armies having been destroyed, there is a song of rejoicing: the poetic Song at the Sea, sung by Moses and the people of Israel. It begins, "I will sing to the Lord, for he has triumphed gloriously; / horse and rider he has thrown into the sea." No sooner has Moses finished than there comes a small fragment of text that appears out of place. The fate of Pharaoh's armies is for some reason quickly retold, and then, with the Israelites once again safely on shore, we learn that "the prophet Miriam, Aaron's sister," begins to sing the very same Song at the Sea. She sings the first two lines. The text then moves on to other business.

Trible paused. There are several interesting things here, she said. One is that we learn for the first time that the sister of Aaron, who must also be the sister of Moses, has a name, and that it is Miriam. We also see that she is called a prophet and that this occurs at a place in the text well before the place where Moses is first called a prophet, though the precise meaning of "prophet" in the context of Exodus remains unclear. What this piece of text about Miriam represents, Trible said, is the dogged survival of an earlier version of the Exodus story. Indeed, she pointed out, scholars have argued that in the most ancient Israelite traditions the singing of the Song at the Sea was ascribed not to Moses but to Miriam. The role was only later shifted away from Miriam. (As an aside, Trible observed that the first work on the attribution of the Song at the Sea to Miriam dates back to the mid-1950s—and was done by men. She added pointedly, "I'm not one to say that you can't use the previous generation of scholarship—not at all.")

Miriam moves with the people of Israel into the desert, whereupon she disappears from the Book of Exodus. But she reappears later in the Bible, in connection with what seems to be a severe clash within the leadership, one from which Miriam emerges the loser—accounting, perhaps, for her diminished prominence. The reappearance occurs amid the jumble of the Book of Numbers, wherein Miriam and Aaron are heard to question the authority of their brother, asking the question that Trible and others ask more broadly: "Has the Lord spoken only through Moses?" The Lord does not punish Aaron, but Miriam is struck down with a skin affliction, possibly leprosy, for her rebelliousness, and later dies in the wilderness of Zin.

And yet there are signs that the memory of Miriam in the Israelite consciousness remains an active and uplifting one. Miriam has always been associated with water, Trible noted—remember the basket among the rushes? remember the Song at the Sea?—and the text immediately following the notice of Miriam's death again brings up the subject of water. It reads, "Now there was no water for the congregation." In standard editions of the Bible that sentence starts a new paragraph, as if the subject is suddenly being changed. Trible said, "Written Hebrew doesn't have such breaks. The paragraph marking after the end of the Miriam story is artificial. It makes you miss the idea that what is happening is connected to Miriam's death. Nature is mourning the loss of Miriam." Henceforward in the Bible, Miriam reappears only in hints and fragments, as in this passage from Deuteronomy: "Remember what the Lord your God did to Miriam on your journey out of Egypt." But she survives in real life—in the form of the continuing popularity of the name Miriam. The New Testament, compiled more than a millennium after Miriam's death, is populated with a multitude of women named Mary—the Hellenized version of the Hebrew Miriam. It is no coincidence, Trible has argued, that the Magnificat, the great canticle of Mary the mother of Jesus, borrows imagery directly from the Song at the Sea.

Miriam, Trible said, is only one of a number of apparently powerful women in the Bible who are alluded to almost in passing, the modesty of the references at odds with the importance of the roles these women seem to play. The references hint, perhaps, at the existence of a class of women in Israel whose history has in essence been lost, or can today be recovered only by means of the most delicate salvage, even then yielding mere wisps of insight. But that the references survive at all—that the editors believed some mention of these women had to be made—is itself suggestive.

Miriam is only one of a number of apparently powerful women in the Bible who are alluded to almost in passing, the modesty of the references at odds with the roles these women seem to play.

"It shows," Trible said, "that the stories just couldn't be squelched."

THE EARLIEST ISRAELITES

During part of almost every year for thirty years Carol Meyers, a professor of religion at Duke University, has left behind the comforts of university life for the rigors of archaeological excavations in the Middle East. For the past five summers she and her husband, Eric, have led excavations at a place called Sepphoris, in Israel, a site with remains as recent as the Crusades and as ancient as the Iron Age. Sepphoris, near Nazareth, in Galilee, is said in Christian tradition to be the birthplace of Mary. This summer Carol and Eric Meyers are excavating an Iron Age site at Sepphoris, one that dates to the earliest years of the Israelite people.

I visited Carol Meyers not long before her latest tour of duty in the Middle East, and she began describing the conditions under which she and her colleagues worked there. We were in her Gothic office at Duke, and the crowded shelves around us held books like *L'architecture domestique du Levant* and *Catalogue of Ancient Near-Eastern Seals in the Ashmolean Museum*—the sort of books that elicit in me a vague yearning for baked earth and native porters. When you step off the plane in Israel, Meyers said, it is always a visual shock. Even with the achievements of modern irrigation—even in the rainy season—much of the landscape is forbidding: barren, rocky, thorny. And in the summer it is *hot*. And in the winter, as people abroad often do not realize, it is *cold*. There is wind and hail and sleet.

These conditions are at their most extreme in the hill country of Judea and Samaria and Galilee, where the Israelites first emerged, inhabiting the unforgiving uplands because the Canaanite city-states controlled the fertile bottomlands. In this marginal ecological niche, where water was scarce and soils were bad, the tribes of Israel clung to a tenuous subsistence. They terraced the hills to make fields. They built cisterns lined with slaked-lime plaster to hold water.

Precisely who the Israelites were and where they came from remain matters of debate, but their appearance in the Land of Canaan can be dated to roughly 1250 B.C. The period of the Israelite monarchy, the kingdom of Saul and David and Solomon and their successors, was two centuries away, and the demands of social organization fell almost entirely upon the family—or, more precisely, upon clusters of related families. There was no central government, no structured politics, no sense of a public domain.

In this inhospitable and tribalized world, Carol Meyers believes, men and women functioned in social parity. The books of the Bible that describe this period of Israel's history—Judges and Joshua, primarily—do not necessarily show this to be the case, of course. Having achieved final form centuries later, they depict a society in which most of the important roles were played by men. But, as Meyers observed, there is frequently a big disjunction between a society's public stance and the everyday social reality; and everyday social reality in ancient Israel has only recently become an object of scrutiny. In biblical studies as in many other kinds of scholarship, social history has been a latecomer, and it is in social rather than political history that women tend at last to emerge from the background.

That Carol Meyers developed an interest in biblical studies at all is an accident of history. When she was an undergraduate at Wellesley, in the mid-1960s, a course in the Old Testament and the New Testament was required for graduation. Wellesley's insistence on biblical education, now long since dropped, had deep historical roots: Wellesley was a college where female biblical scholars had since the late nineteenth century found a congenial home. The first woman to present a paper at a meeting of the Society of Biblical Literature (1913) was a Wellesley professor, as was the first woman to publish a paper in the society's *Journal of Biblical Literature* (1917). Meyers found herself drawn to the world of the Bible and after a summer spent on an archaeological excavation in Wyoming, run by Harvard University, she knew that she wanted to combine biblical studies and archaeology. She began studying biblical Hebrew and then took up Akkadian, a Semitic language with many Hebrew cognates. In graduate school at Brandeis she was the only woman in most of her classes, and she had no female professors.

Needless to say, there was no such thing as feminist biblical studies. Nor did Meyers feel an inner tug in that direction. "It really was only once I began teaching at Duke," she recalled when we spoke, "that I became aware of the need and of the potential for gender studies with respect to Scripture. It really wasn't even at my own initiative—and I'm not embarrassed to say that. When I started teaching here, my colleagues said, 'Listen, you have to put a couple of courses on our curriculum that are of your own design. Why don't you think about doing some course on women and the Bible, or something like that?' This was in the mid-seventies, and I was the only woman in the department. Of course I said yes. When I started trying to put such a course together, I found out that there was no material. No one had done any research on it; no one had written about it. And that's when I started doing work myself."

Much of that work is embodied in *Discovering Eve: Ancient Israelite Women in Context* (1988), a book that draws on biblical sources and, more important, the insights offered by archaeology and social anthropology to reconstruct aspects of life in Israel before the dawn of monarchy and complex political institutions.

The economic functions of men and women at that time would have been separate and distinct, Meyers writes, with the men disproportionately responsible for tasks involving brute strength and the women responsible for tasks requiring technology or specialized skills or social sophistication: shearing wool and weaving cloth, processing and preserving food, teaching children, and managing a complex household whose membership, excavated floor plans suggest, usually went far beyond the nuclear family. In pre-monarchic Israel, as in primitive societies today where the household is the basic political and economic unit, women would have been central and authoritative figures.

Meyers observes further that the God of Israel, in sharp contrast to the gods of all other contemporaneous religions, was perceived at this time as asexual. Moreover, when God had to be described metaphorically, both male and female imagery was used. The prominence of God as father is a very late development in Israelite religion, Meyers argues, and makes only rare appearances in the Hebrew Bible itself (the term "father" is used in association with God just ten times).

The editors of the Bible have preserved traces of what Meyers believes was a relatively egalitarian regime. The Book of Judges, which reached its final form around the time of the Babylonian Captivity (586–538 B.C.), depicts life in Israel half a millennium earlier, and contains material that is very old. It brings to our attention an unusually large number of self-assured and powerful women. One of these, Deborah, is referred to as both a prophet and a judge. The "judges" in these earliest times were not magistrates but rather those few individuals

among the Israelites whose authority extended beyond household and tribe and might be thought of as somehow national. Some scholars have even speculated that one portion of the Book of Judges, the so-called Song of Deborah, may have been composed by a woman. (Resolving such matters of authorship is at this point impossible. It should be noted that the recent and widely publicized *Book of J,* in which the literary critic Harold Bloom entertains the conceit that one of the authors of the Pentateuch, the so-called J source, was a woman, is not held in high regard by biblical scholars, whatever the truth about J's identity may be. An earlier and more reliable book that speculates briefly on the same question is *Who Wrote the Bible?* by Richard Elliott Friedman.)

To Israelite women's economic productivity—at least equal in importance to that of men—must be added the essential element of reproductivity. Meyers reads the Bible mindful of the precarious demographic circumstances confronting the early Israelites. "It's wrong," she said, "to impose our idea of the individual on a society in which that may not have been a driving force in human development. The 'me-ness' or the 'I-ness' of our own contemporary life cannot be superimposed upon another era. The demands of community survival meant cooperation and a sense that what people were doing was in order for the group to survive. I get annoyed at some feminist critics who don't consider the social-history perspective. They see things like 'Be fruitful and multiply, and fill the earth' as meaning that the sole purpose of a woman is to conceive children. And all her interactions with God or with her husband seem to be to bring that fact about. They say, 'Well, a woman is just giving up her body for her husband.' I would counter by saying that in an agrarian society large families are essential. And that the Israelites were settling into marginal lands that had never been developed before. And whether they would make it or not depended on a certain population base. So the injunctions for fertility—and remember, they are addressed to both men and women—can be seen as a way of encouraging something that was beneficial if not essential for community survival."

It was a hard life. Infant mortality approached 50 percent. Excavations of burials show that female life expectancy, owing in part to the risks involved in

repeated pregnancies, was perhaps thirty years, ten years less than life expectancy for men. Meyers told me that whenever she is on an archaeological dig in the Middle East, she inevitably begins to imagine herself as one of those women of ancient Israel. During an excavation Meyers is working the same remorseless terrain as did the Israelites 3,000 years ago, the two sexes side by side. The toil is unremitting and tedious, the environment dry and dusty. The days when scores of local laborers were supervised by aristocrats in pith helmets are long over. Archaeology is a complex enterprise, group-oriented in the extreme. Being a mother, Meyers for years had other responsibilities as well: young children for whom she had to care, on the site, even as the excavations proceeded.

Meyers's research has now moved beyond the formative centuries of Israel to the Israelite monarchy, which was instituted under Saul around 1020 B.C. This is the Israel of the two books of Samuel and the two books of Kings, a unified monarchy until, after the death of Solomon, around 920 B.C., the country was partitioned into northern and southern kingdoms. Under its kings, political structures in Israel became increasingly centralized and urban centers became increasingly important. A market economy grew up alongside the subsistence one. During this period, too, at least in urban settings, the position of women relative to men became more unequal—came more to resemble the kind of society we see in the Bible. It is hard to know how closely the situation in, say, Jerusalem reflected life elsewhere. Jerusalem, Meyers explained to me, was always an anomaly. After the Assyrians overran the Northern Kingdom, in 721 B.C., the population of Jerusalem the capital of the Southern Kingdom, was swollen by refugees. The city grew to be ten times as large as the next largest city in Israel. Its inhabitants no longer had ties to the land, and women no longer had a central role in economic life. There was poverty and chaos and great social stratification. There were large numbers of foreigners. There was something called public life, and it was in the hands of men. This is the time and the place in which much of the Hebrew Bible was fashioned. No wonder, Meyers said, that it is androcentric.

And yet, Meyers went on, some 90 percent of the people of Israel continued to live in agricultural villages in the countryside. She is cautious about applying the label "patriarchal" either too broadly or too loosely. Often the social patterns that prevail in the city are quite different from those that survive in the country. The term "patriarchy" may be legitimate in some places and times and not in others. Who knows what this nineteenth-century construct even means when applied to a pre-modern society like that of ancient Israel? "It does a disservice," Meyers said, "to a complex piece of literature, the Bible, and to a society that existed for a thousand years, and changed and grew."

> Meyers is cautious about applying the label "patriarchal" too broadly. Who knows what this nineteenth-century construct even means when applied to ancient Israel?

Our gaze is deflected, too, Meyers said, by the very focus of the Bible on public life. On the relatively rare occasions when it affords a glimpse of private life, a patriarchal society is not always what we see. The Song of Songs offers such a glimpse. It contains much archaic material, and is especially noteworthy for the amount of text written in a woman's voice, and in the first person. Some of the terminology is suggestively feminine, and even hints at female authority. For example, whereas in most of the Bible the standard term for a household is *bet'ab*, or "father's house," the term used in the Song of Songs is *bet'em*, or "mother's house." Indeed, there has been speculation that the Song of Songs was written by a woman.

My beloved is mine and I am his;
he pastures his flock among the lilies.
Until the day breathes and the shadows flee,
turn, my beloved, be like a gazelle
or a young stag on the cleft mountains.

Regardless of the author's sex, the love poetry in the Song of Songs expresses an emotional bond not between a master and a subordinate but between equals.

PATRONS AND PRESBYTERS

"Do you know what a 'squeeze' is?" Under other circumstances I might have confidently given a reply, but after several hours of conversation with Ross S. Kraemer, a fellow at the University of Pennsylvania's Center for Judaic Studies, I had a feeling that the answer would be unexpected. We had met in Philadelphia, where Kraemer lives, and we talked over lunch and during a drive through town (interrupted by calls to a housekeeper on the car phone). Kraemer spoke about the Greek cult of Dionysus, which, though little attention has been paid to the fact, was in its ecstatic rites the province of women. (A study of the cult of Dionysus had been the nucleus of her doctoral dissertation at Princeton.) She spoke about Mary Magdalene, one of the women who figured most prominently in the circle around Jesus, and noted that, commonplace public assumptions notwithstanding, nowhere do the New Testament writings identify her as a prostitute. (The tradition may have been developed deliberately as part of an attempt to diminish Mary's stature, particularly in comparison with that of the Apostle Peter.) She spoke about the ancient "purple trade"—the trade in expensive purple-dyed fabric, the participants in which could be presumed to enjoy a certain affluence. This information bears on a woman named Lydia, a "dealer in purple cloth" from the city of Thyatira, who appears in the Acts of the Apostles and is an example of the kind of independent woman of means who seems to have played an especially active role in early Christianity.

> Kraemer noted that, commonplace assumptions notwithstanding, nowhere do the New Testament writings identify Mary Magdalene, who was prominent in Jesus' circle, as a prostitute.

A squeeze is a mold of an ancient inscription carved in marble or other stone, obtained by coating the hard surface with a pliable substance—latex has supplanted papier-mâché as the medium most commonly used—and then peeling it off. Epigraphers, as those who study inscriptions are called, typically have a selection of them in their possession, along with files of photographs and transcriptions. The subject of squeezes had come up when Kraemer began describing the types of sources auxiliary to the Bible on which scholars can rely in the study of women and ancient religion. As time moves forward from primitive epochs, the sources become more plentiful. They include works of art and works of history and literature. They include a diverse array of documents involving women: for example, letters, tax receipts, wet-nurse contracts. And they include large numbers of inscriptions and fragments of inscriptions from buildings and monuments. Kraemer pointed to the work of one colleague whose analysis of Greek and Latin epigraphical evidence led her to conclude, contrary to the prevailing scholarly consensus, that at least sometimes Jewish women occupied prominent leadership roles in the ancient synagogue.

That the sources become more plentiful suggests a Mediterranean world that was becoming more complex. By the end of the sixth century B.C. the monarchic period in Israel had drawn to a close. The Israelites had endured a half century of exile in Babylon and then been allowed to return to their homeland. During the several hundred years that elapsed before the birth of Jesus, this homeland would be ruled by Persians, by Greeks, by Romans. The entire region would feel the influence of new economic and cultural systems. This is also the period when, in the Temple precincts of Jerusalem, the Hebrew Bible gradually cohered into the form in which we have it now, a collection of thirty-nine canonical texts, some of them incorporating material of great antiquity passed down through the ages more or less verbatim. (I remember Carol Meyers's once pointing out that the enormous stylistic variety of the Bible's Hebrew is one characteristic that eludes translation.) The canon of the Hebrew Bible was closed—no books would subsequently be added—toward the end of the first century A.D. By then the Romans had razed the Temple in Jerusalem, and the sacred texts of a new religious force, Christianity, were in the process of being compiled.

How egalitarian was that new religious force? More important (and borrowing the title of an influential and controversial 1971 article by Leonard Swidler, a professor at Temple), was Jesus a feminist? Such questions unfailingly stir up a range of scholarly responses. I asked Ross Kraemer to talk about those questions, and the conversation gravitated naturally to the work of Elisabeth Schüssler Fiorenza. Kraemer acknowledged the enormous debt that everyone owed Schüssler Fiorenza, acknowledged that her work had been groundbreaking in providing a new but also comprehensive and coherent way of viewing the Jesus movement and its context. But she added that she was less, well, optimistic than Schüssler Fiorenza. "I'm not as optimistic not so much in terms of her recovery of what she thinks women in early Christianity did, what roles they played—I think she's likely to be right about a lot of that. Where I would part company is with her argument that the earliest theology of Christianity is *intentionally* egalitarian and feminist. I'm really not persuaded of that, though I think that Christianity in many communities may have had egalitarian consequences. Elisabeth wants to locate the intent in Jesus himself. It's not so much that I think she's wrong as that I'm simply not convinced we can know that she's right. It's very hard to argue that we know *anything* about what Jesus really thought, and the few things that any scholar would be willing to attribute to Jesus himself with any confidence don't address this particular issue."

The difficulty is that the Gospels and other early texts are encrusted documents, layered accretions formed out of a mixture of sources and motivations. On women's issues as on other matters, they may be surer guides to the communities in which they were formed than to the community around Jesus that they ostensibly describe. Kraemer used the various Resurrection stories and the part played by women in those stories to illustrate the pitfalls. All four Gospels depict women as having been the first to discover the empty tomb of Jesus, and in two of the Gospels, Jesus first appears after the Resurrection to Mary Magdalene. This would certainly seem to make a point about the position of women in the Jesus movement, some scholars say, and would also bolster a claim to female authority in Christian affairs—at the time of Jesus or later. Others note, however, that the account of the Resurrection in Paul's first letter to the Corinthians, which was written at least twenty years before the Gospels existed in written form, makes no mention of Mary Magdalene or indeed of any

women, and it makes no mention of the empty-tomb tradition.

What is going on? One possibility, of course, is that in his account Paul is deliberately ignoring a tradition he is fully aware of—perhaps so as not to deflect emphasis from the authority of men (and himself). This could suggest that the process of diminishing the authority of women in Christianity began at a very early date. If that is the case, the survival of the women-at-the-empty-tomb tradition in the Gospels—decades after Paul—suggests its sheer durability. Thus we should perhaps take at face value, after all, what the Gospels have to say about the prominent position of women in the Jesus movement.

But wait: What if Paul was unaware of the empty-tomb tradition? What if, indeed, it arose *after* Paul—arose, as some have ventured, in conjunction with a growing belief among Christians in the prospect of a physical resurrection of an uncorrupted body after death, a belief that Paul himself would have regarded as crudely simplistic, whether applied to Jesus' Resurrection or to a more general resurrection of the dead? If the tradition did arise after Paul, Kraemer argues, then casting women as the first to see the empty tomb might have subtly helped to explain why it took so long for the good news about the physical Resurrection of Jesus to spread: because they were women, the original witnesses had been afraid to divulge what they knew, or had been widely disbelieved. In either case, of course, the result is an implicit denigration of women.

The situation is something of a mess. As Kraemer points out in her book *Her Share of the Blessings,* the basic problem is that "early Christian communities, especially after the death of Jesus, experienced considerable conflict over the appropriate roles of women, and tended to retroject their positions about this conflict back onto the stories they told about the women who encountered the earthly Jesus."

Her Share of the Blessings is a wide-ranging exploration of the role of women in Greco-Roman religions—pagan, Jewish, Christian—from about the fourth century B.C. to the fifth century A.D. The comparative approach Kraemer takes has great advantages, allowing her to see how structures in one realm may have influenced those in another. If she believes that, for whatever reason, early Christianity was more egalitarian in

terms of gender than it later became—and she does—it is not only because of the interpretation she accepts of early Christian writings. She knows also from looking at the larger context that it was not unusual for women to hold cultic office in pagan religion, not unusual for them to play the role of patron. In light of the social mores of the time, the emphasis in much of early Christianity on sexual asceticism would also have served to enhance female independence: it offered free women a radical new option, a door to open other than the traditional one of marriage and child bearing and domesticity. Another force conducive to egalitarianism was the expectation among many early Christians that the present earthly order would soon pass—that the Lord was about to return in glory. In such a climate attachment to social structures that were plainly "of the world" was considerably lessened. Did women serve as priests? The formal establishment of a priesthood in Christianity came very late, Kraemer writes, but a diverse body of evidence shows that women in early Christianity held the title *presbytera,* and that people who held this title performed all priestly functions: they taught, they baptized, they blessed the Eucharist.

There are, of course, tensions. One cannot read very far into the writings of Paul without becoming aware of his inner conflict when it came to questions of gender and sexuality. George Bernard Shaw once characterized Paul as the "eternal enemy of woman." In the epistle to the Galatians, Paul embraced an egalitarian formula, but in I Corinthians he showed himself to be clearly disturbed by the powerful and independent women in the Christian community at Corinth. He did not forbid the Corinthian women from prophesying, but he demanded that they cover their heads when they prayed in public, and he added a statement that defines women as subordinate to men. Is this last statement (along with some other problematic passages) a later interpolation, as some scholars believe? Perhaps. But tensions exist nonetheless, Kraemer writes, and they become deeper and more intolerable as Christianity moves further away in time from its origins, and moves closer to the contemporaneous social establishment.

Conflicting perspectives on women are apparent in later writings. One perspective is embodied in the apocryphal Acts of Thecla, probably written in the second century A.D., which celebrates the life of an ascetic female missionary supposedly sent out by Paul himself to teach and spread the word of the Lord. The Acts of Thecla, it must be said, has many decidedly odd elements (for example, Thecla is described as baptizing herself by jumping into a pool of hungry seals), but this text and many others like it enjoyed wide popularity. The other perspective is embodied, for example, in the epistles to Timothy, written in the second century, which contain some of the most stringent passages about women in the New Testament, passages that were then ascribed to Paul:

Let a woman learn in silence with full submission. I permit no woman to teach or to have authority over a man; she is to keep silent. For Adam was formed first, then Eve; and Adam was not deceived, but the woman was deceived and became a transgressor.

This is the perspective that hardened when Christianity became the religion of the Roman state.

WOMEN WHO LEAD

Was Junia, whom Paul, in his epistle to the Romans, called "prominent among the apostles," a man or a woman? What about the person named Jael, who is referred to in an inscription from Aphrodisias, in Asia Minor, as being the presiding officer or patron of a Jewish community there? These questions are not academic. They speak to issues of gender, status, and leadership.

Some would argue that Junia and Jael had to have been men. How, after all, could a woman be a Christian apostle or the presiding officer of a Jewish community, when we know that women were barred from such honors? This is the kind of reasoning that brings a note of both excitement and exasperation to Bernadette Brooten's voice. Brooten is a professor of Scripture and interpretation at the Harvard Divinity School and the woman who made the study of Greek and Latin inscriptions which Ross Kraemer referred to. This fall she will join the faculty at Brandeis University. It is bad enough, Brooten said during a conversation one day, for women to be invisible in ancient Judaism and Christianity because men didn't think to mention them or because they weren't in a position to be mentioned. Must we also argue away the few women in plain sight?

Junia was a common female name in the ancient world, Brooten said. Several ancient religious commentators, such as Origen of Alexandria and John Chrysostom, assumed as a matter of course that the Junia mentioned in Romans was a woman. This assumption prevailed until the Middle Ages. Then a reaction set in. Paul reserved the title "apostle" for persons of great authority—people who had served as missionaries and founded churches. To a medieval mind, such people had to have been men. Junia underwent a change of sex. Later Martin Luther popularized a reinterpretation of Junia as *Junias,* an apparently masculine name—the diminutive, perhaps, as scholars would later speculate, of Junianius or Junilius. There is only one problem, Brooten said. The name Junias cannot be found in antiquity: not on documents, not in inscriptions. It does not exist as a name, diminutive or otherwise. All that we have is Junia, a common name for a woman—in this case, the name of a woman "prominent among the apostles."

As for the name Jael, Brooten said, the only reason the question of gender has come up at all is that there is an important title attached to the name, and the name sits at the top of a list of other names, all of which are male. In less politically charged circumstances, this Jael would simply have been assumed to be a woman. Jael was—is—a well-known woman's name. A woman named Jael is prominent in Judges. But scholars have hunted through Scripture and other ancient sources to see if they can find precedent for a Jael who is a man, because it seems to them so unlikely that this Jael could have been a woman. In some manuscripts of the Book of Ezra, as it appears in the Septuagint, they have found such a Jael. The name is in a list of male exiles who had married foreign women and were now repudiating them upon their return to Israel. The identification is highly tentative, however. The Septuagint is the Hebrew Bible as translated into Greek, and the transliteration of Semitic names from Hebrew into Greek is haphazard and inconsistent. What this means, Brooten went on, is that to take Jael as a man's name one has to accept an instance that may be nothing more than an artifact of transliteration. One has to prefer this to the attestation of Jael as female in a major book of the Bible, the name being that of a well-known figure whose story was probably a staple of synagogue readings.

"All of which," Brooten said, "raises several questions for me. How many women do there have to have been for there to have been any? And if it's part of the marginalization of women that women are very rarely leaders to begin with, then even in those circumstances in which women do occur as leaders, they may be either perceived as not being women or perceived as not being leaders." The note of frustration in Brooten's voice gave way to something slyer as she summoned up an image of scholars one day confronting a document that referred to Prime Minister Margaret Thatcher and the members of one of her all-male Cabinets. It would be only a matter of time, Brooten said, before some scholar came along and pronounced Thatcher a man.

Harvard Divinity School is one of the many divinity schools to whose revival an influx of women has contributed greatly. Applicants are plentiful, with women accounting for well over half the enrollment in the school's various programs. Whatever this portends for the future, women as yet remain distinctly underrepresented among the school's senior faculty.

Brooten joined the Harvard faculty in 1985. She had received her doctorate from Harvard a few years earlier, and in the intervening period had taught at Claremont. Part of her academic training took place in Tübingen, the cobbled and timbered university town in Germany whose name has long been associated with new departures in theology. She describes the German academic environment for women in much the same way Schüssler Fiorenza does. "German theologians," Brooten told me, "will just say outright that they don't want women." Oddly, though, Tübingen is where Brooten took her first women's-studies course: Leonard Swidler, on leave from Temple, happened to be a visiting professor there for a year, and offered a seminar on women and the Church. Brooten was one of two students who signed up for it. "In the university as a whole," she recalled, "there was no interest in such things at all."

Brooten's office at Harvard has the dusky flavor of a Dickensian garret. Narrow pathways thread among tumuli of tables and books. Some of the books are old, spines worn to a dull sheen by centuries of palms. There is not even a computer to suggest the late twentieth century, though Brooten does use one at

5. THE GREAT RELIGIONS

home. It is now standard in the field to have computer software that can print in Greek, Hebrew, and Coptic fonts. Computers have also made some kinds of research much easier for biblical scholars. For example, the great bulk of the writing that survives from antiquity in Greek, Latin, and Hebrew—not just works of literature but also snippets from tens of thousands of papyrus fragments and stone inscriptions—is now available on CD-ROM.

A capsule summary of the implications of Brooten's earliest research might read like this: with respect to roles played by women, there was more differentiation within Judaism in the Greco-Roman world than many scholars acknowledge. This touches on a highly sensitive issue. Some scholars, particularly among those who want a liberalization of Christian church policies concerning women, have argued that if early Christianity fell short of an egalitarian ideal, the cause lay in part in the nature of the Jewish world out of which Christianity emerged. Thus, one argument runs, there might have been more women leaders in Christianity if only there had been more in Judaism. Looking at the matter another way, to the degree that egalitarianism did exist in early Christianity, it is sometimes presented as a sharp break from Jewish tradition. Often implicit, this kind of thinking amounts, in the view of some, to locating the origins of patriarchal misogyny in the Hebrew Bible and those who inhabited its shadow. That is perhaps stating the problem too unsubtly, but it exposes a place where the nerve is raw. Brooten's view is that the spectrum of tolerable practice among Jews in ancient times was broad—just as it is in modern Judaism, just as it was and is in Christianity.

The work of feminist scholars has been greeted by some with impatience, irritation, even contempt. It has also established women's issues as a permanent focus of biblical studies.

In her doctoral dissertation, later published in book form as *Women Leaders in the Ancient Synagogue,* Brooten considered nineteen carved inscriptions dating from as early as 27 B.C. to as late as the sixth century A.D., in which Jewish women are accorded official titles relating to the communal life of a synagogue—titles such as "head of the synagogue," "leader," "elder." Titles like these, when applied to women, had long been interpreted as honorific rather than functional. "Rufina, a Jewess, head of the synagogue, built this tomb for her freed slaves and the slaves raised in her house"—these words come from a marble plaque, inscribed in the second century A.D., that was found in Smyrna. The traditional view has been that Rufina, the "head of the synagogue," the *archisynagogos,* had no real functional authority and was in all likelihood merely the wife of the true *archisynagogos.* Rufina is seen to have the title, as Brooten wryly notes, "*honoris causa.*" In dense, meticulous arguments that cannot be reviewed here, Brooten mounts an assault on that view. She takes up the cases of Rufina and the eighteen other women, and exposes what she deems to be the flawed presuppositions and tortured reasoning necessary to conclude that their titles were not functional. Women leaders of the synagogue were, of course, never the norm and were perhaps always the great exception. But, Brooten states, it is wrong to see the emergence of women leaders in Christianity as unprecedented.

Brooten's more recent work involves the writings of Paul, in particular his views on the proper place of women in society and where those views came from. One clue lies in Paul's condemnations of same-sex love. As Brooten explains, in a discussion that draws not only on religious texts but also on ancient materials as diverse as medical and astrological writings, Paul was in this regard no more than a man of his time. Whatever the exceptions in practice, on the normative gender map of the Roman world some behavior is appropriately masculine and some appropriately feminine, and the line is not supposed to be crossed. In sexual relations between members of the same sex this distinction is violated. One man becomes "like a woman"; one woman becomes "like a man." Underlying all this was a world view that, Brooten argues, saw the distinction between "active" and "passive" as more fundamental even than distinctions of sex. It was the basis of social order and social hierarchy. It was the

origin of the tension in Paul. Forward-looking in many ways, Paul could not let it go.

"Paul was happy to work with women as colleagues, and encouraged them," Brooten said. "So, for example, he mentions Junia, and he acknowledges Prisca and Tryphaena and Tryphosa and Persis and other women. He teaches with them and he recognizes their prophecy, and he works with them as missionaries in the Roman world. On the other hand, while he was very willing to make a religious and societal break with Jewish tradition on points that were considered very central to Judaism, such as the issue of dietary laws and the circumcision of men, in order to permit Jew and Gentile to come together alike to accept Jesus as the Christ, with some customs concerning women he's not willing to make that kind of break. For example, the issue of the hairstyling and veiling of women. And, indeed, at that very point in the text he describes Christ as the head of man, and man as the head of woman, which goes beyond tolerating a custom and gives a theological underpinning to gender differentiation. I see his position as essentially ambivalent. On certain issues—gender, slavery, Roman power—he is very much interested in maintaining social order. But what's fascinating about Paul is that he experiments."

Toward the end of a long conversation we lingered for a moment on the nature of that first-century world of which Paul was a part: a world that those who know it well describe as more alien from our own in its psychology and belief systems and outlook than we imagine. How confident do you feel, I asked Brooten, that we can span the gulf between these two cultures, ours and theirs—can reconstruct something trustworthy about the dynamics of *then*?

"That's something I ask myself about all the time," Brooten said. And then she laughed. "I've often had this thought: that I'll die, and go to heaven, and Rufina will meet me, and I'll greet her as *archisynagogos.* And she'll say, '*Archisynagogos*? Nah. That was just my husband's title.' "

THE WRITING ON THE WALL

To focus on the work of a handful of scholars is necessarily to leave aside the work of scores of others. And there are, literally, scores. Their research by now covers just about every conceivable aspect of the Hebrew Bible and the New Testament. It has spread deeply into the fields of history and theology and literary criticism. I once asked David Tracy, the prominent Catholic theologian, what he thought would be the result of feminism's encounter with religion, and he said simply, "The next intellectual revolution." That assessment may sound overblown, but it isn't. Phyllis Trible used the metaphor of a conversation between feminism and the Bible. Feminism's larger conversation with religion touches every aspect of it, leaves no subject off the table. It engages doctrine, liturgy, ministry, and leadership, and it engages them all at once.

Scholarly work on women and the Bible faces certain inherent problems, certain inherent risks. In my talks with people in the field, the same worries were voiced by one scholar after another. A fundamental one has to do with the distinction between deriving an interpretation *from* a text and reading an interpretation *into* a text. It is one thing for a contemporary personal agenda—a desire, say, to see women enjoy a position of full equality in religious institutions—to direct one's research focus. Agendas of one sort or another frequently drive scholarship. But can't they also get out of hand? Another concern is an issue raised by Bernadette Brooten: the sometimes facile comparisons made between Christianity and Judaism. This has already begun to stir animosity outside the field of biblical studies, as evidenced by an eloquent recent essay in the Jewish bimonthly *Tikkun*.

The range of scholarly output on matters involving women and the Bible has been enormously diverse. As in any academic endeavor, the work has been of uneven quality. Much of the research remains tentative and preliminary, and there are severe limits, given the sparseness of what is likely to be the available evidence, to what can ever be known with certainty. The most we can hope for, Bernadette Brooten has written, is "a quick glimpse through a crack in the door." What has been accomplished thus far? One achievement is simply the staking out of ground. Several decades ago no one was particularly concerned—indeed, the thought rarely occurred to anyone—that the entire academic biblical enterprise was based on what was known about men's lives, was one that generalized from men to all humanity. Those days are gone. Another achievement has been a new emphasis on the sheer variety of thought and practice which sometimes existed within ancient religious groups. Scholars who perhaps went searching after some lost Golden Age—driven by the "earlier-is-better" bias that seems to be a characteristic of human thought—have stumbled into worlds that are more confused and complex than they may have anticipated, worlds that are in that sense not unlike our own. Yet another achievement is simply this: leaving aside the specific details, scholars have gone a long way toward bringing women in biblical and early Christian times into sharper relief. They have also shown how meaning has been shaded by the lacquer of interpretation. A good distillation of much of the research on women can be found in *The Women's Bible Commentary*, edited by Carol A. Newsom and Sharon H. Ringe.

Perhaps the most important lesson offered by the work of feminist biblical scholars comes in the form of a reminder: that in religion, as in other spheres, circumstances have not always been as we see them now. Evolution occurs. Some things, it turns out, are *not* sacred. This point may be obvious, but with respect to religion, especially, it is frequently overlooked—and, in fact, sometimes hotly denied. Whatever one believes about the nature of their origin, the handful of immutable precepts at any religion's core are embedded in a vast pulp of tradition, interpretation, and practice. And that pulp bears an all too human character. It is variously diminished, augmented, scarred, sculpted, and otherwise shaped by powerful human forces in every society and every time period through which it passes. Sometimes the change occurs slowly and almost invisibly. Sometimes it happens quickly and right before one's eyes, as I believe it is happening now—the proliferation of feminist scholarship on the Bible being both consequence and cause.

I write these last words on the day of my daughter's first communion in a denomination that still restricts the role of women, and I write them in the expectation that with respect to the position of women, matters will not remain—will simply not be able to remain—as in some places we see them now; in the expectation, to employ a biblical turn, that the present way's days are numbered.

STATE AND SOCIETY
UNDER ISLAM

Bernard Lewis

Bernard Lewis is professor of Near Eastern Studies (emeritus) at Princeton University and the director of the Annenberg Research Institute in Philadelphia. Born in London, England, he received his A.B. (1936) and Ph.D. (1939) from London University. His books include The Assassins *(1967) and* The Muslim Discovery of Europe *(1982). This essay was presented in August 1989 at a conference on "Europe and Civil Society" at Castel Gandolfo in Italy under the auspices of the* Institut für die Wissenschaften vom Menschen *of Vienna, Austria.*

Christendom and Islam are in many ways sister civilizations, both drawing on the shared heritage of Jewish revelation and prophesy and Greek philosophy and science, and both nourished by the immemorial traditions of Middle Eastern antiquity. For most of their joint history, they have been locked in combat, in an endless series of attacks and counter-attacks, jihads and crusades, conquests and reconquests. But even in struggle and polemic they reveal their essential kinship and the common features which link them

to each other and set them apart from the remoter civilizations of Asia.

As well as resemblances, there are, of course, profound disparities between the two, and these go beyond the obvious differences in dogma and worship. Nowhere are these differences more profound—and more obvious—than in the attitudes of these two religions, and of their authorized exponents, to the relations among government, religion, and society. The founder of Christianity bade his followers "render unto Caesar the things which are Caesar's; and unto God the things which are God's"—and for centuries Christianity grew and developed as a religion of the downtrodden, until Caesar himself became a Christian and inaugurated a series of changes by which the new faith captured the Roman Empire and—some would add—was captured by it.

The founder of Islam was his own Constantine and founded his own empire. He did not therefore create—or need to create—a church. The dichotomy of *regnum* and *sacerdotium*, so crucial in the history of Western Christendom, had no equivalent in Islam. During Muhammad's lifetime, the

Muslims became at once a political and a religious community, with the Prophet as head of state. As such, he governed a place and a people, dispensed justice, collected taxes, commanded armies, waged war, and made peace. For the first generation of Muslims, whose adventures are the sacred and salvation history of Islam, there was no protracted testing by persecution, no tradition of resistance to a hostile state power. On the contrary, the state that ruled them was that of Islam, and God's approval of their cause was made clear to them in the form of victory and empire in this world.

In pagan Rome, Caesar was God. For Christians, there is a choice between God and Caesar, and endless generations of Christians have been ensnared in that choice. In Islam, there was no such choice. In the universal Islamic polity as conceived by Muslims, there is no Caesar, but only God, who is the sole sovereign and the sole source of law. Muhammad was his Prophet, who during his lifetime both taught and ruled on God's behalf. When Muhammad died in A.D. 632, his spiritual and prophetic mission, to bring God's book to man, was completed. What remained was the religious mission of spreading God's revelation until finally all the world accepted it. This was to be achieved by extending the authority and thus also the membership of the community which embraced the true faith and upheld God's law. To provide the necessary cohesion and leadership for this task, a deputy or successor of the Prophet was required. The Arabic word *khalifa*, the title by which that successor came to be known, combines the two meanings. This was the title adopted by the Prophet's father-in-law and first successor, 'Abū Bakr, whose accession to the leadership of the Islamic community marked the foundation of the great historic institution of the caliphate.

Under the caliphs, the community of Medina, where the Prophet had held sway, grew in a century into a vast empire, and Islam became a world religion. In the experience of the first Muslims, as preserved and recorded for later generations, religious belief and political power were indissolubly associated: The first sanctified the second; the second sustained the first.

The late Ayatollah Khomeini once remarked that "Islam is politics or it is nothing." Not all Muslims would go that far, but most would agree that God is concerned with politics, and this belief is confirmed and sustained by the Shari'a, the Holy Law, which deals extensively with the acquisition and exercise of power, the nature of authority, the duties of ruler and subject—in a word, with what we in the West would call constitutional law and political philosophy.

In the Islamic state, as ideally conceived and as it indeed existed from medieval through to Ottoman times almost into the 19th century, there could be no conflict between Pope and Emperor; in classical Middle Eastern Islam, the two mighty powers which these two represented were one and the same, and the caliph was the embodiment of both. As a building, a place of public worship, the Muslim equivalent of the church is the mosque; as an institution, a corporate body with its own hierarchy and laws, there is no church in Islam. For the same reason, there is no priesthood in the true sense of the term, and therefore no prelates or hierarchy, no councils or synods, to define orthodoxy and thus condemn heterodoxy. The ulema, the professional men of religion in the Islamic world, may perhaps be called a clergy in the sociological but certainly not in the theological sense. They receive no ordination, have no parishes, perform no sacraments. There is no priestly mediation between the worshiper and his God, and in early Islam there was no constituted ecclesiastical authority of any kind.

The primary function of the ulema—from a word meaning knowledge—is to uphold and interpret the Holy Law. From late medieval times, something like a parish clergy emerged, ministering to the needs of ordinary people in cities and villages, but these were usually separate from and mistrusted by the ulema, and owed much more to mystical than to dogmatic Islam. In the later Islamic monarchies, in Turkey and Iran, a kind of ecclesiastical hierarchy appeared, but this had no roots in the classical Muslim tradition, and members of these hierarchies never claimed and still less exercised the powers of Christian prelates.

If one may speak of a clergy only in a

limited sociological sense in the Islamic world, there is no sense at all in which one can speak of a laity. The very notion of something that is separate or even separable from religious authority, expressed in Christian languages by such terms as lay, temporal, or secular, is totally alien to Islamic thought and practice. It was not until relatively modern times that equivalents for these terms were used in Arabic. They were borrowed from the usage of Arabic-speaking Christians.

Yet, from the days of the Prophet, the Islamic society had a dual character. On the one hand it was a polity—a chieftaincy which successively became a state and an empire. At the same time, it was a religious community, founded by a Prophet and ruled by his deputies who were also his successors.

Christ was crucified, Moses died without entering the Promised Land, and the beliefs and attitudes of their religious followers are still profoundly influenced by the memory of these facts. Muhammad triumphed during his lifetime and died a conqueror and a sovereign. The resulting Muslim attitudes can only have been confirmed by the subsequent history of their religion.

In the West, barbarian but teachable invaders came to an existing state and religion, the Roman empire and the Christian church. The invaders recognized both and tried to serve their own aims and needs within the existing structures of Roman polity and Christian religion, both using the Latin language. The Muslim Arab invaders who conquered the Middle East and North Africa brought their own faith, with their own scriptures in their own language; they created their own polity, with a new set of laws, a new imperial language, and a new imperial structure, with the caliph as supreme head. This state was defined by Islam, and full membership belonged, alone, to those who professed the dominant faith.

The career of the Prophet Muhammad, in this as in all else the model which all good Muslims seek to emulate, falls into two parts. In the first, during his years in his birthplace Mecca (?570–622), he was an opponent of the reigning pagan oligarchy. In the second, after his migration from Mecca to Medina (622–632), he was the head of a

Islamic civilization, as it spread, accommodated and absorbed other cultures. In this 16th-century Mughal painting, Alexander the Great, wearing an Islamic turban, is shown being lowered into the sea in a glass jar.

state. These two phases in the Prophet's career, the one of resistance, the other of rule, are both reflected in the Qur'an, where, in different chapters, the believers are enjoined to obey God's representative and to disobey Pharaoh, the paradigm of the unjust and tyrannical ruler. These two aspects of the Prophet's life and work inspired two traditions in Islam, the one authoritarian and quietist, the other radical and activist. Both are amply reflected, on the one hand in the development of the tradition, on the other, in the unfolding of events. It was not always easy to determine who was God's representative and who was Pharaoh; many books were written, and many battles fought, in the attempt. Both traditions can be seen very clearly in the polemics and struggles of our own times.

Between the extremes of quietism and radicalism, there is a pervasive, widely expressed attitude of reserve, even of mistrust, of government. An example is the sharp difference, in medieval times, of popular attitudes towards the qadi, a judge, and the mufti, a jurisconsult in the Holy Law. The qadi, who was appointed by the ruler, is presented in literature and folklore as a venal, even a ridiculous figure; the mufti, established by the recognition of his col-

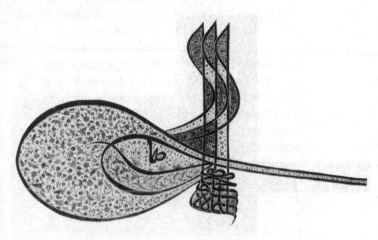

Calligraphic emblem of Süleyman I.

leagues and the general population, enjoyed esteem and respect. A recurring theme in biographies of pious men—of which we have hundreds of thousands—is that the hero was offered a government appointment, and refused. The offer establishes his learning and reputation, the refusal his integrity.

Under the Ottoman sultans there was an important change. The qadi gained greatly in power and authority, and even the mufti was integrated into the public chain of authority. But the old attitude of mistrust of government persisted, and is frequently expressed in proverbs, folk tales, and even high literature.

For more than a thousand years, Islam provided the only universally acceptable set of rules and principles for the regulation of public and social life. Even during the period of maximum European influence, in the countries ruled or dominated by European imperial powers as well as in those that remained independent, Islamic politi-

cal notions and attitudes remained a profound and pervasive influence.

In recent years there have been many signs that these notions and attitudes may be returning, albeit in much modified forms, to their previous dominance. There are therefore good reasons to devote a serious study to these ideas, and in particular to how they deal with the relations among government, religion, and society.

The term "civil society" has become very popular in recent years, and is used in a number of different—sometimes overlapping, sometimes conflicting—senses. It may therefore be useful to examine Islamic perceptions of civility, according to various definitions of that term.

Perhaps the primary meaning of civil, in the Middle East today, is as the converse of military; it is in this sense that civility must begin, before any other is conceivable. This has a special relevance in a place and at a time when the professional officer corps is often both the source and the instrument of power. Understood this way, Islamic society, at the time of its inception and in its early formative years, was unequivocally civil. The Prophet and the early caliphs that followed employed no professional soldiers but relied for military duties on a kind of armed, mostly voluntary militia.

It is not until the second century of the Islamic era (A.D. eighth century) that one can speak, with certitude, of a professional army. The caliph, who in early though not in later times occasionally commanded his armies, was nevertheless a civilian. So too was the wazir, who, under the caliph's authority, was in charge of all branches of the government, both civil and military. The wazir's emblem of office was an inkpot, which was carried before him on ceremonial public occasions. During the later Middle Ages, internal upheavals and external invasions brought about changes which resulted in the militarization of most Islamic regimes. This has persisted to modern times. During the late 19th and early 20th centuries, there was an interlude of civilian, more or less constitutional government, mostly on Western models. During the 1950s and after, these civilian regimes, for the most part, came to an end and were replaced by authoritarian governments under ultimate military control.

This is, however, by no means universal. In some countries, including, for example, Saudi Arabia and Morocco, traditional monarchies still maintain a traditional civilian order; in others, such as Turkey and, later, Egypt and Pakistan, the military themselves have prepared the way for a return to civilian legality. On the whole, the prospects for civilianization at the present time seem to be reasonably good.

In the more generally accepted interpretation of the term civil society, civil is opposed not to religious or to military but to government as such. So construed, the civil society is one in which the mainsprings of organization, initiative, and action come from within the society rather than from above, from the holders of authority, the wielders of power. Islamic precept, as presented by the jurists and theologians, and Islamic practice, as reflected by the historians, offer a variety of sometimes contradictory precedents.

The tradition of private charity, for example, is old and deeply rooted in Islam, and is given legal expression in the institution of *waqf*. A *waqf* is a pious endowment in mortmain, consisting of some income-producing property, the proceeds of which are dedicated to a pious purpose—the upkeep of a place of worship, a school, a bathhouse, a soup kitchen, a water fountain, and the like. The donor might be a ruler or government official; he might equally be, and very often was, a private person. Women, who in Islamic law had the right to own and dispose of property, figure prominently among founders of *waqfs*, sometimes reaching almost half the number. This is perhaps the only area in the traditional Muslim society in which they approach equality with men. By means of the institution of *waqf*, many services, which in other systems are the principal or sole responsibility of the state, are provided by private initiative. One of the major changes brought by modernizing autocrats in the 19th century was to bring the *waqfs* under state control. (Several present-day Muslim states, including Egypt, have departments or ministries of *waqfs*.)

Islamic law, unlike Roman law and its derivatives, does not recognize corporate legal persons, and there are therefore no Islamic equivalents to such Western corporate entities as the city, the monastery, or the college. Cities were mostly governed by royal officers, while convents and colleges relied on royal or private *waqfs*. There are, however, other groupings of considerable importance in traditional Muslim society. Such, for example, are the kin group—family, clan, tribe; the faith group, often linked together by common membership of a sufi fraternity; the craft group, joined in a guild; the ward or neighborhood within a city. Very often these groups overlap or even coincide, and much of the life of a Muslim city is determined by their interaction.

In the Islamic context, the independence and initiative of the civil society may best be measured not in relation to the state but in relation to religion, of which, in the Muslim perception, the state itself is a manifestation and an instrument. In this sense, the primary meaning of civil is nonreligious, and the civil society is one in which the organizing principle is something other than religion, that being a private affair of the individual. This idea received its first classical formulation in the *Letter Concerning Toleration* by the English philosopher John Locke, published in 1689. Locke's conclusion is that "neither Pagan, nor Mahometan, nor Jew, ought to be excluded from the civil rights of the commonwealth because of his religion."

The first European country which actually accorded civil rights to non-Christians was Holland, followed within a short time by England and the English colonies in North America, where extensive, though not as yet equal rights were granted to nonconformist Christians and to Jews. These examples were followed by others, and the libertarian ideas which they expressed contributed significantly to the ideologies of both the American and French Revolutions.

In time, these ideas were almost universally accepted in Western Christendom. Though few nations, other than France and the United States, accepted a formal constitutional separation of religion and the state, most of them in fact accepted secular principles. This virtually ended the earlier situation which Danish scholar Vilhelm Gronbech spoke of as "a religion which is the soul of society, the obverse of the practi-

MUHAMMAD THE PROPHET

The Prophet Muhammad (?570–632) lived only 1400 years ago. Of all the founders of major world religions, he is the closest to us in time. Yet historians have struggled to piece together a complete and accurate biography of the man who Muslims believe is the last prophet in the succession of Abraham. Scarce primary sources include the Qur'an and the *Hadith*, traditional accounts of Muhammad's words and deeds. Early biographies (8th–9th centuries)—the *Sirah* (Life) by Ibn Ishaq, the *Maghazi* (Expeditions) by Al-Waqidi, and the writings of Ibn Sa'd—also remain valuable to scholars.

The Prophet was born in Mecca, a prosperous trading town located in the western part of the Arabian Peninsula. Shortly before his birth around 570, the town's preeminent tribe, the Quraysh, appears to have gained control of the lucrative caravan trade running between Yemen and Syria. This new prosperity, according to some historians, may have created a rift between the great merchants and the lesser Quraysh "clans," undermining an older code that emphasized communal wealth and protection through kinship ties.

Muhammad, the son of a respected Quraysh family, was orphaned at six and raised, successively, by his grandfather and uncle. He himself went on to become a successful caravan merchant, and at 25 he married his employer, Khadijah, a wealthy widow (and the first of several wives). Financially secure, Muhammad turned to other, higher matters, and sometime in his late thirties he began to meditate in a hill cave outside of town. Around 610, the faithful believe, he had a vision of the archangel Gabriel, who pronounced Muhammad the "Messenger of God." To his friends and relatives and later to the entire community, Muhammad began to relate messages that he claimed came directly from God.

The central tenet of Muhammad's teachings posed a threat to the polytheistic creed of most of his fellow Arabs: He declared that there was only one good and all-powerful God. He also preached about the coming of a Day of Judgment and the existence of Heaven (the Garden) and Hell (the Fire). Islam literally means submission, and Muhammad's faith called on Muslims (those who submit) to acknowledge God's might and majesty and to accept Muhammad as the final prophet.

Muhammad's preaching was, above all, religious, but it also contained a social message that was troubling to some of Mecca's wealthier merchants. By A.D. 616, many of the Quraysh leaders had grown alarmed by the Prophet's success, and Muhammad began coming under verbal and then physical attack. By this time, too, the Prophet's reputation had begun to spread beyond Mecca. During the summer of 620, six pilgrims from Yathrib, an oasis town 250 miles north of Mecca, came to hear the Prophet preach. Impressed, they begged him to return with them to arbitrate among the rival tribes in their own community. In 622, Muhammad and some 70 of his followers moved to Yathrib; the *Hijra* (migration) marks year one of the Islamic calendar.

Established in Yathrib (which the Muslims renamed al-Madina, the city), Muhammad and his followers soon came into conflict with the pagan oligarchy in Mecca. War broke out and Muhammad's forces, though greatly outnumbered, outfought their foes. Each victory seemed proof of Allah's will, and the Islamic ranks swelled to some 10,000 fighting men. In 630, Muhammad triumphantly returned to Mecca at the head of his army; the city surrendered and many of its inhabitants converted to Islam. Muhammad now ruled as the most powerful political and religious leader in Arabia.

The Prophet, however, had little time to savor his triumph. He died a natural death in 632. Thereafter, a line of caliphs (successors), beginning with Muhammad's faithful lieutenant and father-in-law, 'Abū Bakr, spread the power and faith of Islam. Within little more than a century, Islam had expanded north as far as the Atlas Mountains, east across Persia and central Asia to the borders of India and China, and west across North Africa and into Spain.

cal, a living and real religion, the practical relationship of the people to God, soul and eternity, that manifests itself in worship and works as a life-giving power in politics and economics, in crafts and commerce, in ethics as in law. In this sense," he concludes, "the modern state has no religion."

Despite the personal devoutness of great and growing numbers of people, Gronbech is right—the Western democratic state has no religion, and most, even among the devout, see this as a merit, not a defect. They are encouraged in this belief by the example of some states in Central and Eastern Europe, yesterday and today, where the principle of unity and direction was retained but with a shift of stress—religion replaced by ideology, and the church by the single ruling party, with its own hierarchy, synods, inquisition, dogmas, and heresies. In such countries, it was not the state that withered away but the civil society.

In the Islamic world, the dethronement of religion as the organizing principle of society was not attempted until much later and resulted entirely from European influences. It was never really completed and is perhaps now being reversed. Certainly in Iran, organized religion has returned to something like the status which it enjoyed in the medieval world, both Christian and Islamic. Indeed, in some ways—notably in the power of the priesthood and the emergence of a political prelacy—the Iranian theocracy is closer to the Christian than to the classical Islamic model.

During the 14 centuries of Islamic history, there have been many changes. In particular, the long association, sometimes in coexistence, but more often in confrontation, with Christendom, led to the acceptance, in the later Islamic monarchies in Iran and Turkey and their successor states, of patterns of religious organization that might suggest a probably unconscious imitation of Christian ecclesiastical usage. Certainly there is nothing in the classical Islamic past that resembles the more recent offices of the chief mufti of the Ottoman empire or the grand ayatollah of Iran.

These Western influences became more powerful and more important after the French Revolution—the first great movement of ideas in Christendom which was not Christian but was even, in a sense, anti-Christian, and could therefore be considered by Muslim observers with relative detachment. Such earlier movements of ideas in Europe as the Renaissance, the Reformation, or the Enlightenment had no impact whatsoever on the Muslim world, and are virtually unnoticed in contemporary Muslim philosophical and even historical writings. The initial response to the French Revolution was much the same, and the first Muslim comments dismiss it as an internal affair of Christendom, of no interest or concern to Muslims and, more important, offering them no threat.

It was on this last point that they were soon obliged to change their minds. The dissemination of French revolutionary ideas in the Islamic world was not left to chance but was actively promoted by successive French regimes, both by force of arms, and, much more effectively, by translation and publication. The penetration of Western ideas into the Islamic world was greatly accelerated when, from the early 19th century, Muslim students in increasing numbers were sent to institutions of higher education in France, Italy, and Britain, and later also in other countries. Many of these, on their return home, became carriers of infectious new ideas.

The revolutionaries in France had summarized their ideology in a formula of classical terseness—liberty, equality, fraternity. Some time was to pass before they, and ultimately their disciples elsewhere, came to realize that the first two were mutually exclusive and the third meaningless. Of far greater effect, in the impact of Western ideas on Islam, were two related notions—neither of them originating with the French Revolution, but both of them classically formulated and actively disseminated by its leaders: namely, secularism and nationalism. The one sought to displace religion as the ultimate basis of identity, loyalty, and authority in society; the other provided an alternative.

In the new dispensation, God was to be doubly replaced, both as the source of authority and as the object of worship, by the Nation. Secularism as such had no appeal to Muslims, but an ideology of change and progress, free—as it seemed then—from any taint of a rival religion, offered attractions to 19th-century Muslims who were increasingly aware of the relatively backward and impoverished state of their own society, as contrasted with the wealth and power of Europe. Liberalism and patriotism seemed to be part of the same progressive ideology and were eagerly adopted by young Muslim intellectuals, seeking arguments to criticize and methods to change their own societies. The West European civic patriotism proved to have limited relevance or appeal, but the ethnic nationalism of Central and Eastern Europe had greater relevance to Middle Eastern conditions, and evoked a much more powerful response. According to the old view, the Muslims are one community, subdivided into such nations as the Turks, the Arabs, the

An illustration from a 13th-century Iraqi manuscript on the pharmaceutical uses of plants. Islamic civilization is known for its contributions to medicine and other sciences.

Persians, etc. But according to the new, the Arabs are a nation, subdivided into Muslims and Christians, to which some were, for a while, willing to add Jews.

For a time the idea of the secular nation, defined by country, language, culture, and descent, was dominant among the more or less Westernized minority of political activists. Beginning with the decline and fall of the old Westernized elites in the mid-20th century, and the entry into political life of more authentically popular elements, the ideal of the secular nation came under challenge and in some areas has been decisively defeated.

Nowadays, for the first time in many years, even nationalism itself is under attack and has been denounced by some Muslim writers as divisive and un-Islamic. When Arab nationalists complain that the religious fundamentalists are creating divisions between Muslim and Christian Arabs, the latter respond that the secular nationalists are creating divisions between Arabs and other Muslims and that theirs is the larger and greater offense.

The attack on secularism—seen as an attempt to undermine and supplant the Islamic way of life—has been gathering force and is now a major element in the writings of religious fundamentalists and other similar groups. For these, all the modernizing leaders—Kemal Atatürk in Turkey, the Shah in Iran, Faruq, Nasser, and Sadat alike in Egypt, the Ba'thist rulers of Syria and Iraq, and their equivalents elsewhere—are tarred with the same brush. They are all apostates who have renounced Islam and are trying to impose neo-pagan doctrines and institutions on the Muslim world. Of all the Muslim states, only one, the Turkish republic, has formally declared itself a secular state and legislated, in its constitution, the separation of religion and government. Indonesia, by far the largest Islamic state, includes belief in one God among the basic constitutional principles but does not formally establish Islam. Virtually all the others either proclaim Islam as the state religion or lay down that the laws of the state shall be based on, or inspired by, the holy law of Islam. In fact, many of them had adopted secular legislation, mostly inspired by European models, over a wide range of civil and criminal matters, and it is these laws that are now under strong attack.

This is of particular concern to the two groups which had, in law at least, benefited most from the reforms, namely women and non-Muslims. Hence the phenomenon, paradoxical in Western but not in Muslim eyes, that such conventionally liberal causes as equal rights for women have hitherto been espoused and enforced only by autocratic rulers like Kemal Atatürk in Turkey and Mohamed Reza Shah in Iran. For the latter,

QUR'AN

Accepted as the word of God by Muslims, the Qur'an, the holy book of Islam, remains the fundamental source of Islamic doctrine, law, thinking, and teaching. It says to its followers, "You are the best nation ever brought forth to men, bidding to honour, and forbidding dishonour, and believing in God" (III, 106).*

During Muhammad's life, observes historian Marshall Hodgson in *The Venture of Islam* (1974), it "served at once as the inspiration of Muslim life and the commentary on what was done under that inspiration; its message transcended any particular circumstances yet at the same time served as a running guide to the community experiences, often down to seemingly petty details." The Qur'an (literally "recitations") touches on everything from manners—"O believers, do not enter houses other than your houses until you first ask leave and salute the people thereof..." (XXIV, 27)—to the largest questions of spiritual import: "O believers, fear God as He should be feared, and see you do not die, save in surrender" (III, 97).

Scholars distinguish between two main parts of the Qur'an, the whole of which consists of 114 *Surahs* (chapters) of varying numbers of *Ayahs* (verses). The early *Surahs*, revealed to Muhammad while at Mecca, focus upon ethical and spiritual teachings: "Then he whose deeds weigh heavy in the Balance shall inherit a pleasing life, but he whose deeds weigh light in the Balance shall plunge in the womb of the Pit" (CI, 6). *Surahs* revealed later at Medina, however, concern social legislation and the politico-moral principles for constituting and ordering the community. Verses such as "God has promised those of you who believe and do righteous deeds that He will surely make you successors in the land..." (XXIV, 54) point to a concern with the rightful rule.

According to tradition, Muhammad received the verses of the Qur'an at irregular intervals from around A.D. 610 to 632. Many of Muhammad's devout followers memorized the

Qur'an, and for a time no comprehensive written collection of the *Surahs* existed. After the Prophet's death, and especially after the battle of Yamamah (633), where many who knew the words by heart fell in combat, fear of losing the record of God's word spurred meticulous collection efforts. Several versions resulted. But a desire for consistency led the third caliph, 'Uthmān (ruled 644–656), to order its consolidation, producing the authoritative 'Uthmānic recension now used. 'Uthmān then had all other copies destroyed.

'Uthmān's version, compiled by a handful of learned Muslims, arranges the chapters approximately according to length (except for the opening chapter, longest first). Yet Qur'anic specialists have assembled a rough chronology and identified a handful of recurring themes. The essential message is that there is only one God, Allah, who will judge men by their earthly deeds on the Last Day. Men, therefore, should endeavor to worship God and to act generously in dealings with others.

As Islam became established during the centuries after Muhammad's death, theological and legal questions inevitably arose. What was the correct way for Muslims to pray, to live, to do business, to govern? To deal with such questions, a succession of distinguished theologians and jurists employed three methods: study of the Qur'an; consideration of the precepts and practices of the Prophet, as handed down by tradition; the use of independent reason to apply the first two to problems that arose. (Sunnis, the majority of Muslims, believed that independent reason ceased to be a valid method after the ninth century; Shiites believe that it still is.) The Qur'an remains the ultimate authority to all Muslims, but pious believers have frequently differed over points of interpretation. For example, the Shiites argue that passages on divorce allow temporary marriages for a fixed dower; the Sunnis, however, find no Qur'anic support for such temporary arrangements.

---

*Qur'anic quotations are from *The Koran Interpreted*, translated by A. J. Arberry (© George Allen & Unwin Ltd., 1955).

this was indeed one of the main grievances of the revolutionaries who overthrew him. It has been remedied under their rule.

Until the recent impact of Western secularist ideas, the idea of a non-religious society as something desirable or even permissible was totally alien to Islam. Other religious dispensations, namely Christianity and Judaism, were tolerable because they were earlier and superseded versions of

God's revelation, of which Islam itself was the final and perfect version, and therefore lived by a form—albeit incomplete and perhaps debased—of God's law. Those who lacked even this measure of religious guidance were pagans and idolaters, and their society was evil. Any Muslim who sought to join them or imitate them was an apostate.

Some medieval Muslim jurists, confronting a new problem posed by the Christian reconquest, asked whether it was lawful for Muslims to live under non-Muslim rule, and found different answers. According to one view, they might stay, provided that the non-Muslim government allowed them to observe the Muslim religion in all its aspects and to live a full Muslim life; according to another school, no such thing was possible, and Muslims whose homeland was conquered by a non-Muslim ruler were obliged to migrate, as the Prophet did from pagan Mecca to Medina, and seek a haven in Muslim lands, until in God's good time they were able to return and restore the rule of Islam.

O ne of the tests of civility is surely tolerance—a willingness to coexist with those who hold and practice other beliefs. John Locke, and most other Westerners, believed that the best way to ensure this was to sever or at least to weaken the bonds between religion and state power. In the past, Muslims never professed any such belief. They did however see a certain form of tolerance as an obligation of the dominant Islamic religion. "There is no compulsion in religion" runs a much quoted verse in the Qur'an, and this was generally interpreted by Muslim jurists and rulers to authorize a limited measure of tolerance for certain specified other religious beliefs, though of course without questioning or compromising the primacy of Islam and the supremacy of the Muslims.

Does this mean that the classical Islamic state was a theocracy? In the sense that Britain today is a monarchy, the answer is certainly yes. That is to say that, in the Muslim conception, God is the true sovereign of the community, the ultimate source of authority, the sole source of legislation. In the first extant Muslim account of the British House of Commons, written by a visitor who went to England at the end of the 18th

The harem, no pleasure-den, was simply where women and children lived in a Muslim house.

century, the writer expresses his astonishment at the fate of a people who, unlike the Muslims, did not have a divinely revealed law and were therefore reduced to the pitiable expedient of enacting their own laws. But in the sense of a state ruled by the church or by priests, Islam was not and indeed could not be a theocracy. Classical Islam had no priesthood, no prelates who might rule or even decisively influence those who did. The caliph, who was head of a governing institution that was state and church in one, was himself neither a jurist nor a theologian but a practitioner of the arts of politics and sometimes of war. There are no popes in Islamic history and no political cardinals like Wolsey or Richelieu or Alberoni. The office of ayatollah is a creation of the 19th century; the rule of Khomeini an innovation of the 20th.

In most tests of tolerance, Islam, both in theory and in practice, compares unfavorably with the Western democracies as they have developed during the last two or three centuries, but very favorably with most other Christian and post-Christian societies and regimes. There is nothing in Islamic history to compare with the emancipation, acceptance, and integration of other-believers and non-believers in the West. But equally, there is nothing in Islamic history to compare with the Spanish expulsion of Jews and Muslims, the Inquisition, the autos-da-fé, the wars of religion, not to speak of more recent crimes of commission and acquiescence. There were occasional persecutions, but they were rare and atypical, and usually of brief duration, related to local and specific circumstances.

Within certain limits and subject to certain restrictions, Islamic governments were willing to tolerate the practice, though not the dissemination, of other revealed, monotheistic religions. They were able to pass an even severer test by tolerating divergent forms of their own. Even polytheists, though condemned by the strict letter of the law to a choice between conversion and enslavement, were in fact tolerated, as Islamic rule spread to most of India. Only the total unbeliever—the agnostic or atheist—was beyond the pale of tolerance, and even this exclusion was usually enforced only when the offense became public and scandalous. The same standard was applied to the tolerance of deviant forms of Islam.

In modern times, Islamic tolerance has been somewhat diminished. After the second Turkish siege of Vienna in 1683, Islam was a retreating force in the world, and Muslims began to feel threatened by the rise and expansion of the great Christian empires of Eastern and Western Europe. The old easy-going tolerance, resting on an assumption not only of superior religion but also of superior power, was becoming difficult for Muslims to maintain. The threat which Christendom now seemed to be offering to Islam was no longer merely military and political; it was beginning to shake the very structure of Muslim society. Western rulers, and, to a far greater extent, their enthusiastic Muslim disciples and imi-

tators, brought in a whole series of reforms, almost all of them of Western origin or inspiration. These reforms increasingly affected the way Muslims lived in their countries, their cities and villages, and finally in their own homes.

These changes were rightly seen as being of Western origin or inspiration; the non-Muslim minorities, mostly Christian but also Jewish, were often seen, sometimes also rightly, as agents or instruments of these changes. The old pluralistic order, multi-denominational and polyethnic, was breaking down, and the tacit social contract on which it was based was violated on both sides. The Christian minorities, inspired by Western ideas of self-determination, were no longer prepared to accept the tolerated but inferior status accorded to them by the old order, and made new demands—sometimes for equal rights within the nation, sometimes for separate nationhood, sometimes for both at the same time. Muslim majorities, feeling threatened, became unwilling to accord even the traditional measure of tolerance.

By a sad paradox, in some of the semi-secularized nation-states of modern times, the non-Muslim minorities, while enjoying complete equality on paper, in fact have fewer opportunities and face greater dangers than under the old Islamic yet pluralistic order. The present regime in Iran, with its ruling clerics, its executions for blasphemy, its consecrated assassins, represents a new departure in Islamic history. In the present mood, a triumph of militant Islam would be unlikely to bring a return to traditional Islamic tolerance—and even that would no longer be acceptable to minority elements schooled on modern ideas of human, civil, and political rights. The emergence of some form of civil society would therefore seem to offer the best hope for decent coexistence based on mutual respect.

CONFUCIUS

Confucianism, once thought to be a dead doctrine,

has made an astonishing comeback during the past 20 years.

Cited as a major force behind East Asia's economic

"miracles," it is now finding a renewed following among

mainland Chinese grown disillusioned with communism.

Yet what exactly Confucianism means is hard to say.

All the more reason, Jonathan Spence urges,

to return to the man himself—

and to the little we know about his life and words.

JONATHAN D. SPENCE

Jonathan D. Spence *is George B. Adams Professor of History at Yale University. His many books include* The Death of Woman Wang *(1978),* The Gate of Heavenly Peace *(1981),* The Search for Modern China *(1990), and, most recently,* Chinese Roundabout *(1992).*

Across the centuries that have elapsed since he lived in northern China and lectured to a small group of followers on ethics and ritual, the ideas of Confucius have had a powerful resonance. Soon after his death in 476 B.C., a small number of these followers dedicated themselves to recording what they could remember of his teachings and to preserving the texts of history and poetry that he was alleged to have edited. In the fourth and third centuries B.C., several distinguished philosophers expanded and systematized ideas that they ascribed to him, thus deepening his reputation as a complex and serious thinker. During the centralizing and tyrannical Ch'in dynasty that ruled China between 221 and 209 B.C., the works of Confucius were slated for destruction, on the grounds that they contained material antithetical to the obedience of people to

their rulers, and many of those who prized or taught his works were brutally killed on the emperor's orders.

Despite this apparently lethal setback, Confucius's reputation was only enhanced, and during the Han dynasty (206 B.C.–A.D. 220) his ideas were further edited and expanded, this time to be used as a focused source for ideas on good government and correct social organization. Despite the pedantry and internal bickering of these self-styled followers of Confucius, his ideas slowly came to be seen as the crystallization of an inherent Chinese wisdom. Surviving the importation of Buddhist metaphysics and meditative practices from India in the third to sixth centuries A.D., and a renewed interest in both esoteric Taoist theories of the cosmos and the hard-headed political realism of rival schools of legalistically oriented thinkers, a body of texts reorganized as "Confucian," with their accumulated commentaries, became the basic source for competitive examinations for entrance into the Chinese civil service and for the analysis of a wide spectrum of political and familial relationships: those between ruler and subject, between parents and children, and between husband and wife. In the 12th century A.D., a loose group of powerful philosophers, though differing over the details, reformulated various so-called Confucian principles to incorporate some of the more deeply held premises of Buddhism, giving in particular a dualistic structure to the Confucian belief system by separating idealist or universalist components—the inherent principles or premises, known as the *li*—from the grosser matter, or manifestations of life-in-action (the *ch'i*).

A final series of shifts took place in the last centuries of imperial China. During the 16th century elements of Confucian doctrine were deepened and altered once again by philosophers who emphasized the inherent morality of the individual and tried to overcome the dualism that they felt Confucians had erected between nature and the human emotions. In the 17th century Confucian scholars confronted the promise and challenge of newly imported scientific ideas from the West, brought by Jesuits and other Catholic missionaries. During the following century Confucian scholars embarked on a newly formulated intellectual quest for the evidential basis of historical and moral phenomena, one that led them cumulatively to peaks of remarkable scholarship. In the 19th century these scholars began to cope with Western technology and constitutional ideas and with the development of new modes of education. But in the 20th century Confucian ideas were attacked from within and without China as contributing to China's economic backwardness, myopic approach to social change, denial of the idea of progress, resistance to science, and a generally stultified educational system.

These attacks were so devastating that as recently as 20 years ago, one would have thought that the chances of Confucius ever again becoming a major figure of study or emulation were slight indeed, in any part of the world. In Communist China, where he had been held up to ridicule or vilification since the Communist victory of 1949, his name was invoked only when mass campaigns needed a symbol of the old order to castigate, as in the "Anti-Confucius and anti-Lin Biao Campaign" of 1973–74. But in that case the real focus of the campaign was Chairman Mao's former "closest comrade-in-arms," General Lin Biao, not the discredited sage of Lu. In Taiwan, though constant lip service was paid to the enduring values of Confucianism, the doctrine that lived on under that name was slanted in content

and attracted few of the brightest young minds. It was a version of Confucian belief that followed along lines first laid down by Nationalist Party ideologues during the 1930s in an attempt to boost their own prestige and give a deeper historical legitimacy to party leader Chiang Kai-Shek. Although in Taiwan as in other parts of Asia there were great scholars who continued to explore the sage's inner meaning, in many Asian schools Confucius was also invoked in support of authoritarian and hierarchical value systems. In Europe and the United States, though Confucian texts were studied in East Asian and Oriental studies centers, they did not arouse much excitement, and the young—if they were interested in earlier Asian studies at all—were likely to be far more interested in Taoism or Buddhism.

Now, however, the revival is in full swing. Confucian study societies have sprung up inside the People's Republic of China, with government approval. In Taiwan, Confucianism is studied as a central aspect of philosophical inquiry, and so-called New Confucians are linking his ideas on conduct and the self to certain preoccupations in modern ethics. In the United States especially, many colleges now teach sophisticated and popular courses in "Confucian belief," and a distinguished stream of "Confucian" academics jet around the world as conference participants and even as consultants to foreign governments on the sage. Translations of Confucius's work, and that of his major followers, are in print with popular presses, often in variant editions. And "Confucian principles" are cited approvingly as being one of the underpinnings of the disciplined work habits and remarkable international economic success of a number of Asian states.

The renewed interest in Confucius is not the result of any rush of new information about him. There has been no newly discovered cache of intimate details about him or his family that could engage the public interest, no fresh sources that can be ascribed to him and thus deepen our sense of his achievement, or that could serve as the basis for new controversies. The scraps of information about Confucius are so slight that they barely give us an outline, let alone a profile, of the man. (The modern name Confucius is an early Western rendering of the sage's Chinese honorific name, "K'ung-fu-tsu.") We are almost certain that he was born in 551 B.C. We have a definite year of death, 479 B.C. He was born in the kingdom of Lu, one of the many small states into which China was then divided and which corresponds roughly to the area of modern Shandong province. His parents might have had aristocratic roots, but they were neither prominent nor wealthy, and though Confucius received a good education in historical and ritual matters, his parents died when he was young, and the youth had to fend for himself. He acquired a number of skills: in clerical work, music, accounting, perhaps in charioteering and archery, and in certain "menial activities" on which we have no other details. Sometime between 507 and 497 B.C. he served in the state of Lu in an office that can be translated as "police commissioner" and that involved hearing cases and meting out punishments. Before and after that stint of service he traveled to various neighboring states, seeking posts as a diplomatic or bureaucratic adviser but meeting with little success. Because of some feud he was, for a time, in mortal danger, but he handled himself with calmness and courage. He married and had one son and two daughters. His son predeceased him, but not before producing an heir. One of his daughters married a student of Confucius who had served time in jail. Confucius approved the match because he believed that the young man had in fact done no wrong. During his later years Confucius was a teacher of what we might now call ethics, ritual, and philosophy; the names of 35 of his students have come down to us.

To compound the problems caused by this paucity of biographical information, we have nothing that we can be completely sure was written by Confucius himself. What we do have is a record of what some of his disciples and students—or their students—said that he said. Usually translated as *The Analects of Confucius*, this collection is brief, aphoristic, and enigmatic. But the *Analects*, despite the problem of indirect transmission, remain our crucial source on Confucius's beliefs, actions, and personality. Not surprisingly, scholars disagree on how to interpret many passages and how much to believe in the authenticity of the different parts of this text. The best and perhaps the only gauges of authenticity are internal consistency, tone, and coherence. One can also look at the construction of each book— there are 20 in all, each running about five pages in English translation—and search for

obvious distortions and later additions. The last five of the books, for example, have lengthy sections that present Confucius either as a butt to the Taoists or as an uncritical transmitter of doctrines with which he can be shown in earlier chapters to have disagreed. It is a fairly safe assumption that these were added to the original text by persons with a special cause to plead. Other books give disproportionate space to Confucius's praise of a particular student whom we know from other passages that he rather disliked. Perhaps in such cases we are witnessing attempts to correct the record by later followers of the student concerned. There does not seem to be any political censorship; indeed, one of the mysteries of the later uses of Confucianism concerns the way that the original text as we now have it has been preserved for two millennia even though it seems quite obviously to contradict the ideological uses to which it was being put. Interpretation and commentary, that is to say, carried more weight with readers than did the original words.

Given the bewildering array of philosophical and political arguments that Confucianism has been called on to support, and given, in particular, the generally held belief that Confucius was a strict believer in hierarchy and the values of absolute obedience to superiors, and that he lacked flexibility and imagination, it is an intriguing task to read the *Analects* with open eyes and without any presuppositions drawn from later interpretative attempts. What was, in fact, the central message of the man Confucius himself?

Personally, almost two and a half millennia after his death, I find that Confucius is still especially valuable to us because of the strength of his humanity, his general decency, and the fervor of his belief in the importance of culture and the act of learning. He emphatically did not feel that he had any monopoly on truth. Rather, he was convinced that learning is a perpetual process that demands flexibility, imagination, and tenacity. He scolded students who would not get up in the morning, just as he scolded those who were unctuous or complacent. He said that he had no interest in trying to teach those who did not have the curiosity to follow up on a philosophical argument or a logical sequence of ideas after he had given them an initial prod in the right direction. He let his students argue among themselves—or with him—and praised those who were able to make moral decisions that might benefit humankind in general. But at the same time he adamantly refused to talk about the forces of heaven or to speculate on the nature of the afterlife, since there was so much that he did not know about life on this Earth that he was convinced such speculations would be idle.

It is clear that Confucius derived great pleasure from life. Once, one of his students could not think what to say to an influential official who had asked what sort of a person Confucius really was. Hearing of the incident, Confucius gently chided his student with these words: "Why did you not simply say something to this effect: He is the sort of man who forgets to eat when he tries to solve a problem that has been driving him to distraction, who is so full of joy that he forgets his worries and who does not notice the onset of old age?"

This brief exchange comes from *The Analects of Confucius*, book VII, section 19, and it is typical of words that Confucius left us, words through which we can in turn analyze his character.* Another example could be taken from Confucius's views concerning loyalty to the state and the value of capital punishment. In later periods of Chinese history, it was commonplace to assert that "Confucian" bureaucrats and scholars should always put their duty to the state and the dynasty they served ahead of personal and family loyalties. Chinese history is also replete with grim details of executions carried out in the name of "Confucian" ideology against those who violated the state's laws. But in the most clearly authenticated books of the *Analects* that we have, we find completely unambiguous views on these central matters of human practice and belief. What could be clearer than this?

> The Governor of She said to Confucius, "In our village there is a man nicknamed 'Straight Body.' When his father stole a sheep, he gave evidence against him." Confucius answered, "In our village those who are straight are quite different. Fathers cover up for their sons, and sons cover up for their fathers. Straightness is to be found in such behavior." (XIII/18)

---

*All citations of the *Analects* are from D. C. Lau's Penguin Books translation, *Confucius, The Analects*. In some cases I have made minor modifications to his translations.

On executions, Confucius was equally unambiguous:

> Chi K'ang Tzu asked Confucius about government, saying, "What would you think if, in order to move closer to those who possess the Way, I were to kill those who do not follow the Way?" Confucius answered, "In administering your government, what need is there for you to kill? Just desire the good yourself and the common people will be good. The virtue of the gentleman is like wind; the virtue of the small man is like grass. Let the wind blow over the grass and it is sure to bend." (XII/19)

If it were humanly possible, Confucius added, he would avoid the law altogether: "In hearing litigation, I am no different from any other man. But if you insist on a difference, it is, perhaps, that I try to get the parties not to resort to litigation in the first place." (XII/13) In the long run, the fully virtuous state would be forever free of violent death: "The Master said, 'How true is the saying that after a state has been ruled for a hundred years by good men it is possible to get the better of cruelty and to do away with killing.' " (XIII/11)

Since the words of Confucius have been preserved for us mainly in the form of aphorisms or snatches of dialogue—or the combination of the two—one way to find a coherent structure in his thought is to track the remarks he made to specific individuals, even if these are widely scattered throughout the *Analects*. Sometimes, of course, there is only one remark, especially in the case of those whose behavior Confucius considered beyond the pale. My favorite example here is his dismissal of Yuan Jang, allegedly once his friend: "Yuan Jang sat waiting with his legs spread wide. The Master said, 'To be neither modest nor deferential when young, to have passed on nothing worthwhile when grown up, and to refuse to die when old, that is what I call being a pest.' So saying, the Master tapped him on the shin with his stick." (XIV/43) That tapping on the shin, perhaps playful, perhaps in irritation, shows an unusual side of Confucius. Was he trying to add physical sting to his sharp words? More commonly with him, it was a laugh or a shrug that ended a potentially confrontational exchange.

With several of his students, Confucius clearly felt a deep rapport, even when they did not see eye to eye. One such student was Tzu-lu, who was more a man of action than a scholar. Confucius loved to tease Tzu-lu for his impetuosity. Thus, after telling his students that if he were on a raft that drifted out to sea, Tzu-lu would be the one to follow him, Confucius added wryly that that would be because Tzu-lu had at once more courage and less judgment than his teacher. On another occasion, when Tzu-lu asked if Confucius thought he, Tzu-lu, would make a good general, Confucius replied that he would rather not have as a general someone who would try to walk across a river or strangle a tiger with his bare hands. (V/7 and VII/11)

Different in character, but still very much his own man, was the merchant and diplomat Tzu-kung. Confucius acknowledged that Tzu-kung was shrewd and capable, and made a great profit from his business deals. He even agreed that Tzu-kung's type of intelligence was especially useful in the world of literature and thought: "Only with a man like you can one discuss the Odes. Tell such a man something and he can see its relevance to what he has not been told." (I/16) But Confucius did not like Tzu-kung's insistence on always trying to put people in a ranked order of priorities, as if they were so many objects—"For my part I have no time for such things," Confucius observed—and he was equally upset if he felt that Tzu-kung was skimping things that really mattered because of his private feelings: "Tzu-kung wanted to dispense with the practice of ritually killing a sacrificial sheep at the announcement of the new moon. The Master said, 'You love the sheep, but I love the Rites.' " (XIV/29 and III/17)

Most readers of the *Analects* feel that the student called Yen Yuan was clearly Confucius's favorite, and the one closest to the Master by behavior and inclination. Yen Yuan was poor but lived his life without complaining. He did not allow poverty to sour or interrupt his search for the Way, and his intelligence was truly piercing. As Tzu-kung, not a modest man, put it, "When he [Yen Yuan] is told one thing he understands 10. When I am told one thing I understand only two." To which Confucius sighed in agreement, "Neither of us is as good as he is." (V/9) In a similar vein, Confucius praised Yen Yuan's prudence, contrasting it with Tzu-lu's bravado. As Confucius phrased it, Yen Yuan was the kind of man who "when faced with a task, was

fearful of failure," and who knew how "to stay out of sight when set aside;" furthermore, Yen Yuan was not above making mistakes, but more important, "he did not make the same mistake twice." (VII/11 and VI/3) When Yen Yuan died young, before being able to achieve his full promise, Confucius gave way to a conspicuous display of immoderate grief. When some of his students remonstrated with him for showing such "undue sorrow," Confucius's answer was brief but powerful: "If not for him for whom should I show undue sorrow?" (IX/10)

Confucius lived to a fine old age, and not even regret over the loss of his favorite student and his own son could blunt the pleasures he felt at his own mounting experience and the attainment of something that might be approaching wisdom. He did not boast about the knowledge he had acquired—indeed he thought he was lucky to have got as far as he had. As he put it once to Tzu-lu: "Shall I tell you what it is to know? To say you know when you know, and to say you do not know when you do not, that is knowledge." (II/17) His own greatest ambition, as he once told Yen Yuan and Tzu-lu jointly, was "to bring peace to the old, to have trust in my friends, and to cherish the young." (V/26) On another occasion he went even further, telling his followers, "It is fitting that we hold the young in awe. How do we know that the generations to come will not be the equal of the present?" (IX/23) In the passage that is perhaps the most famous of his sayings, Confucius gave his own version of the stages of life, and it is as different as anything could be from Shakespeare's "Seven Ages of Man," with its heart-rending account of man's descent into the weakness and imbecility of old age after a brief phase of youthful vigor. Whereas according to the *Analects*, the Master said, "At 15 I set my heart on learning; at 30 I took my stand; at 40 I came to be free from doubts; at 50 I understood the Decree of Heaven; at 60 my ear was attuned; at 70 I followed my heart's desire without overstepping the line." (II/4)

Certainly we should not read Confucius as though he were always right. And as we read through the *Analects* we can find Confucius revealing a fussy and sometimes impatient side. Some of his vaunted arguments seem like quibbles, and he could be punctilious to the point of prudishness. His political motivations are often obscure, and he seems to appreciate various struggling rulers' foibles less than his own. But cleared of the accumulation of unsubstantiated details and textual over-interpretations that have weighed him down across the centuries, we find to our surprise an alert, intelligent, and often very amusing man.

How then did he get the reputation that he did, one at once more austere, more pompous, harsh even, and as a reinforcer of the status quo? Strangely enough, part of the reappraisal resulted from the efforts of the man who is undeniably China's greatest historian, Ssu-ma Ch'ien, who lived from around 145 to 89 B.C., during the Han dynasty. In his life's work, a composite history of China entitled simply *Historical Records*, which was completed between 100 and 95 B.C., Ssu-ma Ch'ien aimed to integrate the histories of all China's earlier states and rulers with the steady and inexorable rise to power of the centralizing Ch'in dynasty (221–209 B.C.), and he determined to give Confucius an important role in this process. Thus Ssu-ma Ch'ien paid Confucius the ultimate accolade by placing his story in the section devoted to the ruling houses of early China, as opposed to placing him with other individual thinkers and statesmen in the 70 chapters of biographies that conclude the *Historical Records*. In the summation of Confucius's worth with which he ended his account, Ssu-ma Ch'ien gave concise and poignant expression to his homage:

> In this world there have been many people—from kings to wise men—who had a glory while they lived that ended after their death. But Confucius, though a simple commoner, has had his name transmitted for more than 10 generations; all those who study his works consider him their master. From the Son of Heaven, the princes, and the lords on down, anyone in the Central Kingdom who is dedicated to a life of learning, follows the precepts and the rules of the Master. Thus it is that we call him a true Sage.

To give substance to this judgment, Ssu-ma Ch'ien took all known accounts written over the intervening three centuries that purported to describe Confucius, following the principle that if there was no clear reason for discarding an item of biographical information, then he should include it, leaving for later generations the task of winnowing the true from the false. Thus was Confucius given cou-

rageous ancestors, his birth described in semi-miraculous terms, his own physical distinction elaborated upon. In one curious addition, Confucius's father was described as being of far greater age than the sage's mother: By one interpretation of the phrase used by Ssu-ma Ch'ien, that the marriage was "lacking in proportion," Confucius's father would have been over 64, while his mother had only recently entered puberty. Confucius's precocious interest in ritual and propriety, his great height and imposing cranial structure, the fecundity of the flocks of cattle and sheep that he supervised in one of his first official posts, his preternatural shrewdness in debate, his instinctive brilliance at interpreting unusual auguries—all of these were given documentary precision in Ssu-ma Ch'ien's account. The result is that Confucius not only emerges as a key counselor to the rulers of his native state of Lu, but the meticulousness of his scholarship and his flair for editing early texts of poetry, history, and music are presented as having attracted an ever-widening circle of hundreds or even thousands of students from his own and neighboring states.

Having constructed this formidable image of a successful Confucius, Ssu-ma Ch'ien was confronted by the need to explain the reasons for Confucius's fall from grace in Lu and for his subsequent wanderings in search of rulers worthy of his service. Being one of China's most gifted storytellers, Ssu-ma Ch'ien was up to this task, presenting a convincing scenario of the way the sagacity of Confucius's advice to the ruler of Lu made him both respected and feared by rival rulers in northern China. One of them was finally able to dislodge Confucius by sending to the ruler of Lu a gift of 24 ravishing female dancers and musicians, along with 30 magnificent teams of chariot horses. This gift so effectively distracted the ruler of Lu from his official duties—most important, it led him to forget certain key ritual sacrifices—that Confucius had no choice but to leave his court.

In various ways, some subtle, some direct, the portrait of Confucius that Ssu-ma Ch'ien wove incorporated diverse levels of narrative dealing with the unpredictability of violence. This was surely not coincidental, for the central tragedy of Ssu-ma Ch'ien's own life had been his court-ordered castration, a savage punishment inflicted on him by the Han dynasty emperor Wu-ti (r. 141–87 B.C.). Ssu-ma Ch'ien's "crime" had been to write a friend a letter in which he incautiously spoke in defense of a man unjustly punished by the same emperor. Despite this agonizing humiliation, which placed the historian in the same physical category as the venal court eunuchs he so deeply despised, Ssu-ma Ch'ien refused to commit suicide; he maintained his dignity by making his history as grand and comprehensive as possible—his presentation of Confucius being a stunning example of his dedication to craft and content. Thus he describes Confucius as a man who had the bureaucratic power to make major judicial decisions but who did so only with care and consideration of all the evidence. When Confucius acted harshly, according to Ssu-ma Ch'ien, it was only when the long-term threat to his kingdom was so strong that leniency would have been folly. This explains one shattering moment in Ssu-ma Ch'ien's biography. One rival leader was planning to overthrow the ruler of Lu, but each of his ruses was seen through and foiled by Confucius. At last, in desperation, the rival ruler ordered his acrobats and dwarfs to perform wild and obscene dances at a ritual occasion that the ruler of Lu was attending. Confucius, according to Ssu-ma Ch'ien, ordered the dwarfs killed.

In another dissimilar but equally powerful comment on violence, Ssu-ma Ch'ien showed that even the descendants of a man of Confucius's integrity could not escape Emperor Wu-ti's willful power. Thus at the very end of his long biography, before the final summation, Ssu-ma Ch'ien lists all of Confucius's direct descendants in the male line. When he comes to the 11th in line, An-kuo, the historian mentions tersely that An-kuo had died "prematurely" under the "ruling emperor." Ssu-ma Ch'ien knew—and knew that his readers knew—that An-kuo had been executed on Wu-ti's orders for involvement in an alleged court coup. The line had not, however, been stamped out, because An-kuo's wife had borne a son before her husband was killed.

Ssu-ma Ch'ien's attempt to reconstruct a convincing psychological and contextual universe for Confucius was a brilliant one, and his version was elaborated upon and glossed by scores of subsequent scholars, even as suitable pieces of the Confucian legacy were seized upon by later rulers and bureaucrats to justify some current policy decision or to prove some philosophical premise. But after more than two millennia of such accretions, it seems time to go back to the earlier and simpler version of the record and try to see for ourselves what kind of a man Confucius was. The results, I feel, in our overly ideological age, are encouraging to those who value the central premises of humane intellectual inquiry.

The Koran, Gita, and Tripitaka

Islam, Hinduism, and Buddhism have their own distinct approaches to their sacred writings

Thomas B. Coburn

Special to The Christian Science Monitor. *Thomas B. Coburn is Charles A. Dana professor of religious studies and classical languages at St. Lawrence University in Canton, N.Y.*

Since all of the world's major religious traditions have produced written documents, it is possible and legitimate to ask: What are the equivalents of the Christian Bible in those different traditions? What and where are the historic copies of their scriptures?

Answers to these questions, however, quickly indicate not only the expected diversity of documents, but also very different *significances* that have been ascribed to the documents.

The written word does not always have the same function in the lives of Buddhists, Hindus, Muslims or others as it does for Christians—even acknowledging that there is variety among Christians themselves.

Verbal literacy has been variously valued in different times and places, and the unique authority that Christians, particularly Protestants, ascribe to a book is elsewhere: in a charismatic individual, in certain ritual behavior, in a self-authenticating mystical experience.

In short, to ask a seemingly simple and obvious question is to move immediately into the fascinating field of the comparative study of religion.

Questioning our assumptions

The first step in attempting to answer these questions is to reexamine the assumptions that lead us to ask them.

As William A. Graham, a historian of religion, has noted, we in the modern West "stand on this side of the epochal transition accomplished to large degree by about 1800 in the urban culture of Western Europe, and now still in progress elsewhere, from a scribal . . . and still significantly oral culture to a print-dominated . . . primarily visual culture. Our alphabetic 'book culture,' like our 'book religion,' is not even the same as the 'book culture' (or 'book religion') of sixteenth- or seventeenth-century Europe, let alone that of classical antiquity, the Medieval or Renaissance West, or the great literary civilizations of Asia past and present."

It is therefore impossible for us to find any "book religions" precisely parallel with those of the modern West, because the quite specific conditions that have produced our "book culture" have not existed elsewhere.

Even as literacy rises around the globe, its significance is shaped by local cultural factors, which are virtually always very different from those of European and American life of the past two centuries.

The following brief overview of Muslim, Hindu, and Buddhist "Bibles," therefore, can only hint at what the relevant documents are—and at the more interesting and complex matter of their religious significance for those who value them.

Islam: the 'corrective' scripture

The Muslim situation is closest to that of Jews and Christians, and for good reason: The religion of Islam sees itself as the fulfillment of the two older traditions, which, like Islam, are rooted in the faith of Abraham. This fulfillment focuses explicitly on scripture, the Koran (or Qur'an; meaning "the recitation").

In Muslim understanding, this scripture was revealed piecemeal to the Prophet Muhammad, in the Arabian cities of Mecca and Medina, between AD 610 and 632. The words are understood as the flawless word of God himself, not as Muhammad's personal utterances.

The Koran stands as the corrective to the faulty scriptures of other "People of the Book": the one God (Allah) had previously spoken through a series of prophets to Jews and Christians, but his message was distorted in the course of writing it down.

The Koran serves to amend these previous partial misunderstandings and to provide comprehensive guidance for human conduct, both individual and social.

Islam is in many ways the most "scriptural" of the world's religions, not just in the comprehensive significance it ascribes to the Koran, but in the rapidity with which a definitive version was assembled.

Within 20 years of Muhammad's death, the third caliph, Uthman, had a definitive codex completed, thereby setting a norm for recitation.

Oral transmission remained crucial, however, because of the incomplete system of writing Arabic, and it was nearly three centuries later that a text with vowel pronunciation was produced.

The Uthmanic version, with very minor variant readings, remains standard throughout the Muslim world. So, too, does emphasis on the Koran's oral, recited quality; a great many Muslims who are functionally illiterate carry the entire "text" verbatim within their hearts.

Hinduism: primacy of oral tradition

The Hindu situation could not be more different. The symbolic center of the tradition is the Rig Veda, a collection of 1,028 Sanskrit hymns, composed for liturgical use over 3,000 years ago. They are among the earliest compositions in any Indo-European language.

Yet Indian culture has consistently affirmed that the power of these (and most other) words lies in their oral and aural quality, and so has resisted reducing them to writing.

The Rig Veda was not, in fact, publicly accessible until its first published edition appeared in the mid-1800s. That work, significantly, was accomplished by an Oxford professor, F. Max Müller, and is of virtually no religious consequence for Hindus themselves: The Rig Veda's significance is symbolic, a cultural and religious reference-point, not literal or applicable to daily life.

In modern times, partly in response to imported Western ideas about "religions" having "scriptures," efforts have been made to present the Bhagavad Gita, Krishna's instruction on knowledge, morality and devotion, as the "Bible" of Hinduism. This text has become, after the Christian Bible, the second-most translated book in world history.

The Gita has doubtless been widely prized over the course of the past 2,000 years, but it has never commanded the exclusive attention of Hindus as a whole.

As it is with gods in Hinduism, so it is with scriptures: There are a very great number, and which one is in the ascendant depends on region, time of year, family tradition, caste, language, century, and so on.

Certain texts may attain a near-canonical status in particular contexts, but the core of Hindu religion lies, not in its texts, but in its stories about deities: Rama, Shiva, the Goddess, Krishna, and others.

It is these stories that lie in Hindu hearts and that get told, and retold, interpreted, and amended, and reinterpreted over and over and over again.

Buddhism: melding the word and experience

Buddhists lie somewhere between Muslims and Hindus in their attitudes toward holy writ. Like Muslims, they have a notion of a standard text, a canon, but like Hindus, they have an open-ended and expansive attitude toward what may appropriately be considered standard.

The decisive measure is what is consistent with "the word of the Buddha," but this does not mean slavish fidelity to the historical founder, Siddhartha Gautama (563 to 483 BC). Rather, it means teachings that accord with the experience of enlightenment, as taught by the historical Buddha and as lived by later followers.

This dynamic quality gives the Buddhist canon great diversity. The Pali canon of Theravada (South and Southeast Asian) Buddhism was composed and written down by the 1st century AD, but it remained in manuscript form until the 19th century. It consists of 31 texts, of varying antiquity, grouped into three "baskets" (Tripitaka): rules for monastic

practice, sayings of the Buddha, and scholastic analysis.

The rise of Mahayana Buddhism, and its spread to East Asia, produced a Chinese canon, whose first block printing was completed in 983. It includes some 1,076 items, and is approximately 70 times the length of the Christian Bible. However, sectarian and individual practice has tended to emphasize one particular text, and such scriptures as the Lotus Sutra have been enormously popular.

Tibetan Buddhism also has a massive canon of over 300 volumes, dating from the 14th century, much of it consisting of translations of Indian sources now lost. Here too, the daily life of both monks and laity focuses on a few, selected texts for meditational, ritual, or philosophical elaboration.

To inquire into "Bibles" elsewhere in the world thus reveals a stunning variety of content, of attitudes toward texts, and of what it means to be religious. This discovery should caution us against a simplistic cross-cultural comparison of scriptures.

At the same time, it should invite us to think more deeply about the distinctive features of the Bible, and of Christian attitudes toward it, while pondering other traditions, and other expressions, of religious faith.

The World of the Middle Ages, 500–1500

World historians have some difficulty with this period of time. In the history of Europe, the Middle Ages, or the medieval period, is a time of retreat after the fall of Rome. The thousand-year span covers feudalism, the growth of nation-states, the bubonic plague called the Black Death, reestablishment of long-distance trade, the domination of the Roman Catholic Church, and the emergence of Western civilization. For world historians, Western developments during this period of time are important for the future but pale in comparison to the achievements of China and Islam and to the changes that people elsewhere in the world were experiencing.

In the Western Hemisphere, Mesoamerican civilization flourished, with magnificent stone cities rising out of the jungles of southern Mexico and Central America. Much of the cultural information was destroyed during the conquest of the Spanish, and it is only recently that the writing of the Maya has been deciphered. The Mayan civilization, however, suffered a precipitous decline 600 years before the coming of the Europeans. Later, the same sort of experience befell the Mogollon people of the American Southwest, as examined in "Tracking a Vanished People through the Sierra Madre." The Aztecs came to dominate Mesoamerica shortly before the onslaught of Hernán Cortés and his soldiers. This civilization was swept away in warfare and disease.

Asian civilization was in a "golden age" in the Middle Ages, as demonstrated by the exhibit "Imperial Tombs of China," which traveled throughout the United States from 1995 to March 1997. The rulers of China needed worldly comforts after death to prevent their remaining spirits from turning malevolent. The artifacts demonstrate the artistry and power of the Chinese emperors. Still, Genghis Khan, with superior war technology, as examined by Morris Rossabi in "All the Khan's Horses," was able to conquer much of Asia, including the Chinese.

At the same time, Islamic civilization burst out of the Arabian deserts and conquered the Middle East, North Africa, India, and the fringes of Europe. There was a cultural flowering, particularly in writing, as explained in "The Master-Chronologers of Islam." The Muslims turned back the attacks of various Christian crusades in the eleventh and twelfth centuries. These assaults, examined in "Reinterpreting the Crusades: Religious Warriors," were motivated by religion, as a sort of penitence, although imperialism and greed are also readily seen as a part of the crusader's incentive. These events brought Europeans into violent contact with the peoples of the Middle East.

Within Europe two important events occurred that helped to shape the future. English barons extracted a statement of personal liberties from King John with the Magna Carta in the thirteenth century. This document became a foundation stone of the principle of rule by law rather than rule at the whim of a monarch. In the same century the first mechanical clocks, invented by an unknown genius, appeared in Europe. This key invention changed attitudes toward time and inspired further developments, such as miniaturization of parts and mass production. It led to the Industrial Revolution. By the fifteenth century Europeans were ready to reach out into the world as no other civilization had done.

Looking Ahead: Challenge Questions

Why caused the decline in Mogollon and Mayan cultures? Why is more known about the Maya than about the Mogollon of Mesoamerica or the Moche of Peru?

What knowledge was gained by breaking the Mayan script?

Why were the Mongols successful warriors while the crusaders were not?

How have the crusades been interpreted by later historians? Which analysis is correct?

What was learned from the Imperial tombs of China?

What was the role of warfare in the writing of the Magna Carta?

What is the importance of Arab scholarship in world history?

Why is the clock considered an important invention?

UNIT 6

Tracking a vanished people through the Sierra Madre

In 1890, Carl Lumholtz pushed into Mexico,
on a search for the ancient culture now known
as the Anasazi. Instead, he found the Mogollon

David Roberts

David Roberts reported on a Mogollon village in
Arizona in March 1992 and became familiar with
the Sierra Madre while doing a book on the Apache.

The dim light of dawn gave shape to the recesses inside the cave. Ranged along its walls, the ruins of a dozen adobe rooms, built by the ancients more than five centuries before, stood as testimony to some vanished lifeway. Soot from campfires immemorial coated the ceiling of the alcove. All across the Southwestern United States I had found cliff dwellings that vaguely resembled this collection of back-to-back mud houses. But never had I seen anything that looked like the bizarre structure standing in the center of the site, dominating the cave.

Twelve feet tall, made of coiled grass rope plastered with mud, it swelled from a small base to bulbous proportions, then tapered to the tiny hoop of its open roof, a few feet below the cave ceiling. The combined efforts of rodents, vandals and the winds of eons had worn holes in it, and the whole thing looked precarious.

That May morning, photographer Terrence Moore and I lingered inside Cueva de la Olla, in the remote Cave Valley in the mountains of the Mexican state of Chihuahua. One hundred and five years before our visit, the Norwegian explorer Carl Lumholtz had made the Western discovery of this remarkable ruin.

Lumholtz's Mexican workers had called the bulging structure (above) an *olla*, or "jar," insisting it must have been used as a cistern. But Lumholtz at once deduced—rightly, we know now—that it had been a granary for storing corn. Terry and I had seen many a granary built by the ancient Anasazi in the Four Corners region of what is now the United States: they tended to be small, neatly mortared cubicles with stone slab doors. The "olla" was not only by far the largest, but certainly the strangest granary we had ever seen. It had been crafted by a different people altogether from the Anasazi. Archaeologists know them as the Mogollon (pronounced muggy-OWN).

On that January day in 1891 when he discovered the granary, Carl Lumholtz had scarcely begun a journey that would last a total of six and a half years and would amount to one of the most glorious wild-goose chases in North America. Four years earlier he had conceived his expedition. Though Cliff Palace on Mesa Verde, the largest cliff dwelling in the United States, would not be discovered until the following year (SMITHSONIAN, December 1993), by 1887 word of the remarkable prehistoric ruins scattered across the Southwest had already reached Europe.

Lumholtz made a logical but fallacious deduction. The builders of those stone-and-mud ruins had vanished, yet Spanish explorers in the 16th century had come across Indians living in kindred villages in Mexico. Perhaps the ancients had retreated into the vast Sierra Madre of northern Mexico, where they still flourished unknown to Mexicans and Anglos alike.

During those six and a half years in northern Mexico, Lumholtz found not a single living Anasazi (as the builders of the great Four Corners ruins would come to be called in the 1930s). Curiously, Lumholtz overlooked the possibility that many of the Pueblo Indians living at Hopi, Zuni and some 20 villages near the Rio Grande might be the descendants of the Anasazi—a possibility that, by 1890, had already been divined by several American ethnographers working in the Southwest.

As he set off into the Sierra Madre, Lumholtz was 39 years old. Raised in Lillehammer, he had studied dutifully for the priesthood, a vocation his father had chosen for him, but the strain of pursuing a theology degree brought on a nervous breakdown. After recuperating, on solo jaunts into the mountains of central Norway, Lumholtz was moved to tears of joy by such sights as sunlight streaming through willow leaves reflected in rainpools. "Love of nature took stronger and stronger hold of me," the explorer recalled at age 70, "and one day it occurred to me what a misfortune it would be to die without having seen the whole earth."

Armed with a second university degree in natural science, in 1880 Lumholtz set off on a zoological expedition into the wilds of northeastern Australia. His journey began as a classic Victorian collecting trip, and the young savant bagged his catch of new species—notably, the tree kangaroo (*Dendrolagus lumholtzii*). Yet, during nearly four years in Queensland, Lumholtz ventured again and again into remote territory inhabited only by aborigines. He claimed to be the first European to dare such forays alone, where the collective wisdom of the British colonists decreed, "Never have a black fellow behind you."

Lumholtz's sojourn among the aborigines was indeed a risky proposition. In his memoirs, the explorer credits his safe passage to the intimidating magic of his revolver, which he often shot off before going to bed as a reminder of "the white man's superiority." But it is clear that his fearless curiosity, his gift for song and language, and his willingness to try out an aboriginal way of life—his favorite dish, he reports dryly, was "the larva, eaten toasted, of a large brown beetle"—served to surround Lumholtz's figure with a charmed aura.

His Australian adventure led to a stirring book, *Among Cannibals*, written in English and published in Copenhagen. As he set out for Mexico in 1890, he had come to realize that "the study of savage and barbaric races has . . . become my life's work."

As that phrase suggests, the young Lumholtz was steeped in the ethnocentric condescensions of his day. Despite his admiration for the skills of the peoples he had visited, he could still refer to the aborigines as "a race of people whose culture—if indeed they can be said to have any culture whatever—must be characterized as the lowest to be found among the whole genus *homo sapiens*." Mexico would profoundly change the smug European.

In New York City, Lumholtz won friends and sponsors: his first Mexican expedition was generously supported by the American Museum of Natural History (AMNH) and the American Geographical Society. With an entourage of scientists, packers and nearly a hundred horses and mules, Lumholtz started south from Bisbee, Arizona, in September 1890. The party passed through such dusty Mexican hamlets as Opoto, Guasavas and Granados. Then they turned east, climbing into "that great and mysterious mountain range called the Sierra Madre," a region "never visited by tourists" and "foreign even to most Mexicans."

Expecting to run across signs of the desperate remnant Apache bands rumored still to be hiding there, and hoping to meet living "cliff dwellers," Lumholtz plunged into the mountains with the joyful verve of a seasoned explorer. The jagged crests, V-shaped gorges and all-but-waterless streambeds of the Sierra Madre sorely tested the party.

Instead of furtive Apaches or flourishing Anasazi, the explorers everywhere found what Lumholtz called "traces of a by-gone race." These ranged from mere scatterings of potsherds and flint flakes to the ubiquitous stone check dams (some as tall as 15 feet) built across rivulets to shore up terraces for planting. On mesa tops, Lumholtz found pueblos of a hundred or more rooms, the walls half collapsed, grinding stones and basins lying discarded in the grass. In midwinter, having crossed the divide from Sonora into Chihuahua, the party began to discover cliff dwellings, such as the extraordinary Cueva de la Olla. Many archaeologists today believe that the people who had built these structures were a Mexican branch of the ancient Mogollon, who once lived in what is now the American Southwest.

In keeping with the practice of the day, Lumholtz dug every promising site, amassing large collections of artifacts and human remains, most of which he shipped back to the AMNH in New York. As the team trundled on, however, the Norwegian grew disenchanted with its unwieldy size. Gradually one scientist after another returned to the United States, and Lumholtz dismissed his Mexican muleteers, until eventually he was alone with only an interpreter.

Lumholtz's six and a half years in Mexico, during which he pushed farther and farther south, actually comprised four separate expeditions stretching over eight years. By 1892 he had realized that the only way properly to understand native peoples was to live alone among them. Eventually he would spend a total of a year and a half with the Tarahumara Indians and ten months among the Coras and Huichols.

6. THE WORLD OF THE MIDDLE AGES, 500–1500

Along with the artifacts sent back to the AMNH, the enduring legacy of Lumholtz's great journey is *Unknown Mexico,* one of the classics of North American travel literature. By 1902, when he published this leisurely 1,013-page narrative, the Norwegian had become a superb writer in his adopted language. The book sketches a matchless adventure with a wry, self-effacing wit.

For all the time Lumholtz spent among living Indians, the prehistoric ruins he found all over the Sierra Madre continued to haunt his thoughts. Who were these ancients who had wrought such wonders, only to disappear? As he wrote in 1902, looking back at the first leg of his journey: "We had just emerged from a district which at that time was traversed by few people; perhaps only by some illiterate Mexican adventurers, though it had once been settled by a thrifty people whose stage of culture was that of the Pueblo Indians of to-day, and who had vanished, nobody knows how many centuries ago. Over it all hovered a distinct atmosphere of antiquity and the solemnity of a graveyard."

In pursuit of our own understanding of the Mogollon, Terry Moore and I made our way last May to Grasshopper Ruin with University of Arizona archaeologist Jefferson Reid. Located on the White Mountain Apache reservation in east-central Arizona, on the northwestern edge of the Mogollon domain, the site ranges across some 30 acres of plateau at 6,000 feet. A perennial spring, the ancient village's water source, serves the Apache cattle that graze the plateau.

For 30 years after 1963, University of Arizona teams dug at Grasshopper, making it one of the last major excavations undertaken in the Southwest. The teams, led after 1979 by Jeff Reid, revealed a 500-room pueblo, housing perhaps 600 people at a time during the years A.D. 1275 to 1400. In 1992, when work at Grasshopper ceased, the site was backfilled for protection, leaving little to see but long, undulating ridges in the ground that mark the outlines of the room blocks. Here and there stray building stones—curious mixtures of pink sandstone and gray limestone—lay in the grass. And we found hundreds of plain brown potsherds lying in the dirt—identical to the ones we would see outside Cueva de la Olla in Mexico, more than 300 miles to the southeast.

The concept of the Mogollon as a separate people dates from the 1930s, from the work of the preeminent Arizona archaeologist Emil Haury, who argued persuasively that something was going on in southeastern Arizona and southwestern New Mexico that did not fit under the hitherto-sweeping rubric of the ancient Bas-

The Gila Cliff Dwellings in New Mexico, dating from A.D. 1270-1300, are considered to be Mogollon. They share qualities both with Anasazi sites like Cliff Palace and with Mogollon cave dwellings in Mexico.

ket Maker-Cliff Dweller culture now known as the Anasazi. Later, researcher Erik Reed would itemize the crucial differences between Mogollon and Anasazi. Reed's distinctions—which are still debated—ranged from ceramic styles (brownware versus grayware) to the shapes of ceremonial structures (Mogollon tend to be quadrangular, Anasazi circular), to burial position (Mogollon laid out flat, Anasazi tucked into fetal position) and even to the characteristic skull deformation caused in infancy by different styles of cradleboards.

As we sat beneath a ponderosa, Reid expanded on his understanding of the ancients. "The Mogollon were above all a mountain people," he said. "They were the supreme hunter-gatherer-gardeners. They were always mobile, far less sedentary than the Anasazi. Their chief source of game was deer, but they also hunted rabbits, squirrels, turkeys, even some fish. Unlike the Anasazi, they never became fully dependent on corn. I imagine their attitude was, 'If it grows, it grows. If it doesn't, we'll go do something else.'"

A golden age of potters without peers

Terry and I spent a week seeking out other Mogollon sites, such as the Gila Cliff Dwellings and the petroglyphs of Pony Hills in New Mexico, as well as Arizona's Canyon Creek ruin, a cliff village just southwest of Grasshopper. And we spent several days in the valley of the Mimbres River in southwestern New Mexico.

Here, during one meteoric surge between A.D. 1000 and 1150, a Mogollon subculture flared into enigmatic brilliance. The ruins of the villages, crude-looking rooms made of unshaped river cobbles gobbed together with mud, are nothing to look at. But the pottery is the most striking ever crafted in the prehistoric Southwest.

Virtually all Anasazi and Mogollon ceramics, when they are decorated at all, are covered with abstract geometric designs. Yet Classic Mimbres pottery bursts into figurative life. The interiors of these black-on-white bowls celebrate a wild diversity of beasts, humans, insects and chimeric fusions of unlike creatures. The painting is often lucidly stylized, so that a mere detail captures the essence of some animal's behavior.

Mimbres bowls seem to have been very personal items, used throughout one's life. They are often found in burials, inverted over the face of the dead person; usually a small hole, called a kill hole, has been deliberately punched through the bottom, as if to ceremonially retire the vessel. In the 1960s, as Mimbres pots began to command huge prices on the black market, vandals launched brutal attacks on Mimbres sites, using backhoes and bulldozers to tear up graves. Extensive looting continues today.

At the Western New Mexico University Museum in Silver City, museum director and archaeologist Cynthia Bettison guided Terry and me through one of the best Mimbres collections in the Southwest. Our minds reeled at the scenes painted so delicately on clay nearly a millennium ago: a wading bird hovering over an upside-down fish, a man swarmed with butterflies bigger than himself, two butterflies with their proboscises intertwined to make a maze, the "Siamese rattlesnake" with twin bodies and one head. By now, some 10,000 Mimbres pots are known, and scholars recognize the surrealistic menagerie as a style—complete with rigid conventions, such as diamond-shaped eyes and receding chins for human figures—that flashed into being in a particular region, then winked out within 150 years.

Mimbres culture remains an enigma. There is virtually no evidence that the pots were traded extensively out-

At Cuarenta Casas, dwellings five to six feet high suggest the small stature of the Mogollon. Lumholtz found the site (its name means "Forty Houses") in the Sierra Madre. Vandals have left their mark.

Intertwined proboscises of two butterflies form a maze on this Mogollon bowl from the Mimbres region.

A stylized bighorn sheep is surrounded by a band of intricate geometric shapes in this Mimbres bowl.

side of the Mimbres region, supporting the view that they were cherished as ceremonial and personal objects.

The Mogollon of New Mexico and Arizona have been relatively well investigated. Their cousins in the Sierra Madre, south of the border, continue to elude archaeology: since the days of Lumholtz, few of the countless mountain sites have been dug and analyzed. One notable exception is the astonishing prehistoric city called Paquimé, near the town of Nuevo Casas Grandes.

Built around A.D. 1300, Paquimé stands on the grasslands of Chihuahua, just east of the Sierra Madre foothills. On a blazing day last May, Terry Moore and I walked the city's lanes with John Roney, Albuquerque Bureau of Land Management archaeologist and an expert on the Mexican Mogollon. Dancing in the heat, the sensuous adobe walls swooped and jutted, defining a maze of rooms and corridors redolent of some arcane ceremonial purpose. We walked through I-shaped ball courts, burial chambers, large plazas, the House of the Macaws (where prized birds had been cooped in bins with stone-ring doorways), and the House of the Skulls (where human craniums hung from the roof).

Jeff Reid had warned us: "Paquimé isn't really Mogollon. They probably still lived there when it was built, but the city is pretty clearly some kind of Mesoamerican overlay." By and large, other Mogollon sites seem innocent of the impact of the great civilizations of central Mexico, like the Toltec or Aztec. At Mogollon sites in Arizona, one finds no ball courts, very few macaws, no rock art clearly portraying such Mexican gods as Quetzalcoatl or Tlaloc.

What, then, to make of Paquimé? Lumholtz was deeply puzzled by the city, which he guessed had housed 3,000 to 4,000 inhabitants. His account is little more than a catalog of the place's paradoxes: a seemingly palatial center with only humble dwellings, no "trace of a place of worship," a "Latin" cross engraved atop an open altar, pottery "far superior in quality and decoration to anything now made in Mexico."

Rumors of Paquimé had lured the first Western visitors to the site more than three centuries before Lumholtz. Francisco de Ibarra was a fame-hungry conquistador who, in the wake of Coronado's bold but fruitless journey to the north, set out himself to find the fabled Seven Cities of Cíbola.

Mad for Cíbola's gold, the expedition made the first European crossing of the Sierra Madre and arrived at Paquimé. The Spaniards were dazzled by the ruins: they reported houses six and seven stories high, magnificent patios paved with jasper, silver mines strewn with slag, big underground *estufas* (steam baths), and painted adobe walls. The "wild, coarse, and roaming people" who dwelt nearby indicated by sign language that the former residents of the great city now lived six days' journey to the north. Ibarra apparently thought Paquimé was the work of ancient Romans.

However impressive, Paquimé was no city of gold. Ibarra headed north, then across the Sierra Madre by a purported shortcut. On this desperate journey, beset by flooding rivers, dying horses, starvation and poisonous mushrooms, the party nearly perished to the last man. Like Coronado before him, Ibarra returned under the shroud of failure.

As I walked through Paquimé, John Roney pointed out the misperceptions that might have led to Ibarra's wild claims. Mescal-baking pits, visible today, gleam with a shiny residue the Spaniards could have mistaken for silver slag. Worked sheets of flint and chert—flakes of which still strew the ground—may have paved the "jasper" patios. The estufas were actually reservoirs.

Yet who were the builders of Paquimé, and what relationship did they bear to the Mogollon? During the next few days, Terry and I pushed his four-wheel-drive vehicle deep into the obscure mountain canyons of Chihuahua. In Cave Valley, Strawberry Valley and Cuarenta Casas, we revisited Mogollon cliff dwellings Lumholtz's party had found more than a century before. Unlike the majority of Anasazi ruins on the Colorado Plateau, which perch on cliff-edge, commanding lordly views—and others built into shallow cliffs—these Mogollon houses in Mexico tended to huddle in the dark nether reaches of deep, gloomy caves, or to claim scanty ledges under frowning overhangs. Sometimes we could see the indentations in the dirt floors from early excavations. And as we prowled through these hidden canyons, we pondered the two central Mogollon mysteries.

The wholesale Anasazi abandonment of the Four Corners region, in the years just before A.D. 1300, is well known. But few visitors to the Southwest realize that the Mogollon suffered their own full-scale abandonment. Archaeologists place the exodus sometime between 1400 and 1450.

We know for a certainty that about 1300 the Anasazi moved south and east, settling on the Hopi mesas, the Little Colorado and the Rio Grande, where they became the Pueblo who live there today. But where the Mogollon went, and why, remain utter mysteries. And we can only guess, after a century of speculation, which people living today are the descendants of the Mogollon. As far as modern science can determine, the Mogollon vanished not only from their ancient homeland but from the surface of the earth.

As Lumholtz pushed farther south in 1892, he began to encounter his first Indians. They were the Tarahumara, and they lived in caves. Dismissing his colleagues, he settled alone among the Tarahumara for a year, acutely observing everything he could about their lives and beliefs. By the time he recorded this visit, the Norwegian had traveled far from the callow social Darwinist who had sneered at the aborigines. He grew to like and admire the Tarahumara, and he came to believe that these "uncivilized"—but remarkably civil—Indians were greatly preferable to the acculturated ones who had acquired a taste for easy money and Mexican liquor.

The obvious hypothesis, that the Tarahumara were the descendants of the ancient cliff dwellers, was one Lumholtz tried out and rejected. His argument smacks of culture-bound Victorianism. Tarahumara rock art, pottery and architecture, he insisted, were too crude to have degenerated so far from the excellent standards of the ancient cultures he had studied, cultures that would later be known as the Anasazi and Mogollon.

Late in his own life's work, Emil Haury, who invented the concept of the Mogollon, speculated that in fact the Tarahumara *were* their descendants. Other archaeologists lean toward an assimilation among the Pueblo to the north, within whose villages today an extraordinary diversity of language and oral tradition points toward complex mixtures of ancient migrants. The jury is out.

For all the vividness of *Unknown Mexico*, the character of its author remains opaque. Essentially a loner, Lumholtz never married. His correspondence reveals little about his inner thoughts. Only in his travel writing did

Lumholtz begin to let down his guard. *Unknown Mexico*'s most moving passage expresses Lumholtz's grief upon the death of his dog, Apache, who had faithfully accompanied him through six years of rugged exploration.

That he was profoundly attracted to the Indian life is unmistakable. He believed that Indians had an "animal magnetism" unmatched by Westerners, and more than one became his loyal friend and companion. Here and there, a fleeting encounter with a woman seems to stir the pangs of loneliness. But he passes on: "With her fine dark eyes, her loose wavy hair and graceful figure, she made a strikingly beautiful picture, and as she called out in a sweet, melodious voice, '*Adios, Señor!*' I took this kindly greeting from a pretty girl as a good omen for my journey."

Later I asked Martha Graham, Registrar for Cultural Resources at the AMNH, whether her careful reading of the voluminous correspondence between Lumholtz and the museum had given her any inklings into the private man. "So much of his letters," she replied, "is aimed at ensuring continued funding. 'I'm finding wonderful things, things nobody's seen before—send more money.' There's no sense of the personal."

From 1915 to 1917, Lumholtz made his third great ethnographic journey, to Borneo, traveling solo deep into the interior, living among peoples rumored to be cannibals and headhunters. Once more, he produced a memorable account of his adventures, called *Through Central Borneo*.

In 1922, at the age of 71, as he planned yet another expedition—this time to New Guinea, a trip he had dreamed of as the "jewel" of his career—Lumholtz became seriously ill. In May of that year, he died of tuberculosis at Saranac Lake, in the Adirondacks.

In Australia, Borneo and Mexico, Lumholtz had been seized with the glum conviction that the people he admired and labored to understand were doomed to vanish, either through extinction or assimilation. As he wrote in the final sentence of his first book, *Among Cannibals*: "Invading civilisation has not brought development and progress to the Australian native; after a few generations his race will have disappeared from the face of the earth."

Happily, Lumholtz's dire predictions have not yet been realized. Though still threatened, the Australian aborigines, the Dayak of Borneo and the Tarahumara remain, their cultures remarkably intact.

Yet the Mogollon are gone, and not even the canniest scholars today can say whether they died out to the last man and woman, or migrated, intermarried and evolved into a people whose joys and sorrows continue to reverberate in some corner of the Southwest. Meanwhile, the startling ruins they left behind in the Sierra Madre, many of which Lumholtz was the first Westerner to see, stand crumbling under the ponderosas, brimming with meaning we have yet to decode.

CRACKING THE MAYA'S CODE

New light on dark history

What the discovery of the Rosetta stone did for the study of ancient Egypt, some inspired detection has done for the Maya people of Central America

"ONE of the greatest intellectual achievements of our century." Thus Michael Coe of Yale University, about the deciphering of the ancient Mayan script. His exaggeration is pardonable. When the Maya's strange, pebble-like writings were rediscovered in 1839, the man who found them, John Lloyd Stephens, lamented that "No Champollion has yet brought to them the energies of his enquiring mind [Champollion had deciphered Egyptian hieroglyphics 17 years before]. Who shall read them?" It has taken 150 years to answer that question.

The Maya were the only pre-Columbus Americans to have developed a sophisticated writing system, and they covered their buildings with it. These buildings, now ruined, lie buried in the fast-eroding jungles of Mexico and Central America. The temples, with their steeply stepped sides and crests of limestone, peer down upon an ebbing sea of trees, which undulates slightly as it rolls over unearthed temples, their coats of jungle waiting to be stripped away. It is like another world—and, indeed, the largest surviving Maya city, Tikal in Guatemala, played the part of an alien fort in the film "Star Wars".

As for the people who built these places, they might indeed have come from another world. Or so the scholars who wrote about them made it appear. According to the traditional view, the Maya were unlike any other people in the annals of mankind: they were men without war, without cities, without kings, and even without history—or rather without any interest in it (which comes to much the same thing).

Two men were largely responsible for this. One was an American, Sylvanus Morley. He thought the limestone in the jungle was not the ruins of cities but of vacant temples, which had been inhabited only by priests and acolytes. When his "The Ancient Maya" was revised in 1956, the word "city" was replaced throughout by "ceremonial centre". Morley was obsessed with the Maya calendar, an extraordinarily elaborate construction with concentric cycles of hundreds and thousands of years wheeling around a 260-day period, made up of a magic number 13 and a base number 20 (the Maya counted in twenties).

The other figure was Sir Eric Thompson, an upper-class Anglican whose powerful mind and waspish, elegant pen dominated Maya studies until his death in 1975. Thompson put religion centre-stage. In his view, the Maya were star-worshippers living at peace in scattered villages, presided over by priests absorbed by astronomical calculation. The writing on the monuments, he thought, was about not kings, but gods: "I do not believe that historical events were recorded on the monuments."

That was hardly surprising: Thompson barely thought the Maya had a history at all—certainly no states or kings or wars. When evidence of cities and states appeared, he dismissed it, saying it showed only barbarian invasion: cities were not really Mayan. As for the script itself, he thought that too was unique. Unlike other writing, it did not express a language ever spoken by anyone. It was a mystical rebus invented by priests for calendrical and religious purposes, not merely unknown but unknowable.

Alas, it was all rubbish: Arcadia did not exist. Over the past decade or so, a fundamentally different way of looking at the Maya has upturned almost every assump-

5 Eb 15 Mac (October 28th 709 AD)

He is letting blood

?

4 Katun Lord

Shield Jaguar the captor of

Ah Ahaual

Lord of Yaxchilan

She is letting blood

Name or titles

Lady Xoc

Lady Batab

The Yaxchilan scene and its inscription

balam   ba-balam   balam-ma   ba-balam-ma   ba-la-ma

Five spellings of "balam" (jaguar): cat's head and syllable-signs

tion of the traditionalists. In the new version, the Maya created an urban civilisation. They were far from peaceful. They had a knowable history. Their collapse came about through internal political failure, not invasion or (as Thompson argued) religious upheaval. Above all, they wrote a real language—and it was the discovery of this that opened the door to the new conclusions. As with many great changes in thinking, the transformation has come about not in a blinding flash, but gradually.

From obscurity to history

The first breakthrough appeared in part of the world about as far from the steamy heat of Central America as you can get: Leningrad, in 1952, where a young scholar, Yuri Knosorov, published an article in Soviet Ethnography.

In 1945, as a young soldier, Mr Knosorov had been present at the fall of Berlin—and had rescued a single book from the flames engulfing the city's National Library. It turned out to be an edition of three of only four surviving Mayan books. He took the tome back to Russia and seven years later announced what Thompson had always declared to be unknowable: how the words were spelled. Mr Knosorov argued that Mayan, like virtually all other early scripts (and like Japanese and Chinese), was partly pictorial and partly phonetic; the technical term is logographic. "The system of Mayan writing", he asserted, "is typically hieroglyphic, and in its principles of writing does not differ from known hieroglyphic systems." Thompson denounced this as Bolshevik propaganda.

The second step, ironically, had nothing to do with the first. In 1960, Tatiana Proskouriakoff, a Russian-American, published an article with the mind-numbing title, "Historical Implications of a Pattern of Dates at Piedras Negras". Using numbers that had already been worked out (mostly by Thompson) and repeating symbols that could only be names, she argued that sequences of names separated by intervals of time conform to human life-cycles—birth, marriage and death. In other words, the inscriptions were personal histories. Thompson had always denied this but the evidence was so compelling that he had to back down.

The third step put these two arguments together with linguistic analysis and came to a new conclusion: the script referred to a spoken language, with an identifiable grammar and syntax. By concentrating on those symbols which were not dates or names, and by looking at the structure of modern Mayan languages, Linda Schele of the University of Texas isolated Mayan verbs. Others then showed that the phonetic bit of the script was more important than had been thought: the Maya routinely wrote the same word using phonetic and pictorial signs interchangeably. This unleashed a torrent of decipherments. During the 1980s, about 80% of the hieroglyphic characters ("glyphs" in scholarly jargon) were translated and most inscriptions read. The Mayan code had been cracked.

The Maya emerge

Maurice Pope, a language expert, wrote that "decipherments are by far the most glamorous achievements of scholarship. There is a touch of magic about unknown writing." True—but the unglamorous reality is that the deciphering is only a start. What matters is understanding what the words say. By the mid-1980s, the scholars knew the script and understood the grammar and syntax. They could see what to look for. The flood-gates opened.

The Maya turn out to have created a world much older and more durable than had been realised. In the old view, their civilisation had lasted about 500 years, from 300AD until 800. It was at its height when Charlemagne was crowned as emperor of Christian Europe on Christmas Day 800 and when Muhammad was fleeing from Mecca to Medina. But the new scholars found glyphs from 200 years earlier, in 100AD, and the first cities seemed earlier still, from the 5th and 6th century BC. In other words, Maya civilisation ran from Periclean Athens to the start of medieval Europe.

This means that the Maya are emerging not as a prehistoric people but as possessors of a very familiar sort of history. As Proskouriakoff had argued, the people on the inscriptions were not priests but kings. In Copan in Honduras, writing experts first worked out the dynastic chain from the carvings, and then archaeologists discovered the bodies. In city after city, scholars reconstructed who ruled when, who his children were, what wars he fought and how he dealt with the neighbours. Like the ancient Egyptians, the Maya wrote their politics and diplomacy on their temples.

Just as important as the length of the history and its nature was the astounding detail in which it is being recovered. The Maya did not worship time but they were concerned to place political actions in their precise historical context in order to make them legitimate. The result is that scholars have worked out not only the year in which an event occurred centuries ago, but also the day and sometimes even the hour. Far from being non-historical, the records yield a chronology whose accuracy was not surpassed until the 19th century.

This onslaught of detail has made it possible to work out both what happened and also, to some extent, why. In "A Forest of Kings" (William Morrow, $17.95), Mrs Schele and David Friedel of Southern Methodist University, in Dallas, Texas, argue that kingship was the central Maya political institution. The royal monuments were not just lists but accounts of new military strategies (as at Tikal); what happens when a woman inherits the throne (as at Palenque); what happens when the succession is disputed (at Yaxchilan); how you create a new system of government after social collapse (at Chichen Itza); and so on. In "The Blood of Kings" (George Braziller, $29.95) Mrs Schele and Mary Miller, now of Yale University, argue that the principal concerns of the rulers were royal blood and bloody conquest. These were expressed literally, with scenes of the most hair-raising sacrifice and self-sacrifice carved in gruesome detail. In a series of carvings from Yaxchilan (now on display in a new gallery in the British Museum after years in its cellar), a woman kneels before her son, pulling a rope-like barbed wire through her tongue. Her son perforates his penis and threads strips of paper through it.

In yet another book, "Maya Cosmos" (William Morrow, $15), Mrs Schele and Mr Friedel examine the system of beliefs behind such things. The Maya, they argue, looked at the world in an unusual way. They tracked their creation stories through the vast movement of the stars across the heavens, and thought that the point at which the Milky Way appeared as a vertical band in the night sky represented both the growth of the maize stalk (their staple crop) and the moment of creation.

And they thought of the world as alive. If you took something from it (by growing food) you had to give something back—and blood was your most precious fluid. The word for blood also meant God and soul and was related to the words for sun and dream. The Maya believed you could summon up sacred ancestors by shedding blood and by inducing trances (sometimes, bizarrely, with hallucinogenic enemas). But the purpose of the blood-letting ceremony at Yaxchilan was dynastic, too: because the succession was disputed, the claimants wanted to contact the first ruler to justify their titles.

The end of the Maya world

At first, the new scholars thought the political arrangements of the Maya world were rather like those of ancient Greece—20 or so city states that co-existed for the most part independently of each other and without any over-arching political organisation. Of these, the biggest was Tikal, with a population of perhaps 40,000 people in the city and 500,000 in the hinterland.

But such is the pace of the change in the field that even this relatively recent theory is now being superseded. Two younger scholars, Nikolai Grube and Simon Martin, argue on the basis of newly-deciphered glyphs that most of the city-states were grouped into two loose alliances centred on Tikal and Kalakmul. The alliances were largely military, held together by payments of tribute (discovered by deciphering another new glyph) and by marriage. Mr Friedel reckons these alliances, and their wars, were a more or less permanent feature of Maya society from start to finish.

The finish is important. These alliances cast new light on what remains one of the great mysteries of the Maya world: its collapse. The Maya were not, like the Aztecs, cut down in their prime by the Spanish conquistadors. Rather, Maya civilisation collapsed of its own accord, in an astonishingly brief space of time, six centuries before the Spaniards arrived. The last dates recorded on monuments in the cities tell their own story: Copan, 820AD; Naranjo, 849AD; Caracol, 859AD; Tikal, 879AD.

Tikal was overrun not by its traditional enemies but by outsiders: portraits of moustachioed warriors start appearing there, along with foreign orange pots. What was left of the Maya world then degenerated into anarchy: the remains of defensive walls can be found thrown up hurriedly in the 9th century AD, first around large areas, then towns and lastly, in a few cases, villages and fields.

By about 1000 there is nothing. In the Copan valley and elsewhere, the population seems to have fallen by 90%. Here was a case, like Europe's Dark Ages, of a world going backwards. The Maya had been wealthy. At their height, their world was more successful than the one that exists today in the Maya area—successful as defined by the number of people able to sustain life there. The Yucatan, the green thumb sticking into the Gulf of Mexico, now has about two people per square kilometre. When the Maya kingdoms were at their height, they sustained a population 150 times greater—a density as great as that of Java today—largely thanks to a complex irrigation system now in ruins.

The Maya have been held up as an example of a society which exploited its environment beyond the possible limits. Certainly, evidence of soil erosion, drought and malnutrition exist in the late period. But so they do at other times. The new research proposes another explanation of the cataclysm: profound political failure.

In 695, the old system of alliances came unstuck when Tikal conquered Kalakmul and sacrificed its king. The first outcome was the dissolution of the Kalakmul alliance. But then, because the alliances never completely overrode the power of local kings, Tikal failed to exert any control over the extended area. The result was Balkanisation, silted canals, anarchy and collapse.

There is a coda to this story. For the most part, the scholarly revolution has wrung history out of the mute stones. But not just history. The rediscovery of the past by western scholars has coincided with a cultural revival among the modern Maya—and indeed is reinforcing it.

The beginning of the Maya world

That revival is partly a response to what some call the third great calamity of the Maya (after the 9th-century collapse and the arrival of the Spaniards, who destroyed those states which had revived after the 10th century). This third calamity was the counter-insurgency launched by the Guatemalan army in the 1980s, in which an estimated 190,000 Maya died and 1m (from a population of 3m) were made refugees.

The Maya recovery under subsequent governments has had repercussions beyond Guatemala. In Mexico, the Zapatist rebellion—usually described as an uprising of economically desperate peasants—in fact has strong Maya roots. In both countries, the first peace accords struck between government and rebels promised the use (for the first time) of Mayan languages in schools and in government. Gary Goosen, of New York State University, has shown that some of the old beliefs outlined in "Maya Cosmos", are still held by modern Maya, particularly the all-important one that links blood, soul and sun. Suddenly, all over Central America, there are diaries using the Maya 260-day calendar; comic books use old Maya stories; even the glyphs are back in commemorative plaques.

So the Maya do, indeed, have an extremely unusual ancient civilisation. Not because it was based on star-worship or peace but because it is neither dead, like those of ancient Greece or Mesopotamia, nor living, like those of China or India. Instead, it is waking up: the old system died but its way of looking at the world still influences Mayan-speakers today. They, like the scholars, are rediscovering history.

Considered to be the portals between the worlds of the living and the dead, these burial sites contained treasures to ensure that members of the royal family could continue their extravagance in the afterlife.

THE LARGEST exhibition from China's mysterious underground palaces ever to come to the U.S., "Imperial Tombs of China," currently is on view at the Memphis (Tenn.) Cook Convention Center's Grand Exhibition Hall. Spanning seven dynasties (500 B.C.-1900 A.D.), it includes more than 250 objects excavated from the tombs of China's most prominent emperors and ancient rulers. WONDERS, The Memphis International Cultural Series, organized the exhibition and selected objects from 18 museums and cultural centers throughout nine Chinese provinces. Sixty percent of the objects are ranked as national treasures.

Tombs were considered to be the portals between the worlds of the living and the dead. The Chinese believed the soul of the departed was divided into two parts—one went to heaven and one resided within the body. The soul remaining in the body had to be appeased or it could turn evil. The soul going to heaven was thought to act on behalf of loved ones by offering protection or even recommending good fortunes. To encourage their ancestors in heaven to do a favorable job on their behalf, the living did everything possible

to ensure the deceased were well-provided for in the afterlife. Tombs also were believed to house the spirits of the world's most powerful emperors, as well as their empresses, concubines, eunuchs, servants, and mighty warriors.

The burial sites were planned carefully. *Fengshui,* the ancient art that uses numerology, astrology, and other systems to determine the best orientation for a structure, guided the location choice and tomb construction. Some Chinese still consult a *fengshui* practitioner before they erect buildings or launch ventures.

Galleries throughout the exhibition are designed to replicate the layout of actual tomb complexes. This puts the objects in context and brings viewers into the atmosphere and environment of the imperial tombs. Visitors are able to enter the re-created tombs.

The treasures are highly symbolic. Stylistic changes in tomb guardians, animals, and decorative patterns show the influence of the major Chinese belief systems based on Animism, Confucianism, Taoism, and Buddhism.

Inside the tombs, furnishings designed to support a comfortable afterlife included the items and people the emperor had used throughout his life. This often meant concubines, servants, and warriors were strangled and placed inside the tomb. Since the

lives of royalty revolved around power and wealth, their mortuary goods reflected their extravagant lifestyles.

In the sixth century B.C., Confucius suggested that effigies could be buried with the emperor instead of living human beings as a more humane approach to providing him with servants. This concept was carried over to miniaturizations of objects that would be impractical to bury, such as houses and courtyards. Objects for religious rites such as sacrificial cooking, storage vessels, and weapons to defend the spirits usually were buried in their actual size. Guardians to watch over the burials were rendered symbolically in terracotta or other ceramics. Precious objects of jade, gold, and silver were included for use by the spirits in the afterlife.

Burial shrouds. An important burial practice was the use of shrouds of precious materials. The exhibition features a rare Han Dynasty jade burial suit made of 2,000 pieces of jade sewn together with more than two pounds of thick gold thread. Accompanying it are jade nose and ear plugs to prevent the escape of vital essences from the body. Jade was believed to have the power to ward off evil and preserve the corpse from decay.

Another important imperial burial garment

is a Ming Dynasty empress' dragon and phoenix headdress dating from 1368 A.D. Its exquisite design verifies the important position of its owner. Gold filigree dragons symbolizing the emperor and brilliant blue feather phoenixes representing the empress are mounted against a background of pale blue enameled clouds with gold thread. More that 100 rubies and sapphires and 2,000 pearls complete the decoration of this crown. This magnificent headdress never had been shown outside Beijing before this exhibition.

Bronze vessels. The tomb of the Marquis Yi, lord of the Warring State of Zeng, yielded more than 10 tons of ornate bronze vessels, the most ever found. By the time of the Warring States Period (475-221 B.C.), the casting of bronze vessels and ornaments had reached its greatest level of sophistication and diversity. Bronze is an alloy of copper and either tin or lead. Since its production involved the exhaustive processes of mining, melting, and casting, most vessels made during the early dynasties could be purchased only by aristocrats. They were used in rituals and funeral ceremonies, as well as for preparing and storing food and wine.

Tomb guardians, often made of tri-color pottery or terra-cotta, played a significant role in burial practices. Different types, ranging from animals to warriors, were placed both outside and inside Chinese tombs. These guardians were believed to have the power to protect the dead from evil spirits and tomb robbers.

The exhibition features a variety of tri-color pottery guardians. This pottery is made

by mixing copper, iron, and cobalt to produce blue, green, red, brown, and yellow. Any combination of three of these creates a tri-color glaze. One of the most dramatic guardians in the exhibition is the Tomb Quelling Beast from the Tang Dynasty (618-907 A.D.). It stands nearly four feet tall and has a semi-human face, cow-like ears, large horns, the body of a hoofed animal, and wings that spring out from its shoulders.

The First Emperor, Qin Shi-huang-di, had the greatest number of tomb guardians. Around his burial chamber, sculpted armies of more that 8,000 life-size soldiers and horses were buried for his protection. Individual details of facial features, expressions, hair styles, gestures, and uniforms denoting rank endow each figure with a unique character or personality. Scholars speculate that the figures were terra-cotta portraits of members of the emperor's army, accompanying him in military glory for the last time—to the afterworld.

The layout of the army reflects a Qin Dynasty military formation. Food soldiers archers, infantrymen, cavalrymen with their officers, commanders, horses, and chariots were positioned according to a configuration found in the military strategy texts of that time. This undertaking required more than 700,000 laborers and artisans. After it wa completed, the interior workers were shut inside the tomb in order to keep this vast army of terra-cotta warriors a secret. Remains of the laborers and artisans and their workshops have been located near the tomb.

The Terra-Cotta Warriors were discovered in 1974 by Xi'an residents who were digging a well. Today, the site is a museum displaying nearly 7,000 warriors, 40 chariots, and 475 horses in three different pits. Archaeologists still are discovering more soldiers and horses Four warriors and one horse are on display in a gallery designed to resembled the actual site of this extraordinary archaeological find.

Throne room. Perhaps the most spectacular part of the exhibition is the last emperors' throne room from the Shenyang Palace. It features a gold lacquered screen carved throne, cloisonne incense burners and many other surrounding objects.

"Imperial Tombs of China" will remain at the Cook Convention Center through Sept. 18, then travel to the Brigham Young University Museum of Art, Provo, Utah (Nov. 1-March 17, 1996); Portland (Ore.) Art Museum (May 1-Sept. 15, 1996); and Denver (Colo.) Museum of Natural History (Nov. 1, 1996-March 17, 1997).

All the Khan's Horses

*With fresh mounts in reserve, Genghis Khan's
warriors could outlast any enemy*

Morris Rossabi

Formerly at Case Western Reserve University's China Institute, Rossabi is now a professor of Chinese and Inner Asian history at City University of New York (Queens College) and a visiting professor at Columbia University. The author of Khubilai Kahn *and* Voyager from Xanadu, *he is [working on] a multivolume history of the Mongols and a study of Roy Chapman Andrews's Mongolian expeditions.*

In August 1227, a somber funeral procession—escorting the body of perhaps the most renowned conqueror in world history—made its way toward the Burkhan Khaldun (Buddha Cliff) in northeastern Mongolia. Commanding a military force that never amounted to more than 200,000 troops, this Mongol ruler had united the disparate, nomadic Mongol tribes and initiated the conquest of territory stretching from Korea to Hungary and from Russia to modern Vietnam and Syria. His title was Genghis Khan, "Khan of All Between the Oceans."

Genghis Khan and his descendants could not have conquered and ruled the largest land empire in world history without their diminutive but extremely hardy steeds. In some respects, these Mongolian ponies resembled what is now known as Przewalski's horse. Mongols held these horses in highest regard and accorded them great spiritual significance. Before setting forth on military expe-

ditions, for example, commanders would scatter mare's milk on the earth to insure victory. In shamanic rituals, horses were sacrificed to provide "transport" to heaven.

The Mongols prized their horses primarily for the advantages they offered in warfare. In combat, the horses were fast and flexible, and Genghis Khan was the first leader to capitalize fully on these strengths. After hit-and-run raids, for example, his horsemen could race back and quickly disappear into their native steppes. Enemy armies from the sedentary agricultural societies to the south frequently had to abandon their pursuit because they were not accustomed to long rides on horseback and thus could not move as quickly. Nor could these farmer-soldiers leave their fields for extended periods to chase after the Mongols.

The Mongols had developed a composite bow made out of sinew and horn and were skilled at shooting it while riding, which gave them the upper hand against ordinary foot soldiers. With a range of more than 350 yards, the bow was superior to the contemporaneous English longbow, whose range was only 250 yards. A wood-and-leather saddle, which was rubbed with sheep's fat to prevent cracking and shrinkage, allowed the horses to bear the weight of their riders for long periods and also permitted the riders to retain a firm seat. Their saddlebags contained cooking pots, dried meat, yogurt, water bottles, and other essentials for lengthy expeditions. Finally, a sturdy stirrup enabled horsemen to be steadier and thus more accurate in shooting when mounted. A Chinese chronicler recognized the horse's value to the

For almost ten days before the Kalka River battle on May 31, 1223, more than 20,000 invading Mongols (dots) feigned retreat before a Russian force (white arrow) of 80,000 men. At the Kalka River, the Mongols finally re-formed their ranks.

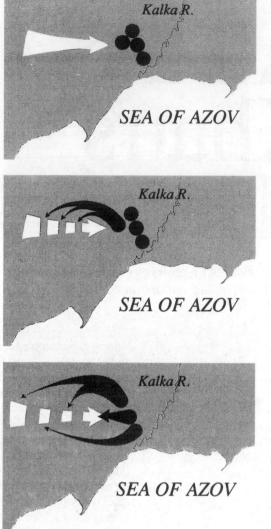

After pursuing the Mongols for days, the exhausted Russian troops were spread out along a twenty-mile line. The Mongols charged, with 5,000 mounted archers (black arrows) in the lead.

Once the leading Russian detachments were separated from their support columns and thrown into disarray, 5,000 Mongol heavy cavalry troops (black arrow) engaged them in close combat. Ten thousand light cavalry troops (gray) followed the retreating Russians, capturing or slaughtering most of them.

Mongols, observing that "by nature they [the Mongols] are good at riding and shooting. Therefore they took possession of the world through this advantage of bow and horse."

Genghis Khan understood the importance of horses and insisted that his troops be solicitous of their steeds. A cavalryman normally had three or four, so that each was, at one time or another, given a respite from bearing the weight of the rider during a lengthy journey. Before combat, leather coverings were placed on the head of each horse and its body was covered with armor. After combat, Mongol horses could traverse the most rugged terrain and survive on little fodder.

According to Marco Polo, the horse also provided sustenance to its rider on long trips during which all the food had been consumed. On such occasions, the rider would cut the horse's veins and drink the blood that spurted forth. Marco Polo reported, perhaps with some exaggeration, that a horseman could, by

nourishing himself on his horse's blood, "ride quite ten days' marches without eating any cooked food and without lighting a fire." And because its milk offered additional sustenance during extended military campaigns, a cavalryman usually preferred a mare as a mount. The milk was often fermented to produce kumiss, or *araq,* a potent alcoholic drink liberally consumed by the Mongols. In short, as one commander stated, "If the horse dies, I die; if it lives, I survive."

Mobility and surprise characterized the military expeditions led by Genghis Khan and his commanders, and the horse was crucial for such tactics and strategy. Horses could, without exaggeration, be referred to as the intercontinental ballistic missiles of the thirteenth century. The battle of the Kalka River, now renamed the Kalmyus River, in southern Russia is a good example of the kind of campaign Genghis Khan waged to gain territory and of the key role of horses.

After his relatively easy conquest of Central Asia from 1219 to 1220, Genghis Khan had dispatched about 30,000 troops led by Jebe and Sübedei, two of his ablest commanders, to conduct an exploratory foray to the west. After several skirmishes in Persia, the advance forces reached southern Russia. In an initial engagement, the Mongols, appearing to retreat, lured a much larger detachment of Georgian cavalry on a chase. When the Mongols sensed that the Georgian horses were exhausted, they headed to where they kept reserve horses, quickly switched to them, and charged at the bedraggled, spread-out Georgians. Archers, who had been hiding with the reserve horses, backed up the cavalry—with a barrage of arrows as they routed the Georgians.

Continuing their exploration, the Mongol detachment crossed the Caucasus Mountains, a daunting expedition during which many men and horses perished. They wound up just north of the Black Sea on the southern Russian steppes, which offered rich pasturelands for their horses. After a brief respite, they first attacked Astrakhan to the east and then raided sites along the Dniester and Dnieper Rivers, inciting Russian retaliation in May of 1223 under Mstislav the Daring, who had a force of 80,000 men. Jebe and Sübedei commanded no more than 20,000 troops and were outnumbered by a ratio of four to one.

Knowing that an immediate, direct clash could be disastrous, the Mongols again used their tactic of feigned withdrawal. They retreated for more than a week, because they wanted to be certain that the opposing army continued to pursue them but was spaced out over a considerable distance. At the Kalka River, the Mongols finally took a stand, swerving around and positioning themselves in battle formation, with archers mounted on horses in the front.

The Mongols' retreat seems to have lulled the Russians into believing that the invaders from the East were in disarray. Without waiting for the remainder of his army to catch up and without devising a unified attack, Mstislav the Daring ordered the advance troops to charge immediately. This decision proved to be calamitous. Mongol archers on their well-trained steeds crisscrossed the Russian route of attack, shooting their arrows with great precision. The Russian line of troops was disrupted, and the soldiers scattered.

After their attack, the archers turned the battlefield over to the Mongol heavy cavalry, which pummeled the already battered, disunited, and scattered Russians. Wearing an iron helmet, a shirt of raw silk, a coat of mail, and a cuirass, each Mongol in the heavy cavalry carried with him two bows, a dagger, a battle-ax, a twelve-foot lance, and a lasso as his principal weapons. Using lances, the detachment of heavy cavalry rapidly attacked and overwhelmed the Russian vanguard, which had been cut off from the rest of their forces in the very beginning of the battle.

Rejoined by the mounted archers, the combined Mongol force mowed down the straggling remnants of the Russian forces. Without an escape route, most were killed, and the rest, including Mstislav the Daring, were captured. Rather than shed the blood of rival princes—one of Genghis Khan's commands—Jebe and Sübedei ordered the unfortunate commander and two other princes stretched out under boards and slowly suffocated as Mongols stood or sat upon the boards during the victory banquet.

The battle at the Kalka River resembled, with some slight deviations, the general plan of most of Genghis Khan's campaigns. In less than two decades, Genghis Khan had, with the support of powerful cavalry, laid the foundations for an empire that was to control and govern much of Asia in the thirteenth and fourteenth centuries. He died on a campaign in Central Asia, and his underlings decided to return his corpse to his native land. Any unfortunate individual who happened to encounter the funeral cortege was immediately killed because the Mongols wished to conceal the precise location of the burial site. At least forty horses were reputedly sacrificed at Genghis Khan's tomb; his trusted steeds would be as important to him in the afterlife as they had been during his lifetime.

The master-chronologers of Islam

ABDESSELAM CHEDDADI

Abdesselam Cheddadi is a Moroccan historian who teaches at the faculty of education sciences at Rabat. An authority on Ibn Khaldun, he has translated into French the great Arab historian's autobiography (Sindbad publishers, Paris, 1984) and extracts from his history (Sindbad, Paris, 1987).

THE most striking feature of Islamic historical writing or *tarikh* is its sheer volume. Only a small part of it has so far been published and new texts are continually being discovered. From the second half of the first century of the Hegira (late seventh century AD) to the thirteenth century (nineteenth century AD) the writing of Islamic history continued almost without a break wherever the Islamic faith was professed. The language used was primarily Arabic, but there were also writings in Persian, Turkish and Malay. Although essentially written by Muslims, it also attracted Christian authors, especially in Egypt and Syria.

A second important feature of Islamic historiography is its very great diversity. It comprises forms and genres ranging from vast universal or general histories and monographs to annals, dynastic and genealogical tables or lists divided into *tabaqat* (classes), as well as biographical dictionaries and local histories. It also covers many fields: religious, political, administrative and social life; scientific, literary and artistic activities; schools of thought and ideological trends; travel, the topography of cities, monuments; natural disasters, famines, epidemics....

The historians who worked in this tradition were also curious about non-Islamic civilizations, western and northern Europe, India, China, the Far East and Africa. They were interested in any information relating to man, his relations with his social and cultural environment and his relations with God. Ibn Khaldun (see box) noted that they wrote just as much for the "crowds" and for "simple folk" as for "kings" and "the great". This view of history as universal in scope and the attempt to reach a wide audience prefigured modern approaches to the subject.

A grasp of time

A further point of similarity with modern historiography lay in the importance attached very early on to time and to chronology. From the first to the fourth century of the Hegira (seventh-tenth century AD) a vast amount of knowledge about time was amassed in Islamic culture. Drawing on earlier Arab tradition, it incorporated Persian, Indian, Greek and Egyptian material and also leaned on the work of astronomers and geographers. The masterly conspectus achieved by al-Biruni in the first half of the fifth/eleventh century is impressive for its tone of objectivity. It represents the most extensive and most rigorous survey of knowledge about time that we possess up to the modern era.

Muslim historians benefited greatly from this knowledge. From the second/eighth century onwards it gradually became common practice to give dates, to follow a chronological order and to provide tables. For most of the facts reported by historians it became a virtually absolute rule

Reprinted with permission from *The UNESCO Courier,* March 1990, pp. 35-39.

Originality and limitations

The originality, but also the limitations of Islamic historiography lie in its conception of historical information (*khabar*). *Khabar* means the fact, the event, as incorporated into discourse, related in a "story". The historian does not deal in raw facts. He starts from a given which is the story as reported by written or oral tradition, or by a living witness (who may be the historian himself). His most important task is therefore to authenticate or validate stories by subjecting accounts and channels of transmission to critical scrutiny. The historian does not seek to discover or establish facts but to gather, classify and organize information while making sure of its validity. The intrinsic truth of stories was a relatively minor concern until Ibn Khaldun, who based historical criticism on knowledge of the laws of *'umran* (the human order, society).

Bound to accept traditional sources, often down to the finest detail, the historian could incorporate them into a wide variety of genres or organize them at will within more or less voluminous compilations, but he could not formulate them in his own way, reconstruct them or recast them according to his own perspective.

In Islamic historiography then, the past is not reconstructed as it was by some Greek historians, nor is there any theological history as there was in the Christian Middle Ages. This accounts for its widely acknowledged impartiality and also for its stationary conception of time, which contains in itself no potential for change or progress but simply gives external order to a sequence of events. It was Ibn Khaldun again who, in considering the emergence, evolution and decline of vast human groups such as the Arabs, Berbers, Persians and the *Rum* (Greeks, Romans and Byzantines) added a new dimension to this vision.

Three major periods

The first major period of Islamic historiography, which extends up to the third century of the Hegira, is crowned by at-Tabari's chronicle *Tarikh ar-Rusul wa al-Muluk (History of Prophets and Kings)* (see box). A calendar based on the Hegira soon came to be adopted generally. The *isnad* method, whereby the names of those who transmitted information from generation to generation are cited, was first developed for the purposes of the religious sciences and then applied

Above, illustration from a Turkish manuscript recording a journey (1605-1606).

to note the year, month and day when they occurred. This contrasts with medieval historiography in the West where it was not until the eleventh century AD that a unified chronological system began to be widely accepted and where, as late as the fourteenth century, the chronology of the main historical events was still uncertain.

At-Tabari

AT-TABARI (839-923) did not invent Islamic historiography but he is its most illustrious figure. His *Tarikh ar-Rusul wa al-Muluk (History of Prophets and Kings)* long served as a model. This chronicle, which relates the history of the Islamic world year by year in the first three centuries of the Hegira, was continued by later authors, and many abridged versions and adaptations were made of its account of the pre-Islamic period. It was incorporated in other general surveys such as Ibn al-Athir's *al-Kamil (The Complete History)* in the thirteenth century AD and Ibn Kathir's *al Bidayah wa an-nihayah (The Beginning and the End)* in the following century.

At-Tabari was trained as a jurist, traditionalist and historian. For close on thirty years he journeyed through the cities and countries of the Middle East in a quest for knowledge which took him to the greatest scholars of his time. He was interested not only in history, Qur'anic exegesis and the traditions of the Prophet, but also in grammar, ethics, mathematics and medicine. His fame also rests on his monumental *Tafsir*, or commentary on the Qur'an.

His *History*, which is the culmination of a process which can be traced back to the first century of the Hegira, is guided by a constant concern to show how each item of information has been passed down through an unbroken line, which is subjected to critical scrutiny. He applied a strict chronological order to the raw material of history, and gave a more ample and finished form to the universal history sketched out by ad-Dinawari in his *Akhbar at-Tiwal (The Long Stories)* and by al-Ya 'qubi in his *Tarikh*.

At-Tabari's *Tarikh ar-Rusul wa al-Muluk* is described as a history of the world from the Creation up to the author's own time. In fact, as he explains in his preface, it is first and foremost a history of the relations between God and His creatures, whether of obedience and gratitude or of rebelliousness and revolt. Its main protagonists, after Iblis/Satan and Adam and his sons, are the prophets and kings. Biblical history is included, and neither Graeco-Roman and Byzantine history nor Persian history is neglected.

It is an irreplaceable mine of information. The author cites his sources for each fact reported and in many cases reproduces the accounts in which they are mentioned, thereby giving us access to early materials that are now lost. In the words of the historian Franz Rosenthal, at-Tabari in his *History* demonstrates "the scrupulousness and untiring inspiration of the theologian, the precision and love of order of the jurist and the perspicacity of the politician versed in law".

ABDESSELAM CHEDDADI

Ibn Khaldun

IBN KHALDUN was one of the greatest historians and thinkers of all time. He wrote a long autobiography thanks to which we are familiar with the details of his life. Born in Tunis in 1332, he came from a line of senior government officials and scholars of Andalusian origin, descended from ancient Yemeni Arab stock. He received a thorough religious, literary and scientific education at the hands of the most eminent scholars in the Maghrib. During his adolescence Ifriqiya was conquered by the Marinid king Abu al-Hasan, who entered Tunis in 1348. The following year his father and mother were carried away by the Black Death. In 1352 he went to Fez where he stayed for some ten years and served as private secretary to the sultan Abu Salim. But neither there nor in Granada, to which he travelled in 1362, nor later in Bejaia or Tlemcen, did he manage to lead a stable life or to achieve his political ideal. He did however acquire detailed knowledge of court life and the workings of the state and observed the world of the Arab and Berber tribes.

In 1375, at the age of forty-three, he withdrew from public life in order to devote himself to science. In the castle of Ibn Salamah, near Frenda in Algeria, he wrote the first version of the *Muqaddimah (Introduction to History)*. The need for more extensive documentation forced him to leave his refuge. He returned to Tunis where he taught and completed the first version of the *Kitab al-'Ibar*, his monumental history of the world. But, fearing the intrigues of his enemies, he left the Maghrib for good in 1384 and settled in Egypt. In Cairo he was given an introduction to the Mamluk ruler as-Zahir Barquq and took on teaching and judicial duties, while continuing to work on his voluminous opus. Five years before his death in 1406, during the siege of Damascus, he met the Mongol Timur, of whom he left a striking portrait.

Ibn Khaldun's concerns were primarily those of a historian. Wishing to give a comprehensive account of his age which might serve as a model for future historians, dissatisfied with traditional methods of authenticating and verifying facts, he formulated a theory of society on which all his historiography was to be based. In the *Muqaddimah* he laid the foundations of what would today be called anthropology. Here we can give no more than a glimpse of the rich fund of concepts he brought into play.

Central to his theory of society is the concept of *'um-*

(continued)

ran. For lack of a more adequate term, this can be translated as "civilization", but only if this word is stripped of any connotation of an opposition between "advanced" societies and "primitive" societies. A more radical concept, based on the religious idea of the Creation, 'umran designates the fact of human life, the human order in general. Fundamentally equal and free, human beings are God's creatures, and as such are the rulers of the Earth, but they differ from one another by virtue of their living conditions, which are themselves determined by geographic and climatic conditions. The term also denotes the forms of social life or, in a more restrictive sense, urban life with its dense concentration of humanity, contrasting with life in mountain or desert regions.

In 'umran Ibn Khaldun distinguishes two states, which are at the same time the two main stages in human evolution. Badawah, the original agro-pastoral phase, close to nature, satisfying only the barest needs, yields to hadarah, the complex urban stage which gives rise to surpluses, in which society fulfils itself and achieves its purpose. It is the fate of 'umran to oscillate in accordance with an implacable law between these two poles.

For Ibn Khaldun, mulk (power) was the basic factor responsible for social and historical dynamics. As a source of the highest prestige, it is the goal of all human aspiration and desire, spurring men to action. Precarious by nature, it passes from one group to another, from one nation to another. As a means of distributing economic surpluses and structuring society, it has a pivotal role in the transition from badawah to hadarah. Around this central principle of social life Ibn Khaldun structured his history. In studying the Arabs and Berbers he concerned himself with those nations that successively held power. His narrative traces the rise of political groups from their Bedouin status to the heights of power, and their subsequent downfall.

These concepts tie in with many others, which include, in the social sphere, cohesion ('asabiyah), kinship (nasab), protection (walah, istinah), honour (nu 'ra); in the political sphere, constraint (ikrah), coercion (Qahr), domination (ghalab or taghallub), prestige (jah); and in the economic sphere, means of subsistence (ma 'ash), gain or profit (kasb), value (qimah) and work (a 'mal).

The concepts he employs, the laws governing the functioning of Arab-Berber society which he identifies, and the bird's-eye view that he provides of many aspects of Islamic history, are still indispensable tools of anthropological and historical research into Islamic society. Far from being superseded, this rigorous, coherent set of theories continues to be a mine of scientific knowledge for modern researchers.

ABDESSELAM CHEDDADI

---

to the biography of the Prophet, to stories of the Muslim conquests and gradually to all kinds of stories.

The earliest historical writing appeared and sometimes crystallized in a number of genres, including *maghazi* and *sira* (the biography and deeds of the Prophet), *futuh* (Muslim conquests), *ahdath* (major political events), *akhbar al-awa 'il* (stories of pre-Islamic kings and nations), *ayyam al- 'arab* (stories of the Arab past), *ansab, ma'athir* and *mathalib* (genealogies, exploits and failures); biographies of scholars, lists of teachers, political and administrative chronicles, history of the Umayyad and 'Abassid dynasties, and collections of secretaries' letters. It gradually became the usual practice to date facts and events precisely and to follow a chronological order.

Numerous compendiums were published, such as al-Waqidi's *Maghazi*, Ibn Ishaq's *Sira*, Ibn Sa 'd's *Tabaqat*, ad-Dinawari's *Akhbar at-tiwal*, al-Baladhuri's *Ansab al-ashrai* and al-Ya 'qubi's *Tarikh*. Together this constituted a vast historical literature, relatively little of which has survived but whose existence is attested by the titles listed in subsequent bibliographies, like Ibn an-Nadim's *Fihrist,* completed in 377 of the Hegira (998 AD).

The second period, known as the classical period, is marked both by the accentuation of these various tendencies with, however, some slackening of the *isnad* method, and by the emergence of new genres. After at-Tabari, but less influential than he, al-Masudi composed the *Golden Meadows,* another universalist history.

From the fourth century of the Hegira onwards the writing of history became a more or less official activity involving greater use of national or provincial archives. This period was notable for the work of a line of historians starting with Hassan Ibn Thabit Ibn Sinan as-Sabi and, later, Miskawayh's *Tajarib al-umam (History of the Buyid Dynasty),* continued in the following century by Abu Shuja'.

The history of cities developed into a major genre. Many works were produced, the best known of which is al-Khatib al-Baghdadi's *History of Baghdad*. Biographical dictionaries relating to religious and intellectual life became more sophisticated and more numerous. They included lists of poets and other specialists, directories

Above, manuscript page from a collection of prose and verse biographies of Sufi saints, written by Hosayn Bayqarah (1469-1506), the last of the Timurid sovereigns of Persia.

Right, page from a 12th-century Arabic manuscript describing the customs of China and India.

of scholars belonging to different juridico-religious schools, catalogues of writers and lives of saints. In the various regions of the Islamic empire a thriving historiographical tradition thus took root.

In the mid-fifth century of the Hegira political upheavals in the Islamic world were not without an effect on historiography. A third period began, marked by an ebb in production until the mid-sixth century. Syria then came to the fore for a while with historians like Ibn at-Tayyi, Ibn Abi ad-Dam and Ibn an-Nazif, who wrote universal histories, followed soon after by Ibn al-Athir, the author of *al-Kamil (The Complete History)*. Then it was the turn of Egypt to produce major historians such as Ibn Hajar, al-Maqrizi, al-'Ayni, Ibn Tighribirdi, as-Sakhawi and as-Suyuti. The same period saw the birth in the Maghrib of Ibn Khaldun whose pioneering work was admired in his time but who had no successors.

REINTERPRETING THE CRUSADES

Religious warriors

Nine hundred years after the first of them was proclaimed, the crusades still resonate—and not just in the Middle East. Jonathan Riley-Smith, professor of ecclesiastical history at Cambridge University and the author of several books on the crusades, reflects on their changing interpretation

THAT the crusades continue to fascinate is obvious from the vast number of books, television programmes and films pouring forth around the world. Nor is the fascination merely historical. The crusades helped shape many notions still current in today's world, ranging from concepts of religious violence, through anti-Semitism, to ethnic cleansing. Interpretation of the crusades has also changed to reflect the mood of the times. Once considered as religiously motivated, the crusades later metamorphosed into an early manifestation of European imperialism; they then became a monstrous enterprise, motivated by greed. Now the pendulum has swung back again to favour a religious interpretation.

That was certainly how the First Crusade was presented by Pope Urban II, who proclaimed it on November 27th 1095, in a field outside the French town of Clermont. The event was stage-managed. The pope had wanted nobles to come from across Western Europe to hear his sermon, and the crowd reacted with obviously rehearsed acclamations. Few nobles turned up, and the theatre must have been risky: it was the onset of winter, and the pope was an old man on an arduous preaching tour. Even so, his appeal for knights to liberate Jerusalem struck a chord in western society. Between 1096 and 1101 a succession of armies, their numbers swelled by non-combatant pilgrims, swept into Asia Minor.

The most significant force, comprising perhaps 60,000 people, of whom about 6,000 were knights, came together in June 1097. Two years later some 15,000, of whom 1,500 were knights, took Jerusalem. They had undergone (and inflicted) the most appalling sufferings. They had struck out on their own, with no system of provisioning; during the eight-month siege of Antioch, a region roughly 50 miles around was stripped bare by foraging parties.

BY INVITATION

Within a year of leaving Europe most of the crusaders' horses were dead; more seriously, their pack animals died as well, forcing them to carry their armour in sacks.

Not surprisingly, the crusaders' march was punctuated by moments of blind panic. There was a continuous trickle of deserters. But there was also a growing sense of wonder at their achievement. From the moment they entered Syria, visions in the heavens multiplied. One victory was attributed to an army of angels, saints and the crusaders' dead, which came galloping up on the left flank—significantly, it was horsed—and routed the Muslims. To contemporaries the success of the First Crusade could be explained only by divine intervention.

Urban II could have had no idea that he was starting a movement that would endure for hundreds of years, involve huge numbers of people from all classes and manifest itself in so many different theatres of war—the Spanish Armada of 1588 was an unsuccessful crusade. It is not surprising that events that impinged so directly on history should attract the interest of a broad public. More to the point, their effects still influence relations between Catholic and Orthodox Christians, and between Christians, Jews and Muslims.

Several centuries of crusading

Many Muslims, for instance, still reckon that the crusades initiated centuries of European aggression and exploitation. Some Catholics want the pope to apologise to the world for them. Liberals of all stripes see the crusades as examples of bigotry and fanaticism. Almost all these opinions are, however, based on fallacies. The denigrators of the crusades stress their brutality and savagery, which cannot be denied; but they offer no explanation other than the stupidity, barbarism and intolerance of the crusaders, on whom it has become conventional to lay most blame. Yet the original justification for crusading was Muslim aggression; and in terms of atrocities, the two sides' scores were about even.

The anti-crusaders draw on, and distort, the views of historians from the late 19th century on, who offered mainly materialistic reasons for the crusades. These historians saw them as early examples of the expansion of Europe, with recruitment for them a response to economic, not religious, impulses. In an imperialist age, the crusades seemed to be forerunners. The conquests in the east were, in a phrase much loved by French historians, "the first French empire". This was picked up by the British at the time of Allenby's victories over the Turks and his entry into Jerusalem in 1917–18; it was then passed on to early Arab nationalists, who turned it on its head.

The First Crusade certainly began the process of European conquest and settlement in the eastern Mediterranean; but this was not planned from the start. The Christian knights assumed they would be joining a larger force that would drive back Muslim Turks who had recently invaded Asia Minor, and restore Jerusalem, lost for 35 years, to the Byzantine empire. It was only a year into the campaign when, finding little support from the Byzantine Greeks, they struck out on their own.

The subsequent decision to settle the Levant comprehensively seems to have been taken not from a desire for land or profit, but to defend the holy places that the crusade had won, and to maintain a Christian presence in the Holy Land. If the kingdom of Jerusalem established by the crusades was a colony, it was in a special category of such enterprises, grounded more on ideology than economics. Another example is modern Israel.

More recently those still looking for an economic explanation of the crusades have argued that rising populations forced European families to take measures to prevent the break-up of their estates, either through primogeniture or through the practice of allowing only one male of each generation to marry. These measures, it was said, produced a surplus of young men with no prospects, who were naturally attracted by the hope of adventure, spoils and land overseas. Yet there is no evidence to support the argument—nor, even, that younger sons tended to crusade rather than older ones. And it can be shown from documents that foremost in the minds of most nobles and knights was not any prospect of material gain but anxiety about the costs.

Warfare is always an expensive business; and this was war of a type never experienced before. The crusaders were volunteers, at least theoretically. Those not ensconced in the household of a great crusading noble had to finance themselves. Meeting the bills often meant raising cash on property or rights. It was to alleviate this burden that European kings, shortly followed by the church, instituted systems of taxation (including the first regular income taxes) to provide subsidies. The argument that the crusades were a response to economic conditions at home turns out to be grounded on dubious assumptions.

Why did these interpretations hold for so long? Charters recording the pledging and selling of property and rights by crusaders have, after all, been in print for at least 100 years. The reason that so many historians overlooked them may have been that they were blinded by an abhorrence of religious and ideological violence, and by their inability to comprehend that it could have had any appeal. They forgot how intellectually respectable the Christian theory of holy war once was. It was easier to believe that the crusaders were too simple-minded to understand what they were doing; or to argue that they had been motivated, whatever they said, by a desire for material gain.

Since 1945 new questions have been asked. Combat psychiatry made great strides during the second world war; it became harder to categorise behaviour in war in the old clear-cut terms of heroism or brutality. There was also a natural revival of interest in the theoretical underpinning of a "just war". The Nuremberg trials, and their assumption that crimes could be committed against humanity, gave new life to the concept of natural law. Similarly, the debate over whether obedience to orders was justified raised questions about the legitimate authority of the state in war. Later on, the doctrine of nuclear deterrence, and a concern with proportionality, brought another just-war criterion, right intention, into the foreground. The 1960s revival of Christian theories of positive force in South American liberation movements also contributed to the debate.

Crusade historians, in short, suddenly discovered that there were sincere and devout contemporaries of theirs holding ideological positions quite like those of the medieval writers they were studying. And, with their eyes opened, the fundamental weakness of arguments for a materialist motivation, and the paucity of the evidence on which they rested, became clearer.

Holy war

The theoreticians at the time of the crusades drew on the work of theologians such as St Augustine of Hippo, the greatest and most influential proponent of Christian violence. For them, violence, when employed as a means of opposing "injuries" and thus achieving justice, could accord with divine providence. All rulers, even pagans, were divine ministers who could proclaim just wars; but God could also personally order violence. Violence specifically commanded by him was not to be distinguished from other just violence, except that it was "without doubt just". The concept of a political Christ, which was to return in the 1960s, passed out of fashion after the late 18th century that in the 1930s one theologian, Jacques Maritain, wrote of sacred violence being an impossibility, because no modern state could be associated with Christ's wishes for mankind.

It is no coincidence that in the decades leading up to the proclamation of the First Crusade a group of brilliant intellectuals were anthologising and reviving St Augustine's ideas. Crusade propagandists took trouble to conform their arguments to the criteria for Christian violence he had laid down, including the need for a just cause and a right intention on the part of the fighters; and they drew on the idea of a war at Christ's command mediated by the pope as his agent on earth.

Yet in one respect crusading was unlike nearly every other manifestation of Christian holy war. The cross was enjoined on men (and women) not as a service, but as a penance. The association of war with penance, in which the assumption was made that combat was so severe and unpleasant an experience for the penitent fighter that it constituted an act of self-punishment, had first been made a decade before the preaching of the First Crusade. It was unprecedented in Christian thought, as conservative opponents pointed out at the time. It was startling because it put fighting on the same meritorious plane as prayer, works of mercy, and fasting. The penitential element was reinforced by associating the First Crusade with pilgrimage to Jerusalem, the most sacred goal of all, and a place where devout Christians went to die.

Although over the centuries the penitential element was to some extent diluted by the notion of chivalric service, it remained at the heart of the crusading ethos. Preparations for crusades were always surrounded by an atmosphere of penitence. From the Fourth Lateran Council in the early 13th century to the Council of Trent in the middle of the 16th, every general council of the Catholic church was summoned on the ground that no crusade could be successful without a reform of the church. Crusaders knew that they were embarking on a campaign in which their obligations constituted an act of condign self-punishment.

In some cases, indeed, men considering entry into monasteries changed their minds on hearing about the First Crusade and joined up instead; they saw in crusading some equivalence to monasticism. Running through many of the documents issued by departing crusaders is a pessimistic piety, expressed in a horror of sin and a fear of its consequences. The crusaders craved forgiveness. They joined up, as one put it, "in order to obtain the pardon that God can give me for my crimes"; or, wrote another, "so that he might gain Christ".

In most expressions of holy war God is at the centre of things; in crusading the crusader was. For him the crusade was only secondarily about service in arms to God or the benefiting of the church; it was primarily about benefiting himself. That was why a Dominican preacher in the later 13th cen-

Waves of crusades

	Dates	Places
First	1095-1102	Asia Minor, Palestine
Second	1147-49	Syria, Palestine
Third	1189-92	Cyprus, Palestine
Livonian	1193-1230 et seq.	Prussia, Lithuania
Fourth	1202-04	Greece, Constantinople
Albigensian	1209-29	France (v heretics)
Fifth	1217-29	Egypt, Palestine
Spanish	1229-53, 1482-92	Spain, North Africa
St Louis	1248-54, 1269-72	Palestine, Egypt
Nicopolis	1396	Balkans
Hussite	1420-31	Bohemia (v heretics)

...ry commented of the crusading dead that, by this kind of death, people make their way to heaven who perhaps would never reach it by another road." Hard as it is to understand, Christian culture had produced an ideology in which fighting was an act of self-sanctification.

But the side-effects

It is necessary not to lose sight of the rest of the picture. Ventures of this sort easily attract psychopaths, and no method was devised whereby the crusades could screen recruits for suitability. Indeed, it could not have been, because crusades were technically pilgrimages that had to be open to all. In any case successive popes were sometimes only too pleased to get any response at all to their appeals.

Because the successful launching of a crusade depended on arms-bearers volunteering to take part, churchmen went to great lengths to address them in a language easy to understand. In doing so, they ran the danger of arousing forces which they could not control. For example, to call on men in an age of extended families and endemic blood-fueds to go to the assistance of their "father" Christ, who has lost his patrimony, or of their "brothers and sisters", who groaned under a Muslim yoke, risked the swift degeneration of any crusade into a vendetta. The passions unleashed, when combined with the stresses of crusading, led to acts of unspeakable horror.

There was even, sometimes, a savage beauty about active service. Think of Richard the Lionheart battling against Saladin; of the glittering coats of arms carved and painted on the walls of fortresses on the shores of the Aegean and the Baltic; of a fleet leaving Venice in the autumn of 1202 with trumpets and horns calling and braying to each other from ship to ship across the water; or, most romantic of all, of the colourful bravado of the Teutonic knights in 14th-century Prussia, who attracted recruits from all over Europe for campaigns against Lithuania that involved long rides through a wilderness of forest, undergrowth and bog, before a ravaging cavalcade in pagan territory, and finally a feast at Marienburg where a Table of Honour was laid for the most prestigious knights, and badges were presented to the most meritorious by the grand master.

This chivalric theatre masked, however, many awful atrocities: ferocious pogroms against Jews that were features of the preliminaries of many crusades, gross examples of ethnic cleansing in which non-Christians were driven from towns of religious or strategic significance by deliberate campaigns of terror, and collapses in military discipline that led to appalling consequences for any wretches unlucky enough to be found in the crusaders' path.

No one could possibly condone a movement that, through its cocktail of idealism, indiscipline, alienation and stress, managed to give birth to such grotesque manifestations of inhumanity. Yet one should not criticise crusaders for being what they were not. They were not imperialists or colonialists. They were not simply after land or booty. And they were not too stupid to know what they were doing. Their scale of values was different from today's. They were pursuing an ideal that, however alien it seemed to later generations of historians, was enthusiastically supported at the time by such heavyweights as St Bernard of Clairvaux and St Thomas Aquinas.

Blindness to reality can be dangerous. Only ten generations have passed since Christian armies, operating within a clear tradition and inspired by a coherent ideology, were winning a land war against the Turks in the Balkans. Modern Christian sacred violence has largely been confined to churches in poor countries. Although the Lebanese Maronites, whose church submitted to Rome in 1180, have always had a folk memory of a golden age under crusader rule, and the Croats—and, from a different perspective, the Orthodox Serbs—have romanticised the disasters and triumphs of the Balkan wars against the Turks, in almost all Christian tribalism in recent years there has been no specific ideology of holy war. The roots of ethnic violence have, in every case, lain rather in nationalism.

Things may be different in Islam, although nationalism obviously plays a large part there as well. Some Muslims now maintain that the *jihad* should be interpreted merely as a battle against evil. But in its traditional form, it was a war for the extension of Islamic territory. Some Muslims still seem to envisage the use of force, not only to counter perceived threats to their way of life, but to bring about world reformation on their own terms.

Indeed, it is conceivable that a situation could arise not unlike that in the 50 years or so before the proclamation of the First Crusade. After a period of quiescence, fanatical Muslims, Turkish religious warriors in Asia Minor and Berber zealots in Spain were destabilising the frontiers between the religions. The development of crusading was in part a response to a huge loss of Christian territory in the east.

History never repeats itself. But if renewed aggressiveness among Muslims were to meet a revival of Christian theories of positive force, the outcome could be nasty. One way to avoid it is to study and interpret the crusades—and the conditions that allowed them to flourish. Understanding should help to bring enlightenment.

THE MAKING OF MAGNA CARTA

Ruth I Mills

On 15th June, 1215, at Runnymede, between Windsor and Staines by the river Thames, King John of England sealed a document called 'The Articles of the Barons'. The charter between the King and his subjects had a life of only about ten weeks and it was a later version that bore the name—Magna Carta—by which they both became known to history.

John was the youngest of the four surviving sons of King Henry II of England and his Queen, Eleanor of Aquitaine, and as such he had not been expected to rule. One by one, however, his brothers died—Henry, Geoffrey, and, finally in 1199, King Richard perished while fighting on the Continent.

Richard had been an exceptional warrior and had joined the 3rd Crusade to the Holy Land but while there he quarrelled with his French and German allies and made a treaty with his enemy, Saladin. On his way back to England he had been captured by the Archduke of Austria and held for ransom by the Emperor of Germany.

During Richard's absence, from 1190 until 1194, John had tried to persuade the barons to support him in an effort to seize the throne. The rebellion failed when Richard returned from captivity to quell the uprising, but when the King died, John gained by lawful succession the crown he had been unable to wrest from his brother. Those barons who had resisted John's rule now feared retribution. They fortified their castles in anticipation of John's wrath, but the influential Earl of Pembroke, William Marshal, persuaded them to pledge fealty to the new King.

Under John's command, the barons defended their Norman and Angevin castles against the

King John ratifying Magna Carta at Runnymede (The Mansell Collection)

From *British Heritage*, October/November 1990, pp. 41-44. © 1990 by Cowles Magazines, Inc. Reprinted by permission of *British Heritage*, P.O. Box 8200, Harrisburg, PA 17105-8200.

Above: Pope Innocent III, who reigned from 1198 to 1216 (The Mansell Collection). Opposite: King John, Innocent's nemesis and later his vassal (The Mansell Collection)

French. According to the French, John had forfeited the right to his French lands by supposedly murdering the son of the Duke of Brittany (who had been a contender for the British throne) and marrying the already-engaged Isabelle of Angoulême. Unfortunately, the barons met with little success and by 1204 the last of the castles had fallen to the enemy. The frustrated barons claimed that John was a poor leader, disinclined toward fighting and inept at it. John accused them of acting irresponsibly after many of them had turned their castles over to the French without a fight.

The cost of John's campaigns in France and his exhorbitant lifestyle, in addition to unpaid bills stemming from Richard's crusade and ransom, swelled England's debts. When John demanded that his barons pay higher taxes, many refused, saying that they had no more to give. The King grew ever more insistent. He imposed fees for the preservation of the 'King's peace', exacted huge fines for trivial offences, increased inheritance and dowry charges and demanded that castles be turned over to him. He took barons' sons as hostage and murdered them whenever his demands were not met. Widows were deprived of rightful inheritances.

On 12th July, 1205, Hubert Walter, the Archbishop of Canterbury, died, bringing the King into conflict with the Church as well. John, as every English King before him, named a successor. Simultaneously, the Canterbury monks, by Canon Law, nominated their own successor. John's envoy and the monks went to Rome to present their choices to Pope Innocent III, but he rejected them both. During December, 1206, he prevailed upon the Canterbury monks to elect Cardinal Stephen Langton, an Englishman born at Langton-by-Wragby, Lincolnshire.

John refused to accept Langton and forced him into exile in France. Pope Innocent retaliated by laying an interdict on England on 23rd March, 1208. English churches were closed and all clerical services were suspended except for baptisms and confession for the dying. Many bishops and monks, fearing John's wrath, fled to France.

In 1209 Innocent realized that John was not repentant and, determined to employ harsher measures, he ordered King John's excommunication. The edict was not announced in England until 30th August, 1211, because most of the clerics remaining in England were either sympathetic towards the King or afraid of incurring his anger.

During the excommunicate years John's actions became even more extreme. Rumours of his cruelty were rampant. The barons kept silent, not knowing who among them were John's spies. Secretly, though, they took heart in the prophesy announced by a hermit, Peter of

Wakefield, in the spring of 1212: 'Within the year King John will lose his crown to one pleasant in God's sight.'

At first John laughed, but when he discovered that his subjects believed the prophecy he became enraged. John imprisoned the hermit and his son and awaited the outcome of the prediction. Frightened that this might presage a French invasion or a baronial uprising, and seeking now to reconcile himself with the Pope and thereby win his support, John sent an envoy to Rome to say that Stephen Langton was welcome in England.

Innocent no longer trusted John, however, and he sent an envoy to France commanding King Phillip to invade England in a 'holy war'. Unknown to Phillip, Innocent's envoy then continued to England, where, in January 1213, he told John that his choices were to irrevocably accept Langton or suffer invasion.

King John was now afraid he would lose all and not only repeated his willingness to accept Langton but also gifted the Kingdoms of England and Ireland to Pope Innocent who, with his successors, would serve as Lord of these lands in perpetuity. The Pope accepted the offer and on Ascension Day, 1212, John was still the ruler of England, even though he was technically now only a vassal of the Pope. The hermit's prophecy had not come true. Tied to horses' tails, Peter and his son were dragged to the gallows and hanged.

At Winchester on 20th July, 1213, Archbishop Stephen Langton removed the excommunication from King John, who swore that he'd act justly toward his subjects. Many barons scoffed. The King's promises, they said, were worthless. Within days John ordered military service for another continental campaign, but many barons refused to go.

Langton realized that a serious break between the King and his subjects was impending and, serving in the Archbishop of Canterbury's traditional rôle as church primate and first adviser to the King, he sought for a surer way of reaching agreement than through another verbal promise. At a meeting with several barons at St Paul's on 25th August, 1213, Langton promised them his support provided they acted legally—by means of a charter. He showed them the King Henry I Coronation Charter, considered 'ancient custom that is just', which promised that the excesses of King William Rufus's reign would not be repeated. That charter, Langton explained, could serve as the precedent for a new charter, one fair to baron, merchant, peasant and King, according to the 'laws of nature's God'—justice.

In May 1214 John was defeated in his attempts to recover the lands he had lost to the French, and, blaming his failures on the barons' lethargy, he again requested that they pay the expenses of his campaigns. He closeted himself with his advisers, whom the barons called 'evil counselors'. The barons met together as well, to sharpen their fighting skills and demand to be heard.

Aware that the malcontents' numbers were growing, John agreed to a meeting in London on the day of the Feast of the Epiphany, 6th January, 1215. There the barons, dressed in battle gear, exacted a promise from John that he would hear their proposal for redress of grievances during Easter week.

During that spring Marshal and Langton acted as intermediaries. At the Easter meeting, John refused to consider draft after draft of the barons' statement of redress whilst complaining to England's Lord, Pope Innocent, about the barons' intransigence. On Ash Wednesday, 1215, John declared himself a holy crusader, thus ensuring by Canon Law that no one could take or destroy his property.

The longer King John delayed, the less the barons trusted Langton's sincerity. At last they decided that force was the only avenue open to them. Assisted by peasants, barons began assaulting Royal castles at the end of April. On 17th May the residents of London opened the city gates to the insurgents and by 6th June, John asked for a truce. He ordered the barons to compose another statement of redress of grievances and granted many of the demands he had previously refused.

Finally, both sides to the argument met at Runnymede on 15th June, 1215. The recalcitrants promised they'd pledge fealty to John were he to seal 'The Articles of the Barons'. After minor details of the charter were worked out, John affixed his seal and 'The Articles of the Barons' became the law of the land. Sixteen years of turmoil seemed over.

Instead, horrendous events took place that rocked the Nation. First the barons refused to pledge fealty to King John and retained their private armies. Threatened with excommunication, they finally disbanded, but once back home, they fortified their castles and prepared for war. On 16th August, word reached England that Pope Innocent, in defence of his crusader-vassal, had issued an order on 18th June for Langton to excommunicate each dissenting baron. Then, on 24th August, the supreme blow came: Pope Innocent, Lord of England, had annulled the charter of liberties.

Langton, however, defied the Pope and refused to excommunicate the barons. He had urged them to seek a charter and knew the Pope had been misinformed. Planning to attend the Lateran Council in Rome, he decided to arrive early and explain the barons' position to Pope Innocent. As Langton embarked, the Pope's envoy suspended him from his see.

The barons now realized that Langton had worked on their behalf and had sacrificed his own position for them. He had failed to establish a charter, but every baron knew St Augustine's dictum: 'When all else fails, war is justified.' They were determined to succeed where Langton had not by defeating John in battle and dividing up the Kingdom amongst themselves. But, not having been actively engaged in warfare for a decade, the rebels were no match for John's supporting barons and mercenaries. From the autumn of 1215 until the spring of 1216, John's forces prevailed. By May the insurgents controlled only London and a few castles.

Meanwhile, in Rome, Pope Innocent refused to heed Langton's pleas. If not for the intervention of his fellow cardinals, the Archbishop would have been expelled from his post. Forbidden by the Pope to return to England, Langton went again into exile in France in January 1216.

In May 1216, the war in England took on a new dimension. Prince Louis of France invaded John's domain at the barons' invitation, in return for a promise of the British throne should he succeed. At the same time, several barons who had been loyal to John deserted him. Louis and his troops easily restored castle after castle to the rebellious barons, while John raced frantically about the Kingdom, doing whatever he could to preserve his lands. His last trip, on 9th October, took him to the Lincolnshire tidal flats where, supposedly, his treasure was lost in quicksand. Ten days later the King died of dysentery. His 10-year-old son became King Henry III.

John's death marked a drastic reversal of the political climate. Many barons who'd opposed John deserted Louis and pledged fealty to King Henry. William Marshal became Regent to the young King and took command of the Royal Army. Within the year Louis was expelled from England. By then Pope Innocent had died and been replaced by Pope Honorious III, who had respected Langton's position.

One of the Marshal's first acts as Regent was to revise the barons' charter, deleting certain offensive clauses and those pertaining to Royal forests. The remaining clauses, those ensuring personal liberties, became the Great Charter, Magna Carta, sealed 12th November, 1216, by the Regent.

During the ensuing years of Henry's reign and that of his son, King Edward I, Magna Carta was further revised and reconfirmed many times and in 1297 it became a part of the Revised Statutes. Almost a century in the making, Magna Carta now stands as a beacon, for under its medieval concerns are found timeless ethical principles that Stephen Langton called the 'laws of nature's God'.

CLOCKS
REVOLUTION
IN TIME

David Landes

Ancient Clepsydra

The question to ask is: Why clocks? Who needs them? After all, nature is the great time-giver, and all of us without exception, live by nature's clock. Night follows day day, night; and each year brings its succession of seasons. These cycles are imprinted on just about every living being in what are called circadian ('about a day') and circannual biological rhythms. They are stamped in our flesh and blood; they persist even when we are cut off from time cues; they mark us as earthlings.

These biological rhythms are matched by societal work patterns: day is for labour, night for repose, and the round of seasons is a sequence of warmth and cold, planting and harvest, life and death.

Into this natural cycle, which all people have experienced as a divine providence, the artificial clock enters as an intruder.

WHEN IN THE LATE SIXTEENTH century Portuguese traders and Christian missionaries sought entry into China, they were thwarted by a kind of permanent quarantine. Chinese officials correctly perceived these foreigners as potential subversives, bringing with them the threat of political interference, material seduction, and spiritual corruption. The ban was not lifted for decades, and then only because Matteo Ricci and his Jesuit mission brought with them knowledge and instruments that the Celestial Court coveted. In particular, they brought chiming clocks, which the Chinese received as a wondrous device. By the time Ricci, after numerous advances and retreats, finally secured permission from the court eunuchs and other officials to proceed to Peking and present himself to the throne, the emperor could hardly wait. 'Where', he called, 'are the self-ringing bells?' And later, when the dowager empress showed an interest in her son's favourite clock, the emperor had the bell disconnected so that she would be disappointed. He could not have refused to give it to her, had she asked for it; but neither would he give it up, so he found this devious way to reconcile filial piety with personal gratification.

The use of these clocks as a ticket of entry is evidence of the great advance

European timekeeping had made over Chinese horology. It had not always been thus. The Chinese had always been much concerned to track the stars for astrological and horoscopic purposes. For the emperor, the conjunctions of the heavenly bodies were an indispensable guide to action, public and private – to making war and peace, to sowing and reaping, to conceiving an heir with the empress or coupling with a concubine. To facilitate the calculations required, court mechanicians of the Sung dynasty (tenth and eleventh centuries) built a series of remarkable clock-driven astraria, designed to track and display the apparent movements of the stars. The clock mechanism that drove the display was hydraulic – a water clock (clepsydra) linked to a bucket wheel. As each bucket filled, it activated a release mechanism that allowed the big drive wheel to turn and bring the next bucket into position. The water clock in itself was no more accurate than such devices can be; but in combination with the wheel, it could be adjusted to keep time within a minute or two a day. By way of comparison, the ordinary drip or flow water clocks then in use in Europe probably varied by a half-hour or more.

These astronomical clocks marked a culmination. The greatest of them, that built by Su Sung at the end of the eleventh century, was also the last of the series. When invasion and war forced the court to flee, the clock was lost and its secret as well. From this high point of achievement, Chinese timekeeping retrogressed to simpler, less accurate instruments, so that when the Jesuits arrived some five hundred years later with their mechanical clocks, they found only objects that confirmed their comfortable sense of technological, and by implication moral, superiority.

Meanwhile European timekeeping made a quantum leap by moving from hydraulic to mechanical devices. The new clocks, which took the form of weight-driven automated bells, made their appearance around 1280. We don't know where – England possibly, or Italy – and we don't know who invented them. What we do know is that the gain was immense and that the new clocks very rapidly swept the older clepsydras aside. Since these first mechanical clocks were notori-

ously inaccurate, varying an hour or more a day, and unreliable, breaking down frequently and needing major overhauls every few years, one can only infer that water clocks left even more to be desired. The great advantage of the mechanical clock lay in its relative immunity to temperature change, whereas the drip or flow of the water clock varied with the seasons while frost would halt it altogether (the temperature did not have to go down to freezing to increase viscosity and slow the rate). In the poorly heated buildings of northern Europe, especially at night, this was a near-fatal impairment. Dirt was another enemy. No water is pure, and deposits would gradually choke the narrow opening. The instructions for use of a thirteenth-century water clock installed in the Abbey of Villers (near Brussels) make it clear that no one expected much of these devices: the sacristan was to adjust it daily by the sun, as it fell on the abbey windows; and if the day was cloudy, why then it was automatically ten o'clock at the end of the morning mass.

Why Europe should have succeeded in effecting this transition to a superior technology and China not is an important historical question. Anyone who looked at the horological world of the eleventh or twelfth century would have surely predicted the opposite result. (He would have also expected Islam to surpass Europe in this domain.) The Chinese failure – if failure is the right word – cannot be sought in material circumstances. The Chinese were as troubled and inconvenienced by the limitations of the water clock as were the Europeans; it can get very cold in Peking. (The Chinese tried substituting mercury or sand for water, but mercury kills and neither behaves very well over time.) Instead the explanation must be sought in the character and purposes of Chinese timekeeping. It was, in its higher forms, a monopoly of the imperial court, as much an attribute of sovereignty as the right to coin money. In this instance, dominion over time and calendar was a major aspect of power, for it laid the cognitive foundation for imperial decisions in every area of political and economic life. So much was this the case that each emperor began by proclaiming his own calendar, often different from that of his predecessor; by so doing,

he affirmed his legitimacy and identity.

Timekeeping instruments were therefore reserved to the court and certain of its officials; there was no civilian clock trade. Such great astronomical clocks as were built for the throne were undertaken as special projects, the work of a team assembled for the occasion. Each of these machines was a *tour de force*, and each built on earlier models, researched in the archives by way of preparation. There was, then, no continuous process of construction and emendation; no multiplicity of private initiatives; no dynamic of continuing improvement. Instead we have these occasional peak moments of achievement, highly fragile, vulnerable to political hostility and adventitious violence, easily buried and forgotten once the team of builders had dissolved or died.

Outside these rarefied circles, the Chinese people had little interest in time measurement for its own sake. Most of them were peasants, and peasants have no need of clocks. They wake with the animals in the morning, watch the shadows shorten and lengthen as the sun crosses the sky, and go to bed once night falls – because they are tired, illumination is costly and they must get up very early. They are not unaware of the passage of time, but they do not have to measure it. Time measurement is an urban concern, and in medieval China the authorities provided time signals (drums, trumpets) in the cities to mark the passage of the hours and warn the residents of such things as the closing of the gates to the separate quarters or neighbourhoods. But such noises could not easily be used to order the daily round of activities, for the Chinese did not number the hours sequentially; rather they named them, so that auditory signals transmitted limited information. Such as they were, they sufficed, for the organisation of work created no need for closer or continuous timing. The typical work unit was the household shop, comprising master, assistants, and apprentices. The day started at dawn, when the youngest or newest apprentice woke to make the fire and wake the rest; and work continued until night imposed its interruption. This mode of production set no artificial *clocktime* limited to labour; nature fixed the bounds.

In contrast, medieval Europe did have a constituency concerned to track and use time. This was the Christian church, especially those monastic orders that followed the rule of Benedict. This rule, which was defined in the sixth century, became over time the standard of monachal discipline in western Europe. The aim of the rule was to ensure that the entire day be ordered and devoted to the service of God – to pray above all, but also to work, which was defined as another kind of prayer. The daily prayer offices numbered seven (later eight), six (later seven) in the daytime and one at night. The institution of a nocturnal office was peculiar to Christianity and sharply differentiated it from the other monotheistic religions. It went back to the prayer vigils conducted by the earliest Christians in imminent expectation of the *parousia*, or second coming. It was these vigils that were later merged with the morning prayer to constitute the canonical hour known as matins.

The obligation to rise to prayer in the dark imposed a special condition on Christian worship. Whereas Jews (and later Muslims) set their times of prayer by natural events (morning, afternoon, and evening) that do not require the use of an artificial timekeeper, Christians needed some kind of alarm to wake to matins. In the cities of the Roman empire, the night watch could give the signal. In medieval Europe such municipal services had long disappeared, and most abbeys were located in rural areas. Each house, then, had to find its own way to satisfy the requirement, usually by means of an alarm device linked to a water clock. This would rouse the waker, usually the sacristan, who would then ring the bells that called the others to prayer. Most house rules – for although the principle was general, there was little uniformity in the details of practice – enjoined the sacristan to be scrupulous in his performance of this duty, for his neglect imperilled the salvation of his brethren (and the larger church) as well as his own. 'Nothing, therefore, shall be put before the Divine Office', says the Rule.

To the ordinary monk, getting up in the dark of the night was perhaps the hardest aspect of monastic discipline. Indeed the practical meaning of 'reforming' a house meant first and foremost the imposition (reimposition) of this duty. The sleepyheads were prodded out of bed and urged to the offices; they were also prodded during service lest they fail in their obligations. Where the flesh was weak, temptation lurked. Raoul Glaber (early eleventh century) tells the tale of a demon who successfully seduced a monk by holding the lure of sweet sleep:

> As for you, I wonder why you so scrupulously jump out of bed as soon as you hear the bell, when you could stay resting even unto the third bell . . . but know that every year Christ empties hell of sinners and brings them to heaven, so without worry you can give yourself to all the voluptuousness of the flesh . . .

The same Glaber confesses to two occasions when he himself woke late and saw a demon, 'come to do business with the laggards'. And Peter the Venerable, Abbot of Cluny in the twelfth century, tells the story of Brother Alger, who woke thinking he had heard the bell ring for nocturns. Looking around, he thought he saw the other beds empty, so he drew on his sandals, threw on his cloak, and hastened to the chapel. There he was puzzled not to hear the sound of voices lifted in prayer. Now he hurried back to the dormitory, where he found all the other monks fast asleep. And then he understood: this was all a temptation of the devil, who had awakened him at the wrong time, so that when the bell for nocturns really rang, he would sleep through it.

These, I suggest, are what we now know as anxiety dreams. They clearly reflect the degree to which time-consciousness and discipline had become internalised. Missing matins was a serious matter, so serious that it has been immortalised for us by perhaps the best known of children's songs:

Frère Jacques, Frère Jacques,
Dormez-vous? dormez-vous?
Sonnez les matines, sonnez les matines,
Ding, dang, dong; ding, dang, dong.

We know far less than we should

A monastic water-driven wheel clock of thirteenth-century Europe. The mechanism is hard to make out, but the picture suggests that water-driven wheel clocks of the Chinese type were used (or at least known) in Europe before the advent of the weight-driven wheel-clock.

Manuscript illustrations from the fifteenth century show the metaphorical importance clocks had in a medieval application of the concept of time. The goddess Attemprance, half-figure in a cloud, grasps a clock with hanging bells in both hands; large bell above. A French manuscript illustration of the late fifteenth century.

(Left) Manuscript illustration of 1450 showing a huge, intricate clock, standing on earth, but with its open and visible wheel-work and dial and bell in heaven. The four traditional symbols of the evangelists are shown on the four corners of the dial. The goddess Attemprance, resting on the clouds, is winding the clock.

the monastic time service. The enhanced temporal consciousness may be related to the revival of monastic life after the millennium and in particular to the needs of the Cistercian order – that economic empire with its agricultural, mining, and industrial enterprises, its ever-turning water wheels, its large labour force of lay brethren, its place in the forefront of European technology.

One of the innovations of this period seems to have been the combination clepsydra/mechanical alarm. This worked as follows: when the water in the recipient vessel reached an appropriate height, it tripped a weight-driven escape wheel, so called because it meshed with pallets that alternately blocked and released it (allowed it to escape). This stop-go motion in turn imparted a to-and-fro oscillation to the rod or *verge* holding the pallets; hence the name *verge escapement*. Attach a small hammer to the end of the verge, and it could ring a bell. Put an oscillating cross bar on the end, and you had a controller for a clock.

The first clocks were probably alarms converted in this manner. The very name *clock* meant bell, and these were essentially machines to sound the passing hours. Their use entailed a drastic change in the character of European timekeeping. Because the mechanical clock beat at a more or less uniform rate, it sounded equal-length

like about monastic horology in the Middle Ages, and such information as we have is confused by the use of the general term *(h)orologium* for any and all kinds of timekeeper. It seems clear, however, that the century or two preceding the appearance of the mechanical clock saw important improvements in technique and a growing emphasis on the details of hours – what later came to be known as mean (average) time. But the standard of medieval Europe was the sun, and the hours were natural, equal fractions of the day and night. Thus as days got longer, daylight hours lengthened and night hours shrank; and vice versa. These seasonally variable hours (often called temporal hours) were easily measured by the water clock; all one had to do was change the scale with the seasons. But an automated bell was another story: changing the times of ringing to take account of changing hours would have been a difficult and time-consuming task. So Europeans learned a new time standard in which the sun rose and set at different hours as the days passed. This seems natural enough to us, but it must have come as a shock at first. (Some places chose to start their day at sunrise, which took care of one end of the problem, though not the other).

In effect the new clock offered a rival time standard in competition with the older church time. It was not only the hours that differed; it was the signals also. The old water clocks did not sound public, tower bells. They told the time for the bell ringer, who usually rang, not the unequal, temporal hours, but the hours of prayer, the so-called canonical hours. These were not equally spaced and did not lend themselves to the kind of calculation we take for granted: how long since? how long until? It was equal hours that made this possible and thereby contributed significantly to the growing numeracy of the urban population. Insofar as the medieval church resisted the new time standard, it gave over an important symbol of authority to the secular power. Where once people punctuated their day by such marks as sext, none, and vespers, now they thought in terms of hours and, very soon, minutes.

The transition from church time to lay time was at once sign and consequence of the rise of a new, urban social order. The new machines appealed from the start to the rich and powerful, who made them the preferred object of conspicuous consumption. No court, no prince could be without one. But far more important in the long run was the rapid acceptance of the new instrument in cities and towns, which had long learned to regulate many aspects of civil life by bells – bells to signal the opening and closing of markets, waking bells and work bells, drinking and curfew bells, bells for opening and closing of gates, assembly and alarms. In this regard, the medieval city was a secular version of the cloister, prepared by habit and need to use the clock as a superior instrument of time discipline and management.

The pressure for time signals was especially strong in those cities that were engaged in textile manufacture – the first and greatest of medieval industries. There the definition of working time was crucial to the profitability of enterprise and the prosperity of the commune. The textile industry was the first to go over to large-scale production for export, hence the first to overflow the traditional workshop and engage a dispersed work force. Some of these workers – the *ciompi* in Florence, the 'blue nails' (stained by dye) in Flanders – were true proletarians, owning none of the instruments of production, selling only their labour power. They streamed early every morning into the dye shops and fulling mills, where the high consumption of energy for heating the vats and driving the hammers encouraged concentration in large units. Other branches of the manufacture could be conducted in the rooms and cottages of the workers: employers liked this so-called putting-out because it shifted much of the burden of overhead costs to the employee, who was paid by the piece rather than by time; and the workers preferred it to the time discipline and supervision of the large shops. They could in principle start and stop work at will, for who was to tell them what to do in their own home?

The bells would tell them. Where there was textile manufacture, there were work bells, which inevitably gave rise to conflict. Part of the problem was implicit in the effort to impose time discipline on home workers. In principle, payment by the piece should have taken care of the matter, with workers responding to wage incentives. In fact, the home workers were content to earn what they felt they needed, and in time of keen demand, employers found it impossible to get them to do more, for higher pay only reduced the amount

(Left) A sketch of a clock tower by Villard de Honnecourt, circa 1225-1250. An early example of a chiming clock tower which kept equal hours and provided regular signals — a constraint for worker and employer alike.

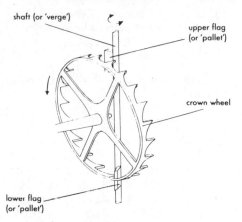

Diagram illustrating the 'verge' escapement. An escapement is the mechanism which could control and slow down the speed at which the weights of a clock dropped. The 'verge' escapement is the earliest surviving form.

of work required to satisfy these needs. The effort to bring the constraints of the manufactory into the rooms and cottages of spinners and weavers made the very use of bells a focus of resentment.

Meanwhile in the fulling mills and dyeshops the bells posed a different kind of problem, especially when they were controlled by the employer. Consider the nature of the wage contract: the worker was paid by the day, and the day was bounded by these time signals. The employer had an interest in getting a full day's work for the wages he paid; and the worker in giving no more time than he was paid for. The question inevitably arose how the worker could know whether bell time was honest time. How could he trust even the municipal bells when the town council was dominated by representatives of the employers?

Under the circumstances, workers in some places sought to silence the *werkclocke*: at Therouanne in 1367 the dean and chapter promised 'workers, fullers, and other mechanics' to silence 'forever the workers' bell in order that no scandal or conflict be born in city and church as a result of the ringing of a bell of this type'. Such efforts to eliminate time signals never achieved success: as soon suppress the system of wage labour. Besides, once the work day was defined in temporal rather than natural terms, workers as well as employers had an interest in defining and somehow signalling the boundaries. Time measurement here was a two-edged sword: it gave the employer bounds to fill, and to the worker bounds to work. The alternative was the open-ended working day, as Chrétien de Troyes observed of the silk weavers of Lyons in the twelfth century:

... nous sommes en grand'misère,
Mais s'enrichit de nos salaires
Celui pour qui nous travaillons.
Des nuits grand partie nous veillons
Et tout le jour pour y gagner

... we are in great misery,
The man who gets rich on our wages
Is the man we worked for.
We're up a good part of the night
And work all day to make our way ..

It was not the work bells as such, then, that were resented and mistrusted, but the people who controlled them; and it is here that the chiming tower clock made its greatest contribution. It kept equal hours and provided regular signals, at first on the hour, later on the halves or quarters, and these necessarily limited the opportunities for abuse. With the appearance of the dial (from the word for day), of course, it was possible for all interested parties to verify the time on a continuous basis.

The early turret clocks were very expensive, even when simple. Wrought iron and brass needed repeated hammering, hence much labour and much fuel. The casting of the bells was a precarious operation. The placement of the mechanism usually entailed major structural alterations. The construction and installation of a tower clock might take months if not years. Teams of craftsmen and labourers had to be assembled on the site and there lodged and boarded. Subsequent maintenance required the attendance of a resident technician, repeated visits by specialised artists, and an endless flow of replacement parts.

These costs increased substantially as soon as one went beyond simple timekeepers to astronomical clocks and/or automata. The medieval accounts show this process clearly: the sums paid to painters and wood-carvers bear witness to the growing importance of the clock as spectacle as well as time signal. The hourly parade of saints and patriarchs; the ponderous strokes of the hammer-wielding *jaquemarts*; the angel turning with the sun; the rooster crowing at sunrise; the lunar disc waxing and waning with the moon – and all these movements and sounds offered lessons in theology and astronomy to the upgazing multitude that gathered to watch and wonder at what man had wrought. The hourly pageant was an imitation of divine creation; the mechanism, a miniaturisation of heaven and earth. As a result, the show clock was to the new secular, urbanising world of the later Middle Ages what the cathedrals had been to the still worshipful world of the high Middle Ages: a combination of a sacrifice and affirmation, the embodiment of the highest skills and artistry, a symbol of prowess and source of pride. It was also a source of income – the lay analogue to the religious relics that were so potent an attraction to medieval travellers. When Philip the Bold of Burgundy defeated the Flemish burghers at Rosebecke in 1382 and wanted to punish those proud and troublesome clothiers, he could do no worse (or better) than seize the belfry clock at Courtrai and take it off to his capital at Dijon.

These public clocks, moreover, were only the top of the market. They are the ones that history knows best, but we know only a fraction of what was made. In this regard, the records are misleading: they have preserved the memory of a spotty, biased selection and largely omitted the smaller domestic clocks made to private order. As a result, it was long thought that the first mechanical clocks were turret clocks, and that the smaller domestic models were the much later product of advances in miniaturisation. Yet there was no technical impediment to making chamber clocks once the verge escapement had been invented. Indeed, since the mechanical clock is a development of the timer alarm, itself made to chamber size, small may well have preceded big.

Whichever came first, the one logically implied the other, so that we may fairly assume that both types of clock were known and made from the start. In the event, the first literary allusion to a mechanical clock refers to domestic timepieces. This goes back to the late thirteenth century, in Jean de Meung's additional verse to *Le roman de la rose*. Jean, a romantic poet of curiously worldy interest, attributes to his Pygmalion a fair array of chamber clocks:

Et puis faire sonner ses orloges
Par ses salles et par ses loges
A roues trop subtillement
De pardurable mouvement.

And then through halls and chambers,
Made his clock chime
By wheels of such cunning
Ever turning through time.

By the end of the fourteenth century, hundreds of clocks were turning in western Europe. A new profession of horologers had emerged, competing for custom and seeking severally to improve their product. There could be no surer guarantee of cumulative technical advance. Few inventions in history have ever made their way with such ease. Everyone seems to have welcomed the clock, even those workers who toiled to its rules, for they much preferred it to arbitrary bells. *Summe necessarium pro omni statu hominum* was the way Galvano Fiamma, chronicler of Milan, put it when he proudly marked the erection in 1333 (?) of a clock that not only struck the hours but signalled each one by the number of peals. And this in turn recalls an earlier inscription on a clock installed in 1314 on the bridge at Caen:

Je ferai les heures ouir
Pour le commun peuple rejouir.

I shall give the hours voice
To make the common folk rejoice.

Even the poets liked the new clocks. That is the most astonishing aspect of these early years of mechanical horology, for no group is by instinct and sensibility so suspicious of technical innovation. Here, moreover, was an invention that carried with it the seeds of control, order, self-restraint – all virtues (or vices) inimical to the free, spontaneous imagination and comtemplation so prized by creative artists. Yet it would be anachronistic to impute these ideals to the thirteenth and fourteenth centuries; they came much later. The medieval ideal was one of sobriety and control, along with due respect for worthy models. Besides, it was surely too soon to understand the potential of the new device for forming the persona as well as dictating the terms of life and work. Instead, the availability of this new knowledge gave all a sense of power, of enhanced efficiency and potential, of ownership of a new a valuable asset, whereas we, living by

(Right The clockmaker at work, from a sixteenth-century wood engraving.

the clock, see ignorance of or indifference to time as a release from constraint and a gain in freedom. Everything depends, I suppose, on where one is coming from. In any event, the early celebrators of the clock were no mere poetasters: thus Dante Alighieri, who sang in his *Paradise* (Canto X) the praises of the 'glorious wheel' moving and returning 'voice to voice in timbre and sweetness' – *tin tin sonando con si dolce nota* (almost surely a reference to a chamber clock, unless Dante had a tin ear), therein echoing the pleasure that Jean de Meung's Pygmalion took in his chiming clocks a generation earlier. And a half-century later we have Jean Froissart, poet but more famous as historian, composer of 'love ditties', among them *L'horloge amoureuse* (1369):

... The clock is, when you think about
it,
A very beautiful and remarkable
instrument,
And it's also pleasant and useful,
Because night and day it tells us the
hours
By the subtlety of its mechanism

Even when there is no sun.
Hence all the more reason to prize one's
machine
Because other instruments can't do this
However artfully and precisely they
may be made
Hence do we hold him for valiant and
wise
Who first invented this device
And with his knowledge undertook and
made
A thing so noble and of such great pride

The invention and diffusion of the mechanical clock had momentous consequences for European technology, culture, and society – comparable in their significance to the effects of the later invention of movable type and printing. For one thing, the clock could be miniaturised and, once small enough, moved about. For this, a new power source was needed, which took the form of a coiled spring, releasing energy as it unwound. This came in during the fifteenth century and gave rise to a new generation of small domestic clocks and, by the early sixteenth, to the watch, that is, a clock small enough to be worn on the person. Domestic clocks and, even more, the watch were the basis of the private, internalised time discipline that characterises modern personality and civilisation – for better or worse. Without this discipline, we could not operate the numerous and complex activities required to make our society go. (We could, no doubt, have recourse to public signals, as in the army. But that would mean a very different kind of collectivity).

For another thing, the mechanical clock was susceptible of great improvement in accuracy, even in its smaller form. This potential lay in its revolutionary principle of time measurement. Whereas earlier instruments had relied on some continuous movement – of shadow (the sundial) or fluid (the clepsydra) – to track the passage of time, the mechanical clock marked time by means of an oscillating controller. This took the form of a bar or wheel swinging to and fro. The swings (pulses or beats) could then be counted and converted to time units – hours, minutes, and eventually sub-minutes. To the ancients who invented the sundial and water clock, a continuous controller on what we would not call the analogue principle seemed only logical, for it was an imitation of time itself, always passing. But in the long run, its possibilities for improvement were limited not only by the inherent flaws of sunlight (no use at night or in cloudy weather) and flowing liquids, but by the difficulty of sustaining an even, continuously moving display. Time measurement by beats or pulses, on the other hand – the digital principle – had no bounds of accuracy. All that was needed was an even, countable frequency. The oscillating controller of the first medieval clocks usually beat double-seconds. Frequency was decidedly uneven, hence the large variation in rate. It took almost four hundred years to invent a vastly superior controller in the form of the pendulum, which in its seconds-beating form could keep time within less than a minute a day. Today, of course, new controllers have been invented in the form of vibrating quartz crystals (hundreds of thousands or even millions of beats per second), which vary less than a minute a year; and atomic resonators (billions of vibrations per second), which take thousands of years to gain or lose a second. These gains in precision have been an important impetus to scientific inquiry; indeed, almost all of them came about because scientists needed better timekeeping instruments. How else to study process and rates of changes?

Finally, the clock with its regularity came to stand as the model for all other machines – the machine of machines, the essence of man's best work in the image of God; and clockmaking became the school for all other mechanical arts. No one has said it better than Lewis Mumford in *Technics and Civilization*:

The clock, not the steam engine, is the key-machine of the modern industrial age... In its relationship to determinable quantities of energy, to standardization, to automatic action, and finally to its own special product, accurate timing, the clock has been the foremost machine in modern technics; and at each period it has remained in the lead: it marks a perfection toward which other machines aspire.

All of this was there in germ in the oscillating controllers of the first mechanical clocks. The builders of those clocks did not know what they had wrought. That the clock was invented in Europe and remained a European monopoly for some five hundred years, and that Europe then built a civilisation organised around the measurement of time; – these were critical factors in the differentiation of West from Rest and the definition of modernity.

FOR FURTHER READING:
David S. Landes, *Revolution in Time: Clocks and the Making of the Modern World* **is published by Harvard University Press; on January, 16th at £17.** Ernest von Bassermann-Jordan, *The Book of Old Clocks and Watches* (4th ed., revised by Hans von Bertele; New York: Crown, 1964); Eric Bruton, *The History of Clocks and Watches* (New York: Rizzoli, 1979); Carlo Cipolla, *Clocks and Culture, 1300-1700* (New York: Walker, 1967); Jacques Le Goff, *Time, Work, and Culture in the Middle Ages* (University of Chicago Press, 1980); Lewis Mumford, *Technics and Civilization* (New York: Harcourt, Brace, 1934); Joseph Needham, Wang Ling, and Derek J. de Solla Price, *Heavenly Clockwork: The Great Astronomical Clocks of Medieval China* (Cambridge University Press, 1960); also articles in *Antiquarian Horology*, the journal of the Antiquarian Horological Society of Great Britain.

1500: The Era of Global Explorations

If the agricultural and industrial revolutions are the most important events in world history, then, perhaps, the beginning of the modern world should start at 1800 and textbooks could divide at that point. That would roughly mark the start of the Industrial Revolution and the liberal political revolts in France and the United States. Yet, 1500 is the time of the Reformation, the Renaissance, and the great global explorations of the West. This is the start of the Western domination of the world that continues into the present. Therefore, most world historians accept 1500 as a breaking point for teaching purposes. So it is with the two volumes of *Annual Editions: World History*.

At the year 1000, the educated people of Europe and the Middle East, though they might know about their own locale, knew very little about the larger world. They did the best they could with limited information, as David Lindberg states, but their maps were grossly misleading. It might have been the Chinese who could have led the way in exploration if it had not been for indifference, internal economic problems, and, perhaps, arrogance. Zheng He, a court eunuch and Muslim, led a powerful fleet westward in the fifteenth century, but his discoveries were left unexploited by the Chinese government, which later instructed the admiral to remain at home.

The abdication of world exploration by the Chinese was a fortuitous turn for Europeans. The Portuguese sailed down the western coast of Africa and found a water route to India, and the Spanish sponsored Christopher Columbus for his fateful voyages westward. Peter Copeland gives insight into the lives of Columbus's men in his essay, "The Sailors of Palos." They were not common thieves and murderers as had been assumed. But, poor Columbus! During the quincentenary of his voyage in 1992 he was vilified by Native Americans, environmentalists, humanists, and others. In contrast, in 1892, there was a great fair organized in his honor in Chicago, and Columbus was regarded as a hero. If nothing else, these events prove the truth of the statement that every generation rewrites history to suit itself. A summary of the various interpretations is included in "Columbus and the Labyrinth of History" by John Noble Wilford.

Further explorations came closely after Columbus's encounter with the New World. Within a generation, Juan Sebastian d'Elcano completed Magellan's circumnavigation of the globe. Simon Winchester captures the difficulty of the original feat in his essay, "After Dire Straits, an Agonizing Haul across the Pacific." Later, one of the places discovered was remote Easter Island, which had been colonized by Polynesians in the fifth century. The islanders erected massive stone heads but devastated the environment. By the time the Europeans arrived, much of the original habitat had vanished and the island was hardly able to sustain human life. Easter Island offered a lesson about overpopulation that was not noticed at the time but that still gives warning to the contemporary world.

Meanwhile, the impact of Columbus and the other intrepid European explorers who were reaching out into the world had no immediate effect. China still dominated the Far East and Islam controlled the Middle East. Through their exploration and technology, however, Europeans were able to sail around the Middle East to open up trade lanes that later gave them command of the globe. Time and technology were on the side of the West.

Looking Ahead: Challenge Questions

Why were people in the Middle East and Europe so limited in their knowledge of the world in the year 1000?

Compare Zheng He and Columbus. Why did Zheng He fail and Columbus succeed in interesting their civilizations to explore?

Was Columbus representative of his world, or was he unique?

Does the history of Columbus and exploration have any current relevance? Explain.

Considering what you have read about historiography, how should historians treat Columbus?

What technology helped Columbus and his sailors succeed?

What is the lesson of Easter Island? Are there comparisons to the Maya, Akkadian, and the Mogollon peoples?

Images of Earth in the year 1000

by David C. Lindberg
University of Wisconsin — Madison

One thousand years ago, people imagined a far different Earth than we do. Here's what people believed about the planet at the beginning of the millennium.

We who live at the end of the 20th century conceive Earth to be an insignificant speck of rock and water orbiting an insignificant star in an incomprehensibly vast universe. Our forebears of a thousand years ago had a very different opinion, viewing Earth as the centerpiece of a far smaller and cozier cosmos, placed there by a providential God. The contrast between these views is dramatic, and it raises the question to which this essay will be devoted: What did learned people in Christian Europe, in the Islamic world, and in Jewish communities scattered throughout Christendom and Islam know or believe about Earth and its inhabitants in the year 1000?

Knowledge throughout the Middle Ages (roughly A.D. 450-1450) was powerfully shaped by Greek ideas, particularly those of Plato and Aristotle (both fourth century B.C.). The latter definitively mapped the cosmos and defined Earth as its central object — a position from which it was not to be dislodged until the 16th and 17th centuries. But what fixes Earth in this central position? Aristotle argued simply that the heavy elements of which Earth is composed move by their very nature toward the center of the universe and collect there in a spherical mass. In effect, the center of the cosmos, which coincides with Earth's center, is "down" relative to all other points.

The claim that medieval people conceived of Earth as a globe may come as a surprise, because it contradicts the claim, now a staple of high school history texts, that they universally regarded Earth as flat. The truth is that Earth was conceived of as a

In the Middle Ages, people in Europe and the Islamic world conceived of their universe as a cozy place created by a providential God, as seen in this 13th-century illustration of the architect of the cosmos.

 From *Earth*, December 1996, pp. 26-29. © 1996 by Kalmbach Publishing Company. Reprinted by permission.

globe by almost every person after Aristotle known to have addressed the issue. Therefore it makes sense that Christians and Jews, who were among the vast majority of people who knew Earth was round, did not allow statements in the Bible seeming to affirm Earth's flatness to overrule either the authority of Aristotle or the testimony of the senses, such as the curved shadow of Earth during a lunar eclipse.

In the Aristotelian scheme that dominated medieval thought, the terrestrial region consisted of Earth and its atmosphere, the latter extending from the surface of Earth to the inner surface of the lunar sphere. The ingredients of this terrestrial region were the four elements: earth, water, air and fire. It was understood that all real substances are composites of two or more of the four elements combined in various proportions. For example, solid or earthy stuff is composed primarily of the element earth and liquids primarily of water.

Earth's atmosphere was held to consist principally of air and fire. These were separated in the ideal case into distinct spherical shells; but in the real world, Aristotle argued, air and fire undergo considerable mixing. Meteorological phenomena in the atmosphere were of great interest to medieval people. Lightning, thunder, rain, snow, rainbows, comets and shooting stars (the latter two judged, like the others, to be meteorological) were all studied and theorized about. Indeed, before the end of the Middle Ages, a correct theory of the rainbow — involving refractions and internal reflections within individual raindrops — had appeared.

Knowledge of Earth's crust in the year 1000 was limited but not insignificant. The globe was typically divided into five climatic zones — the torrid zone straddling the equator, and temperate and frigid zones running in an east-west direction on both sides of the equator. The terrestrial land mass was divided into three continents — Europe, Asia and Africa — surrounded by ocean. This conception was often represented schematically in what are known as T-O maps. These consist of a circle

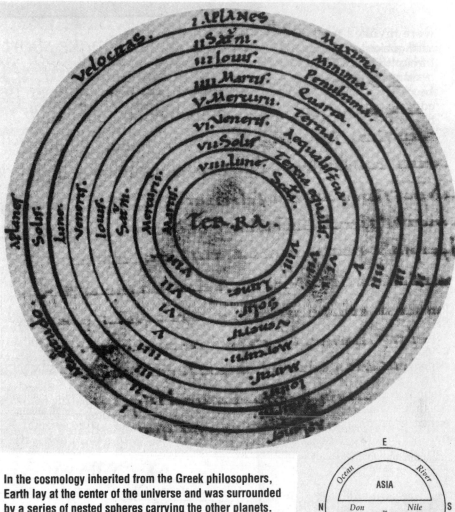

In the cosmology inherited from the Greek philosophers, Earth lay at the center of the universe and was surrounded by a series of nested spheres carrying the other planets.

representing the known world, with an inscribed T representing the major bodies of water (the Mediterranean Sea and the Nile and Don Rivers) that separate the known world into its three continents. (East is at the top in the accompanying illustration.)

Geographical knowledge of a more local sort frequently took the form of coastal surveys listing cities, rivers, mountains and other topographic features in the order in which they would be encountered by a traveler. Of course, medieval people had good knowledge of their native region; and despite the absence during the Middle Ages of anything analogous to our road maps, pilgrims, crusaders and merchants traveled great distances without getting lost.

The principal agents of geological change were judged to be erosion, sedimentation and subterranean winds blowing through hollow cavities in Earth's interior. Such winds

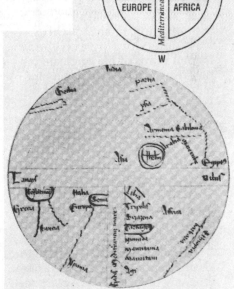

A T-O map is a schematic rendering of Earth's major continents and bodies of water developed by medieval cartographers. More realistic maps based on mathematical coordinate systems were invented in antiquity by Ptolemy and others, but they were lost during the Middle Ages and did not make a reappearance until the 15th century.

were invoked to explain earthquakes, volcanoes and the uplift of the crust that produces mountains. In keeping with Aristotle, the educated medieval person believed that minerals were formed by "exhalations" (something like vapors) arising within Earth's interior — dry exhalations giving rise to rocks, moist exhalations to the various metals.

Medieval people had ample practical knowledge of the oceans in their vicinity — how to catch the fish that inhabited it and how to employ the oceans for coastal transportation — but little theoretical knowledge of their origins or nature. As for the geography of the oceans, a common belief in the year 1000 held that the inhabited portion of the terrestrial globe was encircled by a continuous ocean. Oceanic tides were explained either by astrological influence emanating from the moon or by ocean currents colliding and rebounding at Earth's poles.

Medieval people of the year 1000 also focused considerable attention on the living inhabitants of Earth. It was understood by everybody that all forms of life originated in the creative activity of an omnipotent God. However, this did not forbid subsequent change in living things or even the emergence of forms of life hitherto unknown. Indeed, in an influential theory, the fourth-century Christian scholar Augustine argued that God created all forms of life in the beginning, although some as seeds that would germinate and flower subsequently.

Knowledge of plants existed in several forms. Given the agrarian economy of the Middle Ages, people had an intimate, practical, first-hand knowledge of local flora. Some of this practical botanical knowledge could be found in herbals oriented toward medical purposes. One such herbal, written by Dioscorides during the first century, contained descriptions of some 900 plant, animal and mineral products

It is easy to make sport of medieval ideas. Or, if we prefer, we can ransack the Middle Ages for anticipations of modern ideas. But we waste our time by proceeding along either of those courses.

alleged to have therapeutic value. There was also a tradition of what might be called "theoretical botany" in the medieval world. This grew out of a treatise, *On Plants* (falsely attributed to Aristotle), known in Islam by the year 1000 and somewhat later in Christendom.

Knowledge of animal life followed much the same pattern. Local fauna, including domesticated animals, were well-known. "It could hardly

Medieval knowledge of plants was rooted in the practical, especially medical, uses of plants. This page from a medieval herbal describes couch grass (top), sword lily and rosemary.

be otherwise," the British literary scholar C. S. Lewis wrote, "in a society where everyone who could be was a horseman, hunter, and hawker, and everyone else a trapper, fisher, cowman, shepherd, swineherd, goose-girl, henwife, or beekeeper." There was also a body of theoretical literature emanating primarily from Aristotle, dealing with questions of animal anatomy, physiology and behavior.

Situated alongside these practical and theoretical bodies of zoological knowledge was a genre of literature that has attracted much modern attention: the medieval bestiary. Bestiaries are collections of animal lore and mythology — some factual, some fanciful — arranged in short entries by animal name. These works have been widely misinterpreted as attempts (unsuccessful) to write modern zoological manuals. But the authors had no such intention. Bestiaries were meant to instruct and entertain, and their authors would have been astonished to learn that their success was to be judged by the standards of a 20th-century scientific textbook.

Medieval knowledge of the human race is too large a topic to be delved into here, but there were other forms of life deemed high on the "scale of being." Many medieval people of the year 1000 believed that distant lands were populated by monstrous races. *Natural History*, written by the first-century Roman author Pliny the Elder, was one of the principal sources for such beliefs. In this work Pliny describes the cannibal Scythians, the sexually promiscuous Garamantes, the naked Gamphasantes and the headless Blemmyae, whose mouth and eyes are attached to their chests. It is difficult to know how widespread was belief in fairies, nymphs, elves, satyrs, centaurs and the like — elusive creatures encountered not in scholarly literature and (presumably) not in the field, but in literary sources. However, it appears that skepticism among the educated was

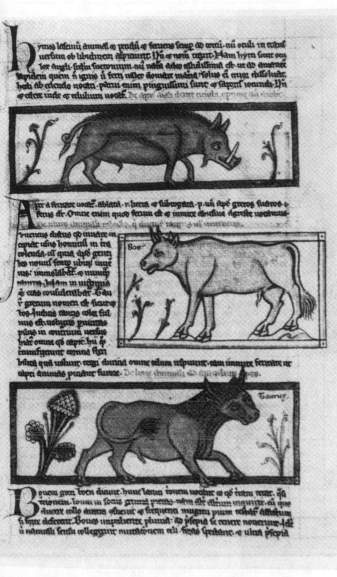

Medieval bestiaries, widely misunderstood as early zoological textbooks, were actually collections of animal lore and mythology meant to instruct and entertain. This page from an early 13th-century bestiary depicts a boar (top), an ox and a bull.

Among the ancient texts available to Medieval scholars was *Natural History*, a compendium of 20,000 facts about the world compiled by the first-century Roman author Pliny the Elder. This page from his book depicts the "monstrous" races of men thought to inhabit parts of the world.

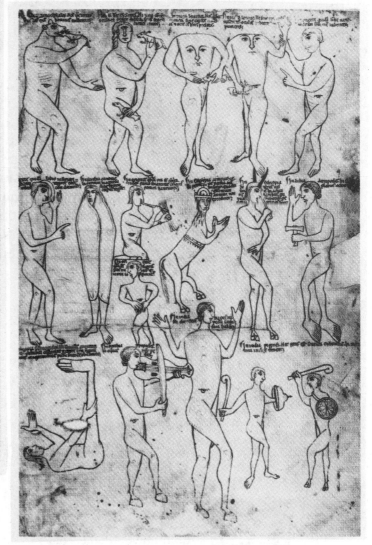

not total. And to round out the population of Earth and its atmosphere, angels and demons, inhabiting the aerial regions, were universally believed to exist.

What are we to make of these medieval beliefs? It is easy to make sport of medieval ideas — the central Earth, the four elements, bestiaries, centaurs and angels. Or, if we prefer, we can ransack the Middle Ages for anticipations of modern ideas and applaud the medieval genius for "discovering" the sphericity of Earth and the refractions and reflections that give rise to the rainbow. But we waste our time by proceeding along either of those courses. In both, we would be judging medieval knowledge by modern criteria, imagining that people who preceded us by a thousand years were answering, or trying to answer, modern questions on the basis of modern evidence. If we want to engage in a useful quest, we would do well to judge medieval people and their achievements within the context of the Middle Ages — recognizing that they struggled with all the resources at their disposal, just as we do, to survive in and make sense of the world in which they lived. ⊕

David C. Lindberg is Hilldale Professor of the History of Science at the University of Wisconsin-Madison. He is a distinguished historian of medieval science and has published several books on the subject, including influential studies of medieval optics and visual theory. Professor Lindberg is past-president of the History of Science Society and has been a Guggenheim Fellow and a visiting member of the Institute for Advanced Study in Princeton. In 1994 he won the Watson Davis Prize of the History of Science Society for his book, The Beginnings of Western Science (University of Chicago Press, 1992).

Columbus and the Labyrinth of History

Every generation creates the Columbus it needs. As the Quincentenary of his 1492 voyage approaches, observers are torn between celebrating a brave visionary and condemning the first representative of an age of imperial exploitation. Here Pulitzer Prize-winning journalist John Noble Wilford explores the various Columbus legends and discovers, beneath them, a very human figure and an adventure unprecedented in boldness.

John Noble Wilford

John Noble Wilford has been a science correspondent for the New York Times *since 1965. Twice winner of the Pulitzer Prize, Wilford is the author of* The Mapmakers *(1981),* The Riddle of the Dinosaur *(1985),* Mars Beckons *(1990), and* Mysterious History of Columbus *(1991).*

History has not been the same since Christopher Columbus. Neither has he been the same throughout history.

During the five centuries since his epochal voyage of 1492, Columbus has been many things to many people: the protean symbol of the adventuring human spirit, the lone hero defying both the odds and entrenched thinking to change the world; the first modern man or a lucky adventurer blinded by medieval mysticism; an icon of Western faith in progress or an object of scorn for his failings of leadership and intellect; a man virtually deified at one time and roundly vilified today for his part in the initiation of an international slave trade and European imperialism. We hardly know the real Co-

lumbus. Such, it seems, is the fate of historical figures whose deeds reverberate through time.

The Columbus story surely confirms the axiom that all works of history are interim reports. What people did in the past is not preserved in amber, a moment captured and immutable through the ages. Each generation looks back and, drawing from its own experiences, presumes to find patterns that illuminate both past and present. This is natural and proper. A succeeding generation can ask questions of the past that those in the past never asked themselves. Columbus could not know that he had ushered in what we call the Age of Discovery, with all its implications, any more than we can know what two world wars, nuclear weapons, the collapse of colonial empires, the end of the Cold War, and the beginning of space travel will mean for people centuries from now. Perceptions change, and so does our understanding of the past.

Accordingly, the image of Columbus has changed through the years, sometimes as a result of new information, more often because of changes in the lenses through which we view him. Once a beneficiary of this phenomenon, Columbus in times of reigning optimism has been exalted as a mythic hero. Now, with the approach of the Quincentennial, he has fallen victim to a more self-critical society, one prone to hero-bashing and historical pessimism.

As recently as 1974, Samuel Eliot Morison, the biographer of Columbus, concluded one of his books with a paean to European influence on America: "To the people of the New World, pagans expecting short and brutish lives, void of hope for any future, had come the Christian vision of a merciful God and a glorious heaven." It is hard to conceive of those words being written today. In a forward to the 1983 edition of Morison's *Admiral of the Ocean Sea: A Life of Christopher Columbus*, British historian David Beers Quinn criticizes Morison for ignoring or dismissing Columbus's failings. Columbus, Quinn writes, "cannot be detached from the imperialist exploitation of his discoveries and must be made to take some share of responsibility for the brutal exploitation of the islands and mainlands he found."

By and large, this new perspective has produced a more realistic, demythologized version of the Columbus story. The temptation, though, is to swing too far in the other direction, rewriting history as we wish it would have been or judging people wholly by anachronistic political standards. This has happened all too often regarding Columbus, producing myth and propaganda in the guise of history.

All the more reason for us to sift through the romantic inventions and enduring misconceptions that have clouded the real Columbus and to recognize that so much of the man we celebrate or condemn is our own creation. He is the embodiment of our running dialogue about the human potential for good and evil.

* * *

Some of the facts about Columbus—who he was and what he did—are beyond serious dispute. This mariner of humble and obscure origins was possessed of an idea that became an obsession. He proposed to sail west across the uncharted ocean to the fabled shores of the Indies, the lands of gold and spices celebrated in the tales of Marco Polo and the goal of an increasingly expansionist Europe in the 15th century. The Portuguese had sought a route around the tip of Africa. Some Florentine cosmographers had pondered the prospect of a westward sea route. But Columbus was apparently the first with the stubborn courage to stake his life on the execution of such a daring scheme.

After years pleading his case before the courts of Portugal and Spain, dismissed as a hopeless visionary or a tiresomely boastful nuisance, Columbus finally won the reluctant support of Ferdinand and Isabella. At the little Andalusian port of Palos de la Frontera, he raised a fleet of three ships and enlisted some 90 seamen. Whatever the sailors' trepidations or their opinion of Columbus when he arrived at Palos, their destiny was to share with him a voyage "by which route," Columbus wrote in the prologue to his journal, "we do not know for certain anyone previously has passed."

Columbus was never more in command of himself and his destiny than on that day, August 3, 1492, when he weighed anchor at Palos. He was a consummate mariner, as all his contemporaries agreed and historians have not contradicted, and here he was doing what he did best and so sure of his success. Of course, he never made it to the Indies, as head-shaking savants had predicted, then or on any of his three subsequent voyages. His landfall came half a world short of them, on an unprepossessing island inhabited by naked people with no knowledge whatsoever of Marco Polo's Great Khan.

On the morning of October 12, Columbus and his captains, together with their most trusted functionaries, clambered into armed launches and headed for the sandy beach and green trees. They carried the flags of the Christian monarchs of Spain. A solemn Columbus, without so much as a thought that it was anything but his to take, proclaimed possession of the island for the king and for the queen. Columbus and his officers then dropped to their knees in prayer.

It did not escape Columbus that these islanders "go around as naked as their mothers bore them; and the women also." This was not prurience but culture shock. Columbus was generally admiring in his initial descriptions of the people. They were

'GARDENS THE MOST BEAUTIFUL I EVER SAW'

The following account of October 10–13, 1492, is taken from Columbus's Diario, *as abstracted by Bartolomé de las Casas and adapted by William Carlos Williams.*

Wednesday, 59 leagues, W.S.W., but counted no more than 44. Here the people could endure no longer. All now complained about the length of the voyage. But I cheered them as best I could, giving them good hopes of the advantages they might gain by it. Roused to madness by their fear, the captains declared they were going back but I told them then, that however much they might complain, I had to go to the Indies and they along with me, and that I would go until I found them, with the help of our Lord. And so for a time it passed but now all was in great danger from the men.

Thursday, 11th of October. The course was W.S.W. More sea [spilling over the deck] than there had been during the whole of the voyage. Sandpipers and a green reed near the ship. And for this I gave thanks to God as it was a sure sign of land. Those of the *Pinta* saw a cane and a pole, and they took up another small pole which appeared to be worked with iron; also another bit of cane, a land plant, and a small board. The crew of the caravel *Niña* also saw signs of land, and a small plant covered with berries.

....I admonished the men to keep a good lookout on the forecastle and to watch well for land and to him who should first cry out that he had seen land I would give a silk doublet besides the other rewards promised by the Sovereigns which were 10,000 *maravedis* to him who should first see it. Two hours past midnight, the moon having risen at eleven o'clock and then shining brightly in the sky, being in its third quarter, a sailor named Rodrigo de Triana sighted the land at a distance of about two leagues. At once I ordered them to shorten sail and we lay under the mainsail without the bonnets, hove to waiting for daylight.

On Friday, the 12th of October, we anchored before the land and made ready to go on shore. Presently we saw naked people on the beach. I went ashore in the armed boat and took the royal standard, and Martin Alonzo and Vincent Yañez, his brother, who was captain of the *Niña*. And we saw the trees very green, and much water and fruits of diverse kinds. Presently many of the inhabitants assembled. I gave to some red caps and glass beads to put round their necks, and many other things of little value. They came to the ship's boats afterward, where we were, swimming and bringing us parrots, cotton threads in skeins, darts— what they had, with good will. As naked as their mothers bore them, and so the women, though I did not see more than one young girl. All I saw were youths, well made with very handsome bodies and very good countenances. Their hair short and coarse, almost like the hairs of a horse's tail. They paint themselves some black, some white, others red and others of what color they can find. Some paint the faces and others paint

"guileless and generous." Bringing cotton, parrots, and javelins to trade, they paddled out to Columbus's ships in their dugouts, each made from a single tree and so long that they held 40 men; the West Indian term for these dugouts was *canoa*—and thus a New-World word entered European speech. Columbus was pleased to note that they had no firearms. When he had shown them some swords, "they took them by the edge and through ignorance cut themselves." "They should be good and intelligent servants," he concluded, "for I see that they say very quickly everything that is said to them; and I believed they would become Christians very easily, for it seemed to me that they had no religion." Columbus

the anthropologist had his priorities.

Unfortunately, we have no record of the first impressions that the people Columbus called Indians had of the Europeans. What did they think of these white men with beards? Their sailing ships and their weapons that belched smoke? Their Christian God and their inordinate interest in gold and a place beyond the horizon called the Indies? We will never know. They could not put their feelings into writing; they had no writing. And the encounter itself doomed them. Within a generation or two, they became extinct, mainly through exposure to European diseases, and so could not pass on by word of mouth stories about the moment white men entered their lives.

the whole body, some only round the eyes and others only on the nose. They are themselves neither black nor white.

On Saturday, as dawn broke, many of these people came to the beach, all youths. Their legs are very straight, all in one line, and no belly. They came to the ship in canoes, made out of the trunk of a tree, all in one piece, and wonderfully worked, propelled with a paddle like a baker's shovel, and go at marvelous speed.

Bright green trees, the whole land so green that it is a pleasure to look on it. Gardens of the most beautiful trees I ever saw. Later I came upon one man in a canoe going from one island to another. He had a little of their bread, about the size of a fist, a calabash of water, a piece of brown earth, powdered then kneaded, and some dried leaves which must be a thing highly valued by them for they bartered with it at San Salvador. He also had with him a native basket. The women wore in front of their bodies a small piece of cotton cloth. I saw many trees very unlike those of our country. Branches growing in different ways and all from one trunk; one twig is one form and another is a different shape and so unlike that it is the greatest wonder of the world to see the diversity; thus one branch has leaves like those of a cane, and others like those of a mastic tree; and on a single tree there are five different kinds. The fish so unlike ours that it is wonderful. Some are the shape of dories and of the finest colors, so bright that there is not a man who would not be astounded, and would not take great delight in seeing them. There are also whales. I saw no beasts on land save parrots and lizards.

On shore I sent the people for water, some with arms, and others with casks; and as it was some little distance I waited two hours for them.

During that time I walked among the trees, which was the most beautiful thing which I had ever seen . . . .

Columbus made certain by his words and actions that his discovery would not be lost to history. On the homeward voyage, after visiting a string of other islands and more people, he composed a letter to the court of Ferdinand and Isabella in which he announced his discovery. He had made good his boast to one and all. He may have harbored some disappointment in not reaching the Asian mainland, but he had sailed across the Ocean Sea and found lands and peoples unknown to Europeans. And he wanted the court to read about it in his own words, especially since this justified his own claim to the titles and wealth due him pursuant to the deal he had struck with the court.

The letter Columbus wrote was also his bid for a place in history. He understood that the achievement would go for naught unless the news got back to others. To explore (the word, in one version of its etymology, comes from the Latin "to cry out") is to search out and exclaim discovery. Simply reaching a new land does not in itself constitute a discovery. It must be announced and then recorded in history so that the discovery can be acted upon.

Others besides the indigenous people preceded Columbus in finding parts of America. This is no longer an issue of consuming dispute in Columbian studies. Almost certainly the Norse under Leif Ericson landed at some northern islands and established a short-lived settlement at New-foundland. Ericson and others may have reached America, but they failed to discover it. For nothing came of their deeds. Columbus, in writing the letter, was making sure his deeds would have consequences and his achievement would enter history.

The letter eventually reached the court in Barcelona and had the desired effect. The king and queen received Columbus with pomp and listened to his story with genuine interest and pleasure. They instructed him to return to the new-found lands with a larger fleet including soldiers and settlers. America had entered world history, though Columbus insisted to his dying day that he had reached the Indies.

* * *

This familiar story of Columbus has been embellished to create an enduring popular legend. Some of the tales (though not all of them) have been laid to rest through historical research.

Columbus did not, for example, have to prove that the world was round: All educated people in Europe at the time accepted this as a given. Isabella did not have to pawn her jewels to raise money for the expedition; though the Crown, following its wars against the Moors, was strapped for cash, the financial adviser Luis de Santangel arranged a loan from the ample coffers of the state police and from some Italian merchant bankers. And Columbus did not set sail with a crew of hardened criminals. Only four men, accused of murdering a town crier, took advantage of a promised amnesty, and even they were seasoned mariners and acquitted themselves well on the voyage.

More troublesome for historians have been certain other mysteries and controversies.

Where, for example, did the first landfall occur? We know it was a small island the inhabitants called Guanahani and Columbus christened San Salvador. It was in the Bahamas or thereabouts, far from the Asian mainland he was seeking, but which island? No fewer than nine different possible islands have been identified from the few ambiguous clues in Columbus's journal. The site favored by most experts is the Ba-

hamian island once called Watling's but renamed San Salvador in 1924 to help solidify its claim.

Did Columbus really come from Genoa? Nearly every European nation has at one time or another laid some claim to him. Was he Jewish? Such conjecture originated in the 19th century and was promoted in 1940 in Salvadore de Madriaga's vivid biography, *Christopher Columbus*. But the evidence is circumstantial. Records in Genoa indicate that, whatever his more remote ancestry, Columbus's family had been Christian for several generations.

When and how in the mists of his rootless life did Columbus conceive of his audacious plan? Was it sheer inspiration bolstered by rational research? Or did he come into some secret knowledge? Was he really seeking the Indies? How was he finally able to win royal backing? What were his ships like?—no caravel wreck from that period has ever been recovered. Scholars and amateur sleuths have spent lifetimes trying to resolve these questions, usually without notable success.

Part of the problem lies with the passage of time. Although the record of Columbus by contemporaries is more substantial than that of any other 15th-century explorer, surviving accounts are often difficult to assess from this distance. Whose version is to be trusted? The letters of Peter Martyr, the courtier in Spain who never ventured to the New World? The biography by Hernando Columbus, the devoted son protective of his father's fame? The history of the New World by Bartolomé de las Casas (1474–1566), the Dominican friar and champion of the Indians who never missed a chance to condemn the brutality of the early explorers and colonists? Even the few extant writings of Columbus himself, who could be vague, contradictory and self-serving?

Hero worship has further distorted history. We want—or used to want—our heroes to be larger than life. The result can be a caricature, a plaster saint inviting iconoclasts to step forward with their own images, which can also ignore the complexity of human reality.

We are left, therefore, with enough material to mold the Columbus we choose to extol or excoriate, but not enough ever to feel sure we truly know the man.

* * *

Nothing better illustrates history's changing images of Columbus than the succession of portraits of him that have appeared over the centuries. They show a man of many faces—handsome and stalwart, heavy and stolid, shadowed and vaguely sinister. Artistic interpretation, like history, changes with the times.

Yet, there should be little confusion over the man's physical appearance. His son Hernando, who should have known, said he was "a well-built man of more than average stature, the face long, the cheeks somewhat high, his body neither fat nor lean. He had an aquiline nose and light colored eyes; his complexion too was light and tending to be red. In youth his hair was blond, but when he reached the age of 30 it all turned white."

The son went on to describe his father's character: "In eating and drinking, and in the adornment of his person, he was very moderate and modest," Hernando wrote. "He was affable in conversation with strangers and very pleasant to the members of his household, though with a certain gravity. He was so strict in matters of religion that for fasting and saying prayers he might have been taken for a member of a religious order."

Hernando may be guilty of some exaggeration. Columbus could not be too gentle and modest if he were to promote his vision before skeptical courts and if he could control a crew of rough seamen who suspected they might be headed to their deaths. He could be harsh in meting out punishment to seamen and in ordering punitive raids against Indian villages. Like others of that time, and to this day, he presumably saw no contradiction between his behavior and his religious beliefs. By all accounts Columbus was a demonstrably pious man. Late in life, his writings portrayed a mind filled with mysticism and a belief in his divine mission to carry Christianity to all people and prepare them for the impending end of the world.

Of this mysticism, Hernando has nothing to say. He is also frustratingly reticent or misleading about the genesis of his father's consuming dream and even about his origins. Columbus himself chose to reveal very little about his early life.

Every verifiable historical document, however, indicates that Columbus was born in Genoa, which was an independent city-state (the lesser rival to Venice) whose ships traded throughout the entire Mediterranean world. He was probably born in 1451, and both his father Domenico and his father's father were wool weavers; his mother, Susanna Fontanarossa, was a weaver's daughter. Christopher was probably their eldest child. Bartholomew, the chart-maker who would share many of Columbus's adventures, was a year or two younger. The other children who grew to adulthood were a sister named Bianchetta and a brother Giacomo, better known by the Spanish equivalent, Diego, who joined Christopher on the second voyage. All in all, the Columbuses of Genoa were fruitful and humble tradespeople—and nothing for a young man to be ashamed of.

At a "tender age," as Columbus once wrote, he cast his lot with those who go to sea. At first, he probably made short voyages as a crewman, and then longer ones on trading ships to the Genoese colony of Chios in the Aegean Sea. But even more crucial to Columbus's development than his ancestry or his birthplace was the timing of his birth. He was born two years before the fall of Constantinople, Christendom's eastern capital, to the Ottoman Turks in 1453. Young Columbus was to grow up hearing about the scourge of Islam, the blockage of regular trade routes to the spices of the East, and the parlous times for Christianity. Priests and popes were calling for a new crusade to recapture Constantinople and Jerusalem. All of this could have nourished the dreams of a great adventure in an ambitious young man with nautical experience.

The most significant mystery about Columbus concerns how he came up with his idea for sailing west to the Indies. As in everything else, Columbus's own words on the subject obfuscate more than elucidate. It was his practice, writes the Italian historian Paolo Emilio Taviani, "never to tell everything to everyone, to say one thing to one man, something else to another, to reveal only portions of his arguments, clues, and evidence accumulated over the years in his mind." Perhaps Columbus told so many partial stories in so many different versions that, as Morison suspects, he himself could no longer remember the origins of his idea.

In all probability he formulated the idea in Portugal sometime between 1476 and 1481. Columbus had come to Portugal quite literally by accident. When the Genoese fleet he had shipped with was attacked and destroyed in the summer of 1476, Columbus was washed ashore at the Portuguese town of Lagos. He made his way to Lisbon, where the talk of seagoing exploration was everywhere. He heard stories of westering seamen who found islands far out in the ocean and saw maps sprinkled with mythical islands. On voyages north perhaps as far as Iceland and south along the coast of Africa, he gained a taste for Atlantic sailing. There may even be something to the story of the unknown pilot from whom Columbus supposedly obtained secret knowledge of lands across the ocean. But as far as anyone can be sure—and volumes have been written on the subject—there was no sudden revelation, no blinding flash of inspiration.

Nor did Columbus derive his plan from a careful reading of scholars. He was not then, and never became, a man who read to learn; he read to gather support for what he already thought to be true. His familiarity with the travel accounts of Marco Polo and the *Travels of Sir John Mandeville*, a 14th-century collection of travelers' tales from around the world, did not so much inform his concept as inflame a mind already stoked with the dry tinder of desire. From other sources—from a recent Latin translation of Claudius Ptolemy's second-century *Geography*, which described many Southeast Asian spice islands, to Pierre d'Ailly's *Imago Mundi*, a compendium of contemporary knowledge about the world which argued that the Western Sea was not very wide—Columbus made some calculations of global distances. Like d'Ailly, he conveniently managed to constrict the unknown he proposed to challenge, grossly underestimating the distance from Europe to Japan. Had he unwittingly deceived himself? Or had he deliberately contrived calculations to deceive those he looked to for support? All that can be said with assurance

is that Columbus was by then a man consumed by an enthusiasm that willed away obstacles and brooked no doubt.

His marriage in Portugal may have indirectly contributed to his growing conviction. In 1479, he wed Felipa Perestrello de Moniz, a daughter of lesser nobility. Her widowed mother showed Columbus the journals and maps left by her husband, who had sailed for Prince Henry the Navigator. From the papers of Bartolomeo Perestrello and other Portuguese seamen, Columbus concluded, his son Hernando wrote, "for certain that there were many lands West of the Canary Islands and Cape Verde, and that it was possible to sail to, and discover them." The social position of his wife's family also smoothed the way for Columbus's introduction to the court of Portugal's King John II.

When Columbus finally laid out his plan before John II, probably in 1483 or 1484, the court cosmographers, a Portuguese historian wrote, "considered the words of Christovae Colom as vain, simply founded on imagination, or things like that Isle Cypango of Marco Polo."

Columbus refused to accept rejection. By this time, his wife had died, and in 1485 he took their son, Diego, and left Portugal for Palos, across the border in Spain. Tradition has it that Columbus and little Diego, penniless and hungry, got off the ship and trudged along a dusty road to the Franciscan monastery of La Rabida. He knocked at the portal to beg for water and bread. If the legend is true, the father may have been taking the son there to be a boarding student, freeing himself to pursue his dream.

Though a secretive man and often portrayed as a loner, Columbus must not have been without charm, even charisma. He had insinuated himself into the influential society of Lisbon and would do so again in Spain. "Columbus's ability to thrust himself into the circles of the great was one of the most remarkable things about him," writes Harvard historian John H. Parry. It was also in his character that he seldom acknowledged the help of others.

At La Rabida, Columbus won the friendship and confidence of a Franciscan official knowledgeable in cosmography and through him gained introductions to wealthy patrons and eventually his first audience with Ferdinand and Isabella. They referred his proposal to a commission of learned men at the University of Salamanca. Washington Irving, in his fanciful biography, has the commissioners saying that the "rotundity of the earth was as yet a matter of mere speculation." Many of them no doubt deserved Irving's condemnation as a "mass of inert bigotry," but they were right (and Columbus wrong) in their judgment that Asia could not be reached by ships sailing west. They recommended that the monarchs reject the venture.

Columbus was nothing if not persistent. With a modest retainer from the court, he continued to solicit support from influential courtiers. While in Cordoba, waiting for some sign of royal encouragement, he met Beatriz Enriquez de Arana, a peasant woman, and they became lovers. In August 1488 she gave birth to an illegitimate son, Hernando. (They never married, and sometime after his first voyage, they drifted apart. He likely felt a peasant woman was beneath his station.)

Through another friar at La Rabida, Columbus gained other audiences with the monarchs in 1491 and again in early 1492, just after the Moorish capital of Granada fell to the Christian forces. He had been led to believe that, after the burden of the prolonged war was lifted, the queen especially might be disposed to give her approval. Some writers have let themselves imagine that Isabella saw more in Columbus than an insistent supplicant. Such speculation of a sexual relationship between the two, Taviani says, is "a sheer fairy-tale, rejected by all historians."

Nothing seemed to change with the fall of Granada. Columbus was turned away, this time with an air of finality. Behind the scenes, however, Luis de Santangel, the chief financial adviser, interceded with assurances to the queen that financing the expedition need not be an insurmountable obstacle. No one knows why the king and queen finally relented. They might have been persuaded by the argument that they had little to lose and much to gain if this importunate foreigner just happened to be on to something.

* * *

After his first voyage, when he was the toast of Barcelona, Columbus supposedly faced down his first critics. At a banquet, some noblemen insisted that if Columbus had not undertaken the enterprise, someone else, a Spaniard and not a foreigner, would have made the same discovery. At this, Columbus called for an egg and had it placed on the table. "Gentlemen," he was reported to have said, pointing to the egg, "you make it stand here, not with crumbs, salt, etc. (for anyone knows how to do it with meal or sand), but naked and without anything at all, as I will, who was the first to discover the Indies." When it was Columbus's turn, he crushed one end of the egg and had no trouble making it stand up on the table.

The anecdote has proved irresistible to historians and storytellers to illustrate the singular role of Columbus in history. But it never happened—one more Columbian myth. The story was not only apocryphal, Morison points out, but it "had already done duty in several Italian biographies of other characters."

In reality, Columbus would not so easily put down the critics who dogged him the rest of his life—and through history. If only he had stopped with the first voyage, the echo of those fanfares in Barcelona might not have faded so fast.

A fleet of 17 ships, carrying some 1,200 people, left Cadiz in the autumn of 1493 with instructions to establish a permanent settlement on the island of Hispaniola. There, near the present city of Puerto Plata in the Dominican Republic, Columbus built a fort, church, and houses for what would be his colonial capital, La Isabela. The experiment was disastrous. The site had no real harbor, insufficient rainfall, and little vegetation. Sickness and dissension brought work to a standstill and the colony to the point of starvation. Expeditions into the mountains failed to find any rich lodes of gold. As Las Casas wrote, they "spread terror among the Indians in order to show them how strong and powerful the Christians were." Bloody warfare ensued.

With little gold to show for his efforts, Columbus ordered a shipment of Taino Indians to be sold as slaves in Spain. The best that can be said in defense of Columbus is that he was now a desperate man. His power to rule La Isabela was waning. His

Columbus disgraced, 1500. Charged with malfeasance as governor of Hispaniola, Columbus returned to Spain a prisoner in chains.

visions of wealth were fading. He feared that his influence back in Spain would be irreparably diminished by critical reports from recalcitrant officers who had returned to Spain. And he had failed again to find a mainland. His desperation was such that he forced all his crew to sign a declaration that, at Cuba, they had indeed reached the mainland of Cathay. Sick and discouraged, he sailed home in 1496.

The third voyage did nothing to restore his reputation. Departing from Seville in May 1498, he steered a southerly course and reached an island off the northeastern coast of South America, which he named Trinidad, for the Holy Trinity. A few days later, he saw a coastline to the south. Columbus recognized that the tremendous volume of fresh water flowing from the Orinoco River was evidence of a large land, but he failed to appreciate that this might be a continent or to pursue his investigations. Instead, his mind drifted into speculation that the river must originate in the Earthly Paradise. Bound to medieval thinking, the man who showed the way across the ocean lost his chance to have the New World bear his name. The honor would soon go to a man with a more open-minded perspective, Amerigo Vespucci, who on his second voyage

of exploration (1501–2) concluded that the South American landmass was not Asia but a new continent.

Columbus turned his back on South America and sailed to Santo Domingo to attend to the colony there. He found that his brothers, Bartholomew and Diego, had lost control. Some of the colonists had mutinied, and the crown had dispatched a new governor empowered to do anything necessary to restore order. It was then that Columbus was arrested, stripped of his titles, and sent back in irons to Spain in October 1500.

It was an ignominious end to Columbus's authority and to his fame in his lifetime. The crown eventually restored his titles, but never again was he allowed to serve as viceroy. The monarchs now were under no illusions about Columbus. He had failed as a colonial administrator, and they had strong doubts about the validity of his claims to have reached the Indies.

Columbus was given permission for one final voyage, which lasted from 1502 to 1504. He was specifically barred from returning to Santo Domingo. Instead, he explored the coast of Central America and attempted without success to establish a settlement in Panama.

Historians cite the last voyage as one of his many "missed opportunities." With luck and more persistence, Columbus might have stumbled upon the Maya civilization or the Pacific Ocean. As it was, he barely made it back to Spain. He was marooned a year on Jamaica, where he wrote a pathetic letter to the monarchs. "I implore Your Highnesses' pardon," he wrote. "I am ruined as I have said. Hitherto I have wept for others; now have pity upon me, Heaven, and weep for me, earth! I came to Your Highnesses with honest purpose and sincere zeal, and I do not lie. I humbly beg Your Highnesses that, if it please God to remove me hence, you will aid me to go to Rome and on other pilgrimages."

* * *

Columbus in his last years was a dispirited man who felt himself to be misunderstood and unappreciated. He sought to define himself in a remarkable manuscript now known as *Libro*

COLUMBUS'S MYSTERIOUS SIGNATURE

In 1498, Columbus instructed all of his heirs to continue to "sign with my signature which I now employ which is an X with an S over it and an M with a Roman A over it and over them an S and then a Greek Y with an S over it, preserving the relation of the lines and the points." At the top, thus, is the letter S between two dots. On the palindromic second row are the letter S A S, also preceded, separated, and ended with dots. The third row has the letters X M and a Greek Y, without dots. Below that is the final signature, Xpo Ferens, a Greco-Latin form of his given name.

To this day no one can decipher the meaning Columbus had in mind, but it almost certainly bears on his religious outlook. The simplest explanations hold that the letters stand for seven words. It has been suggested that the four letters stand for "Servus Sum Altissimi Salvatoris," for "Servant I Am of the Most High Savior." The three letters of the third line could be an invocation to Christ Jesus and Mary, or to Christ, Mary, and Joseph. Another proposed solution is that the seven letters are the initials for "Spiritus Sanctus Altissimi Salvator Xristus Maria Yesus."

John Fleming, a medievalist at Princeton University, believes he has cracked the code, finding it to be an "acrostic of considerable complexity committed to a more or less learned and hermetic mystical theology." Columbus, he concludes, was borrowing from two medieval traditions in formal signatures, that of the church worthies, like St. Francis, who devised intricate crucigrams, and that of the church mariners who often included in their craft marks anchors, masts, fishhooks, and so forth. For his signature, Fleming says, Columbus seems to have combined religious and nautical symbolism. The unifying idea is the medieval association of the Virgin Mary with Stella Maris, the indispensable navigational star also known as Polaris, or the North Star. The first cross bar stands for StellA MariS. The vertical "mast" stands for "Stella Ave Maris," after the vesper hymn *"Ave, stella maris."* By design, the structure represents both a Christian cross and a ship's mast. The line X M Y may have one meaning, *"Jesus cum Maris sit nobis in via"* (an invocation with which Columbus opened much of his writing), with the Y representing the fork in the road and the symbolism for his having chosen the hard way to destiny's fulfillment. Fleming suggests a double meaning. The X and Y at either end of the bottom line could also stand for "Christophorus," his name and destiny, and "Jacobus," for "St. James," whose feast day and Christopher's are the same and who is, not incidentally, the patron saint of Spain, Santiago—Sant Yago.

Fleming's cryptographic skills have uncovered other clues in the signature to Columbus's "religious imagination." But, for understanding Columbus the mystical discoverer, Fleming draws insight from his associations with Mary, Christopher, and Santiago. He writes: "In Columbus's heavenly city, the Virgin Mary stands ever firm between her two Christ-bearing guards, Christophorus on the one hand, San Yago the Moorslayer on the other. And in the larger meaning of these two saints, both celebrated by the Roman church on a single day, which was of course Columbus's name-day, we may see adumbrated much of the glory, and much of the tragedy, of the European encounter with the New World."

From The Mysterious History of Columbus, *copyright © 1991 by Alfred A. Knopf. Reprinted by permission of the publisher.*

---

de las profecías, or *The Book of Prophecies*. Between the third and fourth voyages, Columbus collected passages of biblical scriptures and the words of a wide range of classical and medieval authors. According to his own description, this was a notebook "of sources, statements, opinions and prophecies on the subject of the recovery of God's Holy City and Mount Zion, and on the discovery and evangelization of the islands of the Indies and of all other peoples and nations."

The document reveals the depth and passion of Columbus's belief that he had a special relationship with God and was acting as the agent of God's scheme for history. He marshaled evidence from the prophecies of the Bible to show that his recent discoveries were only the prelude to the realization of a greater destiny. It was as if he saw his role as being not unlike John the Baptist's in relation to Christ. The wealth from his voyages and discoveries had given the king and queen of Spain the means to recover the Holy Land for Christendom, and thereby he had set the stage for the grandiose climax of Christian history, the salvation of all the world's peoples and their gathering at Zion on the eve of the end of time.

Most historians who studied the document have tended to dismiss it as the product of his troubled and possibly senile mind. His other writings at the time sometimes betrayed a mind verging on paranoia. Delno C. West, a historian who has recently translated the *Book of Prophecies*, suspects that historians were "reluctant to admit that the first American hero was influenced by prophetic ideas." If the book indeed reflects Columbus's thinking even before 1492, it undermines the popular image of Columbus as a man of the modern age who applied reason in conceiving his venture. It exposes him as a person thoroughly mired in the medieval world, obsessed with eschatology, and driven by a supposed call from God to carry out a mission of apocalyptic dimensions.

West contends that this spirituality, which fed Columbus's apocalyptic view of history, lay at the heart of the man and shaped his actions. Rather than some map or unknown pilot's tale, this may have been the "secret knowledge" that inspired Columbus. Certainly, without his unwavering belief in himself and his destiny, Columbus might not have sustained the single-minded persistence it took to win support for the enterprise and to see it through. "The Lord purposed that there should be something clearly miraculous in this matter of the voyage to the Indies," Columbus wrote in the *Prophecies*, "so as to encourage me and others in the . . . Household of God." Beginning in 1493, he began signing nearly all of his letters and documents *Christoferens*, a Latinization of his given name that means "Christ-bearer."

New attention to the spiritual side of Columbus does not, however, necessarily bring this complex man into focus. Images of a superstitious spiritualist and the modern explorer must be superimposed to produce a stereoscopic picture of Columbus, revealing the depth and heights of the mental terrain through which he traveled as he found America and then lost his way in failure, self-pity, and a fog of mysticism.

* * *

Columbus was probably no more than 55 years old when he died on May 20, 1506, in Valladolid, Spain. But he was much older in body and in tormented mind. His last voyages had left him crippled with arthritis and weak from fever. He was reduced to a sad figure, spending his last years in disgrace while stubbornly pressing his claims for the restoration of titles and the wealth due him.

Contrary to legend, he was neither destitute nor alone at the end. His two sons were with him, in a comfortable home. We cannot be sure of the traditional story, that he died believing he had reached the Indies. He never gave explicit expression to any recognition that he had found something other than Asia. All the evidence, though, suggests that he died unsatisfied.

His death went unheralded. There was no public ceremony of mourning and no recorded expressions of grief at the royal court. The man who rose from obscurity died in obscurity. His remains have been moved so many times over the centuries, from Spain to the New World and presumably back again, that no one is sure of his final resting place.

In the first century after his voyages, Columbus languished in the backwaters of history. His reputation suffered from his many failures as a colonial governor. The 1519–1522 Magellan circumnavigation left no doubt about the magnitude of Columbus's error in thinking he had reached the Indies. Conquering explorers such as Cortes and Pizarro won greater immediate fame by their dazzling exploits against the Aztecs and Incas. Cartographers saw fit to name the New World after Vespucci, not Columbus. Books of general history scarcely mentioned Columbus or ignored him altogether.

Within 50 years of Columbus's death, Bartolomé de las Casas, the Dominican bishop who extolled and defended the Indians, produced the first revisionist history. In his *History of the Indies*, Las Casas wrote eloquently of the atrocities committed against the Indians. To sail to the islands Columbus had discovered, Las Casas wrote, one needed only to follow the floating corpses of Indians that marked the way. His accounts of torture and killings documented the so-called Black Legend of Spanish cruelty that was seized upon by the English, Dutch, and French to fan the fires of national rivalries and religious hatreds.

As the Age of Discovery flourished during the late 16th century, Columbus began to be rescued from oblivion. He was celebrated in poetry and plays, especially in Italy and later in Spain. A glimmer of history's future hero could be seen in a popular play by Lope de Vega in 1614. In *The New World Discovered by Christopher Columbus*, he portrayed Columbus as a dreamer up against the establishment, a man of singular purpose who triumphed, the embodiment of that spirit driving humans to explore and discover.

It was in the New World, though, that Columbus would be transformed almost beyond human recognition into an icon.

By the late 17th century, people in the British colonies of North America were beginning to think of themselves as Americans and sought to define themselves in their own terms and symbols. Samuel Sewell, a Boston judge, suggested that the new lands should rightfully be named for Columbus, "the magnanimous hero . . . who was manifestly appointed by God to be the Finder out of these lands." The idea took root. In time, writers and orators used the name "Columbia" as a poetic name for America. Joel Barlow's poem *The Vision of Columbus*, appearing in 1787, has an aged Columbus lamenting his fate until he is visited by an angel who transports him to the New World to see what his discovery had brought to pass. There he could glimpse the "fruits of his cares and children of his toil."

Indeed, the young republic was busy planning the 300th anniversary of the landfall, in October 1792, when it named its new national capital the District of Columbia—perhaps to appease those who demanded that the entire country be designated Columbia. Next to George Washington, Columbus was the nation's most exalted hero. In him the new nation without its own history and mythology found a hero from the distant past, one seemingly free of association with the European colonial powers and Old-World tyranny. Americans invoked Columbus, the

solitary individual who had challenged the unknown, as they contemplated the dangers and promise of their own wilderness frontier. "Instead of ravaging the newly found countries," Washington Irving wrote in his 1828 biography, Columbus "sought to colonize and cultivate them, to civilize the natives."

This would be the Columbus Americans knew and honored throughout the 19th and into the present century. With the influx of millions of immigrants after the Civil War, he was even made to assume the role of ethnic hero. In response to adverse Protestant attitudes and to affirm their own Americanism, Irish Catholic immigrants organized the Knights of Columbus in 1882. The fraternity's literature described Columbus as "a prophet and a seer" and an inspiration to each knight to become "a better Catholic and a better citizen." Catholics in both America and Europe launched a campaign to canonize Columbus on the grounds that he had brought the "Christian faith to half the world." The movement failed not because of Columbus's brutal treatment of Indians but mainly because of the son he had sired out of wedlock.

Columbus's reputation was never higher than on the 400th anniversary of his first voyage. There were parades and fireworks, the naming of streets and dedicating of monuments. The World's Columbian Exposition in Chicago, with its lavish displays of modern technology, was less a commemoration of the past than the self-confident celebration of a future that Americans were eager to shape and enjoy. Americans ascribed to Columbus all the human virtues that were most prized in that time of geographic and industrial expansion, heady optimism, and unquestioning belief in progress. A century before, Columbus had been the symbol of American promise; now he was the symbol of American success.

The 20th century has dispelled much of that. We have a new Columbus for a new age. He is the creation of generations that have known devastating world wars, the struggle against imperialism, and economic expansion that ravages nature without necessarily satisfying basic human needs. In this view, the Age of Discovery initiated by Columbus was not the bright dawning of a glorious epoch but an invasion, a conquest, and Columbus himself less a symbol of progress than of oppression.

Columbus scholarship has changed. More historians are writing books from the standpoint of the Indians. They are examining the consequences—the exchange of plants and animals between continents, the spread of deadly diseases, the swift decline of the indigenous Americans in the face of European inroads. The Quincentennial happens to come at a time of bitter debate among Americans over racism, sexism, imperialism, Eurocentrism, and other "isms." Kirkpatrick Sale's 1990 book about Columbus said it all in its title, *The Conquest of Paradise*.

* * *

Was Columbus a great man, or merely an agent of a great accomplishment, or perhaps not a very admirable man at all? His standing in history has varied whenever posterity re-evaluated the consequences of Europe's discovery of America. Ultimately, Columbus's reputation in history is judged in relation to the place that is accorded America in history.

Europeans took a long time appreciating their discovery. Columbus and succeeding explorers looked upon the islands and mainland as an inconvenience, the barrier standing in their way to Asia that must be breached or circumnavigated.

As early as Peter Martyr, Europeans tried to assimilate the new lands into what they already knew or thought, rejecting the utter newness of the discovery. This was, after all, during the Renaissance, a period of rediscovering the past while reaching out to new horizons. And so the peoples of the New World were described in terms of the Renaissance-ancient image of the "noble savage," living in what classical writers had described as the innocent "Golden Age." The inhabitants of the New World, Martyr wrote, "seem to live in that golden world of which old writers speak so much, wherein men lived simply and innocently without enforcement of laws, without quarreling, judges and libels, content only to satisfy nature, without further vexation for knowledge of things to come."

The innocence of the indigenous Americans was more imagined than real. To one degree or another, they knew warfare, brutality, slavery, human sacrifice, and cannibalism. Columbus did not, as charged, "introduce" slavery to the New World; the practice existed there before his arrival, though his shipments of Tainos to Spain presaged a transoceanic traffic in slaves unprecedented in history.

This idealized image of people living in nature persisted until it was too late to learn who the Americans really were and, accepting them for what they were, to find a way to live and let live. Disease and conquest wiped out the people and their cultures. In their place Europeans had begun to "invent" America, as the Mexican historian Edmundo O'Gorman contends, in their own image and for their own purposes. They had set upon a course, writes historian Alfred W. Crosby, of creating "Neo-Europes." This was the America that took its place in world history.

In the 18th century, however, European intellectuals did engage in a searching reappraisal. A scientific movement, encouraged by the French naturalist Georges-Louis Leclerc de Buffon (1707–1788), spread the idea that America was somehow inferior to the Old World. As evidence, Buffon offered denigrating comparisons between the "ridiculous" tapir and the elephant, the llama and the camel, and the "cowardly" puma and the noble lion. Moreover, Old-World animals introduced there fared poorly, declining in health and size, with the sole exception of the pig. It was Buffon's thesis that America suffered an arrested development because of a humid climate, which he attributed to its relatively late emergence from the waters of the Biblical flood.

Buffon's ideas enjoyed a vogue throughout the 18th century and inspired more extreme arguments about "America's weakness." Not only were the animals inferior, so were the Americans, and even Europeans who settled there soon degenerated.

Unlike the proud patriots in colonial and post-Revolutionary North America, European intellectuals began expressing strong reservations about the benefits of the American discovery. There was no gainsaying its importance. Few disputed the opinion of Adam Smith: "The discovery of

1992: CEREBRATION, NOT CELEBRATION

It was in 1982 that I first became aware that the 500th anniversary of Columbus's 1492 Voyage of Discovery was a minefield, where the prudent celebrant stepped lightly and guardedly.

To my long-time friend Ramon, in an institute attached to the foreign ministry in Madrid, I said on the telephone one day that year, "Ramon, here at Florida we're beginning to get interested in the Columbus Discovery Quincentenary."

"Why do you say Columbus?" he responded. "He was an Italian mercenary. It was Spain that discovered America, not Columbus."

"But, Ramon," I protested, "we can't celebrate 1492 in the United States without mentioning Columbus."

"In your country," he lectured me, "Columbus Day is an Italian holiday. But the ships, the crews, the money were all Spanish. Columbus was a hired hand."

"But—"

"So when Cape Canaveral space center holds its 100th anniversary, are you going to call it the Werner von Braun celebration?"

I was grateful to Ramon for alerting me, in his way, to the sensitive character of this anniversary. Soon afterwards I learned that "Discovery," too, is a term freighted with ethnic and cultural contentions, as many descendants of the native peoples in the Americas argue against its Eurocentric and paternalistic coloring. "We were already here," they reminded me. And they were here so long ago, 10 to 25,000 years the anthropologists say. I was left to wonder, which was the Old World and which was the New?

As the past ten years have shown, the Spanish-Italian tension has softened, but the European-Native American disjunction has hardened, as historians, epidemiologists, moralists, romanticists, and native spokespersons have clashed over the benefits, if any, that European entrance onto the American stage brought the societies of both worlds, particularly this one.

Certainly huge numbers of indigenous people died as a result of the collision: some, it is true, from the sword, but by far the majority from the Europeans' unwitting introduction of pathogens—smallpox, measles, tuberculosis, the plague—to which the native peoples had no immunities. Recognizing the dimensions of that calamity, many Westerners acknowledge that there is little to celebrate. In Spain, where a 500th Year World's Fair will open in Seville, many of that country's intellec-

tuals are decrying what they call a 15th- and 16th-century *genocidio*.

In the margins of the debate, native descendants and their advocates are publicizing a long list of grievances against the Caucasians who abused their liberties, expropriated their lands, and despoiled an environmental paradise. On July 17–21, 1990, some 400 Indian people, including a delegation from the United States, met in Quito, Ecuador, to plan public protests against 500 years of European "invasion" and "oppression." Even before that, the first sign of reaction in the United States had already come when, in December 1989, representatives of the American Indian Movement, supported by a group of university students, began picketing the "First Encounters" archaeology exhibition mounted by the Florida Museum of Natural History as it traveled from Gainesville to Tampa, Atlanta, and Dallas. (In Tampa, their presence was welcomed because it boosted paid attendance.) In 1992, a loose confederation of North American Indian groups will picket in all U.S. cities where the Columbus replica ships will dock. They seek, one of their leaders told me, "not confrontation but media attention to present-day Native American problems."

African Americans also remind their fellow citizens that the events of 1492 and afterwards gave rise to the slave trade. And Jews appropriately notice that 1492 was the year when they were forcibly expelled from their Spanish homeland. In a counter-counteraction in all this Quincentenary skirmishing, however, the National Endowment for the Humanities decided not to fund a proposed television documentary about the early contact period because, reportedly, it was too biased against the Europeans. (Spain, by contrast, is acting uncommonly large-minded: It has agreed to fund the Smithsonian–Carlos Fuentes television production, "The Buried Mirror," a show that is highly critical of Spain's colonial practices.)

It is this "politically correct" dynamic that, most likely, will keep 1992 from being quite the exuberant and careless celebration that the Bicentennial as in 1976.

Anglo-Saxon and Celtic Americans felt comfortable with the Bicentennial because it reinforced their ethnic and cultural givens (Plymouth Rock, Virginia, Washington, Jefferson, the English language, Northern European immigration, etc.). Today, nervous about what is happening to "their" country and learning that citizens of His-

panic origins are projected soon be the largest U.S. minority, the old line white majority may not be enthusiastic about celebrating the 500th coming of the Hispanics—especially since they sense no continuing need for Columbus as a unifying principle or symbol.

What is likely to happen in 1992? Occasional public celebrations and observances will be produced by civic, ethnic, and cultural bodies. Reproductions of Columbus's ships will arrive in various ports from Spain. Tall ships may parade in New York harbor. Fireworks will explode here and there. People will view two television mini-series and read countless ambivalent newspaper stories.

The Federal Quincentenary Jubilee Commission that was appointed to superintend our exultations is in disarray, its chairman forced out on a charge of mishandling funds, its coffers empty of federal dollars, its principal private donor, Texaco, pulling the plug. Some states, and numerous individual cities (especially those named after Columbus, 63 at last count), have plans for observances, large or small. Florida which has the best reasons, geographically and temporally, to do something, has no state-wide plans, two commissions having collapsed and a third now being stripped of its funds.

But now the good news: In anticipation of the 500th anniversary an enormous amount of intellectual activity has occurred, in the form of archival discoveries, archaeological excavations, museum and library exhibitions, conferences, and publications. Some 30 new and upcoming adult titles have been enumerated by *Publishers Weekly*. Over 100 exhibitions and conferences have been counted by the National Endowment for the Humanities. This remarkable efflorescence of original research and scholarship will leave a lasting legacy of understanding and good. On the twin principles that cerebration is more valuable than celebration and that correcting one paragraph in our children's schoolbooks is worth more than a half-million dollars worth of fireworks exploded over Biscayne Bay, 1992 should be the best 1492 anniversary ever.

—Michael Gannon

Michael Gannon *is Director of the Institute for Early Contact Period Studies at the University of Florida.*

America, and that of a passage to the East Indies by the Cape of Good Hope, are the two greatest and most important events recorded in the history of mankind."

But there were negative assessments, not unlike today's. The anti-imperialist Samuel Johnson (1709–1784) wrote: "The Europeans have scarcely visited any coast but to gratify avarice, and extend corruption; to arrogate dominion without rights, and practice cruelty without incentive." He was also one of the first to make an unflattering connection between the conquest of America and its original conqueror. Columbus, Johnson said, had to travel "from court to court, scorned and repulsed as a wild projector, an idle promiser of kingdoms in the clouds: nor has any part of the world had reason to rejoice that he found at last reception and employment."

The French philosopher Abbé Guillaume-Thomas Raynal (1713–1796) challenged others to consider the following questions: Has the discovery of America been useful or harmful to mankind? If useful, how can its usefulness be magnified? If harmful, how can the harm be ameliorated? He offered a prize for the essay that would best answer those questions.

The respondents whose essays have survived were evenly divided between optimists and pessimists. Although "Europe is indebted to the New World for a few conveniences, and a few luxuries," Raynal himself observed, these were "so cruelly obtained, so unequally distributed, and so obstinately disputed" that they may not justify the costs. In conclusion, the abbé asked, if we had it to do over again, would we still want to discover the way to America and India? "Is it to be imagined," Raynal speculated, "that there exists a being infernal enough to answer this question in the affirmative?"

Pangs of guilt and expressions of moral outrage were futile, however; nothing stayed the momentum of European expansion in America. Most of the immigrants had never heard of the "American weakness" or read the intellectuals who idealized or despised the Indians or deplored Europe's bloodstained seizure of the lands. By the millions—particularly after the introduction of the steamship and on through World War I—immigrants flocked to a promised land where people could make something of themselves and prepare a better life for their children. There had been nothing quite like this in history. This was reflected in the image of Columbia. Little wonder that Columbus's standing in history was never higher than it was when the achievements and promise of America seemed so bright and were extravagantly proclaimed at home and abroad.

The "primary factor behind our [current] reassessment of the encounter," Crosby writes,"is a general reassessment of the role of rapid change, even catastrophe, in human history, and even the history of the earth and of the universe." The earlier faith in progress was founded on a Western belief that change came gradually and almost invariably for the better. In 19th-century science, the uniformitarian geology of Charles Lyell and the evolutionary theory of Charles Darwin were widely accepted because they seemed to confirm the idea of progress: The present world and its inhabitants were the products not of global disasters and multiple creations but of slow and steady change.

By contrast, Crosby observes, the 20th century has experienced the two worst wars in history, genocide, the invention of more ominous means of destruction, revolutions and the collapse of empires, rampant population growth, and the threat of ecological disaster. Catastrophism, not steady progress, is the modern paradigm. Even the universe was born, many scientists now believe, in one explosive moment—the Big Bang.

"The rapidity and magnitude of change in our century," Crosby concludes, "has prepared us to ask different questions about the encounter than the older schools of scientists and scholars asked."

* * *

If Abbé Raynal held his essay contest today, the pessimists might outnumber the optimists. Indeed, almost everything about Columbus and the discovery of America has become controversial.

And perhaps the greatest controversy of all is whether or not to celebrate the Quincentennial. The critics who advocate not celebrating it are correct, if to celebrate perpetuates a view of the encounter that ignores the terrible toll. This must be acknowledged and memorialized in the hope that nothing like it is ever repeated. Even so, it would be unhistorical to ignore the more salutary consequences. The New World, for example, changed Europe through new ideas, new resources, and new models of political and social life that would spread through the world. William H. McNeill is one of many historians who believe this led to the Enlightenment of the 18th century and thus to the philosophical, political, and scientific foundations of modern Western civilization. It should not be overlooked that this is the kind of society that encourages and tolerates the revisionists who condemn its many unforgivable transgressions in the New World.

Of course, attributing so much to any one historical development makes some historians uneasy. In cautioning against the "presentism" in much historical interpretation, Herbert Butterfield recalled "the schoolboy who, writing on the results of Columbus's discovery of America, enumerated amongst other things the execution of Charles I, the war of the Spanish Succession and the French Revolution." No one will ever know what the world and subsequent events would have been like if the discovery had not been made, or if it had not occurred until much later. But the impact of that discovery can hardly be underestimated. And it did start with Christopher Columbus.

That brings up another issue central to the Quincentenary debates: Columbus's responsibility for all that followed. It must be remembered who he was—not who we wish he had been. He was a European Christian of the 15th century sailing for the crown of Spain. There can be no expiation, only understanding. His single-mindedness and boldness, as well as the magnitude of his achievement, give him heroic standing. Others did not have Columbus's bold idea to sail across the unknown ocean, or if they did, they never acted upon it. Columbus did. In so many other respects, he failed to rise above his milieu and set a more worthy example, and so ended up a tragic figure. But he does not deserve to bear alone the blame for the consequences of his audacious act.

We must resist the temptation to shift blame for our behavior to someone dead and gone. Mario Vargas Llosa, the Peruvian novelist, finds little to admire in the early Spanish conquerors but recognizes the dangers inherent in transferring to them an inordinate share of the blame for modern America.

"Why have the post-colonial republics of the Americas—republics that might have been expected to have deeper and broader notions of liberty, equality, and fraternity—failed so miserably to improve the lives of their Indian citizens?" Vargas Llosa asks. "Immense opportunities brought by the civilization that discovered and conquered America have been beneficial only to a minority, sometimes a very small one; whereas the great majority managed to have only a negative share of the conquest.... One of our worst defects, our best fictions, is to believe that our miseries have been imposed on us from abroad, that others, for example, the conquistadores, have always been responsible for our problems.... Did they really do it? We did it; we are the conquistadores."

* * *

People have choices, but they do not always choose well. One wishes Columbus had acquitted himself more nobly, in the full knowledge that, even if he had, others who came after would have almost surely squandered the opportunity presented to them to make a truly fresh start in human history—a new world in more than the geographic sense. But wishes, yesterday's self-congratulation or today's self-flagellation, are not history.

Columbus's failings, as well as his ambitions and courage, are beyond historical doubt—and are all too human. The mythic Columbus of our creation is something else. His destiny, it seems, is to serve as a barometer of our self-confidence, our hopes and aspirations, our faith in progress, and the capacity of humans to create a more just society.

The Sailors of Palos

SAILORS IN PORT, 1492.

Text and illustrations Peter F. Copeland

Sometime merchant seaman, treasure diver, and author and illustrator, Peter F. Copeland has made a lifelong study of the working life and social history of sailors through the ages.

When Christopher Columbus's two surviving ships arrived back in Europe from the New World in March 1493, the Admiral of the Ocean Sea returned to lasting but troubled fame. But the mariners who had accompanied him across unknown seas and through storm and shipwreck remained virtually forgotten to history. Here an artist-historian tells us who some of these sailors were and what their seafaring lives were like.

From *American History Illustrated*, March/April 1993, pp. 58-68. © 1993 by Cowles Magazines, Inc. Reprinted by permission.

It was early March 1493, and the great voyage was nearly over. En route back to Spain from the far-off Indies, the storm-beaten *Niña*, flagship of Christopher Columbus, had put into Lisbon. Her consort, the original flagship *Santa María*—or what was left of her—lay shattered on a reef off the island of Hispaniola.*

The *Niña*'s sailors were at work, repairing and renewing their weathered ship, and anticipating a speedy return to Spain and their home port of Palos. They had little time to speculate on the fate of the *Pinta*, the sister caravel last seen one stormy night a month before in mid-ocean.** There was much to be done. A new set of sails must be laid out, cut, and sewn. Running rigging must be renewed; standing rigging needed repair. Already shoreside carpenters were measuring and sawing aloft and on deck, while caulkers worked at sealing the leaky hull. Other sailors turned-to to clean and wash down the hold. Soon they would load sacks and barrels of stones from the banks of the River Tagus, to be packed as ballast in the now lightly laden vessel.

Within a few days, news of Columbus's epochal seven-month voyage and discovery of a sea route across the Western Ocean to the Indies and far Cathay would begin to reverberate across Portugal and Spain, and indeed be trumpeted throughout Europe. Greeted as a hero by all who heard of his enterprise, the admiral already basked in his celebrity. It was, at least for the moment, everything for which the determined explorer could hope.

Columbus returned to Europe in 1493 to lasting but troubled fame for achievements that still cast an imposing shadow today, five hundred years later. But what of the nearly ninety officers and sailors who accompanied him across unknown seas, enduring storm and shipwreck? Unlike Columbus, his mariners have passed the succeeding centuries in virtual obscurity. Who were these sailors and what were their lives like—both in port and during their odyssey of discovery?

A HARBOR SCENE.

Most of the men and boys who signed on for the Voyage of Discovery during the summer of 1492 came from Palos and the other seaside towns and villages of Andalusia in southern Spain. A few, however, were Basques and Gallicians from the northern part of the country, and five—a Portuguese, a Venetian, a Calabrian, and two Genoese—were foreigners.

The crewmen ranged in age and experience from seasoned veterans of the sea accustomed to the rigors of shipboard life to youths no older than twelve years of age. They included skilled specialists such as boatswains, carpenters, caulkers, coopers, gunners, pilots, stewards, and surgeons, as well as untrained boys.

Legend suggests that Columbus's sailors were criminals and convicts,

*On Christmas Eve 1492, as the flagship sailed along the coast of Hispaniola, Columbus, who had been on deck for several days, went below for a few hours of sleep. The night being fine and the sea calm, the officer of the watch also went below, and the watch on deck settled down to sleep—with the helmsman (disobeying the admiral's standing orders) leaving the tiller in the hands of one of the ship's boys. During the night, with the youth at the helm, the *Santa María* went aground on a coral bank, wedging in so firmly that all efforts to kedge her off proved fruitless. Her seams eventually opened and she had to be abandoned.

**The two ships and their crews were unexpectedly reunited on March 15, when both entered the harbor of Palos on the same tide.

WORKING ALOFT.

and hides. Windlasses cracked and groaned as gangs of chantey-singing sailors, clad only in wide-bottomed underdrawers, strained at the capstan bars.

Some of the vessels anchored in the harbor or tied alongside the wharves might have hailed from such far-off places as Denmark and Egypt. Most were lateen-rigged caravels built in western Andalusia—familiar sights along the shores of Spain, Portugal, and throughout the Mediterranean.

A large three-masted deep-sea ship loading horses through a side-port opening also might be seen on the waterfront, tied up alongside tiny coastal trading vessels manned by crews of two men each, or near a fishing boat newly arrived from Iceland and deeply laden with a cargo of dried codfish. Here also might be a ship-of-war, with banners fluttering from her fore and aft castles, taking aboard chests of arms and casks of salt-meat and wine.

Columbus's flagship *Santa María* was a Gallician-built *nao*—a round-bellied, three-masted, square-rigged former merchantman of the type commonly seen in the Mediterranean. Heavy and unwieldy, she measured about eighty-five feet long, had a beam of thirty feet, and displaced more than one hundred tons. Columbus called her "a dull sailor, and unfit for discovery." During the voyage of discovery the *Santa María* shipped a crew of forty men and boys.

The *Niña* and *Pinta* both were caravels, small, lightly-built, broad-bowed vessels that had begun life as lateen-rigged ships with no square sails—a typical Mediterranean rig. Both ultimately were re-rigged as *caravela redondas*, with square sails on the fore and mainmasts, and lateen sails on their mizzens. The *Niña* had a fourth mast aft of the mizzen, called a *bonaventura* mast, upon which was shipped a smaller lateen sail; it is possible that the *Pinta* did also. The *Niña* was about sixty-seven feet long, with a beam of twenty-one feet; tradition tells us that the *Pinta* was somewhat larger. The *Niña* carried a crew of twenty-four men and boys, and the *Pinta* shipped twenty-six crewmen.

A typical merchant ship of the era was described as a "grim and dark city, full of bad odors, filth, and uncomfortable living

dragooned for a desperate enterprise, but in fact only one man among them was a convicted murderer. He and two cohorts were pardoned on condition of volunteering to serve. The vast majority of the sailors joined the expedition—after initial hesitation—for the adventure of the voyage and the hope of gaining riches in the far-off Indies.

Strange and picturesque to the shore-folk he encountered, the seaman of Columbus's time lived apart in his own world of ships and seaports. He had been to distant lands and seen fascinating sights. He wore odd clothes and spoke a language that sounded peculiar and sometimes even incomprehensible.

To landsmen unfamiliar with the fifteenth-century sailor's world, the bustling seaports he frequented must have seemed exciting and exotic places. In many harbors the waterfront itself was called the "lowere city" and sometimes was separated by a tall wooden palisade from the rest of the town—the "upper city"—where dwelt the merchants and well-to-do tradesmen.

This lower city—with its population of fisherfolk, chandlers, peddlers, shipwrights, rogues, slatterns, and drunks—was a place of noise and smells and mud. Packs of half-wild dogs roamed through the narrow, filthy alleys that led down to the ships. The air was filled with the raw stench of hides, fish, and sewage and the sounds of wine vendors, soap sellers, and other street peddlers crying their wares. Here, too, one might hear the chanted prayers of a black-robed priest—his pious petitions for the mariners laboring on the seas occasionally interrupted by songs and shouts emanating from nearby taverns.

The waterfront itself was crowded with merchants, beggars, sailors, and itinerant laborers looking for odd jobs. Ships at the quayside loaded and discharged such cargoes as fish, salt, oil, grain, wine, conditions." At sea the vessel's masts and hull creaked and groaned continually as, with her short keel and round bilges, she pitched and rolled heavily even in a moderate sea. Built with timber from the high Pyrenees, Columbus's ships were fastened with wooden pegs and hand-wrought iron spikes, and they leaked like weathered wash-tubs.

The captain of a Spanish ship of the fifteenth century was commander of the vessel and crew, but not necessarily a seaman. He might be a military officer of the crown, a member of a noble family, or, like Columbus, the holder of a Royal Commission that in Columbus's case declared him "Captain General" of the fleet as well as captain of the *Santa María*.

Second to the captain in line of command stood the master—the man who actually supervised the operation of the ship. He was an experienced seaman in overall charge of each day's sailing, getting the vessel underway, stowing cargo, and anchoring. Sometimes the master also was the ship's captain; occasionally he was its owner as well.

Below the master was the first mate or pilot (*piloto* in Spanish), the navigation officer responsible to the master for the operation of the ship and the work of the seamen. He was, ideally, an experienced ship handler, wise in the ways of the weather, the tides, and the sea. The pilot brought aboard with him such navigational materials as charts, compass, sandglasses, astrolabe or quadrant, and sounding leads. Both master and pilot received a rate of pay about twice that of the sailors.

The *Santa María*, as flagship of Columbus's expedition, carried several additional officials to fulfill special assignments. There was an interpreter to converse with the Asians the explorer expected to meet; a secretary of the fleet to record the discovery of new lands that might be found and claimed; and two royal agents to note expenses and take charge of the Crown's portion of any treasure recovered. There were also a comptroller of the fleet and a silversmith.

Also serving aboard the *Santa María* was the *alguazil de la armada*, or marshal of the fleet. Each of the two other vessels had a marshal of the ship. These men were responsible for maintaining

discipline and administering punishment as required.

A surgeon aboard each vessel served the medical needs of the crew, and a steward was responsible for the food stores, firewood, water, and wine. The steward saw to trimming and maintaining lamps and tending the fires over which hot meals were prepared.

Equal in rank with the steward was the boatswain, who led the seamen in their daily tasks and who reported to the mate. The boatswain carried out the orders of the master and mate in the stowing of cargo; he continually inspected masts, spars, rigging, and sails for wear and repair; and he had charge of all the ship's cable and lines. He also was responsible for keeping the deck clean and shipshape; for maintaining the good condition of the ship's boat; and for making sure that the galley fire was put out each night.

Next below the steward and boat-

swain were the ship's petty officers, or *oficiales*—sailors who practiced special trades such as carpentry, caulking, or cooperage. The caulker, responsible for keeping the deck and hull watertight, had a store of rope yarn, oakum, tallow, oil, pitch, scupper nails, and lead sheets for stopping leaks. He also was in charge of the ship's pumps. The cooper had the important job of making up, caulking, and repairing the ship's casks and barrels, buckets, tubs, hogsheads, and other such wooden containers—all vital for the storage of water, wine, and oil.

Next in this shipboard hierarchy were the experienced seamen or *marineros*, and finally, at the bottom, the apprentices and boys or *grumetes*. There were twenty-six watch-standing sailors aboard the *Santa María*, fourteen aboard the *Niña*, and fifteen aboard the *Pinta*.

Columbus was captain of the *Santa*

RAISING THE MAIN YARD.

María as well as admiral of the fleet. The ship's owner, Juan de la Cosa, sailed as master, with Peralonso Niño as his mate. Juan Sánchez was surgeon, and Pedro de Terreros was Columbus's personal steward. Diego de Arana was marshal of the fleet, and Rodrigo de Escobedo was secretary or *escrivano* of the armada. Luis de Torres, a converted Jew, was the official interpreter. He spoke Hebrew, Aramaic, and some Arabic.

Thirty-year-old Vicente Yáñez Pinzón was captain of the *Niña*, and Juan Niño was master. Sancho Ruiz de Gama served as pilot; Bartolomé García was the boatswain; and Alonso de Moguer was surgeon.

Martín Alonzo Pinzón—brother of Vicente—was captain of the *Pinta*, and his other brother Francisco Martín Pinzón sailed as master. Cristóbal García Sarmiento was pilot, and Juan Quintero was boatswain. García Fernández was steward, and a man named Diego was surgeon.

Most of the ordinary seamen and apprentices whose names appeared on the rosters of Columbus's ships were listed only by their first name and place of origin. Among those assigned to the *Santa María*, for example, was a boy known to us only as Juan, who was listed as a servant. Juan could have been a ship's boy,

an apprentice seaman, or the personal servant of one of the officials aboard the ship. Probably coming from a village in Andalusia, he may have been recommended by a brother or cousin among the members of the crew. His parents could have been peasants who worked the stony coastal land, or possibly fisherfolk. In any case, the social standing of Juan's family would have been very near the bottom of medieval society.

The average seafarer of Columbus's time was illiterate, as were the great majority of people ashore. His life expectancy was short due to his exposure to the perils of the sea, warfare, and waterfront life. Accustomed to coping with primitive conditions, he was tough and cynical, with not much respect for the law but a realistic fear of the strong arm of authority.

Sailors are mentioned briefly here and there in the reminiscences of travelers of the medieval world—ship's passengers, pilgrims, merchants, and clerics. They also appear in some of the works of authors and playwrights of the day. In his *Canterbury Tales*, fourteenth-century writer Geoffrey Chaucer described a "shipman" who was traveling to the shrine to make a votive offering, perhaps in obedience to a vow made in time of peril on the sea. The sailor's rough and homely attire, his awkwardness on horseback, his weather-beaten complexion, and his seafaring speech made him a subject of jest to his fellow pilgrims. He nevertheless was a jovial and welcome companion for the travelers and "certainly he was a good felawe."

Medieval seamen also appeared in a morality play given by the Guild of Shipwrights for the pageant of Corpus Christi in London in the year 1415. Portrayed as being distinctly different from shore folk, the sailors were distinguished by the "quaint expressions of

THE "SANTA MARIA."

their profession," their rough and boisterous humor, and their contempt for the soft and sheltered life of their shoreside cousins.

Superstitious, as so many seafarers through the ages have been, the typical sailor of Columbus's time deeply believed in omens and portents of doom. He accepted the existence of gigantic sea monsters that lived far out in the depths of the unknown ocean. He looked with a child's eyes upon odd things seen in far places and had a great faith in the miraculous. Anything that frightened him or seemed unexplainable, he believed to be of supernatural origin. If a strange bird alighted upon his ship, he took it as an unfavorable omen; and he feared the presence on board of a priest or woman as a sure way to raise up the devil. One medieval ocean traveler recalled that "during the night hours when the wind was high, the sailors would think they could hear sirens singing, wailing and jeering, like insolent men in their cups."

Columbus's sailors were as superstitious as any. They had been skeptical and uneasy about this voyage of exploration to the far Indies. There were old-timers among them who had sailed down the African coast to Guinea and out into the Western Ocean to the Canary Islands and the Azores. They knew that the Portuguese had sailed far reaches of the Atlantic in quest of the mythical islands of Brazil, Antilla of the Seven Cities, and the fabled isles of St. Brendan, but without success.

The same circumstances that made the sailor prone to superstition tended to make him more religious than his kinfolk ashore. His religious convictions conformed to a deeply devout though violent and authoritarian period. The cruelty and amorality of his time did not shake his belief in the existence of an avenging deity or in the strict authority of the Holy Church.

Although lacking in formal education, the able-bodied sailor of the fifteenth century was proficient at the peculiar skills of his trade through years of apprenticeship. He had to be able to steer at the tiller, splice line, caulk seams, make and mend sails, take accurate soundings, and be adept at small-boat handling. He was required, among his other duties, to work at loading and discharging the ship's cargo and to make and take in sail in all weather. He had to be familiar with the process of weighing and letting go the anchors and of securing them when brought aboard. He also had to be fairly skilled at rough carpentry and to be practiced in the use of weapons and in gunnery, for he would be called upon to defend his ship in time of need. Hardy and strong, he was as agile as a monkey; when going aloft he often climbed hand-over-hand up the lines of the standing rigging.

The sailors of Columbus proved as talented as any in the skills of the *marinero*. Before the expedition departed from the Canary Islands on its outbound voyage, Columbus decided to convert the *Niña* from a lateen to a square rig. With no shipyards or skilled artisans available, Captain Pinzón chose a gang from among the ship's own crew to do the job, which included cutting and sewing new sails for the fore and main yards. The work began on August 26, and the *Niña* was ready to sail just three days later. It is a tribute to Columbus's sailors that the only complaint voiced by the admiral about poor workmanship concerned the shipwrights of Palos, whose faulty caulking caused the *Niña* and *Pinta* to leak badly.

The clothing of Columbus's sailors was simple and their possessions few. Typical garb consisted of wide-bottomed knee-length breeches; a loose-fitting hooded blouse of coarse linen or old sail cloth; and, perhaps, a sleeveless vest-like overgarment slit at the sides and tied with laces. Although the sailor sometimes wore stockings and shoes, in milder climes he usually went barefoot. Most seamen wore red woolen stocking caps of the type made in Toledo. Columbus gave several of these caps as gifts to the natives he encountered in the New World.

The Spanish seaman's foul-weather garment has been described as a brown

THE "PINTA."

cloth robe or overcoat called *papahigo* or "storm sail" in sailors' slang, that resembled the habit of the Franciscan friars. This, the sea gown worn by mariners all over western Europe, was the distinctive garment that identified them as seafarers. Chaucer's shipman of the *Canterbury Tales,* for example, wore "a gown of falding (a coarse cloth) to the knee." This, plus the pilgrim's habit of wearing his sailors' knife hung from a thong slung over his shoulder, marked him as a seaman in the eyes of his fellow travelers.

The sailor tightened his sea gown at the waist with a belt or perhaps a bit of ships' hempen line; when working on deck he often knotted the front or tucked it through his waist belt to keep it out of the way.

Ships' officers wore cloaks, jackets, or doublets of cloth or dressed leather that laced down the front; hose and a variety of styles of hats or caps, all in brighter colors than the rough simple clothing of the sailors. At his belt, the ship's officer wore a dagger rather than a sailor's

sheath knife. At sea the officers sometimes reverted, in part at least, to more common sailors' garb. Columbus is reported habitually to have worn a brown sea gown, which was mistaken by some observers as being the hooded brown habit of a Franciscan monk. It is interesting that a man so vain of his rank and titles would choose to wear a garment so rough and uncouth in medieval eyes.

Sleeping and sanitary accommodations aboard Columbus's ships were primitive. The captain and sailing master probably had small cabins, each barely large enough to contain a narrow wooden bunk. Other officers slept on mattresses under the quarterdeck, forward of the helmsman. When not in use, the mattresses were rolled up in grass sacks and lashed along the bulwarks.

The ordinary sailors generally had to

MANNING THE PUMP.

sleep in the open on the cambered deck, where hatch covers offered the only flat surfaces and coils of line served as pillows—or if more fortunate, to huddle under the shelter of the forecastle. On many vessels of that time the sailors were forbidden to sleep in the protection of the ship's hold, even during stormy weather, as it would take too long to roust them out in an emergency. In the *Santa María*, with her large crew, this rule may not have been enforced.

To relieve a call of nature the sailor had to swing up over the bulwarks and hang in the rigging over the ship's lee side, "making reverence to the sun," as the saying was, and hope that he would not be swept away by a visiting wave. The lower rigging had to be washed down each day as a consequence of this necessity.

When the ship was becalmed, the men might bathe themselves on deck, scooping up sea water in buckets; the more adventurous might, in calm weather, even go over the side if there were no sharks about. Most sailors wore whiskers or a full beard, because the average man of that day shaved only once a week if he shaved at all.

The staples of the Spanish sailor's diet were hard biscuit; bacon; salt meat and fish; chick peas and beans; garlic and olive oil; rice and raisins. No cook was carried to prepare the sailors' meals; this duty probably fell to one of the ships' boys. The officers ate aft, their food prepared by the captain's servant.

Hot meals, when they were available, always were soups or stews prepared with salt meat or fish, broken ship's biscuit, rice, and whatever spices were available, with rare additions of onions or potatoes. One such stew, called *lobscouse*, was eaten by seafaring men until the end of the age of sail. On Fridays, if the weather held, the sailors' hot meal was bean soup seasoned with garlic and peppers.

Columbus described his idea of the stores to be carried on a voyage of discovery thus: good biscuit seasoned and not old, flour salted at the time of milling, wine, salt meat, oil, vinegar, cheese, chick peas, lentils, beans, salt fish, honey, rice, almonds, and raisins. The salted flour could be mixed with water or wine, made into cakes of unleavened bread, and baked in the ashes at the bottom of the open iron firebox in which the hot meals were prepared. This primitive stove, called a *fogón*, was brought up from below in fair weather and set on deck near the lee rail. The fire was kindled upon a bed of earth or sand that covered the bottom of the firebox. Supplies of firewood were stowed in every available corner of the ship.

When conditions permitted, a hot meal was prepared before noon so that the watch below could eat before turning to and the watch on deck could dine after being relieved. Gathering around the smoking firebox, the hungry sailors extended their bowls for stew or soup and then found a place on the crowded, cluttered deck or on the hatch. Sprawling or kneeling or sitting as conditions allowed, and with a knife their only utensil, they ate "from their lap" in the fashion of the poor folk in the Middle Ages. As one observer noted, they "pull out their knives of different shapes made to kill hogs or skin lambs or for cutting bags, and then grab in their hands the poor bones and peel them clean of their sinews and meat as if all their lives they had practiced anatomy in Guadelupe or Valencia. In a prayer, they leave them clean as ivory."

It did not take many days at sea for the food supplies to become wormy and rancid in the damp shipboard environment. And the casks of fresh water soon became foul and stinking—though when laced with wine the brackish liquid became at least barely palatable. Sometimes sailors carried their ration below decks to eat in the dark—to avoid seeing the maggots that infested it.

To supplement their diets, the sailors caught fish as often as possible. On Columbus's outward voyage, when supplies were still relatively plentiful and fresh, such catches were a luxury. During the return, however, they became a dire necessity. The admiral recorded in his *Diario* on January 25—more than three weeks before reaching the Azores—that the crew of the *Niña* had "killed a porpoise and a tremendous shark . . . [they] had quite some need of it because they were carrying nothing to eat except bread and wine and yams from the Indies."

Mariners marked the passage of time at sea with the turning of a sandglass, which was done by an apprentice sea-

A MEAL ON DECK IN FAIR WEATHER.

man. As the sand ran out at the end of each half-hour, the helmsman rang a bell to remind the apprentice to turn the glass. This was the origin of the ship's-bell time used to this day.

With each turning of the glass during the night watch, the *grumete* called out to the lookout in the masthead "*Ah! de proa! Alerta, buena guardia!*" to which the lookout called back "*Buena guardia!*" to prove he was awake—a procedure still followed aboard some merchant ships in recent times.

Ceremony and formality accompanied the passage of each watch at sea. Just before sundown and before the first night watch, the crew was called to evening prayers. An apprentice carried the binnacle lamp aft along the deck, singing "Amen and God give us a good night and a good sailing. May the ship make a good passage, captain and master and good company." Then the apprentices led the sailors in prayer, chanting the *Pater Noster*, the *Ave Maria*, and the *Credo*, after which all hands sang the *Salve Regina*. For the sailors these chanted rituals of the church were comforting and expected, their only link to their distant homeland.

The night watches also had their moments of formal spoken reverence, as described by Felix Fabri, a traveler of 1480: "When the wind is quite fair and not too strong all is still save only he who watches the compass and he who holds the handle on the tiller, for these, by way of returning thanks for a voyage and good luck, continually greet the breeze, praise God, the Blessed Virgin and the Saints, on answering the other, and they are never silent so long as the wind is fair. Anyone on board who hears this chant of theirs would fall asleep."

At daybreak the youngest boy of the watch sang or chanted a prayer that invoked a blessing of the True Cross, the Holy Trinity, and the true God, keeper of the immortal soul, concluding:

Blessed be the light of day
And he who sends the night away.

Then the boy recited the *Pater Noster* and the *Ave Maria* and added a plea to God for a good voyage and the hope that he would grant good days to the officers of the after guard and to the sailors forward.

The sailors and apprentices were divided into two watches, each group alternating at watch-standing duties of four hours each. If he was not already on watch, the sailor's day began at seven in the morning when the deck boy sang out "*Al quarto!*" (on deck) and the men of the morning watch crawled out from whatever sheltering spot they had found to sleep away their few hours of rest. No one needed time to dress, for all hands slept in their clothes. One sailor went aft to relieve the helmsman, who steered from his position under the quarterdeck in an enclosed, gloomy little space cut off from the rest of the ship. He handled the heavy tiller below decks, without any view of the sea or the sails; his orders were shouted down to him through a small hatch by the mate standing on the quarterdeck above. Before him, secured to the mizzenmast, was the binnacle, a box containing the compass and its lantern.

In maintaining his assigned compass course the helmsman was aided by the feel of the ship under his feet and the orders of the mate from above. Steering was a rough job. When a heavy sea slammed against the rudder, the swinging tiller might knock the helmsman off his feet. To minimize this, a relieving tackle, which could be adjusted to allow for the set of the sea, was rigged to the tiller. Not every sailor was a skilled helmsman. Columbus noted in his journal that his sailors sometimes steered

badly, carelessly allowing the *Santa María* to run as much as several points off the ordered course.

The first duty of the men of the morning watch was to man the wooden pumps that stood just forward of midships on the main deck, to remove the water that had accumulated in the bilges during the night. The bilge water came up "foaming like hell and stinking like the devil." Seamen believed, however, that if the bilges stank they would enjoy a lucky voyage; the stale water sloshing about in the bottom of the hold ensured that the beams and planks would remain swollen tight and that the crew would not be laboring forever at the pumps.

The men then scrubbed the deck with buckets of sea water and stiff-bristled brooms. In hot, dry climates this scrubbing and sloshing of water over the decks was repeated several times a day to keep the planking from drying out and shrinking in the hot sun. With their buckets, the men then washed down the lower rigging, deadeyes, and main shrouds where they had been soiled by men relieving themselves over the side during the night.

Those on the morning watch were responsible for taking up the slack in the running gear so that all the lines were taut. The sailors also regularly tarred all of the standing rigging, stays, and shrouds. The deck boys were put to making up spun yarn and chafing gear out of old lines and making oakum from old rope yarns for the caulker's use.

When sail was to be taken in, the main yard was quickly lowered to the deck and the sailors gathered the canvas and secured it to the yard with lashings, after which all hands manned the topping lifts and hauled the yard and its furled sail back up to the masthead. In good weather there was no need to raise and lower the heavy yard because sailors could climb the rigging and straddle the yard while gathering up the sail.

When rain was expected and the wind permitted, the sailors manned the mainsail clew lines and raised a corner of the sail to form a belly in the canvas with which to catch some of the precious rainwater, which then would be drained into buckets and casks.

During a storm at sea, life was a nightmarish struggle, with the sailors fight-

ing to take in sails and all hands laboring constantly at the crude hand pump, or (when as often happened, the pump broke down) forming bucket brigades to bail the ship out by hand. Steering with the heavy wooden tiller in bad weather was a brutal wrestling match that left the helmsman exhausted and covered with bumps and bruises.

In storm and howling winds many among the crew were both sick and terrified, and the sailors were not reluctant to pray to God and call upon the saints for mercy. During Columbus's homeward voyage, when the *Niño* fought to survive a February storm off the Azores, the admiral himself "ordered that lots should be drawn for a pilgrimage to Santa María de Guadalupe and to take a five-pound wax candle [and] for another pilgrim to go to spend a night at vigil in Santa Clara de Moguer and to have a Mass said. . . After this the admiral and all the men made a vow that, as soon as they reached the first land, all would go in their shirtsleeves in procession to pray in a church dedicated to Our Lady."

During such miserable times there were no hot meals and little sleep. At the end of his watch the sailor, soaked to the skin, rolled himself in his rough gown and napped, perhaps curled up in a sodden coil of mooring line among the rats and roaches under the forecastle, until the boatswain's whistle rousted him out for another emergency. After the storm passed, the mariners often discovered to their further dismay that the sea stores had suffered storm damage or that wine or water casks had been stove in, requiring that both food and drink thereafter be severely rationed.

During most of his time at sea, the sailor had precious little leisure time that was not spent in trying to sleep or tending to necessary personal chores. When in port or at anchor, however, or in gentler hemispheres where emergencies were infrequent, the seamen found time for entertainment. Storytelling was a universal pastime among mariners and included tall tales of adventures past and hardships endured, of feats of gluttony and drinking bouts ashore, and of romances in different ports. The board game of checkers (*damas* in Spanish) was widely played, and men off watch squandered many a

1401: "Among all the occupations of seafarers there is one which, though loathsome, is yet very common, daily and necessary. I mean the hunting and catching of lice and vermin. Unless a man spends several hours in this work when he is on pilgrimage, he will have but unquiet slumbers."

Although there always have been men who loved the sea in spite of all of its hardships and dangers, there was one feature of the fifteenth-century sailor's calling that probably attracted him more than anything else—the lure of money. The peasant farmer seldom saw hard cash in his life. What his family could not grow, weave, or craft itself must be obtained through barter. To a youth growing up in such a world the idea of regular wages was most attractive. The sailor was paid in cash for his time and labor.

A sailor's monthly wage of eight hundred *maravedis*—enough to buy two fat pigs—was about the same as that earned by the manservant to a nobleman. A ship's master earned more than double that amount—the price of a cow. For those who sailed with Columbus, the enterprise held both the distant promise of a fortune to be discovered in the Indies and also a stipulated monthly salary to be earned in hard money paid from the Royal treasury.

Despite all they had experienced and endured, the crews of the *Niña* and *Pinta* who returned to Palos in March 1493 were in remarkably good shape. None had been lost due to disease or accidents at sea.* Before setting out in August 1492 they had received four months' pay in advance. Now, as they prepared to drop anchor, the seamen could look forward to collecting the balance owed them and to telling all who would listen of the strange sights they had seen. Although history would focus its gaze on the man who commanded the expedition, the seamen whose labors brought the two surviving ships back to their home port could bask, at least for a time, in his reflected glory.

SAILORS IN PORT.

hard-earned coin gambling with dice under the forecastle head.

Singing was another popular recreation for sailors far from home. We are told that after sighting the islands of the New World, the crew of the *Pinta* sang and danced around the mainmast to the accompaniment of pipes and a tambourine. Shipmates also passed their free hours at sea fishing with hand line and harpoon; gathering flying fish that landed on deck; and spotting and identifying types of birds that approached the ships.

Yet another leisure-hour activity was described by a seafaring pilgrim in

*Sadly, more than a third of Columbus's sailors did not survive to enjoy their hard-won rewards. When the *Santa María* ran aground and was wrecked off Hispaniola, the admiral, having insufficient room aboard the remaining ships for all of his crewmen, built a fort—named La Villa de Navidad in honor of the Christmas feast day—and left thirty-nine men behind. When his second expedition returned to Villa de Navidad in November 1493, Columbus found the fort in ashes and the men dead at the hands of local Taino tribesmen—the Navidad garrison having allowed greed and lust to destroy the good relations that Columbus had established with the natives.

After dire straits, an agonizing haul across the Pacific

*It was only a generation after Columbus
that Magellan's tiny fleet sailed west,
via his strait, then on around the world*

Simon Winchester

Simon Winchester is the author of eight books that combine history and travel, including The Pacific *(Hutchinson), from which this article was adapted.*

Balboa found the ocean. Then, in their droves, explorers emerged to circle and probe and colonize it, but first, in that most daring of all endeavors, to cross it.

No one could be sure how wide it was. No one could be sure where lay the Terra Australis Incognita, which Ptolemy had postulated and which Mercator would argue was a necessary balance for a spherical world—without it the whole planet might simply topple over, to be lost among the stars. No one knew the weather or the currents or the winds. But one small certainty spurred the would-be circumnavigators onward. It was that the Spice Islands, the Moluccas, lay at the farthest side of whatever might lie beyond the waters, pacific or unpacific, that Balboa had discovered.

Traders buying nutmegs and cloves from Arabian merchants had known about the Spice Islands for centuries; in the 1200s Marco Polo knew roughly where they were, for he saw junk traffic in the ports of North China loaded with spices and manned by crews who had come from the south. In 1511 a Portuguese expedition led by Antonio d'Abreu actually discovered them by moving eastward, after passing the tip of Africa, to Malacca, thence down the strait and past the immense island of Borneo to the confused archipelago where nearly all known spices grew in wild profusion.

To reach their goal, d'Abreu's men had gone halfway round the world from Europe to the Orient.

The geographical fact they established was of great political and imperial importance. Since 1494, when the Treaty of Tordesillas was signed, all of the unknown world to the east of an imaginary line that had been drawn 370 leagues west of the Cape Verde Islands would belong to Portugal. Everything to the west of that line would belong to Spain. So far as the Atlantic and the Indian oceans were concerned, there was no problem; but what about the other side of the world? Conquest, squatter's rights, annexation, force majeure—these cruder tools of geopolitics might well dictate its eventual position. Thus the Moluccas, if discovered by going eastward around the globe, would belong to Portugal—at least by the logic of some explorers. But the Moluccas claimed by a party going westward might belong to Spain. So while d'Abreu and his colleagues went off eastward, even braver or more foolhardy men, carrying the banner of Castile, were determined to discover—heroically and, as it turned out for many of them, fatally—the way to reach this same Orient by traveling westward across the vast unknown.

There is thus a nice irony in the fact that the man who undertook the seminal voyage, and did so in the name of Spain, was in fact Portuguese. He was born Fernao de Magalhaes, and the Portuguese—"He is ours," they insist—rarely care to acknowledge that he renounced his citizenship after a row, pledged his allegiance to King Charles I (later to become Emperor Charles V) and was given a new name: Hernando de

Magallanes. The English-speaking world, which reveres him quite as much as does Iberia, knows him as Ferdinand Magellan.

He set off on September 20, 1519, with a royal mandate to search for a passage to El Mar del Sur, and thus to determine for certain that the Spice Islands were within the Spanish domains. He had not the foggiest notion of how far he might have to travel. For all Magellan's 237 men in their five little ships knew, Balboa's Panama and the northern coast of South America, which Columbus had sighted in 1498 on his third voyage, might be the equatorial portions of a continent extending without a break to the Antarctic pole, making the southern sea they sought quite unreachable from the west. Johann Schöner's globe of the world, then the best known, placed Japan a few hundred miles off Mexico. The historian López de Gómara asserts that Magellan always insisted that the Moluccas were "no great distance from Panama and the Gulf of San Miguel, which Vasco Núñez de Balboa discovered." Magellan would rapidly discover precisely what "no great distance" was to mean.

The five vessels that would soon make history—the *Victoria*, the *Trinidada* (the *Trinidad*), the *San Antonio*, the *Concepción* and the *Santiago*—were small, the largest being 120 tons, and hopelessly unseaworthy. ("I would not care to sail to the Canaries in such crates," wrote the Portuguese consul in Seville, with obvious pleasure. "Their ribs are soft as butter.")

They set sail from the Guadalquivir River under the proud corporate title of the Armada de Molucca, amply armed but hopelessly provisioned, with crews composed of men of nine different nationalities including a lone Englishman. There was one Moluccan slave, Enrique, who would act as an interpreter if the crossing was accomplished. There was a journalist, too, Antonio Francesca Pigafetta, who may also have been a Venetian spy. In any case, Pigafetta's diaries remained the source for all future accounts of the voyage; he had joined the ships, he said, because he was "desirous of sailing with the expedition so that I might see the wonders of the world."

The sorry tales of sodomy and mutiny, of yardarm justice and abrupt changes of command, and of all the other trials that attended the armada on its path south and west across the Atlantic do not belong here. The truly important phase of the journey starts on February 3, 1520, when the vessels left their anchorage near today's Montevideo and headed south. No charts or sailing directions existed then. The sailors were passing unknown coasts, and confronting increasingly terrifying seas and temperatures that dropped steadily, day by day.

They began to see penguins—"ducks without wings," they called them, *patos sin alas*—and "sea-wolves," or seals. Seeking a way to the Pacific, they explored every indentation in the coast off which they sailed, and with depressing regularity each indentation—even though some were extremely capacious and tempted the navigators to believe that they might be the longed-for straits—proved to be a cul-de-sac. They spent much of the winter, from Palm Sunday until late August, in the center of a chilly and miserable bay at what is now Puerto San Julian (see map on page 88). The winter was made doubly wretched by an appalling mutiny and the consequent executions and maroonings that Captain-General Magellan ordered; by the wrecking of the *Santiago*, which he had sent on a depth-sounding expedition; and by the realization of the dreadful damage done to the remaining ships by the chomping of those plank-gourmets of the seas, teredo worms.

But one important discovery was made at Puerto San Julian: these southern plains were inhabited by enormous nomadic shepherds who herded not sheep, but little wild llamas known as guanacos, and who dressed in their skins. Magellan captured a number of these immense people—one pair by the cruel trick of showing them leg-irons and insisting that the proper way to carry the shackles was to allow them to be locked around their ankles. Magellan's men also liked the giants' tricks: one, who stayed aboard only a week but allowed himself to be called Juan and learned some biblical phrases, caught and ate all the rats and mice on board, to the pleasure of the cook and the entertainment of the men. Magellan called these men "*patagones*"—"big feet"; the land in which he found them has been known ever since as Patagonia.

By late August the fleet set sail again. Two men had been left behind, marooned for mutiny by Magellan's orders. They had a supply of wine and hardtack, guns and shot, but when other, later expeditions entered the bay, no trace of them was found. They may have been killed by the giants; they may have starved to death. All that the men of the armada remembered were their pitiful wails echoing over the still waters as the ships sailed out of the bay into the open sea, and then south.

By the time the flotilla had reached 50 degrees south latitude (not far from the Falkland Islands), the men were restive. Their artless plea now was: If the expedition wanted to reach the Spice Islands, why not turn east toward them and pass below the Cape of Good Hope, as others had? Magellan, sensible enough to know this would make a nonsense of the whole plan to render the Spice Islands Spanish, refused. But he promised that if no strait was found by the time they had eaten up another 25 degrees of latitude, he would turn east as they wished. The murmurs stilled. The Captain-General clearly had no idea of the utter impossibility of navigating at 75 degrees south latitude, for on that longitudinal track his ships would get stuck fast in the thick ice of what is now the Weddell Sea, hemmed in by the yet unimagined continent and the unendurable cold of the Antarctic.

The Captain-General sights a virgin cape

On October 21, 1520, Magellan sighted a headland to starboard. Cabo Virjenes, which today is equipped with a lighthouse that flashes a powerful beam and a radio direction beacon, is an important navigation point on the South American coast. It marks, as Magellan was soon to discover, the eastern end of the strait that bears his name—the tortuous entrance, at long last, to the Pacific.

Ranges of immense, snow-covered mountains crowded into view; there could be, Magellan must have thought, no possible exit. Still, he ordered the *San Antonio* and the *Concepción* into the headwaters of the bay—only to be horrified when he saw them being swept into a huge maelstrom of surf and spindrift by unsuspected currents and winds. But he had no time to dwell on such miseries, for an immense storm broke over his own ship, the *Trinidad*, as well as the *Victoria*, alongside. Men were hurled overboard. One vessel was dismasted; the other nearly turned turtle several times. The storm went on and on and on. When relief finally came to the exhausted crews, the only recourse, it seemed, was to turn tail and head for home. The expedition was over, an abject failure.

Yet just at that moment (one occasionally suspects that the mythmakers have been at work on the story) the lookout sighted sails on the western horizon. They were indeed what they could only have been: the two scouting vessels had returned. Not shattered and aground, they were safe and sound. The joy Magellan must have felt at realizing his men were still alive was, however, as nothing when, as the *San Antonio* and the *Concepción* drew closer, he saw their yardarms hung with bunting, music being played, and the crews dancing and singing.

As an account of the long voyage puts it, "Suddenly, they saw a narrow passage, like the mouth of a river, ahead of them in the surf, and they managed to steer into it. Driven on by wind and tide they raced through this passage and into a wide lake. Still driven by the storm they were carried west for some hours into another narrow passage, though now the current had reversed, so what appeared to be a great ebb tide came rushing towards them. They debouched from this second strait into a broad body of water which stretched as far as the eye could see toward the setting sun. . . ."

By tasting the water and finding it salty, and then making sure that both the ebb tides and flood tides were of equal strength (tests that argued against this body of water being a river), the captains of the scout ships realized they had, indeed, discovered the way through. Magellan, believing that his ultimate goal was within his grasp, brushed aside the persistent doubter's view that he should, despite the discovery, turn back *eastward* for the Moluccas. "Though we have nothing

to eat but the leather wrapping from our masts," he declared, "we shall go on!"

The Strait of Magellan is as darkly beautiful as it is useful. Before I first visited the strait I supposed, wrongly, that since its latitude to the south is more or less the same distance from the Equator as Maine's latitude is to the north, the coastline would also be vaguely similar. But it is much starker, more hostile, more grand. Heading west, as Magellan did, the land begins flat, and wind reduces such trees as there are to stunted survivors. Even today the strait is not an easy place for sailing vessels: ". . . both difficult and dangerous, because of incomplete surveys, the lack of aids to navigation, the great distance between anchorages, the strong current, and the narrow limits for the maneuvering of vessels," says the pilot manual.

"A cargo of falsehood against Magellan"

For Magellan and his men it was a nightmare. The currents were treacherous. Unexpected winds, now known as williwaws, flashed down steep cliffs, threatening to drive the little fleet onto the rocks. He lost another ship; though he did not know it at the time, the *San Antonio* had turned tail and was heading back to Spain, "bearing a cargo of falsehood against Magellan." She also took away supplies vital for all of the fleet—one-third of the armada's biscuits, one-third of its meat and two-thirds of its currants, chickpeas and figs. The men began begging to turn back.

Days passed. Finally, on November 28, 1520, *Trinidad*, *Victoria* and *Concepción* passed beyond the horrors of the strait, and sailed westward into an evening that became, suddenly, magically serene. We are told that "the iron-willed Admiral" broke down and cried. Then he assembled his men on deck. Pedro de Valderrama, the *Trinidad*'s priest, stood on the poop deck and called down on the crew of all three remaining vessels the blessing of Our Lady of Victory. The men sang hymns. The gunners fired broadsides. And Magellan proudly unfurled the flag of Castile.

"We are about to stand into an ocean where no ship has ever sailed before," Magellan is said to have cried (though it has to be emphasized that there is no hard evidence that he did so). "May the ocean be always as calm and benevolent as it is today. In this hope I name it the Mar Pacifico." And just in case it was not Magellan who first uttered the name, then perhaps it was Pigafetta: "We debouched from that strait," he later wrote, "engulfing ourselves in the Pacific Sea."

The European dawn breaks on the Pacific

The concept of the Pacific Ocean, the greatest physical unit on Earth, had been born. Balboa had seen it. D'Abreu had ventured onto its western edges. Magellan had reached its eastern periphery. Now it was up to the explorers to try to comprehend the enormity of their discovery. But before they could do that, Magellan had to sail across it. This was his determined aim, and the aim of those who sponsored his venture.

So the Captain-General ordered the sails set to carry the shrunken, but now at long last triumphant, armada northward. He thought it might take three or four days to reach the Spice Islands. It was a savage underestimate—a tragically optimistic forecast, based quite probably on the terrible inability of long-distance navigators to calculate longitude (an inability that insured that not a single estimate then available to Magellan was even 80 percent of the true size of the ocean).

Not that anyone suspected tragedy as they breezed to the north of Cape Desado. Far from it. Once the armada had reached the lower southern latitudes, the winds began to blow balmily and unceasingly from the southeast. They were trade winds, just like those well known in the southern Atlantic and Indian oceans, and they were pleasantly warm. Their effect produced nothing but splendid sailing: no undue swells, no angry squalls, no cyclonic outbursts. Just endless days and nights of leisured running before a steady, powerful breeze. "Well was it named Pacific," wrote Pigafetta later, confirming his master's choice of name, "for during this period we met with no storms."

And for weeks and weeks, simply by wafting before the winds with sails unchanged, the fleet managed to miss every single one of the islands with which the Pacific Ocean is littered. Magellan's course, sedulously recorded by his pilot, Francisco Albo, shows him—almost uncannily—leading his vessels past the Juan Fernández Islands, past Sala y Gómez and Easter islands, past Pitcairn, Ducie, Oeno and Henderson and, indeed, past everything else. His astrolabe, his crude speed recorder, his hourglass (a watchkeeper would be flogged for holding it against his chest, since to warm it made the sand flow faster, the hour pass more quickly, the watch be more rapidly over) served Magellan admirably: he plotted the likely course to the Spice Islands, and his ships took him there, more or less.

Any deviation could have caused disaster. Had he strayed just 3 degrees north of Albo's recorded track, he would have hit the Marquesas; 3 degrees south, he would have come to Tahiti. He was a hundred miles off Bikini Atoll. He passed within half a day's sailing of razor-sharp coral reefs—thundering surfs, huge spikes and lances that would have ruined his ships forever. At this distance in time, it seems as if some guardian angel had Magellan's tiny fleet under benevolent invigilation for days and nights too numerous to count. Yet this providence had a less kindly face. Six weeks out of the strait, Magellan's men began to die. In the monotony of a long, landless passage, what proved unbearable was the lack of food aboard the sea-locked ships.

Much of the stores had already gone, carried off on

the treacherous *San Antonio*. Such food as the three ships carried began to rot under the soggy tropical airs. The penguins and seals they had killed and salted in Patagonia started to turn putrid; maggots raged through the ships, eating clothes and supplies and rigging; water supplies turned scummy and rank. Men began to develop the classic symptoms of scurvy—their teeth loosened in their gums, their breath began to smell horribly sour, huge boils erupted from their shrunken frames, they sank into inconsolable melancholia.

In January men began to die. One of the Patagonian behemoths whom Magellan had persuaded aboard was, despite his immense physique and power, the first to go; he begged to be made a Christian, was baptized "Paul" and then died. By mid-January a third of the sailors were too sick to stagger along the decks. Their food was limited to scoops of flour stained yellow by the urine of rats, and biscuits riddled with weevils.

The depression and deep anxiety afflicted Magellan too. At one point he flung his charts overboard in a fit of rage. "With the pardon of the cartographers, the Moluccas are not to be found in their appointed place!" he cried. The fleet did, in fact, strike land in late January—a tiny island they called St. Paul's, and which seems to be the minute atoll now known as Pukapuka, in the French Tuamotu group. (Four centuries later, Pukapuka was the first island to be spotted by Thor Heyerdahl aboard the balsa raft *Kon-Tiki* after his long drift westward from Callao in Peru.) They stayed a week, replenishing their water butts and feasting on turtle eggs. They left in an optimistic mood; surely, they surmised, this island must be the first of a vast skein of atolls and lagoons stretching to the now close Moluccas. But it was not to be; the ships had barely traversed a third of their ocean. Soon the hunger pains, the racking thirst and the sense of unshakable misery began anew, and the dying began once more.

After meals of leather—land!

More and more terrible the voyage steadily became. By March 4 the flagship had run out of food completely. Men were eating the oxhides and llama skins used to prevent the rigging from chafing (not too bad a diet—so long as the crew's scurvy-ridden teeth hung in). The smell of death, the knowledge that it was both inevitable and impending, gripped Magellan's sailors. And then dawned March 6, when a seaman called Navarro, the only man still fit enough to clamber up the ratlines, spied what everyone was waiting for—land.

A great cheer went up. Cannon were fired. Men fell to their knees in prayer. A squadron of tiny dugouts sped from shore to meet the Spaniards. Magellan had reached the islands he first called Las Islas de las Velas Latinas and later, after much of his cargo had been filched, Las Islas de Ladrones, the Islands of Thieves. He had made his landfall at what we now call Guam. It was March 6, 1521. Magellan had crossed the Pacific. A voyage the Captain-General had supposed might take three or four days had, in fact, occupied three and a half months.

The fleet stayed in Guam for only three days—to rest, make minor repairs and take on food (such as the "figs, more than a palm long," which must have been bananas) and fresh water. Then Magellan set off, still toward the Moluccas, standing down for the southwest and to the Philippines, islands of which all travellers to these parts had often heard, but which no European had ever seen. Though the Spice Islands, it must be recalled, were the armada's prescribed goal, the official mandate and ambition of Magellan was to discover, name and seize in the name of Spain the immense archipelago that lay north of them.

The only Briton on the expedition, Master Andrew of Bristol, died on this last, short passage. He was never to see the islands that, a novelist was later to write, were "as fair as Eden, with gold beaches, graceful palms, exotic fruits and soil so rich that if one snapped off a twig and stuck it into the ground it would start straightway to grow."

Magellan made his landfall on March 16 on an island at the southern end of the large Philippine island of Samar. Two days later, the first contact was made with Filipinos, though the name "Philippines" was not to be given to the place until 1543, when explorer Ruy López de Villalobos named one after the Infante, later to become King Philip II, the Spanish monarch whose reign made the words "Spanish Armada" infamous. (The name "Philippines" caught on later to mean the entire island group.) The significant moment came two days later still, when the ships sailed down the Gulf of Leyte and the Surigao Strait, where, more than four centuries later in World War II, one of the world's last great naval battles was fought, and Adm. William F. Halsey reduced the Japanese Imperial Navy to vestigial strength.

Once through the strait, Magellan landed at the island that guarded its entrance, Limasawa. Eight inhabitants sailed out to the *Trinidad* in a small boat. On orders from the Captain-General, his Moluccan slave, Enrique, hailed them. In a moment that must have seemed frozen in time, it became clear that the men in the approaching boat understood the words of the Moluccan perfectly.

Their language was being spoken to them by a man on a huge ship that had come to them from the east. The linguistic globe—even if not necessarily the physical globe—had been circumnavigated. A man who had originated in these parts had traveled across Asia and around Africa to Europe as a slave, and had now returned home by the Americas and the Pacific. Enrique de Molucca may well have been, strictly speaking, the first of humankind to circumnavigate the world; he was never to be honored for so doing.

Nor, by the unhappy coincidence of ill-temper and wretched misfortune, was Ferdinand Magellan ever to be able to savor his own triumph. Just six weeks after landing he was dead, cut down on a Philippine island in a skirmish that is as unremembered as the place in which it happened is unsung—a flat and muddy little island called Mactan, where an airport has now been built to serve the city of Cebu.

The circumstances of the Captain-General's end, however, are riven into every Iberian schoolchild's learning, even today. Despite his crew's objections, Magellan insisted on exploring. He was pleased at the relative ease with which the people took to Christianity. (It is perhaps worth remembering that the Catholic faith, which Magellan and his priests brought to Samar and Cebu and northern Mindanao, flourishes there still today. The Philippines, in fact, is the only predominantly Christian country in Asia, and the influence of the church contributed significantly to the recent overthrow of President Ferdinand Marcos.)

But the successful sowing of the seeds of Christianity were to be Magellan's undoing. His horribly inglorious end came in late April. The precise circumstances were chronicled. Magellan had demonstrated what he felt was his superior status to the local raja of Cebu, and had made Christians of him and all his followers. But significantly, the rest of the Philippine nobility did not go along. Many local junior rajas objected, especially the minor raja of Mactan, a man named Cilapulapu and now known to all Filipinos simply as Lapu Lapu. He declared that he was not going to pay fealty to this Christian interloper, come what may. He cared little enough for the raja of Cebu, let alone the Cebuano's newfound foreign friends.

The Spaniards soon got wind of this rebellious mood, and on April 27 Magellan and 60 of his men paddled across the narrow strait to Mactan, in an attempt to bring Lapu Lapu to heel. "You will feel the iron of our lances," Lapu Lapu was told by Magellan's interlocutor. "But we have fire-hardened spears and stakes of bamboo," replied a defiant chieftain. "Come across whenever you like."

The last stand at Mactan Island

The waters at the northern end of Mactan are very shallow and degenerate into warm swamps. A selected 48 of the Spaniards, dressed in full armor, had to wade the last few hundred yards to do battle with the Mactan warriors. They fought for an hour, thigh-deep in the water. Then Magellan plunged his lance into the body of an attacker and was unable to withdraw it quickly enough. It was a fatal delay. Another islander slashed Magellan's leg with a scimitar. He staggered. Scores of others crowded around him as he fell, and as Pigafetta was to write, "thus they killed our mirror, our light, our comfort and our true guide."

It is worth remembering that Fernao de Magalhaes was a native Portuguese—of whom it used to be said, because they were such energetic explorers, "they have a small country to live in, but all the world to die in." There is a monument near the spot where he fell, a tall white obelisk, guarded solicitously for the past 15 years by a man with the splendid name of Jesus Baring. There are two accounts of the event, one engraved on either side of the cross. Señor Baring derives much amusement from showing his occasional visitors—and there are very few, considering how globally important this spot should be—how markedly they differ.

The one on the monument's eastern side—the side that pedant geographers will recognize as marginally nearer to the Spanish Main—records the event as a European tragedy. "Here on 27th April 1521 the great Portuguese navigator Hernando de Magallanes, in the service of the King of Spain, was slain by native Filipinos. . . ." On the other side, by contrast, it is seen as an Oriental triumph—a heroic blow struck for Philippine nationalism. "Here on this spot the great chieftain Lapu Lapu repelled an attack by Ferdinand Magellan, killing him and sending his forces away. . . ." Baring points to the latter and roars with laughter. "This is the real story. This is the one we Filipinos like to hear!"

Lapu Lapu is thus the first, and to many Filipinos the greatest, of Filipino heroes. These days his memory is being revived, his exploits retold, his adventures made the stuff of comic strips, films and popular songs. Each April there is a full-scale reenactment of the Battle of Mactan on the beach, with an improbably handsome Cebuano film star playing the part of the seminaked hero and, when I was last there, the Philippine Air Force officer Mercurion Fernandez playing the role of the armor-clad Magellan. The two sides struggle gamely in the rising surf until that epic moment when Officer Fernandez contrives to collapse into the shallow sea and grunts his last. The assembled thousands then cheer. Such is Filipino pride in the raja of Mactan that there are firebrands—in Manila as well as in Cebu—who believe their country should shed its present name, a reminder that it is a colonial conquest, and be reborn as LapuLapuLand.

Little more needs to be said of the tiny armada now, save to note what most popular historians choose to forget. The *Concepción* was scuttled; the flagship *Trinidad*, which tried to make for home via the Pacific once more, was blown north as far as Hakodate in Japan, captured by a Portuguese battle group and became a total loss in the Spice Islands, which had been its original goal. But one of the ships, the doughty little *Victoria*—at 85 tons she was the second smallest of the original five—did make it back to Spain.

The *Victoria* scudded home under the charge of Juan Sebastian d'Elcano, previously the executive officer of the *Concepción*. She made Java. She made it round the top of Africa, through waters where freak waves sometimes cause modern oil tankers to founder. She made the Cape Verde Islands, where the crew realized that despite meticulous log-keeping, they had lost an entire day from their calendar: the concept of crossing the international date line was unknown—and profoundly unimaginable—to them.

On September 6, 1523, the *Victoria* made the harbor of Sanlucar de Barrameda, from where she had set off almost exactly three years before. Juan Sebastian d'Elcano had brought just 17 men back with him: 237 had started out. Circumnavigation, it happened, was a most costly business.

But well rewarded. D'Elcano was given an annual pension and a coat of arms as handsome as it was aromatic: a castle, three nutmegs, 12 cloves, two crossed cinnamon sticks, a pair of Malay kings bearing spice sticks, and above all, a globe circled by a ribbon emblazoned with the motto *Primus Circumdedisti me*. "Thou first circumnavigated me."

Easter's End

In just a few centuries, the people of Easter Island wiped out their forest, drove their plants and animals to extinction, and saw their complex society spiral into chaos and cannibalism. Are we about to follow their lead?

Jared Diamond

Jared Diamond is a contributing editor of Discover, *a professor of physiology at the UCLA School of Medicine, and a recipient of a MacArthur genius award. Expanded versions of many of his* Dis-cover *articles appear in his book* The Third Chimpanzee: The Evolution and Future of the Human Animal, *which won Britain's 1992* copus *prize for best science book and the* Los Angeles Times *science book prize.*

Among the most riveting mysteries of human history are those posed by vanished civilizations. Everyone who has seen the abandoned buildings of the Khmer, the Maya, or the Anasazi is immediately moved to ask the same question: Why did the societies that erected those structures disappear?

Their vanishing touches us as the disappearance of other animals, even the dinosaurs, never can. No matter how exotic those lost civilizations seem, their framers were humans like us. Who is to say we won't succumb to the same fate? Perhaps someday New York's skyscrapers will stand derelict and overgrown with vegetation, like the temples at Angkor Wat and Tikal.

Among all such vanished civilizations, that of the former Polynesian society on Easter Island remains unsurpassed in mystery and isolation. The mystery stems especially from the island's gigantic stone statues and its impoverished landscape, but it is enhanced by our associations with the specific people involved: Polynesians represent for us the ultimate in exotic romance, the background for many a child's, and an adult's, vision of paradise. My own interest in Easter was kindled over 30 years ago when I read Thor Heyerdahl's fabulous accounts of his *Kon-Tiki* voyage.

But my interest has been revived recently by a much more exciting account, one not of heroic voyages but of painstaking research and analysis. My friend David Steadman, a paleontologist, has been working with a number of other researchers who are carrying out the first systematic excavations on Easter intended to identify the animals and plants that once lived there. Their work is contributing to a new interpretation of the island's history that makes it a tale not only of wonder but of warning as well.

Easter Island, with an area of only 64 square miles, is the world's most isolated scrap of habitable land. It lies in the Pacific Ocean more than 2,000 miles west of the nearest continent (South America), 1,400 miles from even the nearest habitable island (Pitcairn). Its subtropical location and latitude—at 27 degrees south, it is approximately as far below the equator as Houston is north of it—help give it a rather mild climate, while its volcanic origins make its soil fertile. In theory, this combination of blessings should have made Eas-ter a miniature paradise, remote from problems that beset the rest of the world.

The island derives its name from its "discovery" by the Dutch explorer Jacob Roggeveen, on Easter (April 5) in 1722. Roggeveen's first impression was not of a paradise but of a wasteland: "We originally, from a further distance, have considered the said Easter Island as sandy; the reason for that is this, that we counted as sand the withered grass, hay, or other scorched and burnt vegetation, because its wasted appearance could give no other impression than of a singular poverty and barrenness."

When Europeans arrived, the native animals included nothing larger than insects—not a single species of bat, land snail, or lizard.

The island Roggeveen saw was a grassland without a single tree or bush over ten feet high. Modern botanists have identified only 47 species of higher plants native to Easter, most of them grasses, sedges, and ferns. The list includes just two species of small trees and two of woody shrubs. With such flora, the islanders Roggeveen encountered had no source of real firewood to warm themselves during Easter's cool, wet, windy winters. Their native animals included nothing larger than insects, not even a single species of native bat, land bird, land snail, or lizard. For domestic animals, they had only chickens.

European visitors throughout the eighteenth and early nineteenth centuries estimated Easter's human population at about 2,000, a modest number considering the island's fertility. As Captain James Cook recognized during his brief visit in 1774, the islanders were Polynesians (a Tahitian man accompanying Cook was able to converse with them). Yet despite the Polynesians' well-deserved fame as a great seafaring people, the Easter Islanders who came out to Roggeveen's and Cook's ships did so by swimming or paddling canoes that Roggeveen described as "bad and frail." Their craft, he wrote, were "put together with manifold small planks and light inner timbers, which they cleverly stitched together with very fine twisted threads. . . . But as they lack the knowledge and particularly the materials for caulking and making tight the great number of seams of the canoes, these are accordingly very leaky, for which reason they are compelled to spend half the time in bailing." The canoes, only ten feet long, held at most two people, and only three or four canoes were observed on the entire island.

With such flimsy craft, Polynesians could never have colonized Easter from even the nearest island, nor could they have traveled far offshore to fish. The islanders Roggeveen met were totally isolated unaware that other people existed. Investigators in all the years since his visit have discovered no trace of the islanders' having any outside contacts: not a single Easter Island rock or product has turned up elsewhere, nor has anything been found on the island that could have been brought by anyone other than the original settlers or the Europeans. Yet the people living on Easter claimed memories of visiting the uninhabited Sala y Gomez reef 260 miles away, far beyond the range of the leaky canoes seen by Roggeveen. How did the islanders' ancestors reach that reef from Easter, or reach Easter from anywhere else?

Easter Island's most famous feature is its huge stone statues, more than 200 of which once stood on massive stone platforms lining the coast. At least 700 more, in all stages of completion, were abandoned in quarries or on ancient roads between the quarries and the coast, as if the carvers and moving crews had thrown down their tools and walked off the job. Most of the erected statues were carved in a single quarry and then somehow transported as far as six miles—despite heights as great as 33 feet and weights up to 82 tons. The abandoned statues, meanwhile, were as much as 65 feet tall and weighed up to 270 tons. The stone platforms were equally gigantic: up to 500 feet long and 10 feet high, with facing slabs weighing up to 10 tons.

Roggeveen himself quickly recognized the problem the statues posed: "The stone images at first caused us to be struck with astonishment," he wrote, "because we could not comprehend how it was possible that these people, who are devoid of heavy thick timber for making any machines, as well as strong ropes, nevertheless had been able to erect such images." Roggeveen might have added that the islanders had no wheels, no draft animals, and no source of power except their own muscles. How did they transport the giant statues for miles, even before erecting them? To deepen the mystery, the statues were still standing in 1770, but by 1864 all of them had been pulled down, by the islanders themselves. Why then did they carve them in the first place? And why did they stop?

The statues imply a society very different from the one Roggeveen saw in 1722. Their sheer number and size suggest a population much larger than 2,000 people. What became of everyone? Furthermore, that society must have been highly organized. Easter's resources were scattered across the island: the best stone for the statues was quarried at Rano Raraku near Easter's northeast end; red stone, used for large crowns adorning some of the statues, was quarried at Puna Pau, inland in the southwest; stone carving tools came mostly from Aroi in the northwest. Meanwhile, the best farm-

land lay in the south and east, and the best fishing grounds on the north and west coasts. Extracting and redistributing all those goods required complex political organization. What happened to that organization, and how could it ever have arisen in such a barren landscape?

Easter Island's mysteries have spawned volumes of speculation for more than two and a half centuries. Many Europeans were incredulous that Polynesians—commonly characterized as "mere savages"—could have created the statues or the beautifully constructed stone platforms. In the 1950s, Heyerdahl argued that Polynesia must have been settled by advanced societies of American Indians, who in turn must have received civilization across the Atlantic from more advanced societies of the Old World. Heyerdahl's raft voyages aimed to prove the feasibility of such prehistoric transoceanic contacts. In the 1960s the Swiss writer Erich von Däniken, an ardent believer in Earth visits by extraterrestrial astronauts, went further, claiming that Easter's statues were the work of intelligent beings who owned ultramodern tools, became stranded on Easter, and were finally rescued.

Heyerdahl and Von Däniken both brushed aside overwhelming evidence that the Easter Islanders were typical Polynesians derived from Asia rather than from the Americas and that their culture (including their statues) grew out of Polynesian culture. Their language was Polynesian, as Cook had already concluded. Specifically, they spoke an eastern Polynesian dialect related to Hawaiian and Marquesan, a dialect isolated since about A.D. 400, as estimated from slight differences in vocabulary. Their fishhooks and stone adzes resembled early Marquesan models. Last year DNA extracted from 12 Easter Island skeletons was also shown to be Polynesian. The islanders grew bananas, taro, sweet potatoes, sugarcane, and paper mulberry—typical Polynesian crops, mostly of Southeast Asian origin. Their sole domestic animal, the chicken, was also typically Polynesian and ultimately Asian, as were the rats that arrived as stowaways in the canoes of the first settlers.

What happened to those settlers? The fanciful theories of the past must give way to evidence gathered by hardworking practitioners in three fields: archeology, pollen analysis, and paleontology.

Modern archeological excavations on Easter have continued since Heyerdahl's 1955 expedition. The earliest radiocarbon dates associated with human activities are around A.D. 400 to 700, in reasonable agreement with the approximate settlement date of 400 estimated by linguists. The period of statue construction peaked around 1200 to 1500, with few if any statues erected thereafter. Densities of archeological sites suggest a large population; an estimate of 7,000 people is widely quoted by archeologists, but other estimates range up to 20,000, which does not seem implausible for an island of Easter's area and fertility.

Cannibalism replaced only part of Easter's lost foods. Statuettes with sunken cheeks and visible ribs suggest people were starving.

Archeologists have also enlisted surviving islanders in experiments aimed at figuring out how the statues might have been carved and erected. Twenty people, using only stone chisels, could have carved even the largest completed statue within a year. Given enough timber and fiber for making ropes, teams of at most a few hundred people could have loaded the statues onto wooden sleds, dragged them over lubricated wooden tracks or rollers, and used logs as levers to maneuver them into a standing position. Rope could have been made from the fiber of a small native tree, related to the linden, called the hauhau. However, that tree is now extremely scarce on Easter, and hauling one statue would have required hundreds of yards of rope. Did Easter's now barren landscape once support the necessary trees?

That question can be answered by the technique of pollen analysis, which involves boring out a column of sediment from a swamp or pond, with the most recent deposits at the top and relatively more ancient deposits at the bottom. The absolute age of each layer can be dated by radiocarbon methods. Then begins the hard work: examining tens of thousands of pollen grains under a microscope, counting them, and identifying the plant species that produced each one by comparing the grains with modern pollen from known plant species. For Easter Island, the bleary-eyed scientists who performed that task were John Flenley, now at Massey University in New Zealand, and Sarah King of the University of Hull in England.

Flenley and King's heroic efforts were rewarded by the striking new picture that emerged of Easter's prehistoric landscape. For at least 30,000 years before human arrival and during the early years of Polynesian settlement, Easter was not a wasteland at all. Instead, a subtropical forest of trees and woody bushes towered over a ground layer of shrubs, herbs, ferns, and grasses. In the forest grew tree daisies, the rope-yielding hauhau tree, and the toromiro tree, which furnishes a dense, mesquite-like firewood. The most common tree in the forest was a species of palm now absent on Easter but formerly so abundant that the bottom strata of the sediment column were packed with its pollen. The Easter Island palm was closely related to the still-surviving Chilean wine palm, which grows up to 82 feet tall and 6 feet in diameter. The tall, unbranched trunks of the Easter Island palm would have been ideal for transporting and erecting statues and constructing large canoes. The palm would also have been a valuable food source, since its Chilean relative yields edible nuts as well as sap from which Chileans make sugar, syrup, honey, and wine.

What did the first settlers of Easter Island eat when they were not glutting themselves on the local equivalent of maple syrup? Recent excavations by David Steadman, of the New York State Museum at Albany, have yielded a picture of Easter's original animal world as surprising as Flenley and King's picture of its plant world. Steadman's expectations for Easter were conditioned by his experiences elsewhere in Polynesia, where fish are overwhelmingly the main food at archeological sites, typically accounting for more than 90 percent of the bones in ancient Polynesian garbage heaps. Easter, though, is too cool for the coral reefs beloved by fish, and its cliff-girded coastline permits shallow-water fishing in only a few places. Less than a quarter of the bones in its early garbage heaps (from the period 900 to 1300) belonged to fish; instead, nearly one-third of all bones came from porpoises.

Nowhere else in Polynesia do porpoises account for even 1 percent of discarded food bones. But most other Polynesian islands offered animal food in the form of birds and mammals, such as New Zealand's now extinct giant moas and Hawaii's now extinct flightless geese. Most other islanders also had domestic pigs and dogs. On Easter, porpoises would have been the largest animal available—other than humans. The porpoise species identified at Easter, the common dolphin, weighs up to 165 pounds. It generally lives out at sea, so it could not have been hunted by line fishing or spearfishing from shore. Instead, it must have been harpooned far offshore, in big seaworthy canoes built from the extinct palm tree.

In addition to porpoise meat, Steadman found, the early Polynesian settlers were feasting on seabirds. For those birds, Easter's remoteness and lack of predators made it an ideal haven as a breeding site, at least until humans arrived. Among the prodigious numbers of seabirds that bred on Easter were albatross, boobies, frigate birds, fulmars, petrels, prions, shearwaters, storm petrels, terns, and tropic birds. With at least 25 nesting species, Easter was the richest seabird breeding site in Polynesia and probably in the whole Pacific.

Land birds as well went into early Easter Island cooking pots. Steadman identified bones of at least six species, including barn owls, herons, parrots, and rail. Bird stew would have been seasoned with meat from large numbers of rats, which the Polynesian colonists inadvertently brought with them; Easter Island is the sole known Polynesian island where rat bones out-number fish bones at archeological sites. (In case you're squeamish and consider rats inedible, I still recall recipes for creamed laboratory rat that my British biologist friends used to supplement their diet during their years of wartime food rationing.)

Porpoises, seabirds, land birds, and rats did not complete the list of meat sources formerly available on Easter. A few bones hint at the possibility of breeding seal colonies as well. All these delicacies were cooked in ovens fired by wood from the island's forests.

Such evidence lets us imagine the island onto which Easter's first Polynesian colonists stepped ashore some 1,600 years ago, after a long canoe voyage from eastern Polynesia. They found themselves in a pristine paradise. What then happened to it? The pollen grains and the bones yield a grim answer.

Pollen records show that destruction of Easter's forests was well under way by the year 800, just a few centuries after the start of human settlement. Then charcoal from wood fires came to fill the sediment cores, while pollen of palms and other trees and woody shrubs decreased or disappeared, and pollen of the grasses that replaced the forest became more abundant. Not long after 1400 the palm finally became extinct, not only as a result of being chopped down but also because the now ubiquitous rats prevented its regeneration: of the dozens of preserved palm nuts discovered in caves on Easter, all had been chewed by rats and could no longer germinate. While the hauhau tree did not become extinct in Polynesian times, its numbers declined drastically until there weren't enough left to make ropes from. By the time Heyerdahl visited Easter, only a single, nearly dead toromiro tree remained on the island, and even that lone survivor has now disappeared.

(Fortunately, the toromiro still grows in botanical gardens elsewhere.)

Earth's inhabitants have no emigration valve. We can no more escape into space than the Easter Islanders could flee into the ocean.

The fifteenth century marked the end not only for Easter's palm but for the forest itself. Its doom had been approaching as people cleared land to plant gardens; as they felled trees to build canoes, to transport and erect statues, and to burn; as rats devoured seeds; and probably as the native birds died out that had pollinated the trees' flowers and dispersed their fruit. The overall picture is among the most extreme examples of forest destruction anywhere in the world: the whole forest gone, and most of its tree species extinct.

The destruction of the island's animals was as extreme as that of the forest: without exception, every species of native land bird became extinct. Even shellfish were overexploited, until people had to settle for small sea snails instead of larger cowries. Porpoise bones disappeared abruptly from garbage heaps around 1500; no one could harpoon porpoises anymore, since the trees used for constructing the big seagoing canoes no longer existed. The colonies of more than half of the seabird species breeding on Easter or on its offshore islets were wiped out.

In place of these meat supplies, the Easter Islanders intensified their production of chickens, which had been only an occasional food item. They also turned to the largest remaining meat source available: humans, whose bones became common in late Easter Island garbage heaps. Oral traditions of the islanders are rife with cannibalism; the most inflammatory taunt that could be snarled at an enemy was "The flesh of your mother sticks between my teeth." With no wood avail-

able to cook these new goodies, the islanders resorted to sugarcane scraps, grass, and sedges to fuel their fires.

All these strands of evidence can be wound into a coherent narrative of a society's decline and fall. The first Polynesian colonists found themselves on an island with fertile soil, abundant food, bountiful building materials, ample lebensraum, and all the prerequisites for comfortable living. They prospered and multiplied.

After a few centuries, they began erecting stone statues on platforms, like the ones their Polynesian forebears had carved. With passing years, the statues and platforms became larger and larger, and the statues began sporting ten-ton red crowns—probably in an escalating spiral of one-upmanship, as rival clans tried to surpass each other with shows of wealth and power. (In the same way, successive Egyptian pharaohs built ever-larger pyramids. Today Hollywood movie moguls near my home in Los Angeles are displaying their wealth and power by building ever more ostentatious mansions. Tycoon Marvin Davis topped previous moguls with plans for a 50,000-square-foot house, so now Aaron Spelling has topped Davis with a 56,000-square-foot house. All that those buildings lack to make the message explicit are ten-ton red crowns.) On Easter, as in modern America, society was held together by a complex political system to redistribute locally available resources and to integrate the economies of different areas.

Eventually Easter's growing population was cutting the forest more rapidly than the forest was regenerating. The people used the land for gardens and the wood for fuel, canoes, and houses—and of course, for lugging statues. As forest disappeared, the islanders ran out of timber and rope to transport and erect their statues. Life became more uncomfortable—springs and streams dried up, and wood was no longer available for fires.

People also found it harder to fill their stomachs, as land birds, large sea snails, and many seabirds disappeared. Because timber for building seagoing canoes vanished, fish catches declined and porpoises disappeared from the table. Crop yields also declined, since deforestation allowed the soil to be eroded by rain and wind, dried by the sun, and its nutrients to be leeched from it. Intensified chicken production and cannibalism replaced only part of all those lost foods. Preserved statuettes with sunken cheeks and visible ribs suggest that people were starving.

With the disappearance of food surpluses, Easter Island could no longer feed the chiefs, bureaucrats, and priests who had kept a complex society running. Surviving islanders described to early European visitors how local chaos replaced centralized government and a warrior class took over from the hereditary chiefs. The stone points of spears and daggers, made by the warriors during their heyday in the 1600s and 1700s, still litter the ground of Easter today. By around 1700, the population began to crash toward between one-quarter and one-tenth of its former number. People took to living in caves for protection against their enemies. Around 1770 rival clans started to topple each other's statues, breaking the heads off. By 1864 the last statue had been thrown down and desecrated.

As we try to imagine the decline of Easter's civilization, we ask ourselves, "Why didn't they look around, realize what they were doing, and stop before it was too late? What were they thinking when they cut down the last palm tree?"

I suspect, though, that the disaster happened not with a bang but with a whimper. After all, there are those hundreds of abandoned statues to consider. The forest the islanders depended on for rollers and rope didn't simply disappear one day—it vanished slowly, over decades. Perhaps war interrupted the moving teams; perhaps by the time the carvers had finished their work, the last rope snapped. In the meantime, any islander who tried to warn about the dangers of progressive deforestation would have been overridden by vested interests of carvers, bureaucrats, and chiefs, whose jobs depended on continued deforestation. Our Pacific Northwest loggers are only the latest in a long line of loggers to cry, "Jobs over trees!" The changes in forest cover from year to year would have been hard to detect: yes, this year we cleared those woods over there, but trees are starting to grow back again on this abandoned garden site here. Only older people, recollecting their childhoods decades earlier, could have recognized a difference. Their children could no more have comprehended their parents' tales than my eight-year-old sons today can comprehend my wife's and my tales of what Los Angeles was like 30 years ago.

Gradually trees became fewer, smaller, and less important. By the time the last fruit-bearing adult palm tree was cut, palms had long since ceased to be of economic significance. That left only smaller and smaller palm saplings to clear each year, along with other bushes and treelets. No one would have noticed the felling of the last small palm.

By now the meaning of Easter Island for us should be chillingly obvious. Easter Island is Earth writ small. Today, again, a rising population confronts shrinking resources. We too have no emigration valve, because all human societies are linked by international transport, and we can no more escape into space than the Easter Islanders could flee into the ocean. If we continue to follow our present course, we shall have exhausted the world's major fisheries, tropical rain forests, fossil fuels, and much of our soil by the time my sons reach my current age.

Every day newspapers report details of famished countries—Afghanistan, Liberia, Rwanda, Sierra Leone, Somalia, the former Yugoslavia, Zaire—where soldiers have appropriated the wealth or where central government is yielding to local gangs of thugs. With the risk of nuclear war receding, the threat of our ending with a bang no longer has a chance of galvanizing us to halt our course. Our risk now is of winding down, slowly, in a whimper. Corrective action is blocked by vested interests, by well-intentioned political and business leaders, and by their electorates, all of whom are perfectly correct in not noticing big changes from year to year. Instead, each year there are just somewhat more people, and somewhat fewer resources, on Earth.

It would be easy to close our eyes or to give up in despair. If mere thousands of Easter Islanders with only stone tools and their own muscle power sufficed to destroy their society, how can billions of people with metal tools and machine power fail to do worse? But there is one crucial difference. The Easter Islanders had no books and no histories of other doomed societies. Unlike the Easter Islanders, we have histories of the past—information that can save us. My main hope for my sons' generation is that we may now choose to learn from the fates of societies like Easter's.

Index

Credits/Acknowledgments

Cover design by Charles Vitelli

1. Natural History: The Stage for Human History
Facing overview—NASA photo. 18-19—*Scientific American* graphics by
David Starwood. 20-21—*Scientific American* graphics by Patricia J.
Wynne.

2. The Beginnings of Culture, Agriculture, and Cities
Facing overview—United Nations photo.

3. The Early Civilizations to 500 B.C.E.
Facing overview—United Nations photo by John Isaac.

4. The Later Civilizations to 500 C.E.
Facing overview—United Nations photo by Rothstein. 89—American
Museum of Natural History map by Joe LeMonnier.

5. The Great Religions
Facing overview—Aramco photo. 144—Illustration from The
Metropolitan Museum of Art, Gift of Alexander Smith Cochran, 1913.
145—Illustration from The Metropolitan Museum of Art, Rogers Fund,
1938. 149—Illustration courtesy of the Arthur M. Sackler Gallery,
Smithsonian Institution, Washington, DC. Iraq painting from a copy
of the *Materia medica* of Pedanius Dioscorides, A.H. Rajab 621.

150—Illustration courtesy of the Arthur M. Sackler Gallery,
Smithsonian Institution, Washington, DC. Iran painting from ca. 1550
Double-page Illuminated Frontispiece from a Koran. 151—Illustration
from The Metropolitan Museum of Art, The Theodore M. Davis
Collection, Bequest of Theodore M. Davis, 1915.

6. The World of the Middle Ages, 500–1500
Facing overview—WHO photo. 166-168—Photos by Terrence Moore.
179, 182—Illustrations courtesy of Bibliotheque Nationale, Lisbon.
190—Illustration from *The Cyclopaedia of Arts, Sciences, and Literature*
by Abraham Rees, London, 1920. 192-193—Illustrations courtesy of
Bodleian Library Film Strip Service, Oxford. 194—Illustration courtesy
of Bibliotheque Nationale, Lisbon. 196—Mansell Collection Library.

7. 1500: The Era of Global Explorations
Facing overview—Reproduced from the collections of the Library of
Congress. 208, 212—Illustrations from the Granger Collection, New
York. 213—Reproductions from the collection of the Library of
Congress.

ANNUAL EDITIONS ARTICLE REVIEW FORM

■ NAME: _____ DATE: _____

■ TITLE AND NUMBER OF ARTICLE: _____

■ BRIEFLY STATE THE MAIN IDEA OF THIS ARTICLE: _____

_____

■ LIST THREE IMPORTANT FACTS THAT THE AUTHOR USES TO SUPPORT THE MAIN IDEA:

_____

_____

_____

_____

■ WHAT INFORMATION OR IDEAS DISCUSSED IN THIS ARTICLE ARE ALSO DISCUSSED IN YOUR
TEXTBOOK OR OTHER READINGS THAT YOU HAVE DONE? LIST THE TEXTBOOK CHAPTERS AND
PAGE NUMBERS:

_____

_____

_____

_____

_____

■ LIST ANY EXAMPLES OF BIAS OR FAULTY REASONING THAT YOU FOUND IN THE ARTICLE:

_____

_____

_____

_____

_____

■ LIST ANY NEW TERMS/CONCEPTS THAT WERE DISCUSSED IN THE ARTICLE, AND WRITE A SHORT
DEFINITION:

_____

_____

_____

_____

*Your instructor may require you to use this ANNUAL EDITIONS Article Review Form in any number of ways: for articles that are assigned, for extra credit, as a tool to assist in developing assigned papers, or simply for your own reference. Even if it is not required, we encourage you to photocopy and use this page; you will find that reflecting on the articles will greatly enhance the information from your text.

WORLD HISTORY VOLUME I

Prehistory to 1500

Fifth Edition

Editor

David McComb
Colorado State University

David McComb received his Ph.D. from the University of Texas at Austin and is currently a professor of history at Colorado State University. Dr. McComb has written 8 books and over 100 articles and book reviews, and he teaches courses in the history of the United States, sports, and the world. He has traveled twice around the world as a Semester at Sea faculty member of the University of Pittsburgh, and he has spent additional time in India and Mexico. Currently, he is a member of the executive council of the World History Association.

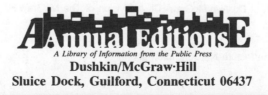

A Library of Information from the Public Press
Dushkin/McGraw-Hill
Sluice Dock, Guilford, Connecticut 06437

*Visit us on the Internet—*http://www.dushkin.com/

The Annual Editions Series

ANNUAL EDITIONS, including GLOBAL STUDIES, consist of over 70 volumes designed to provide the reader with convenient, low-cost access to a wide range of current, carefully selected articles from some of the most important magazines, newspapers, and journals published today. ANNUAL EDITIONS are updated on an annual basis through a continuous monitoring of over 300 periodical sources. All ANNUAL EDITIONS have a number of features that are designed to make them particularly useful, including topic guides, annotated tables of contents, unit overviews, and indexes. For the teacher using ANNUAL EDITIONS in the classroom, an Instructor's Resource Guide with test questions is available for each volume. GLOBAL STUDIES titles provide comprehensive background information and selected world press articles on the regions and countries of the world.

VOLUMES AVAILABLE

ANNUAL EDITIONS
Abnormal Psychology
Accounting
Adolescent Psychology
Aging
American Foreign Policy
American Government
American History, Pre-Civil War
American History, Post-Civil War
American Public Policy
Anthropology
Archaeology
Astronomy
Biopsychology
Business Ethics
Child Growth and Development
Comparative Politics
Computers in Education
Computers in Society
Criminal Justice
Criminology
Developing World
Deviant Behavior
Drugs, Society, and Behavior
Dying, Death, and Bereavement
Early Childhood Education

Economics
Educating Exceptional Children
Education
Educational Psychology
Environment
Geography
Geology
Global Issues
Health
Human Development
Human Resources
Human Sexuality
International Business
Macroeconomics
Management
Marketing
Marriage and Family
Mass Media
Microeconomics
Multicultural Education
Nutrition
Personal Growth and Behavior
Physical Anthropology
Psychology
Public Administration
Race and Ethnic Relations

Social Problems
Social Psychology
Sociology
State and Local Government
Teaching English as a Second
   Language
Urban Society
Violence and Terrorism
Western Civilization,
   Pre-Reformation
Western Civilization,
   Post-Reformation
Women's Health
World History, Pre-Modern
World History, Modern
World Politics
GLOBAL STUDIES
Africa
China
India and South Asia
Japan and the Pacific Rim
Latin America
Middle East
Russia, the Eurasian Republics,
   and Central/Eastern Europe
Western Europe

Cataloging in Publication Data
Main entry under title: Annual editions: World history, vol. I: Prehistory to 1500.
        1. World history—Periodicals. 2. Civilization, Modern—Periodicals. 3. Social problems—Periodicals. I. McComb, David, comp. II. Title: World history, vol. I: Prehistory to 1500.
905   ISBN 0-697-39293-7   90–656260   ISSN 1054–2779

Fifth Edition

Cover: Stonehenge, England. © David Ryan/Picture Network International

Printed on Recycled Paper

Printed in the United States of America